"*The Global Human Resource Management Casebook* is an excellent source of real-life case studies from organizations around the world, which will undoubtedly help students, scholars, and practitioners alike to understand better the regional and national intricacies of managing human resources in the global context. Both the scope and the breadth of cases included, as well as their outstanding contributors, will ensure continued success of the book."

Vlad Vaiman, *California Lutheran University, USA*

"The casebook's first edition has been an invaluable resource for teaching and learning and this second edition is even more impressive. The wide-ranging global perspectives present real insight into the HR challenges organizations face around the world and emphasize unique context-driven issues in particular countries as well as more universal concerns that matter regardless of location. A notable array of international scholars, case questions, and teaching notes makes this an indispensable resource on global HR management."

David G. Allen, *Rutgers University, USA*

The Global Human Resource Management Casebook

This casebook is a collection of international teaching cases focusing on contemporary human resource management issues. Each case centers primarily on one country and illustrates a significant challenge faced by managers and HR practitioners, helping students to understand how the issues they learn about in class play out in the real world.

The cases emphasize the national and cultural contexts of HR management, providing readers with a global understanding of employee motivation, reward systems, recruitment and selection, career development, and more. In this edition, the editors and authors have made significant updates to reflect recent developments in the field and cover a broader range of countries in Eastern Europe and Africa. The authors also delve into new industries like food service, clothing manufacturing, and transportation as well as IT and academia. Recommendations for further reading and relevant videos provide readers with practical insights into the modern HRM field.

With more than 30 cases followed by questions and tasks to encourage reflection, this is a valuable companion for any student of human resource management.

Liza Castro Christiansen is an Associate Professor at Business Academy Aarhus, University of Applied Sciences, Denmark, and a Visiting Academic Fellow of the Doctoral Program at Henley Business School, UK.

Michal Biron is a Senior Lecturer and Head of the MBA Program and the MBA Program for Not-for-Profit Organizations at the University of Haifa, Israel, and an affiliate of the HR Studies Department at Tilburg University, the Netherlands.

Elaine Farndale is an Associate Professor of Human Resource Management at The Pennsylvania State University, USA, and is affiliated with the HR Studies Department at Tilburg University, the Netherlands.

Bård Kuvaas is a Professor of Organizational Psychology and Associate Dean of the Doctoral Program at BI Norwegian School of Management, Norway.

Routledge Global Human Resource Management Series
Edited by Randall S. Schuler, Susan E. Jackson, and Paul Sparrow

Routledge Global Human Resource Management is an important series that examines human resources in its global context. The series is organized into three strands: Content and issues in global human resource management (HRM); Specific HR functions in a global context; and comparative HRM. Authored by some of the world's leading authorities on HRM, each book in the series aims to give readers comprehensive, in-depth and accessible texts that combine essential theory and best practice. Topics covered include cross-border alliances, global leadership, global legal systems, HRM in Asia, Africa and the Americas, industrial relations, and global staffing.

Dedication: The late Professor Michael Poole was one of the founding series editors, and Professors Schuler, Jackson, and Sparrow wish to dedicate the series to his memory.

For a full list of titles in this series, please visit www.routledge.com

Manager-Subordinate Trust
A global perspective
Edited by Pablo Cardona and Michael J. Morley

Managing Human Resources in Asia-Pacific (second edition)
Edited by Arup Varma and Pawan S. Budhwar

Human Resource Management and the Institutional Perspective
Edited by Geoffrey Wood, Chris Brewster, and Michael Brookes

International Human Resource Management (fifth edition)
Policies and practices for multinational enterprises
Ibraiz Tarique, Dennis Briscoe, and Randall S.Schuler

Contemporary HR Issues in Europe (third edition)
Michael Dickmann, Chris Brewster, and Paul Sparrow

Globalizing Human Resource Management (second edition)
Paul Sparrow, Chris Brewster, and Chul Chung

The Global Human Resource Management Casebook (second edition)
Edited by Liza Castro Christiansen, Michal Biron, Elaine Farndale, Bård Kuvaas

The Global Human Resource Management Casebook

Second Edition

Edited by
Liza Castro Christiansen
Michal Biron
Elaine Farndale
Bård Kuvaas

Routledge
Taylor & Francis Group

NEW YORK AND LONDON

First published 2018
by Routledge
711 Third Avenue, New York, NY 10017

and by Routledge
2 Park Square, Milton Park, Abingdon, Oxon OX14 4RN

Routledge is an imprint of the Taylor & Francis Group, an informa business

Library of Congress Cataloging-in-Publication Data
Names: Christiansen, Liza Castro, editor.
Title: The global human resource management casebook / edited by Liza Castro
    Christiansen, Michal Biron, Elaine Farndale, Bêard Kuvaas.
Description: Second edition. | Abingdon, Oxon ; New York, NY : Routledge, 2017.
Identifiers: LCCN 2016045961 | ISBN 9781138949966 (hbk) |
    ISBN 9781138949973 (pbk) | ISBN 9781315668888 (ebk) |
    ISBN 9781317362432 (mobi/kindle)
Subjects: LCSH: Personnel management—Case studies. | Industrial relations—
    Case studies. | Human capital—Management—Case studies.
Classification: LCC HF5549 .G5388 2017 | DDC 658.3—dc23
LC record available at https://lccn.loc.gov/2016045961

ISBN: 978-1-138-94996-6 (hbk)
ISBN: 978-1-138-94997-3 (pbk)
ISBN: 978-1-31566-888-8 (ebk)

Typeset in Minion
by Apex CoVantage, LLC

Visit the companion website: www.routledge.com/textbooks/globalhrm

Contents

Illustrations

Figures

Tables

Contributors

Austria

Wolfgang Mayrhofer (PhD). Full Professor and Head of the Interdisciplinary Institute of Management and Organisational Behaviour, Department of Management at WU (Vienna University of Economics and Business), Austria. He conducts research in comparative international Human Resource Management and leadership, work careers, and systems theory and management.

Katharina Pernkopf (PhD). Assistant Professor at WU (Vienna University of Economics and Business), Austria. Her research projects are located in the wider field of organisational institutionalism and comparative Human Resource Management and talent management.

Azerbaijan

Dave Doughty (PhD). Director of International HR Development at Nottingham Business School, United Kingdom. His research interests include power and influence of HR specialists in organisations within "transitional societies", HR specialists and line-management relationships, localisation of employment, and developing trust relationships between local and expatriate managers.

Helen Shipton (PhD). Professor of Human Resource Management and Director of the NBS Centre of People, Innovation, and Performance at Nottingham Business School, Nottingham Trent University, United Kingdom. Her research interests centre on Human Resource Management, creativity and innovation, leadership and leadership development, informal learning at work and employee performance and well-being.

Veronica Lin (PhD). Lecturer in Management at Queen's Management School, Queen's University Belfast. Her research interests include Strategic Human Resource Management, creativity and innovation, research methods, and leadership.

Belgium

Britt De Soete (PhD). Industrial and Organizational Psychologist and Talent Management Consultant at Aon Hewitt, Singapore. Her main interests are talent assessment through innovative selection instruments, leadership development, cross-cultural selection, and the diversity–validity dilemma in personnel selection.

Filip Lievens (PhD). Professor at the Department of Personnel Management, Work and Organisational Psychology at Ghent University, Belgium. His research interests focus on organisational attractiveness and alternative selection procedures including assessment centres, situational judgment tests, and web-based assessment.

Christoph Nils Herde. PhD Candidate at the Department of Personnel Management, Work and Organisational Psychology at Ghent University, Belgium. His research interests include personnel selection, especially assessment centres, psychological assessment, and research methods.

Botswana

Dorothy Mpabanga (PhD). Director of the Centre of Specialisation in Public Administration and Management and Senior Lecturer at the University of Botswana. Her research interests include Human Resource Management, Industrial Development, NGO management, Higher Education Management, Public Sector Reforms, ICT, governance, and elections/electoral processes.

Bulgaria

Lucia F. Miree (PhD). Professor of Business and Director of the EMBA Programme at the American University in Bulgaria. Her research interests include costing stress-related behaviours in the workplace, post-layoff psychological trauma, and the management of health care organisations.

John E. Galletly (PhD). Professor of Computer Science at the American University in Bulgaria. His research interests include modern software development methods, intelligent systems, novel, nature-inspired optimisation techniques, parallel and distributed processing, and modern teaching methods for computer science education.

Canada

Maria Rotundo (PhD). Professor of Organisational Behaviour and Human Resource Management at the Joseph L. Rotman School of Management, University of Toronto, Canada. Her research interests include discretionary performance behaviours such as co-operative acts and deviance, social identities, leadership, and Human Resource Management.

Chile

Andrés Raineri (PhD). Associate Professor of Human Resource Management at the Business School of Pontificia Universidad Católica de Chile, Santiago, Chile. His research interests include change management, Human Resource Management, leadership, and behavioural decision-making.

China

Shiyong Xu (PhD). Full Professor, Director of the Enterprise Behavior Research Centre and Affiliate of the School of Human Resources and Labor Relations at Renmin University of

China in Beijing. His research interests include stress and burn-out, counter-productive work behaviour, employee relations, ethical leadership, and Human Resource Management.

Huan Wang. PhD candidate at Renmin University of China and Research Fellow at the Institute of China's Economic Reform and Development. His research interests include organisational justice and corporate social responsibility.

Ning Li. PhD candidate at Renmin University of China. His research interests include Strategic Human Resource Management and corporate social responsibility of SOEs in China.

Lihua Zhang (PhD). Full Professor at Renmin University of China and Associate Chair of Beijing Behaviour Science Society. Her research interests include qualitative case studies, cross-cultural Human Resource Management and transformational leadership.

Cyprus

Eleni Stavrou (PhD). Associate Professor of Management and Chair of the Department of Business and Public Administration at the University of Cyprus. Her research interests include work-life issues, strategic and comparative Human Resource Management, and inter-generational transitions in family firms.

Nicoleta Nicolaou Pissarides (BSc, MSc). Head of the School of Economics and Management at the University of Cyprus. Her current research interests include employee relations, equality, performance evaluations, use of innovation and knowledge, business evaluation, and Human Resource Management.

Czech Republic

Martina Fejfarová (PhD). Assistant Professor at the Department of Management at the Faculty of Economics and Management of the Czech University of Life Sciences, Prague. Her research interests include Human Resource Management, Risk Management, and Crisis Management.

Denmark

Liza Castro Christiansen (MBA, DBA). Associate Professor at Business Academy Aarhus, University of Applied Sciences, Denmark. Visiting Academic Fellow at Henley Business School, University of Reading, United Kingdom. Her research interests include change leadership behaviours, middle managers' trust in top management, diversity management, HR business alignment and HR competencies.

Finland

Adam Smale (PhD). Professor and Head of the Department of Management at the Faculty of Business Studies at the University of Vaasa, Finland. His research interests focus on International Human Resource Management, talent management, and careers in multinational firms.

Ingmar Björkman (PhD). Professor and Dean of the Aalto University School of Business, Finland. His research interests focus on International Human Resource Management, knowledge creation and transfer in multi-national corporations, and the integration of international mergers and acquisitions.

Risto Säntti. Post-doctoral researcher and e-Learning specialist at the University of Vaasa, Finland. His research interests include diversity management and knowledge management.

Narashima Boopathi Sivasubramanian. Doctoral researcher at the Department of Management at the University of Vaasa, Finland. His research interests are in leadership and cultural intelligence.

Germany

Marion Festing (PhD). Professor of Human Resource Management and Intercultural Leadership and Rector of ESCP Europe's Berlin Campus in Germany. Her current research interests are concerned with International Human Resource Management with a special emphasis on strategies, careers, rewards, performance, and talent management in various institutional and cultural contexts.

Hong Kong

Christina Sue-Chan (PhD). Associate Head of the Department of Management, City University of Hong Kong, Hong Kong, S.A.R., China. Her research interests include self-regulatory processes in motivation, coaching in the context of leadership and (social) entrepreneurship, creativity, and Human Resource Management.

Clara To (PhD). Director and Principal Consultant at Talent Link Global Limited, Hong Kong.

Hungary

József Poór (PhD). Full Professor of Management at Szent István University, Hungary.

Iris Kassim. PhD candidate at Szent István University, Hungary.

Lajos Reich (PhD). CEO and Co-Founder of Healcloud, Hungary.

Iceland

Ingi Runar Edvardsson (PhD). Professor in Management and Head of the School of Business at the University of Iceland. His research intreests include Human Resource Management, knowledge management, outsourcing, and labour markets.

Gudrun Berta Danielsdottir. Business Operations Manager at Marel, Seattle, USA.

India

Radha R. Sharma (PhD). Dean, Centre of Excellence, Case Centre and Chair Professor, OB/HRD at Management Development Institute, India. Her research interests include emotional intelligence, executive burn-out, gender equity, competencies, positive scholarship, spirituality, well-being, and sustainability.

Sonam Chawla (PhD). Scholar, Organisational Behaviour at Management Development Institute, India. Her research interests include female leadership and career success of women.

Ireland

Brian Harney (PhD). Senior Lecturer in Strategic Human Resource Management and Programme Director of the MSc in HRM at Dublin City University Business School, Ireland. His research interests reside at the intersection of Strategy and HRM with a particular focus on SMEs and knowledge intensive contexts.

Israel

Michal Biron (PhD). Head of the MBA Programme and the MBA Programme for Not-for-Profit Organisations at the University of Haifa, Israel. Affiliate of the HR Studies Department at Tilburg University, the Netherlands. Her research interests include stress and burn-out, employee relations with co-workers and supervisors, withdrawal behaviour, and Human Resource Management.

Jordan

Muhsen Makhamreh (PhD). Dean of the Jordan Applied University College of Hospitality Management. Affiliate with the Business School, the University of Jordan and ISCTE Business School, Portugal. His research interests are in the areas of Human Resource Management, strategic management, and international business.

Mexico

Jacobo Ramirez (PhD). Assistant Professor in Latin American Business Development at the Department of Management, Society and Communication, Copenhagen Business School, Denmark. His research initiatives focus on business development in emerging markets and Human Resource Management.

Laura Zapata-Cantú (PhD). Associate Professor of the Management Department at EGADE Business School, Mexico. Her research work focuses on strategic management and knowledge management.

Netherlands

Corine Boon (PhD). Associate Professor of Human Resource Management at the University of Amsterdam Business School, the Netherlands. Her research interests include strategic HRM and person–environment fit.

Deanne N. Den Hartog (PhD). Full professor of Organisational Behaviour and Head of the Leadership and Management Section of the University of Amsterdam Business School in the Netherlands. Her research interests include leadership, proactive and innovative work behaviour, trust, and HRM.

Norway

Bård Kuvaas (PhD). Professor of Organisational Psychology and Associate Dean of the doctoral programme at BI Norwegian Business School, Norway. His research interests include behavioural decision-making, motivation, leadership, and Human Resource Management.

Anders Dysvik (PhD). Professor of Organisational Psychology at BI Norwegian Business School, Norway. His research interests include Human Resource Management and organisational behaviour.

Poland

Peter Odrakiewicz (PhD). Scientific Director at GPMI Research Institute, Poland.

David Odrakiewicz (PhD). His research interests are at the confluence of economics, efficient management, integrity competences, entrepreneurship and corporate social responsibility.

Magdalena Szulc (MSc). Consultant at McKinsey & Company, Poland.

Romania

Kinga Kerekes (PhD). Associate Professor at the Faculty of Economics and Business Administration, Babeş-Bolyai University in Cluj-Napoca, Romania. Her research interests include the effective use of human resources both at the micro and macro levels, HR practices, and labour market trends.

Russia

Anna Gryaznova (PhD). Associate Professor at Lomonossov Moscow State University Business School, Russia. Her research interests include the evolution of the concepts of leadership and ethics in the Russian business environment, cross-cultural management, psychological contracts, leader–follower and group dynamics, and Human Resource Management.

Singapore

Audrey Chia (PhD). Associate Professor of Management & Organisation, National University of Singapore Business School with a joint appointment at the Saw Swee Hock School of Public Health at the National University of Singapore. Her current research focuses on how social and health problems can be addressed by social entrepreneurship and innovative philanthropy.

Angeline Lim. Research Fellow in the Division of Engineering & Technology Management at the National University of Singapore. Her research interests include gender and diversity, inter-personal relationships and leadership, and their impact on individuals, teams, and organisations.

Slovenia

Robert Kaše (PhD). Associate Professor of Management and Organisation at the Faculty of Economics, University of Ljubljana, Slovenia. His research interests include Human Resource Management, intra-organisational social networks, careers, and emergence in teams.

Sweden

Magnus Hansson (PhD). Associate Professor and Researcher at Örebro University, Sweden. His research interests include organisational restructuring, downsizing, closedowns, corporate governance, and board interlocks.

Thailand

Chaturong Napathorn. PhD candidate in International Human Resource Management and Employment Relations at ILR School, Cornell University, New York. Lecturer of Human Resource Management at Thammasat Business School, Thailand. His research interests include International Human Resource Management, Strategic Human Resource Management, and international and comparative labour relations.

UAE

Scott L. Martin (PhD). Leader and Associate Professor of the Human Resource Management Department at Zayed University, UAE. His research focuses on understanding and managing performance.

Zainab Habeeb Abdulla (BS). Graduate Manager in the Learning and Development Department at Etihad Airways, Abu Dhabi, UAE.

Hashil Abdalla ZamZam (BS). Officer in the Reward and Policy department at Etihad Airways, Abu Dhabi, UAE. He completed his undergraduate degree in Human Resource Management at Zayed University, UAE.

Uganda

John C. Munene (PhD). Professor of Industrial and Organisational Psychology and Director of the PhD Programme at Makerere University Business School, Uganda.

His research interests include organisational and institutional development using a competence framework.

Florence Nansubuga (PhD). Senior Lecturer in Industrial and Organisational Psychology at Makerere University, Uganda. Her research areas include organisational learning focusing on competence development and reflection, talent management, and employee engagement.

Foreword

Global HRM is a series of books edited and authored by many of the best and most well-known scholars in the field of human resource management. The **Global HRM** series provides students and practitioners with accessible, comprehensive, and up-to-date knowledge that is useful for anyone interested in understanding human resource management in a global context. To be used individually or together, books in the **Global HRM** series examine the major topics relevant to international and comparative HRM. Each book takes an in-depth look at one important and complex topic. Together, the groundbreaking **Global HRM** series answers a real need for useful and affordable textbooks on global HRM.

Several books in the **Global HRM** series focus on a specific aspect of human resource management in multinational enterprises, including global leadership, global compensation, global talent management and global labour relations. Other books address special topics that arise in multinational enterprises, such as managing human resources in cross-border alliances, managing global legal systems, and the structure of a global HR function.

This book, the second edition of *Global Human Resource Management Casebook*, edited by Liza Castro Christiansen, Michal Biron, Elaine Farndale and Bård Kuvaas, is unique in the **Global HRM** field in that it is a collection of HRM cases that span the globe. Like the companies represented in these cases, the authors also are located all around the world. The cases address a variety of HR policies and practices in many different types of companies. Some of the companies represented in the cases are multinational firms while the operations and markets of other companies are mostly local. As with all the books in the Series, the cases utilize the most recent and classic research and are grounded in what companies around the world are doing today.

This second edition of *Global Human Resource Management Casebook* has been revised in important ways. First, the editors have replaced approximately 25 percent of the cases; second, cases that were retained from the first edition have been updated; and third, very importantly, the second edition now includes companies from several additional countries in Eastern Europe and Africa.

Like the second edition of *Global Human Resource Management Casebook*, several other books in the **Global HRM** series adopt a comparative approach to understanding human resource management. The comparative human resource management textbooks describe HRM topics found at the country level in selected countries, particularly within regions such as the Middle East, Europe, Central and Eastern Europe, Africa, North America, and Latin America. Thus, the comparative textbooks in the **Global HRM** series can be used quite effectively in conjunction with the second edition of the *Global Human Resource Management Casebook*. The Routledge **Global HRM** series effectively serves the growing global market of scholars and practitioners who are seeking a deeper and broader understanding of the role and importance of human resource management in companies that operate throughout the world. All textbooks in the **Global HRM** series provide thorough reviews of existing research and numerous examples from companies around the world. Some of the examples take the form of short company stories that are used to illustrate specific ideas found in a particular chapter. In addition, many textbooks in the **Global HRM** series include at least one detailed case description that serves as a convenient and more comprehensive example of topics discussed in the book.

A vast array of authors from all around the world have worked to produce the numerous books included in the **Global HRM** series. The scholarly perspectives and the practical company examples cited in these books are exceptionally diverse. Many **Global HRM** authors are pioneers in their areas of expertise and all are deeply knowledgeable about the topics they address. We are very grateful to all of these authors and appreciate their efforts on behalf of the Routledge **Global HRM** series.

The publisher and editors also have played major roles in making this Series possible. Routledge has provided its global production, marketing and reputation to make this Series feasible and affordable to faculty, students, and and practitioners throughout the world. In addition, Routledge has provided its own highly qualified professionals to make this Series a reality. In particular, we express our deep appreciation for the work of our Series editor, Sharon Golan. Her encouragement, expertise and support have been invaluable to us as editors of the **Global HRM** as well as to authors of specific books. She, along with Erin Arata and the entire staff, has helped ensure that the work of producing this Series has been both stimulating and enjoyable. For everything they have done, we thank them all. Together we are all very excited about the Routledge **Global HRM** series and hope you find an opportunity to use *Global Human Resource Management Casebook 2e,* as well as all the other **Global HRM** books.

Randall S. Schuler, Rutgers University, the Lancaster University School of
Management and the Center for HRM at the University of Lucerne
Susan E. Jackson, Rutgers University, the Lancaster University School of
Management and the Center for HRM at the University of Lucerne
Paul Sparrow, Lancaster University Management School
August 2016

Preface

The second edition of this Casebook is intended for those interested in learning about the international practice of Human Resource Management (HRM) from case studies of real companies and real situations. Unsurprisingly, given a particularly strong history in the USA, a large number of popular HRM-focused case studies originate from that context. Unfortunately, for those teaching HRM outside of the USA, there are numerous constraints and contingencies that need to be considered when discussing HRM practice beyond US borders. This book is designed to address this challenge. International cases can also provide a useful support for those teaching International HRM as a specific field of study. In addition, international cases are very appealing to an increasingly international and globally aware student body.

The cases in this volume demonstrate a number of universal concerns and challenges facing HRM practitioners around the world. No matter where in the world you look, there are concerns with recruitment and selection (see the cases from Belgium, Hungary and Thailand), training and development (see the cases from Austria, Azerbaijan, Denmark and the United Arab Emirates), pay and compensation (see the cases from Israel, Poland and Romania), diversity management and cross-cultural issues (see the cases from Botswana, Canada, Finland, Iceland, India, Mexico, Singapore and Slovenia), talent retention (see the cases from Germany and Russia), perennial organisational change, restructuring, and crisis (see the cases from Chile, China, the Czech Republic, Germany, the Netherlands, and Sweden), and the strategic alignment of HRM systems (see the cases from Bulgaria, Cyprus, Hong Kong, Ireland, Jordan, the Netherlands, Norway, and Uganda). This bodes well for the notion that the HRM profession requires a specific and predictable body of knowledge to be practised effectively.

Table 0.1 Cases and topics

	Country	Case	Industry	Topics
1	Austria	McDonalds	Food & Hospitality	• Talent development • Employee training
2	Belgium	Port of Antwerp	Shipping	• Staffing/selection testing • HR innovation
3	Germany	Robert Bosch	Manufacturing	• HRM characteristics • Response to economic crisis • Employee retention

	Country	Case	Industry	Topics	
4	Ireland	Creativity Co.	Industrial Design	• Employee re • Work force m • Managing cre	
5	The Netherlands	RetailCo	Retail	• HRM and cul • Merger and re • Increasing fina	
6	Denmark	Grundfos	Manufacturing	• Talent managen • Employee development • Talent innovation	
7	Finland	'Petrocom'	Energy	• Global Diversity Management • Workforce diversity • Diversity & Inclusiveness • Global versus Local	
8	Iceland	Marel and Stork	Manufacturing	• International Merger and Acquisition • Organisational Culture	
9	Norway	Airport Express Train and Southwest Airlines	Transportation services	• Strategic HRM • Internal consistency • High performance work-system	
10	Sweden	Gusab Stainless	Manufacturing	• Downsizing • Restructuring • Productivity • Labour relations	
11	Bulgaria	Telerik	Software	• HR in an entrepreneurial setting • Organizational culture • Work organization	
12	Czech Republic	The LIQUEUR Company	Food & Hospitality	• Crises management • Leadership styles • Economic crisis	
13	Hungary	General Electric Healthcare	Information technology (IT)	• Employee selection/ recruitment	
14	Poland	Alfa I Omega	Security/Safety Industry	• Employment regulations • Employment contracts • Compensation	
15	Romania	Textico Romania Ltd.	Manufacturing	• Employee motivation	
16	Russia	Eldorado	Retail (electronics)	• Transitional economy • Employee retention	
17	Slovenia	Trimo	Engineering (Pre-fabricated Buildings	• Global talent management • Workforce composition	
18	Azerbaijan	Nottingham Trent University (NTU)/ British Petroleum (BP)	Education/Oil and gas	• HR professionalism • HR training • Cross-national training • Local learning	
19	Botswana	University of Botswana (UB)	Education	• Diversity management policies • Recruitment	
20	Cyprus	Zenon University	Higher education	• People management • Organisational change	
21	Israel	"Foodco"	Food manufacturing	• Organisational structuring • Compensation & rewards	
22	Jordan	Jordan Company of Hospitality Education	Higher education	• Employee turnover • Organisational change	

(Continued)

	Country	Case	Industry	Topics
23	Uganda	NBL Uganda	Food & Hospitality	• Developing economy • Strategic HR alignment
24	United Arab Emirates	United Bank	Finance & Insurance	• Oil-state economy • Employee training and development
25	China	DL Automobile (Group) Co. Ltd.	Manufacture	• State capitalist economy • Labour Relations Structure • Outsourcing • Employee exit strategy
26	Hong Kong	MostClean Ltd.	Technology & services	• Employee Engagement • HRM in a multinational corporation • Talent development
27	India	ICICI bank	Finance & Insurance	• Gender diversity • Talent management
28	Singapore	Alexandra Hospital	Healthcare	• Innovative HR practices • Employee Re-training • Older workers
29	Thailand	ZZZ	Manufacturing	• Employee selection practices
30	Canada	Royal Bank of Canada (RBC)	Finance & Insurance	• Aboriginal workforce • Diversity management
31	Chile	SC Johnson's	Production/ Manufacturing	• Developing economy • Organisational Change • Self-managed teams
32	Mexico	Global Care	Healthcare	• National business cultures • People management • Cross cultural management • Scandinavian model

National differences are, however, also in evidence, and a set of 32 cases from around the world does a fine job of highlighting these differences in a comparative fashion. Differences emerge largely from two primary sources: the nature and trajectory of the economy within which HRM is being practised; and the national, cultural, and, especially, institutional context within which the HRM system develops. In this second edition of the Casebook, the editors encouraged the case authors to include such information in addition to case questions and teaching notes. This edition includes a range of new country cases, as well as cases from the first edition which have been updated.

A further common thread is the significant role played by multiple stakeholders: employees, government, society, unions, managers, owners and customers. The need for HRM managers to balance multiple competing stakeholder interests is a characteristic that strongly marks the profession and the function. This characteristic is consistent around the world. What is distinct within specific contexts is the balance of attention that is paid, for example, to unions, legislative requirements, or social expectations. These differences and similarities are well illustrated in the cases in this book. The social role played by the HR function is particularly apparent in these case studies. Several cases highlight the significant contribution played by the HR function in developing human capital not only for the firm, but also for economies or societies more widely. We hope that these cases contribute to a global understanding of the HRM profession and its activities.

Acknowledgments

The first edition of this book was the result of a novel collaboration among members of the Human Resources Division of the Academy of Management: the HR Division Ambassadors Programme. The Ambassadors Programme was designed to achieve three goals. First, to involve the worldwide membership of the HR Division through contributions by a representative scholar from each country in which the organisation has members. Second, to promote the activities of the organisation to its international membership. Third, to make a practical contribution to the field of Human Resource Management through collaborative research projects. The first edition of the Casebook was the result of the first such project.

The Ambassadors Programme was the brainchild of John Hollenbeck (Michigan State University), Past Chair of the HR Division. The programme falls under the remit of the Division's International Committee, which was then chaired by Steve Werner (University of Houston). The editors of the second edition of this book, Liza Castro Christiansen, Michal Biron, Elaine Farndale and Bård Kuvaas, are also members of the Ambassadors Programme Sub-Committee. However, the editors reserve the real acknowledgment for the contributors to the book, without whom this innovative project would not have been completed.

Part I
Western Europe

1

Austria

Talent Development at McDonald's Austria: A Compromise Between Local Demands and Global Standards

Wolfgang Mayrhofer and Katharina Pernkopf

Together with our franchisees, we make targeted investments in our employees, the focus is always on the personal development of each individual employee. With the opening of the academy for system catering we take an important step for our apprentices throughout Austria and offer a high-quality, uniform training.
Press release, Andreas Schmidlechner, Managing Director of McDonald's Austria (Privatschule für Lehrlingsausbildung / McDonald's, 2014)

McDonald's is the world's largest fast-food chain with substantial recent employer branding activities and in-house talent development practices across the globe. McDonald's has not only successfully positioned itself as the biggest fast-food service industry player on the planet, the Illinois-based company has also increasingly taken advantage of being a transnational organisation, one that constantly adapts itself to the prevailing zeitgeist by combining global and local elements across the countries in which it operates. Especially when it comes down to managing its human resources, McDonald's uses its international network of specialists to discuss problems, enable mutual learning, and find globally informed but locally adjusted solutions. According to its mission statement, McDonald's invests in talent, creates career paths starting from the grill and sets up internal training centres around the world. Global standards guide these activities. Similar to many other global players McDonald's faces the inevitable tensions between global standards, most often set by headquarters, and local demands such as legal regulations, cultural specifics or organisational idiosyncrasies.

Our case shows how setting up a training centre tailored to the demands of the Austrian context is the result of the interplay between the USA-based headquarters' global idea of developing future managers, national requirements in terms of legal regulations, the current labour market situation, and the competitive landscape with regard to attracting young people. This local version of the more general idea of training centres builds on Austria's vocational education system and aligns itself with political interests making vocational training more attractive by educating apprentices to a high level of competence.

After briefly characterising McDonald's both on a global scale and in its Austrian specificity, we will first highlight relevant elements of the Austrian context, in particular the employment legislation, labour market dynamics, and the Austrian system of dual vocational training. In a second step, we will outline the process of setting up a private vocational training school as the Austrian version of a McDonald's training centre, emphasising the various competing demands within the Austrian context and how McDonald's dealt with them. In a final step, we will briefly outline lessons to learn for other contexts.

Organisational Setting

McDonald's operates in more than 36,000 locations across the globe, serving almost 70 million customers in more than 100 countries a day. About 80 percent of restaurants are independently owned and run by local business women and men; in total McDonald's employs more than 420,000 people. According to Forbes, McDonald's ranks sixth on the world's most valuable brands list; only Apple, Microsoft, Google, Coca-Cola and IBM get better ratings. Nonstop optimisations in the delivery of products and related services as well as professionalisation through advanced training are crucial for the continuation of the McDonald's success story. Since the so-called good old days when McDonald's used to be the uncontested number one family fast-food restaurant in the USA, business has become tougher. In the USA, McDonald's struggled with a sales slump in 2015. This resembles episodes in the past where the burger-serving company had to deal with legal cases related to the quality of its products (e.g., "Super Size Me", slow food, and other food movements), allegedly mistreating their employees (e.g., minimum wage debate, strikes and unionisation activities organised by employees), or violations of child labour law. For these reasons McDonald's in the USA has been perceived more or less as a place to buy cheap food and as a low-end employer you do not want to be associated with. People even admit to hiding their lunch bag, making sure nobody would see the "Golden Arches" logo (see also a YouTube video at http://bit.ly/1LD00tZ). However, this image is something McDonald's plans to change, with an emphasis on being a good employer, serving quality products, and developing their human resources. Regarding the latter, they heavily invest in training in their own educational institution, Hamburger University, where only 1 percent of applicants get accepted which makes it more competitive to enter than Harvard.

McDonald's in Austria – colloquially called "Mäci" or "Schachtelwirt" ("box pub") by the local population – is not only the largest fast-food chain in Austria and the biggest host in the local food service industry, but also a major employer. It runs 194 restaurants – 85 percent operated by 43 franchisees – and employs 9,500 people. McDonald's was the first fast-food chain to enter Austria in 1977. It encountered critical media coverage back then, ranging from the problematic impact of fast food on local eating habits to the dangers of standardisation and franchise systems. After more than 35 years of operations, 85 percent of Austrians eat at McDonald's.

Background to the Case

Austria is a well-developed country in the heart of Europe. In 2014 it had a GDP of approximately 329.3 billion euros, ranking about twenty-seventh in the world and fifth in the European Union. Its economy consists of a large service sector (70.6 percent of GDP), a sound industrial sector (28 percent of GDP) with "hidden champions" prominent on the world market such as Swarovski (jewellery), Doppelmayer (cable cars) or Red Bull (beverages), and a small (1.4 percent of GDP), but highly developed agricultural sector. Austria's population amounts to 8,584,926, with about 1.8 million living in Vienna, a city regularly coming up as one of the most liveable places worldwide when measured in terms of political, social and economic climate, medical care, education, infrastructure (e.g., public transportation, power and water supply), and recreational offers such as restaurants, theatres, cinemas, sports facilities as well as the availability of diverse consumer goods from food to cars, along with environmental conditions – from green space to air quality.

Austrian Employment Legislation, Employee Relations and Labour Market Dynamics

Generally, harmony is a highly valued principle in Austria. Austrians are committed to promoting corporate success while paying attention to people's welfare. Reaching a compromise is important in political decision making, reflected most prominently in the system of Social Partnership, a voluntary system of negotiations between parties representing opposite interests, e.g., trade unions and employer's associations. The Austrian workforce traditionally benefits from worker protection because of a strong post-World War II labour movement. Establishing and maintaining fair working conditions is the primary task of the social partnership, an institution that local and globally operating organisations like McDonald's cannot ignore.

Austria has one of the lowest unemployment rates in Europe. Nevertheless, due to the financial crisis and its consequences, Austria is also currently facing the highest number of unemployed since the end of World War II. Traditionally, the labour market consists of people from various countries of origin. Almost 13 percent of people living in Austria were born abroad, which is beyond the comparable figure for classical immigration countries such as the USA (11 percent). This includes not only the 2015 influx of refugees from the Middle East, but also individuals from former Yugoslavian states, Germans, Turks, Slovaks and Czechs since Austria has a long tradition of sheltering refugees from nearby countries. Traditionally, immigrants have been an important group for McDonald's. As in other countries such as Denmark, minority groups have not only become integrated into the labour market through McDonald's, but have also been promoted to leadership roles. Thus one can assume that the fast-food chain will also play an important role as an employer in Austria and across Europe in the future.

Apprenticeship training has lost some of its attractiveness due to the lack of choice in educational pathways, the concentration of apprentices in a few occupations and the steadily decreasing willingness of Austrian companies to provide training opportunities. Thus, there has been a strong demand for reform in the apprenticeship system in order to make apprenticeship trades more attractive again. Reform measures are already being carried out in cooperation with all parties involved including financial support for companies which train apprentices, removal of bureaucratic impediments, and more information about less popular and non-gender-specific occupations. Since these reforms, more companies have been willing to take on apprentices and the government is prepared to follow up with adapting its programmes to make apprenticeship more attractive.

The Apprenticeship System in Austria

In Austria apprenticeship training takes places at two different sites: at the company and at the part-time vocational school ("Berufsschule"). Thus, it is also referred to as a "dual vocational training system" or, in its shortened form, as a "dual system". Currently about

40 percent of all Austrian teenagers enter the apprenticeship system upon completion of their compulsory education. After finishing their apprenticeship, about 40 percent of these young people, now known as "journeymen" (Gesellen), continue to work for the company where they had been trained. The most popular apprenticeship trades among girls are retail-trade merchant, followed by hairdresser and office clerk. Among male apprentices the most popular occupations are motor-vehicle mechanic, followed by electrician.

Students may apply for admission to vocational training after compulsory education (9 years). Apprentices may only be trained in the legally recognised apprenticeship trades. In the food service industry, for instance, you can apply for vocational training to become a catering specialist, assistant in the catering and hotel industry, assistant in the hotel and restaurant industry, chef, system catering specialist, and restaurant specialist. Apprenticeship training lasts from two to four years, but in most cases three years. Companies that train apprentices are obliged to provide them with the skills and know-how specified in the occupational profile. This ensures a uniform minimum standard of training. On-the-job training constitutes the major part of apprenticeship, and because apprentices are company employees, the company also provides them with insurance – as required by law – e.g., full social insurance including health, accident, retirement and unemployment insurance. The aim of the part-time vocational schools for apprentices is the provision of theoretical basics related to the respective occupation, to promote and complement on-the-job training and to deepen the general knowledge of apprentices.

At the moment only six private vocational schools exist in Austria. One belongs to the ÖBB, the Austrian Federal Railways which is owned entirely by the Republic of Austria. Another one is run by Spar, a major retail chain in Austria. Spar's vocational school evolved out of the Meinl-Academy, which is more than 100 years old. Meinl is a traditional Austrian manufacturer and retailer of coffee, gourmet foods and other grocery products which also operates three coffee shops in the USA, all three on the north side of Chicago, Illinois. The other three schools are run by Swarovski, known for its crystals and high-end optics, Plansee, a group of companies focusing on manufacturing powder metallurgical materials, and a public prison.

McDonald's: Handling Global Standards and Local Demands

In 1977 McDonald's opened its first restaurant in the city centre of Vienna, and kicked off a cultural revolution in the land of Wiener Schnitzel. However, at first it was viewed rather sceptically by locals and was seen as an unnecessary competitor to Vienna's well known sausage stands ("Würstelstand"), the still beloved Austrian version of fast food. Besides burgers and co, the chain introduced a new business model, the franchise system, into the country. Despite or even because of all this novelty, McDonald's Austria managed to achieve a market share of 39 percent in the system catering industry in 2013. By comparison Burger King's share only amounted to 3 percent. Other chains like Pizza Hut also opened restaurants in Austria, but have never really gained a foothold. This situation shows how weak the competition has been in that sector of the Austrian economy. Measured by the number of residents, Austria has the highest concentration of McDonald's restaurants in Europe. In 2014 the fast-food chain served 156 million customers with a turnover of about 562 million euros. This success mainly has to do with the quality of their products, as they mostly use domestic produce (note: serving genetically modified food is forbidden in Austria).

McDonald's has had an impact on Austria and its food service industry, but Austria has also had some influence on McDonald's on a global scale. Andreas Hacker, former managing director of McDonald's Austria, was crucially involved in the process of introducing the concept of McCafé into the chain. Moreover, he was the first non-American on the Board of Directors at the USA-based headquarters. Several years ago Austria also managed to soften the strict rules of the group and added beer to its menu, as the absence of beer had been identified as one reason why especially male customers avoided the fast food chain. These examples from marketing and product development already hint towards the transnational HRM approach of McDonald's. The product or the brand is very much interrelated with the labour process or the employer brand and McDonald's allows competent country HR managers to meet local demands as long as global standards such as product quality are ensured.

As outlined above, McDonald's is an important employer for the country. Criticism directed towards working conditions was successfully fended off by introducing a first collective wage agreement in 2011, which is regularly adjusted. The apprenticeship salary exceeds the common rate in Austria and is considerably more than in other similar programmes. In light of its success in the country and its investments in training, McDonald's is seen as a secure (unshakeable) company to work for. Their training programmes provide transparent and accessible career chances and collective wage agreements guarantee an appropriate stable income.

McDonald's Austria does not rest on its laurels. It constantly develops its (employer) brand and accordingly updates its website at http://www.mcdonalds.at/. Besides information on new products, restaurant concepts, basic company information and contact details, a subsite is dedicated to McDonald's as an employer. For the second year in a row, McDonald's received the award "Investors in People", an international accreditation awarded by the Austrian Federation of Industry, the Federal Ministry of Economics and Labour and the European Social Fund. McDonald's uses the award logo on their website. Furthermore, every user can download the collective wage agreement. Apprentices at McDonald's earn more than in other trades. The national website also serves as a means of recruitment, providing information on career opportunities and vacant jobs. They emphasise their flexible work time and promote McDonald's Austria as a secure workplace in times of economic downturn.

Setting Up a Private Vocational School in Austria

Referring to the words of Hamburger University founder Ray Kroc, the company purposefully invests in people: "If we are going to go anywhere, we've got to have talent. And I'm going to put my money in talent" (Hamburger University/AboutMcDonalds.com, 2016). In addition, the McDonald's Corporation founder claimed: "We are not a hamburger company serving people, we are a people company serving hamburgers" (ibid.). In 1961, McDonald's first major internal training centre was established, the Hamburger University in Illinois, USA. Since then training at Hamburger University has emphasised consistent restaurant operations procedures, service, quality and cleanliness. It has turned into the company's global centre of excellence. McDonald's operations training and leadership development has spread out from there. So far six international campuses have followed: Tokyo (1971), London (1981), Munich (1982), Sydney (1989), São Paolo (1996), and Shanghai (2010). Those centres have the purpose of training people working for McDonald's; generally they do not serve the public interest by educating system-catering experts. But credits can be transferred to other bachelor study programmes. According to a recent article on BusinessInsider.com, Hamburger University has had more than 275,000 graduates since 1961 and has already celebrated its 55th anniversary.

For many years McDonald's Austria has been offering apprenticeship positions. Why did they start that in the first place? As a small country Austria only sends the more advanced talents to the Hamburger University campus in Munich. The initial talent development had always taken place locally. Apprentices received vocational training in system catering and were educated to be the restaurant managers of the future. Most of this three-year programme they would spend with company-relevant training, but for the theoretical component they would have to go to a general vocational school ("Berufsschule") in a part of Austria where the apprentice was placed. In that vocational school they would sit together with cooks, waiters and people from other trades. Little wonder that this was not the optimal solution for McDonald's Austria. They would argue, like other companies before, that they were willing to found a private school not because of their discontent with public schools, but because of the beneficial aspects of a tailor-made programme they could then offer their apprentices. They wanted to provide more education than "necessary", for example language courses and further training in culture and ethics. For these reasons McDonald's opened a private vocational school at the beginning of 2014. This tailor-made programme is based on the company-wide curriculum. With running a private vocational school a compromise could be reached that met the organisational evaluative criteria of increasing productivity and was strongly linked to local customs as well as market and civic principles by providing competitive products through training that also contributes to the common good of society.

Yet, it took McDonald's a number of years to finally open up this so-called "academy for system catering". Together with the Austrian Federal Economic Chamber (WKO) McDonald's was the one company in Austria to initiate system catering as a trade in the first place. This was happening more than ten years before the fast-food chain considered running its own vocational school. The local managers responsible for HR were aware of the public debate on a growing shortage of skilled labour in Austria. They also knew that the Austrian government had an interest in making learning a trade more attractive again. Still it had taken local HRM about three years of negotiations to convince school authorities and political decision makers to find a solution. To reconcile the need for being responsive to local demands (strengthening the apprenticeship system in Austria and being in line with the legal regulations) with the need to adhere to global standards of the organisation (centralised McDonald's-specific training), McDonald's set up a private vocational school.

The McDonald's private vocational school was and still is unique. It is a private training centre for all system catering specialists and therefore future restaurant managers at McDonald's where costs are fully covered by and shared among McDonald's Austria and its franchisees. Still the academy for system catering is embedded within Austrian culture and its institutional environment, and aligned with the overall dual vocational training system. Apprentices receive an official certificate that they have become "Gesellen" (journeymen) which certifies that they know their trade, and they can use that to work elsewhere. They can even obtain a high school degree during that time. Graduates are not obliged to stay with McDonald's after completion of the vocational training. Furthermore, the academy for system catering can be regarded as an "elite training centre". Every year it only accepts 50 apprentices. To put that into perspective: in 2012 McDonald's received 24,000 applications. McDonald's Austria has the opportunity to select the most promising applicants, develop them in a tailor-made vocational training system and make a decision whether to invest more into this talent or not. The apprentice, on the other hand, gets the chance to know the world of McDonald's and its products very well. A strong identification with the products provided is key for establishing a meaningful win-win situation between employer and employee. Therefore, it can be argued that the headquarters in the USA accepts local adaptations to HRM practices as long as the product quality remains in line with the global standards.

Generally speaking HR country managers are usually the ones who adjust global HRM practices in response to local expectations. In our case, the Austrian country management had to fulfil competing demands. The global headquarters had its concept of developing in-house talent, Austrian politicians had their understanding of quality vocational training, and potential apprentices also had their individual educational expectations. Setting up a private vocational school, therefore, was a compromise: developing experts, equipping them with a sense of hospitality and other qualities which are highly valued in the Austrian context, at the same time enabling them to deliver competitive products and ensuring the good reputation of McDonald's through customer satisfaction. As a further plus in combination with the employer brand McDonald's also can present their employees as well trained ("Investors in People") and being taken care of ("Belonging to the McDonald's family").

Consequences Beyond Austria

Does this Austrian talent development practice have any consequences for other countries outside of Austria? To answer this we extend our perspective towards Austria's closest neighbours and take a comparative look at the local training programmes of McDonald's Germany and Switzerland.

Although Austria, Germany and Switzerland share the same language and are related in their heritage and customs, vocational training only takes place at McDonald's Germany and Austria. This is surprising since vocational training is common in Switzerland as well. However, it has not worked out for McDonald's Switzerland yet, even though the local HR manager once considered setting up a private vocational school there. According to the HR manager from McDonald's Austria who has good relations with his Swiss colleagues, a major reason is that young Swiss employees apparently do not bother to become experts in system catering, but are primarily attracted by job security and earning good money from day one. They also appreciate flexible working hours and wish for an employer who offers a job that is compatible with family life.

According to official corporate websites and company informants, the product quality is defined the same way in all three countries (excellent product quality through people). In people terms, there are different emphases on how to get there. Besides the classic apprenticeship and on-the-job crew and management training, McDonald's Austria offers the "McMatura" – apprenticeship training with a high school degree. This represents a current trend in the Austrian context. In Germany, the apprentice tends to be called "expert" and as a large country it has its own Hamburger University where a Bachelor of Arts degree may be obtained by the more advanced talents. On the Swiss website, we hardly find any information on training; instead it is important to present the company as a place with manageable careers for parents and other special groups such as students who would like a side job.

Thus even in these apparently very similar contextual settings HRM is challenged and has to find ways to adapt globally defined practices, such as in-house talent development, to local demands. Local HRM builds up competence and has the opportunity to share experiences through a transnational organisation. Learning and benefiting from cultural diversity is the ultimate competitive advantage.

Our empirical illustration has focused on McDonald's, the world's largest fast-food restaurant chain, and its in-house training programme. As illustrated above, McDonald's is eager to invest in its own talent by creating career paths "starting from the grill" and setting up its internal training centres accordingly. Among other things, our case has portrayed the local version of a training centre in contrast to the USA-based headquarters' global idea of developing future managers. This local version has taken into account Austria's apprenticeship system and political interests in making vocational training more attractive, combining it with a high school degree and educating people to a high level. In addition we have briefly contrasted the Austrian training programme with the programmes in Germany and Switzerland in order to hint towards the differences and similarities the actual context makes.

Acknowledgements

The authors would like to thank Johanna Weißensteiner, a research assistant who has helped us with data collection.

Case Study Tasks

Questions for Group/Class Discussion

1 In your opinion, why did McDonald's decide to run a private vocational school?
2 Given what you know about the Austrian cultural and legal environment regarding vocational training:

(i) what are the benefits of running a private vocational school?
(ii) would you see alternative ways to develop talent at McDonald's?

3 If Ray Kroc were still alive, what would his opinion be on the situation in Austria?
4 As a global HR manager, to which countries could you transfer this model?

Role-play Exercise

Imagine a job interview situation. Two 17-year-old students apply for the system catering vocational training at McDonald's. There is only one spot left. McDonald's takes only 50 apprentices a year. One of them has already worked at a McDonald's restaurant during the summer time and knows pretty well what is going on behind the curtains. Simulate a group job interview and justify why the recruiter and the restaurant owner will pick one or the other person.

> *Recruiter*: As a recruiter from the Austrian HRM department your job is to identify talent. This person could become a member of the company's own management team. He or she should therefore make the impression of caring for the world of McDonald's, the quality of products as well as for customers and colleagues.

Restaurant owner: As a franchisee you are interested in getting a well-trained apprentice who is willing to learn and work hard. You share the cost of training that person and want to benefit from the high-quality education. This person might be your future restaurant manager.

Applicant A: Actually you wanted to be an apprentice in a bank, but could not find a position. You have heard of the private vocational school and career opportunities at McDonald's and already see yourself as the next managing director of McDonald's Austria. You are not the biggest fan of burgers, but once in a while you join friends to eat there.

Applicant B: You already worked at a McDonald's restaurant in the summer and really liked it there: nice colleagues, clear processes, and flexible working time arrangements. Belonging to the "family" felt very good. You would be interested in graduating with a "McMatura", because this would give you the opportunity to work at other places after your time at McDonald's.

References and Further Reading

£12,400 child labour fine on McDonald's / UK News / The *Guardian* (2001, August 1). Retrieved June 9, 2016, from http://www.theguardian.com/uk/2001/aug/01/childprotection.society

150 Jahre Wiener Kaffeehauskultur: Julius Meinl Kaffee feiert vom 14. bis 24. Juni am Wiener Graben (2012, June 6). Retrieved June 9, 2016, from http://www.ots.at/presseaussendung/OTS_20120606_OTS0246/150-jahre-wiener-kaffeehauskultur-julius-meinl-kaffee-feiert-vom-14-bis-24-juni-am-wiener-graben-bild

Annual Data (2015, May 30). Retrieved June 9, 2016, from http://www.statistik.at/web_en/statistics/Economy/national_accounts/gross_domestic_product/annual_data/index.html

Arbeitslosigkeit in Österreich: Das Ende eines Musterschülers – Arbeitsmarkt – derStandard.at > Wirtschaft (2016, May 9). Retrieved June 9, 2016, from http://derstandard.at/2000015434074/Arbeitslosigkeit-in-Oesterreich-Das-Ende-eines-Musterschuelers

Company Overview & Segment Information: AboutMcDonalds.com (2014, December 31). Retrieved June 9, 2016, from http://www.aboutmcdonalds.com/mcd/

Denmark: The occupational promotion of migrant workers Eurofond (2009, March 24). Retrieved June 9, 2016, from http://www.eurofound.europa.eu/observatories/eurwork/comparative-information/national-contributions/denmark/denmark-the-occupational-promotion-of-migrant-workers

Geography and Population. Retrieved June 9, 2016, from http://www.migration.gv.at/en/living-and-working-in-austria/austria-at-a-glance/geography-and-population.html

Hamburger University McDonald's: AboutMcDonalds.com. Retrieved June 9, 2016, from http://www.aboutmcdonalds.com/mcd/corporate_careers/training_and_development/hamburger_university.html

Inside McDonald's Hamburger University – Business Insider (2015, October 24). Retrieved June 9, 2016, from http://www.businessinsider.com/mcdonalds-hamburger-university-2333?IR=T

McDonald's. Retrieved June 9, 2016, from http://www.mcdonalds.at/presse

McDonald's Aufstieg zum Staatsburger – trend.at (2012, August 1). Retrieved June 9, 2016, from http://www.format.at/wirtschaft/business/mcdonald-s-aufstieg-staatsburger-336632

McDonald's lawsuit (2011–2016). Retrieved June 9, 2016, from http://www.huffingtonpost.com/news/mcdonalds-lawsuit/

McDonald's Profit Drops 13% As Sales Slump Persists – Forbes (2015, June 23) Retrieved June 9, 2016, from http://www.forbes.com/sites/laurengensler/2015/07/23/mcdonalds-second-quarter-earnings/

Mercer 2016 Quality of Life Rankings. Retrieved June 9, 2016, from https://www.imercer.com/content/mobility/quality-of-living-city-rankings.html

New York Plans $15-an-Hour Minimum Wage for Fast Food Workers – *The New York Times* (2015, July 22). Retrieved June 9, 2016, from http://www.nytimes.com/2015/07/23/nyregion/new-york-minimum-wage-fast-food-workers.html

Privatschule für Lehrlingsausbildung / McDonald's (2014, February 15). Retrieved June 9, 2016, from htttp://www.mcdonalds.at/privatschule-fuer-lehrlingsausbildung

The World's Most Valuable Brands List – Forbes (2016). Retrieved June 9, 2016, from http://www.forbes.com/powerful-brands/list/

Vienna voted the most liveable city in the world for the seventh time! – Vienna – Now or Never!. Retrieved June 9, 2016, from https://www.wien.info/en/lifestyle-scene/most-livable-city

Volkszählungen, Registerzählung, Abgestimmte Erwerbsstatistik. Retrieved June 9, 2016, from http://www.statistik.at/web_de/statistiken/menschen_und_gesellschaft/bevoelkerung/volkszaehlungen_registerzaehlungen_abgestimmte_erwerbsstatistik/index.html

www.oegb.at – English. Retrieved June 9, 2016, from http://www.oegb.at/cms/S06/S06_11/english

2

Belgium

Get Innovative in Personnel Selection:
The Case of the Port of Antwerp

Filip Lievens, Britt De Soete and Christoph Nils Herde

Organizational Setting

Thanks to its central location and its large storage and distribution capacity, the Port of Antwerp can be regarded as a key gateway to Europe. Concerning international maritime transport, Antwerp is ranked as the second harbor of Europe and the seventh harbor worldwide. The Port of Antwerp is the European market leader in terms of the transportation of steel, fruit, forest products, coffee, tobacco, and other products. In 2009, it dealt with almost 160 million tons of goods. Each year, over 14,000 sea-going vessels and 55,000 inland navigation vessels are passing through the Port of Antwerp. As nearly every important European consumption and production center can be reached easily by train, vessel or truck from the Port of Antwerp, it is considered to be a crucial player in the international trade business. Over the centuries, the Port area has grown to exactly 13,057 hectares, or about 20,000 soccer fields.

Each day, about 150,000 people contribute to the operation of the Port of Antwerp. This includes lorry drivers, ships' agents, and customs officials. The majority of these people work for private organizations in and around the port area. In addition, there is the Antwerp Port Authority. As an organization, the Antwerp Port Authority numbers about 1,650 employees who play an important role in the day-to-day operation of the port (e.g., managing and maintaining docks, bridges, locks, quay walls, and land; efficient passage and safety of the shipping traffic).[1]

Since the first Belgian social laws were voted in 1887, there has existed a growing necessity for Antwerp harbor employers as well as employees to gather in occupational associations to facilitate the social bargaining process. The harbor employees joined trade unions who acted on their members' behalf during collective bargaining and social conflicts. Nowadays, every blue-collar harbor worker in the Port of Antwerp is obliged to become a union member because the trade unions not only represent their members in the social debate but also organize the sequence in which all applicants can participate in the port's selection process. The trade unions also provide each selected blue-collar harbor worker with a registration card which gives the owner the official right to perform harbor labor.

In a similar vein, the employers of the Port of Antwerp joined an employers' federation: CEPA (Center of Employers at the Port of Antwerp), which was founded on March 22, 1929. CEPA's main purpose was to optimize the organization of the harbor labor. Each employer in the Port was obliged to become a CEPA member and to pay a yearly contribution to the organization. In turn, CEPA provided its members with, among other things, a social administration service, a medical service organization, a training center, and a compensation fund. This fund was intended to pay the wages of the blue-collar workers in case of economic or technical unemployment. Until now, the responsibilities of CEPA have been threefold. Most importantly, CEPA represents all harbor employers during the social bargaining process with the trade unions and during social conflicts. Second, CEPA is held responsible for the organization and administration concerning the selection and wage payment of all 9,300 Antwerp blue-collar dock workers. The third task of CEPA as an umbrella organization is the daily management of the above-mentioned service organizations and organisms.

HRM in Belgium: A Culture of Compromise

As the Belgian culture is an essential determinant of the HRM processes in Belgium, it is important to describe the broader cultural context (Sels, Janssens, Van Den Brande, & Overlaet, 2000). However, answering this question is not simple, as a united Belgian culture is almost nonexistent. King Albert I found himself confronted with the same observation in 1911 when one of his senators noted: 'Sire, il n'y pas de Belges!' ('Sire, there are no Belgians!' [Sels et al., 2000, p. 21]). Rather than by uniformity, the country is characterized by numerous contrasts. Examples are ideological (Catholic versus liberal), linguistic (French versus Flemish) and economic (labor versus capital) discrepancies. Box 2.1 presents more facts and figures about the economic, political, demographic, and educational context of Belgium.

These opposites, together with the shared Belgian history – rather than the shared Belgian culture – have molded the current relationships between employers and employees. The Catholic influences, and Belgium's pioneer contribution to the second industrial revolution and its inherent social conflicts, have substantially influenced the formal employment agreement and the psychological contract between employers and employees. Individual employment agreements are considered as membership certificates with limited room for negotiation. Therefore, most Belgian employees – especially blue-collar workers – have joined trade unions and changes in employment conditions have been realized by collective bargaining. The long Belgian tradition of social negotiation and collective bargaining was created and is currently fostered by the psychological contract between employers and employees and the accompanying cultural values.

Nowadays, Belgian psychological contracts are characterized by high power distance, high uncertainty avoidance, and, as a consequence, also high loyalty and low exit intentions (Hofstede, 1980). In practice, this implies that Belgian employees highly respect their employer's authority (power distance). However, as a return, they count on their supervisors to meet their expectations, which primarily deal with labor conditions and job security (uncertainty avoidance) and which are subject to collective bargaining. As both employers and employees place great value on the continuity of the production process, job security, social peace, and good-quality long-term relationships, they constantly strive to reach a compromise during the negotiations. As the aforementioned Belgian contrasts have continuously threatened harmony and social peace, the Belgian culture of compromise and consensualism became a strategy to survive – also in the domain of HRM. Therefore, addressing and informing unions, inviting them as a partner in the collective bargaining process, and maintaining good union relationships are inherent parts of the management tasks of Belgian employers.

Box 2.1. Facts and Figures about Belgium

Belgium is a federal state that is governed by a representative democratic, constitutional monarchy. Whereas the royal dynasty represents the Head of State, the Prime Minister serves as head of government. Regarding the separation of powers, the government acts as the executive power, whereas the government as well as the parliament share the legislative power (Belgian Federal Government, 2016). Belgium's population size amounts to 11,209,044, which represents 2.2% of the overall population of the European Union. 61.6% of all Belgian residents are between 18 and 64 years old. Similar to many European countries, Belgian society faces an increasing senescence (the 18.1% of people who are 65 or older). 11.2% of all Belgian residents held a foreign nationality in 2015 (Algemene Directie Statistiek - Statistics Belgium, 2015).

Belgium comprises geographical regions that represent different communities with distinct languages, slight cultural divergences, and even unique governments. In 2015, 57.5% percent lived in the Dutch speaking part (Flanders), 10.5% lived in the French as well as Dutch speaking region of Brussels, 31.3% lived in the French speaking part (Wallonia), and finally, 0.7% lived in the German speaking region/community (Algemene Directie Statistiek - Statistics Belgium, 2015; Belgian Federal Government, 2016).

Altogether, these different communities generate a Gross Domestic Product of 400.6 billion €, which represents 2.9% of the Gross Domestic Product of the European Union. With a share of 69% in 2014, the service sector represents the most important contributor to the overall Gross Domestic Product in Belgium. Within the service sector, trade, transport & catering, government & education, as well as business services are the three leading branches of industry (Algemene Directie Statistiek - Statistics Belgium, 2015).

Regarding the level of education, 29.3% successfully achieved a university diploma, a college diploma or a comparable degree. The percentage of Belgians between 30 and 34 years old with such a higher educational degree was 43.8% in 2014, which is above the average of countries in the European Union (Algemene Directie Statistiek - Statistics Belgium, 2015).

The above-average educational level in Belgium also contributes to its high level of human development. That is, the Human Development Index (HDI), which is based on the dimensions of (1) the ability to lead a long and healthy life, (2) the ability to acquire knowledge, and (3) the ability to achieve a decent standard of living, equals 0.890, which makes Belgium rank 21 in the world. So, Belgium's HDI indicates very high human development (United Nations Development Programme, 2015).

The Port of Antwerp: Towards an Innovative Selection Approach

Problems and Challenges in the Port

From the 1990s until October 2004, CEPA outsourced the whole selection process for blue-collar harbor workers to a government-owned selection company. External consultants were responsible for the acquisition of the test battery, which consisted of an interview and numerous paper-and-pencil tests. The selection tests were rather old-fashioned and no feedback reports were provided to the candidates. Twice a week, Tom Wolters, one of the consultants, visited the Port of Antwerp to communicate his decisions about the applicants and to provide face-to-face feedback when the candidates explicitly requested it.

In light of this state of affairs, both the candidates applying for a job in the Port of Antwerp and the associated unions displayed an extremely negative attitude towards the selection procedure as it was organized in those days. The main critique expressed dealt with its troublesome job-relatedness, namely its perceived lack of a connection between the content and format of the selection methods used on the one hand and the target job on the other hand. This lack of a conceptual link between the test battery and the job led to reduced motivation on the part of the applicants because they perceived the result of the process as merely arbitrary instead of being based on a thorough assessment of their abilities. As the test battery was perceived to be an invalid predictor of job performance, the selection decision was also often challenged by candidates. Frequently, Tom had to deal with complex and emotional feedback conversations with rejected candidates, who received the full support of the trade unions, whereby union representatives often attended the feedback meetings and criticized the entire selection process. At that point, any glimmer of constructiveness and effectiveness in the selection and feedback process of the Antwerp blue-collar harbor workers was in the distant future . . .

In 2004, Sophie Ryan joined CEPA as the new head of the selection department of the blue-collar harbor workers. In the past, she had worked as a consultant in the domain of personnel selection, which had made her aware of the importance of standardized, up-to-date, and valid selection procedures. Sophie's assessment of the selection situation at the Port of Antwerp revealed that CEPA was faced with multiple challenges. First, as the selection battery was questioned and criticized by applicants, harbor workers, and unions, the reputation of the CEPA selection procedure was in jeopardy. Second, the low motivation of the applicants often led to a decline in their test performance. The feedback meetings subsequent to the testing procedure were frustrating both for CEPA – which could not explain why certain candidates were not shortlisted for the job as blue-collar dock workers – and for the candidates – who did not consider their testing results as a sufficient explanation for their rejection. The traditional selection procedure also caused the relationship between the harbor and the union to deteriorate. As the trade unions fundamentally disagreed on the use of the test battery, they displayed a rather inflexible attitude during numerous negotiations with the CEPA management, which slowed down the social bargaining process and complicated it significantly. Another difficulty inherent in the old selection procedure was that the test did not meet the changing nature of the job. In fact, the job demands had modified and increased over the years as a result of the changing legal and technological environment. Last but not least, Sophie noticed that the current selection process was too stringent and demanding so that remaining vacancies were not filled. As the different selection instruments required a high level of literacy and language understanding (even though that was not needed for of the job), many applicants were wrongfully rejected. Especially members of non-traditional applicant (minority) groups faced difficulties in being selected as dock workers because of the high reading and writing demands of the test battery, irrespective of their technical skills. Thus, members of the minority applicant pool had significantly fewer chances to be selected than members of a majority applicant pool (Zedeck, 2010). This adverse impact not only raised ethical, deontological, and legal questions, but also led to practical organizational problems such as the aforementioned shortfalls in applicant pools. This was especially important in times of increasing labor shortages on the one hand and growing globalization and international mobility of employers and employees on the other hand.

In short, Sophie concluded that the Port of Antwerp in general and CEPA in particular were challenged to develop a new, job-related, and transparent selection test battery. First, the selection procedure had to predict the performance of the blue-collar harbor workers, while taking the current job demands into account. Second, it was supposed to elicit positive perceptions among applicants and trade unions, which in turn should improve the image of the Port and its relationships with the union. Third, it had to be an appealing selection procedure for traditional (majority) as well as non-traditional (minority) applicant groups.

The Switch

After careful consideration of the possible options, the chairman of the division, Sophie and her staff decided to transform the current test battery entirely in order to meet the above-mentioned challenges. The development of a novel selection test battery consisted of numerous steps. First, an extensive job analysis was conducted to determine the KSAOs (knowledge, skills, abilities and other competencies) of each blue-collar employee profile. Therefore, interviews were undertaken with the head and the trainers of the training center, co-workers from the prevention and protection department, and trade union representatives. These job analyses resulted in an adaptation of the existing job profiles to the current needs of the harbor and a list of corresponding KSAOs per profile. The next step consisted of determining which selection procedures should be included in the selection process based on the KSAOs to be assessed. CEPA's aim was to shift from traditional test methods to a new test battery that consisted of computer-based tests and simulation exercises. To compose the selection battery, computerized tests used by other maritime organizations were purchased and supplemented with tailor-made computer exercises developed by an external consultancy firm. The former consisted of a 187-item personality questionnaire, an abstract cognitive reasoning test, and a speed-and-accuracy test. All exercises developed by the external consultancy firm used a visual presentation of the test content instead of a written presentation. Some exercises could be defined as simulation exercises or sample-based selection instruments as applicants were put in a simulated work situation and expected to realistically perform job-related tasks and solve problems.

Although most blue-collar dock workers went through the same selection process, attention was also paid to the development of specific selection instruments for specific harbor worker profiles. The crane operator test, a simulation exercise that was developed to test applicants for the job of crane operator, serves as a good example. During this exercise, the candidate is placed in a simulated container crane on a harbor terminal and is subsequently asked to unload an inland navigation vessel. To do so, each candidate has a computer screen and two joysticks at his disposal, which serve to present the simulated situation and to carry out the accompanying tasks respectively. There are two tasks: first of all, the candidate needs to reach out for the container and afterwards he is expected to place the container on the dock. While performing this latter task, it is important that the applicant takes the position of other harbor container transporters into account and does not obstruct them in their movement. Figure 2.1 presents the reader with a screenshot of the crane operator test. The crane operator test measures four different KSAOs: concentration ability (speed-and-accuracy), sense of responsibility, sense of safety, and stress resilience. An important asset of this computer test is its ability to assess these KSAOs in an objective way. By using an automated scoring key which was developed in advance, the subjective element in the assessment process was reduced. Concentration ability was measured by the speed by which a candidate was able to work with the spreader (i.e., container lifting device). The hindering of other vehicles in the harbor served as a proxy for the candidate's sense of responsibility. The applicant's sense of safety was determined by the number of safety mistakes displayed during the test, for example, colliding with containers, ships or other transport vehicles. Finally, stress resilience was measured by the candidate's performance during test situations with increasing demands (e.g., via the manipulation of time limits). Since 2005, the crane operator test has been successfully used in the selection process of Antwerp crane operators.

An important aspect that Sophie took into account while modifying the selection process was improving and maintaining good long-term relationships between CEPA and the trade unions. In order to develop a personal connection with the trade unions and to lower the communication threshold, Sophie decided to introduce herself personally to all harbor union representatives shortly after she joined CEPA. To gain union commitment, Sophie presented the plans to adapt the CEPA selection system and discussed them with the unions already in the earliest stages of the switch. As mentioned earlier, the trade unions participated to develop the new job profiles of blue-collar harbor workers. Although the unions were strong advocates of changing the traditional testing method, the development of a new test battery also induced a new perceived threat to a fair selection process. As Sophie found out during her conversations with union representatives, they feared that the PC-based

Figure 2.1 Screenshot of computerized crane operator simulation

nature of the battery required applicants to possess more computer skills than needed for performing blue-collar worker jobs. Especially older job applicants feared they would not be able to perform the tests properly and be selected out. Both Sophie and the external consultancy firm took this feedback into account when developing the new selection battery. It was ensured that neither computer skills nor a specialized educational background was required to complete the selection instruments. Finally, to familiarize the unions with the new test battery, trade union representatives were invited to pretest the new computerized selection instruments.

In the end, not only the selection battery but also the accompanying feedback process was thoroughly adapted. As opposed to the early days, from 2004 every applicant has been receiving a feedback report. In addition to this written report, each candidate has been entitled to ask for a face-to-face feedback appointment and has had the opportunity to look into his/her tests. Every rejected candidate also has the right to sign up for a retest at an external selection office selected by CEPA.

The Current Situation at the Port of Antwerp

The switch from the traditional test battery to a modern, job-related, and computerized version implied numerous direct and indirect advantages for the Port of Antwerp. Logical consequences resulting from the computerized selection procedure were faster and more efficient test administration and an up-to-date item banking/norming. Apart from these practical benefits, the use of fancy technological devices in selection also tends to generate positive applicant perceptions (Hausknecht, Day, & Thomas, 2004). Taken together, this led to a substantial image improvement of the Port of Antwerp and CEPA in general and its selection process in particular.

One of the most important consequences of the renewed test battery is the development of a job-related selection process for the blue-collar harbor workers. As the test development was based on an extensive job analysis and made use of practical and visual (simulation) exercises, the link between the selection procedures and the job became evident. As researchers have already demonstrated, this job-relatedness or face validity of a selection instrument serves as an important determinant of applicant test motivation and test performance (Chan & Schmitt, 1997; Hausknecht et al., 2004). Accordingly, simultaneously with the switch towards the new selection battery, Sophie noticed an increase in motivation at the applicant level. Hence, CEPA received considerably fewer complaints concerning the selection process. In addition, the feedback meetings went more smoothly as the rejection of candidates could be objectively argued, thereby increasing feedback acceptance. Trade unions also notified the enhanced job-relatedness of the new testing battery and no longer criticized the selection process. This significantly improved the relationships between unions and the harbor management and facilitated the social bargaining process at the Port.

Another benefit of the test battery adaptation was its opportunity to take into account the changing needs at the Port of Antwerp. Due to changes in the legal and technological harbor context, the job of blue-collar harbor worker faced increased demands concerning the KSAOs required. The modernization of the test procedure permitted Sophie and her staff to include these changed job demands when developing the new selection procedure, which resulted in a better assessment of the harbor worker's abilities. This fits with one of the most important goals of the Port of Antwerp, namely ensuring the quality of harbor labor and service.

A last important benefit of the renewed selection process in the Port of Antwerp is its reduced reading and writing demands and enhanced visual presentation of the stimulus material. By omitting unnecessary test demands (i.e., test demands that are not related to the job), the Port of Antwerp has nowadays the chance to enlarge its applicant pool by targeting non-traditional applicant groups.

Conclusion

This case exemplifies how HRM has to invest in developing sophisticated and innovative solutions to tackle current selection challenges such as altering applicant perceptions, responding to changing work environments, improving the company image, and making the selection battery attractive for traditional as well as non-traditional applicant pools. The case further exemplifies the growing importance of "gamification" in contemporary selection (Fetzer & Tuzinski, 2014), training (Fetzer, 2015), and recruitment (Lievens & Slaughter, 2016). Box 2.2 presents more information on gamification. Finally, this case study demonstrates the importance for HRM of taking its country's cultural background into account while developing and implementing a solution. Accordingly, at the Port of Antwerp, the Belgian history of unionization and its culture of consensualism significantly influenced the process of developing a new selection approach.

Box 2.2 Gamification as a Trend in HRM

The computerized crane operator mirrors several game-like elements, such as the engagement in interactive problem solving, test-takers' possibility of controlling the dynamics within the simulation to a reasonable albeit limited extent, and the availability of explicit feedback regarding test-takers' performance during the simulation (Fetzer, 2015). Recent developments to enrich simulation exercises by implementing game-like features aim to enhance the test-takers' engagement in simulation exercises. It is expected that an increase in engagement is related to a decrease in the awareness of one's KSAOs being assessed (Fetzer, 2015; Shute, Ventura, Bauer, & Zapata-Rivera, 2009). The use of serious games within organizational settings has most recently spread across a variety of different areas of application. Most prominently, serious games have been introduced to serve training purposes (Fetzer, 2015). In addition, organizations have started to take advantage of serious games in recruitment (recruitment games) that intend to attract new applicants and to screen potential applicants at the same time (Lievens & Slaughter, 2016). Finally, the use of serious games in personnel selection is also growing (Fetzer, 2015; Ryan & Ployhart, 2014). To the best of our knowledge, however, extensive evaluations of the use of serious games in personnel selection are still lacking (Ryan & Ployhart, 2014). Therefore, in-depth empirical investigations of serious games in personnel selection, especially regarding their validity, adverse impact or applicant perceptions are needed (Fetzer, 2015; Ryan & Ployhart, 2014).

Questions

1 In what ways does the Port of Antwerp resemble or differ from your own national port or large organizations? Is the solution presented applicable in your country of origin?

2 Compare the Belgian unionization to the tradition of unionization in your own country. What implications does this have for the development of staffing solutions in general and a new selection procedure in particular?

3 Do you know of organizations in your country that faced similar problems to those of the Port of Antwerp? How did they solve these problems and what were the outcomes? In what ways did the solutions these organizations proposed differ from the ones adopted by the Port of Antwerp?

4 What are the possible drawbacks of this new selection procedure? What are the challenges it might face in the future?

Note

The authors have permission to publish this case study and to make small factual changes. For privacy reasons only fictional names were used.

1 More information can be found at http://www.portofantwerp.com

References

Algemene Directie Statistiek – Statistics Belgium (2015). *Kerncijfers. Statistisch overzicht van België.* Retrieved from http://statbel.fgov.be/nl/binaries/NL_kerncijfers_2015_WEB_COMPLET_tcm325-275721.pdf

Belgian Federal Government (2016). *Government.* Retrieved from http://www.belgium.be/en/about_belgium/government

Chan, D., & Schmitt, N. (1997). Video-based versus paper-and-pencil method of assessment in situational judgment tests: Subgroup differences in test performance and face validity perceptions. *Journal of Applied Psychology, 82*, 143–159.

Fetzer, M. S. (2015). Serious games for talent selection and development. *The Industrial-Organizational Psychologist, 52*, 117–125.

Fetzer, M. S., & Tuzinski, K. (2014). *Simulations for personnel selection.* New York, NY: Springer.

Hausknecht, J. P., Day, D. V., & Thomas, S. C. (2004). Applicant reactions to selection procedures: An updated model and meta-analysis. *Personnel Psychology, 57*, 639–683.

Hofstede, G. (1980). *Culture's consequences. International differences in work-related values.* Beverly Hills: Sage.

Lievens, F., & Slaughter, J. E. (2016). Employer image and employer branding: What we know and what we need to know. *Annual Review of Organizational Psychology and Organizational Behavior, 3*, 407–440.

Ryan, A. M., & Ployhart, R. E. (2014). A century of selection. *Annual Review of Psychology, 65*, 693–717.

Sels, L., Janssens, M., Van Den Brande, I., & Overlaet, B. (2000). Belgium: A culture of compromise. In D. M. Rousseau & R. Schalk (Eds.), *Psychological contracts in employment: Cross-national perspectives* (pp. 47–66). Thousand Oaks: Sage.

Shute, V. J., Ventura, M., Bauer, M., & Zapata-Rivera, D. (2009). Melding the power of serious games and embedded assessment to monitor and foster learning: Flow and grow. In U. Ritterfeld, M. Cody, & P. Vorderer (Eds.), *Serious games: Mechanisms and effects* (pp. 295–321). New York, NY: Routledge/Taylor and Francis.

United Nations Development Programme (2015). *Human Development Report 2015: Work for human development.* Retrieved from http://hdr.undp.org/en/2015-report/download

Zedeck, S. (2010). Adverse impact: History and evolution. In J. L. Outtz (Ed.), *Adverse impact: Implications for organizational staffing and high stakes selection* (pp. 3–27). New York, NY: Routledge/Taylor & Francis.

3

Germany

Learning about Talent Rentention in Times of Crisis – Opportunities for the Robert Bosch Group in the Context of the German Industrial Relations System

Marion Festing

Country Background: Germany

The Federal Republic of Germany is the largest national economy in the European Union (EU). At the end of 2014, it had 81.2 million inhabitants and a competitive labour market characterised by a strong demand for qualified labour (rising percentage of persons in employment: 43.47 million in 10/2015, and a historically low unemployment rate of 4.4 percent in 10/2015). Growth rates stood at 1.6 percent and inflation at 0.9 percent in 2014 (Statistisches Bundesamt, 2016).

The backbone of the German economy is the small- and medium-sized enterprises (SMEs) sector and the so-called "Mittelstand", including family businesses, which represents more than 90 percent of German enterprises and more than 50 percent of economic production. The most important sectors in the country's economy include medicine and healthcare, transport and logistics (including, for example, automotive), chemicals and pharmaceuticals, technology and innovation, energy, and financial services (German Convention Bureau, n.d.). With a gross domestic product (GDP) of 3,478 billion US dollars (2012), Germany is the world's fourth largest economy and invests important amounts in education and healthcare (Frankfurter Societäts-MedienGmbH, 2014).

It is a land of writers and composers and is home to around 370 higher education establishments, including universities, fostering academic excellence (German National Tourist Board, n.d.). Together with the so-called "dual vocational training system" (an explanation is provided in the ensuing case study) this leads to a relatively high level of education for a large part of society. Typical German values include affording high priority to structure, privacy and punctuality, and hard work and industriousness are often mentioned in the context of the nation's working environment. Another dimension, which is often ascribed to Germans, is uncertainty avoidance – a notion reflected in a strong need for regulations, for example in labour law. With respect to gender equality there are strong initiatives; however, the gender pay gap still sits at 22 percent, and the number of females in top management is low and has a great deal of room for improvement. However, at the same time, Germany – and especially

Berlin – is a place where start-ups, creativity and entrepreneurship are of major importance. Moreover, the picture is not complete if the typical activities in a German's leisure time are not mentioned. They include holiday time and travelling, wine and beer events as well as musical events and carnivals.

Like many industrialised countries, Germany is characterised by important demographic changes caused by decreasing birth rates and increasing life expectancy, and it is supposed that in-migration from abroad might slow down the process of ageing in the population living in the country. Furthermore, migration and the integration of relatively high numbers of refugees, who came to Germany in 2015 and are expected also for the coming years, will be central socio-political issues for the foreseeable future (Statistisches Bundesamt, 2016).

The Environment of HRM in Germany: A Historical Perspective and the Present Situation

Human resource management (HRM) in Germany can only be understood in connection with the unique institutional heritage specific to the country and by considering historical developments and the socio-cultural environment. In this context, it is important to point out three major features of the German business system and their implications for HRM.

First, due to their ownership structure, most German companies have a *long-term orientation* and are not under the same pressure to achieve short-term business success as many companies whose shares are traded on the stock market (for an overview see Dickmann, 2003; Festing, 2012). This is especially true for the company on which this case study focuses, namely Bosch. Despite being a large multinational company, it is due to its legal form (a limited liability company) that it is not restricted by stock market regulations, which emphasise short-term success. For an understanding of the long-termism dimension in the German HRM model it is important to know that labour is often interpreted rather as a fixed production factor. This may be the result of the fact that a complex labour law does not allow a "hire & fire" policy, i.e. labour contracts cannot be terminated easily. Therefore, investment in human resources (on this perspective see Streeck, 1995), for example by developing talents in various training programmes, is a key success factor of the German economy and is expected to provide a high return on investment.

This notion is in line with the second major feature of the German business system, namely its *strong developmental orientation*. One such example is the initial dual vocational training arrangement, which combines simultaneous theoretical learning in professional schools with on-the-job learning in firms. Each year, two-thirds of school pupils in Germany are trained within this system (for a current overview see Gericke, Uhly & Ulrich, 2011), and this vocational qualification is highly accepted in corporations as well as in society. The well-known German "Facharbeiter" (skilled worker) is one result of this system – these are individuals who are well-trained professionals in their field and are seen as one of the backbones of the German economy (for a summary see Festing, 2012). Developmental orientation is further displayed in many single HRM practices such as long-term-oriented training schemes and career planning, or from a long-term perspective in rewards, as depicted in Table 3.1.

The third key principle of the German economy, which is of high importance for HRM, is the social market economy model. Among other things, this emphasises a *cooperative approach between employers and employees* at various levels of the firm, region, industry and

Table 3.1 Selected features of the German national business system, and HRM issues and practices

Selected HRM-relevant features of the German economy	Selected HRM issues and practices in Germany
Long-termism	Turning labour into a more fixed production factor encourages investment in human capital
Management – employee cooperation Co-determination	• Works councils have strong information, participation and decision-making rights with respect to all HRM practices, thus restricting management discretion • Works councils safeguard employment relations, including employment security, by making employee dismissal difficult • The co-determination system ensures communication and the integration of labour issues in strategic planning (via a labour director on the board and works councils)
Collective bargaining	• Collective bargaining ensures a collective orientation • Leads to comparably low wage differentials between various groups of employees

Developmental orientation	Developing and retaining talents is of major importance:
	Employee development:
	  • Initial dual vocational training system
	  • Other educational schemes
	Employee retention:
	  • Staff development through training on various jobs
	  • Long-term career planning, with technical competence and functional expertise as core values based on performance appraisals and high investment in training and career development measures, including team effectiveness
	  • Long-term-oriented rewards, with the emphasis on individual rewards and profit-sharing

Source: Adapted from Festing (2012), p. 47.

state. Cooperation between management and employees is based on the understanding that consensus and collectivism in employment relations are important in German society. Collective bargaining and co-determination at the regional, industry, company and plant levels are supported by regulations at the state level, including the principle of non-interference of the state in the bargaining process between employers and employees ("Tarifautonomie"), the latter of which addresses, for instance, working hours, wage levels and salaries as well as pay mix. The regulation of industrial and employment relations extends to the individual and work contracts level, stipulating the rights of the employed (based on Dickmann, 2003; Festing, 2012; Giardini, Kabst, & Müller-Camen, 2005; Morley, 2004). The various levels of management – employee cooperation based on legislation and regulation, promulgated by the German state – are depicted in Table 3.1.

During the *global economic and financial crisis* – which is the focus of this case study – the positive effects of the highly institutionalised German labour market environment became evident in connection with the outcomes of short-time working legislation ("Gesetzgebung zur Kurzarbeit") enforced by the German government. In addition, the commitment of trade unions and works councils to the primary goals of employment stability, reflected in their cooperative attitude and eagerness to contribute to solving the crisis together with employers, increased the positive effect of labour market policy measures. Thus, the effect of the short-time working schemes enacted at the state level was accelerated significantly by reducing working times within the framework of additional collective agreements for employment security ("Tarifvertrag zur Beschäftigungssicherung") at the regional and industrial levels, as well as agreements between the employer and works councils on working time reduction at the company and plant levels. This measure, as one example of the regulations inherent in the German industrial relations system, resides within the focus of this case study and will be explained later in further detail.

In terms of *evaluation*, in the past, the institutional environment in Germany was perceived as having a rather negative impact on HRM. For example, one of the first empirical studies on German HRM at the beginning of the 1990s (Lawrence, 1993) criticised the fact that managerial discretion concerning the management of people was restricted. The authors claimed that the rigidity of the encompassing industrial relations system prevented managers from using innovative HR techniques and detracted from employment creation in the country. While managerial discretion is indeed somewhat restricted, this does not question the basic principles of German labour market institutions. On the contrary, while the role of the HR department in creating a strategic HRM approach may not be as important in many cases in Germany as in other countries, such as, for example, in the USA, consensus-oriented collective alignment based on state legislation plays a critical role and replaces the HR department, to some extent. It is often argued that the constraints imposed by the rigid industrial relations system are offset by important positive effects normally associated with successful HRM: competitive advantages result from this system of employment relations mainly in the areas of training and associated highly valuable human capital, communication and employment stability. This leads to low turnover rates as compared to other Western European countries (for further discussion see Morley, 2004; Giardini et al., 2005; Festing, 2012).

In the past, there have been several major *challenges to the traditional German institutional context*, including market changes relevant to the reunification of East and West Germany and the completion of the European Union's internal market. Nonetheless, neither initiative led to major changes in the principles of the German institutional environment, including the industrial relations system. On the contrary, this system may have especially positive effects in times of crisis, as will be discussed in this case study (for further discussion see Festing, 2012).

The Bosch Group: Organisational Setting

The Bosch Group (www.bosch.com) is a leading global manufacturer of automotive and industrial technology, consumer goods and building technology. As per April 1, 2015, it employed around 360,000 employees worldwide and generated sales of €49 billion in the fiscal year 2014: "The sales figure disclosed for 2014 does not include the former joint ventures BSH Bosch und Siemens Hausgeräte GmbH (now BSH Hausgeräte GmbH) and ZF Lenksysteme GmbH (now Robert Bosch Automotive Steering GmbH), which have since been taken over completely" (Robert Bosch GmbH, 2015, p. 10).

Set up in Stuttgart, Germany, in 1886 by Robert Bosch (1861–1942) as a "Workshop of Precision Mechanics and Electrical Engineering," the Bosch Group today comprises a network of some 440 subsidiaries and regional companies in over 60 countries, including 94 development and engineering locations. Through its sales and service partners, Bosch has extended its worldwide presence to about 150 countries. With a more than €5-billion annual budget for research and development, and around 4,600 patents applied for worldwide each year, Bosch places great importance on innovation. Today, 53 percent of its sales are achieved in Europe, 20 percent in America and 27 percent in Asia Pacific, including other countries.

At present, the majority shareholder (92 percent) of the Group is Robert Bosch Stiftung GmbH, a charitable foundation which uses the share dividend exclusively for charitable purposes, e.g. to support medical, international, social and educational programmes. Robert Bosch GmbH holds only 1 percent of the shares and does not have any voting power. Instead, Robert Bosch Industrietreuhand, a legally independent unit, has 93 percent of the votes. This entity acts as a kind of board, which in turn provides strategic advice to Robert Bosch GmbH and ensures compliance (Robert Bosch GmbH, 2015, p.4).

Historical Background to the Case

The major phenomenon shaping economic activity and employment between 2007 and 2010 was the global economic and financial crisis, at which time, driven initially by the liquidity crisis, the global economy witnessed a dramatic recession (see Table 3.2).

Among the industries hit most severely by the crisis was the automotive sector. While Bosch is also active in industrial technology (representing 14 percent of its sales in 2014), consumer goods (4 percent) and energy and building technology (9 percent), the major source of the sales at 68 percent of total revenue is "mobility solutions", which is the new name for the group's former automotive technology activities (Robert Bosch GmbH, 2015, p. 11). Therefore, a major part of the firm focused on in this case was heavily threatened by the financial crisis.

Despite programmes introduced by governments across the globe, to encourage car purchases, the automotive industry suffered greatly from a dramatic decrease in revenues. While in Germany it has now fully recovered (and achieved sales of nearly €370 billion in 2014),

Table 3.2 Macroeconomic effects of the global economic and financial crisis (OECD area, unless stated otherwise)

	Average 1997–2006	2007	2008	2009	2010
	Percent				
Real GDP growth[a]	2.8	2.7	0.6	−3.5	1.9
United States	3.2	2.1	0.4	−2.5	2.5
Euro area	2.3	2.7	0.5	−4.0	0.9
Japan	1.1	2.3	−0.7	−5.3	1.8
Unemployment rate[b]	6.5	5.6	5.9	8.2	9.0
Inflation[c]	3.0	2.3	3.2	0.5	1.3
Fiscal balance[d]	−2.0	−1.3	−3.5	−8.2	−8.3

[a] Year-on-year increase
[b] Percentage of labour force
[c] Private consumption deflator. Year-on-year increase
[d] Percentage GDP

Source: Based on OECD, 2009, p.12.

the weakest year was 2009, with a total turnover of slightly more than €260 billion (compared to €330 billion in 2008) (Statista GmbH, 2016b). However, while revenue dropped by more than 20 percent from 2008 to 2009, employment "only" dropped by 3.5 percent in the first year and 3 percent in the second year of the crisis, or in absolute numbers from 750,000 in 2008 to 700,000 in 2010 (Statista GmbH, 2016a). Of course, this economic downturn represented a major challenge, not only for the financial situation of the companies in this sector, but also for the labour market. Given the importance of human capital in this sector, employers did their best to explore all possible avenues to minimise costs in the short term and, at the same time, to retain their skilled workforce in the long term. Driven by a steep global vehicle production slowdown (12 percent compared to 2008 and 17 percent compared to 2007), for Bosch this meant in 2009 that the sales revenues of the company's automotive technology business sector fell by 18 percent to €21.7 billion.

The HR Context at Bosch

The following statement by the founder Robert Bosch is helpful in understanding the HR philosophy particular to this organisation: "It is my intention, apart from the alleviation of all kinds of suffering, to promote the moral, physical and intellectual development of the people." Up to the point at which this statement was made, Bosch had paid special attention to recruiting, retaining, motivating and training talents. Education and lifelong learning were viewed as the major principles of HRM. Thus, investing in human capital, supported with long-term employee and management development measures, represented strategic goals for the firm.

It was extremely difficult to act according to this philosophy during the economic crisis, though, when all costs, including personnel costs, had to be reduced to ensure the survival and the long-term competitiveness of the firm. Workplace security ("With the core workforce through the crisis") was the company's declared goal. The crisis hit the automotive division at the end of 2008, and in September of the same year, the first discussions with the works councils on possible reactions to the predicament took place. The subject of negotiations was the reduction of working time in accordance with decreased production volume.

According to "short-time" regulations in Germany, companies affected by a significant loss of work can reduce the working time of their employees, who are then provided with short-time working allowances by the German state. These allowances amount to 60 percent of net income loss for single persons, or up to 67 percent of the respective net wage cut for employees with children.

Usually, the firm and the employees agree on short-time work for a period of six months. Changes are subject to short-term notice, i.e. within 14 days, and other rules can apply if new production orders arrive. These regulations are an important device for a company to maintain flexible employment during a crisis, and from the employee's perspective they enable individual workers to not only plan their time schedule, but also better organise their personal income situation. During the financial crisis, the maximum period of short-time work was increased tremendously by the German state, when it went up to 24 months stipulated by law.

However, the application of these regulations does not result in a proportional reduction in the non-labour costs of the employer; the company still has to bear additional costs, such as vacation pay or bonuses, as well as – depending on the duration of short-time work – a proportion of social security contributions. Thus, this solution is rather expensive for the employer, due to these so-called 'residual costs', and at Bosch they originally constituted about 47 percent of the regular hourly personnel expenditure. After several amendments to the law, these costs now amount to 36 percent of personnel costs within the first six months of short-time work (with 50 percent of the employer's social security contributions borne by the Federal Employment Agency [*Bundesagentur für Arbeit, BA*]) or to 26 percent, either starting from the seventh month of short-time work or if the employee is being trained during this period (with 100 percent of employee social security contributions covered by the state). At the same time, this scheme is quite attractive for employees, because in times of short-time work they usually receive a wage/salary for the hours worked from their employer (Bosch), 60–67 percent short-time working allowance, i.e. for the time they have not worked they nevertheless receive a certain amount of money from the German state, and, additionally, an adjustment by Bosch based on a separate collective agreement regulation.

The calculations that resulted from the short-time work regulations imposed during the financial crisis represented a true challenge to Bosch's HR department. New software had to be created, and the whole process was very time-consuming. Furthermore, before related expenses were partially reimbursed by the state, they had to be borne by the firm. Sometimes this is a challenge to the liquidity situation of a firm.

Thus, it was important for the company to find alternative ways of reducing working time, without placing an additional financial burden on the employer. The respective separate regional tariff agreement for employment security allowed for a reduction in working time from 35 hours to 30, or – in some tariff zones – even to 29 hours per week. For the company, this option was more attractive, as it allowed for decreasing personnel costs almost proportionally to the reduction in working time.

The collective agreement on employment security stipulates that working time reductions should be agreed upon at the site level. The result of the negotiations between Bosch and the company works council ("Gesamtbetriebsrat") in October 2008 was that the first 15 to 20 percent of the working time reduction should be based on the tariff agreement, while the remainder could be based on legal and additional tariff regulations for short-term work. At the end of 2008, these regulations were applied at several locations. Thus, from late 2008 – when the after-effects of the crisis became even worse – various groups of employees started short-time work. Of course, these measures only applied after the overtime accumulated on flexible time accounts had been considered.

At the same time, the working time of full-time employees (with 40 hours per week contracts) was reduced from 40 to 35 hours per week. Overall, by the end of 2009, 31 percent of the working time of 32,700 employees had been reduced based on the short-time work regulations and tariff agreements. While the first target group included production employees, i.e. those who were actively involved in the value chain, from 2009, non-production employees working in administrative functions and at the company's headquarters were also affected.

By the end of 2009, the crisis was still ongoing. At this point the differentiation between structural and economic problems was more important. In this situation, there was an intense ongoing dialogue between the company and employee representatives. In order to maintain long-term competitiveness, and to keep the core workforce despite cyclical employment problems, further negotiations with the company works council were initiated. It was intended to find a solution in line with Bosch's values.

Outcomes at Bosch

The major advantage of short-time work for Bosch is that it allowed the company to maintain a core value with respect to HRM: although the financial situation of the firm forced it to react to the crisis, it was still committed to the long-term development of its employees and sought to maintain this philosophy as long as possible. It is very expensive to create an in-depth, firm-specific knowledge base of employees, and so return on this very specific investment is at stake if they are made redundant.

The advantage of short-time work for an individual employee is that he or she keeps his or her job, while for the company the advantage is that it does not lose precious human capital. For the wider society the social advantage is that unemployment rates can be kept as low as possible. However, short-time work is a solution only for a limited time during an economic downturn, as it is an expensive compromise, both for the state and for the company.

In 2010, the economic situation of the German automobile industry again changed dramatically; however, this time, the development was extremely positive. Customer orders increased sharply, and Bosch was virtually able to attain the successful economic figures of 2007. The company was now able to pay back its employees for their flexibility during the crisis. A first measure announced in October 2010 was that a tariff-based salary increase would be granted to 85,000 non-exempt employees of Bosch, earlier than negotiated under the respective industry-wide collective agreement (Heller, 2010).

In total, in the German economy in the fourth quarter of 2010, the amount of short-time work was reduced by 80 percent as compared to the peak of the crisis. In addition, unemployment rates dropped dramatically and reached levels seen at the beginning of the 1990s. These figures indicate that the consensus-oriented industrial relations system in Germany had a positive influence on the recovery of the German economy (Bundesregierung, 2010), which is underlined by Bosch's case. As the layoff of qualified employees was avoided, the firm was well-prepared from a human capital perspective, and five years after the crisis it now continues its success story by displaying significant growth figures in terms of sales, numbers of employees and numbers of patents, just to measure one indicator of innovation.

Case Study Questions/Activities

1 Please characterise the basic features of HRM in Germany and of the German industrial relations system.
2 Please describe the advantages and disadvantages of German short-time working schemes for employers and employees.
3 Critics of the short-time working regulations state that, in the long run, such arrangements hamper the reallocation of human resources to other more productive activities. Is there such a danger for Bosch?
4 Although supported by the state, Bosch employees affected by reduced working time had to put up with substantial income loss. Give recommendations on incentives (including long-term compensation) that could be implemented along with the described short-time measures to motivate employees in this situation.
5 During the crisis Bosch and its employees had to exchange different perspectives, in order to negotiate an agreement on short-time work. Please build two groups: one group represents the delegation of the employer, the other represents the works council. First, develop your arguments on options about how to overcome the crisis, with special consideration of short-time work within your respective group. Then, engage in a discussion with the other group, with the goal of reaching an agreement. Please present the cornerstones of your agreement at the end of the session.

Case Summary

This case addresses the specificities of the German industrial relations system and outlines its positive impact on the specific situation of Bosch as a major supplier to the automotive industry during the global financial crisis, which hit Bosch mainly between 2008 and 2009. Since the crisis, Bosch has been a major success story through important increases in all key growth indicators.

References and Further Reading

Bundesregierung. (2010). *Der robuste zukunftsfaehige Arbeitsmarkt.* Retrieved November 12, 2019 from http://www.bundesregierung.de/Content/DE/Artikel/2010/10/2010–10–27-der-robuste-zukunftsfaehige-arbeits markt-.html

Dickmann, M. (2003). Implementing German IHRM abroad: Desired, feasible, successful? *International Journal of Human Resource Management, 14*(2), 265–283.

Festing, M. (2012). Strategic Human Resource Management in Germany: Evidence of Convergence to the U.S. Model, the European Model, or a Distinctive National Model? *Academy of Management Perspectives, 26*(2), 37–54.

Frankfurter Societäts-Medien GmbH. (2014). *Facts and figures about Germany.* Retrieved March 22, 2016, from https://www.deutschland.de/en/topic/politics/germany-europe/facts-and-figures-about-germany

Gericke, N., Uhly, A., & Ulrich, J. G. (2011). Wie hoch ist die Quote der Jugendlichen, die eine duale Berufsausbildung aufnehmen? Indikatoren zur Bildungsbeteiligung. *Berufsbildung in Wissenschaft und Praxis (BWP), 1*(2011), 41–43.

German Convention Bureau. (n.d.). *Discover German Expertise.* Retrieved March 22, 2016, from http://www.gcb.de/en/key-industries/key-industries-in-germany

German National Tourist Board. (n.d.). *Germany at a glance: A brief summary of important facts.* (n.d.). Retrieved March 22, 2016, from http://www.germany.travel/en/travel-information/germany-at-a-glance/germany-at-a-glance.html

Giardini, A., Kabst, R., & Müller-Camen, M. (2005). HRM in the German Business System: A Review. *Management Revue, 16*(1), 63–80.

Heller, M. (2010, October 26). *Bosch: Erholung schneller als gedacht.* Retrieved March 22, 2016, from http://www.stuttgarter-zeitung.de/inhalt.bosch-erholung-schneller-als-gedacht.6483c4d4–5b6d-4648-b372-c4e7d0a6ae64.html

Lawrence, P. (1993). Human Resource Management in Germany. In S. Tyson, P. Lawrence, P. Poirson, L. Manzolini & C. Soler Vicente (Eds.), *Human Resource Management in Europe* (25–41). London: Kogan Page.

Morley, M.J. (2004). Contemporary Debates in European Human Resource Management: Context and Content. *Human Resource Management Review, 14*(2004), 353–364.

OECD. (2009). *OECD Economic Outlook.* Volume 2009/2, No. 86, November.

Robert Bosch GmbH. (2015). *Quality of Life – Bosch Today 2015.* Retrieved March 22, 2016, from http://www.bosch.com/worldsite_startpage/en/Bosch_Today.aspx

Statista GmbH. (2016a). *Automobilindustrie Beschäftigtenzahl in Deutschland.* Retrieved March 22, 2016, from http://de.statista.com/statistik/daten/studie/30703/umfrage/beschaeftigtenzahl-in-der-automobilindustrie/

Statista GmbH. (2016b). *Umsatz Automobilindustrie Deutschland.* Retrieved March 22, 2016, from http://de.statista.com/statistik/daten/studie/160479/umfrage/umsatz-der-deutschen-automobilindustrie/

Statistisches Bundesamt. (2016). *Facts & Figures.* Retrieved March 22, 2016, from https://www.destatis.de/EN/FactsFigures/FactsFigures.html

Streeck, W. (1995). *German Capitalism: Does It Exist? Can It Survive?* Köln: Max-Planck-Institut für Gesellschafts-forschung.

Further Related Web Sources

Federal Ministry of Labour and Social Affairs, Germany

- http://www.bmas.de/EN/Home/home.html

This English-language version of the official internet site of the ministry provides concise and up-to-date information on labour market policies and programmes as well as labour regulations in Germany. It also contains a number of publications on employment, industrial relations and social security, including short-time work.

European Foundation on Improvement of Living and Working Conditions (Eurofound)

- http://www.eurofound.europa.eu/

This web page of Eurofound, a European Union body established by the European Council, contains information on employment, industrial relations, labour markets and laws, and it also hosts online sources such as the European Industrial Relations Observatory Online (eironline) and European Working Conditions Observatory (EWCO).

4

Ireland

Prospects and Challenges in Managing Creativity to Realise Ireland's Knowledge-based Aspirations

Brian Harney

Introduction

Michael, the Managing Director of Creativity Co.,[1] looks out over the high-spec open plan office, noting that the organisation was fortunate to weather the storm of global recession, and in particular the dramatic economic decline experienced in Ireland. It has certainly been an interesting few years for Creativity Co., a small indigenous Irish organisation operating in the creative space of industrial design. Creativity Co. is exemplary of the knowledge-intensive and creative firms said to hold the key to the Irish government's knowledge-based agenda. While technically the organisation is small, employing some 45 employees, in industry terms it is a relatively big player. Success to date is credited to its highly skilled staff and international focus. Both were critical in protecting the firm from the severest consequences of the economic crisis in Ireland. Michael is very conscious that economic revival will once again provide attractive opportunities for his talented workforce to work elsewhere. He also knows that with 45 employees the organisation is an optimal size for an informal approach to managing staff, but how should the organisation manage the growth that might come with success? He puts down his coffee and points to a recent international design award achieved by the organisation; laughing, he notes 'the problem of success, now that's a nice problem to have'.

This case explores the role of an HRM system in managing a workforce whose key task is creative output. HRM solutions are inevitably shaped by the labour market conditions and organisational constraints. Specifically, the case provides an overview of key HR practices in operation at Creativity Co. with respect to recruitment and selection, training and development, performance and rewards and employee voice. Key points to emerge from the case include the long-standing issues that confront small firms with growth aspirations, i.e. whether existing relations can remain intact in the context of increased numbers and more formal practices. This question also finds additional significance in the context of managing creative professionals, in particular whether formal practices will sap the innovation and creativity deemed critical for organisational success.

Organisational Setting

Creativity Co. is a small indigenous Irish organisation operating in the creative space of industrial design. The company designs consumer products for mass production, something deemed 'as important as car design, just not as recognised'. The organisation was founded in the 1980s by two partners, both of whom had previously worked in Asia. The organisation remained a small, 'tight ship' until the early 1990s when one of the founders retired and was bought out by the remaining partner (the current Managing Director). Since then the owner-ship base has expanded to include a Director of Creativity and a Director of Industrial Design. The organisation describes itself as a 45-person 'multidisciplinary team' working from a top-of-the-range studio workshop. Having this many employees was said to be something that 'makes us big in this industry . . . we have gone above small in getting to where we are now' (MD). Except for two administrative positions, and a more recent marketing recruit, Creativ-ity Co. employs a male workforce of relatively early-career industrial designers and engineers.

Excluding the prototype workshop which is located at the back of the premises, the office at Creativity Co. is striking because of its open plan layout. While the three partners do have designated office space these are loosely separated from the rest of the studio by transparent sliding glass doors. Creativity Co. aspires to 'design and realise products with winning quali-ties. Products that build brands.' Rather than being viewed as a 'hot Creativity Consultancy' the company distinguishes itself on its ability to follow through with the necessary techni-cal and engineering prowess 'to get the creative bit to production'. Reflective of its focus on innovation and intense expertise-based collaboration, Creativity Co. is an extremely flat organisation with the task of people management shared evenly across the Directors. Staff work together on each project in multidisciplinary teams with work comprising three key tasks: industrial design, model making and mechanical engineering. The early concept stage of a project involves brainstorming and loose sketches which evolve into designs explored via photomodel. In turn, coherent proposals are communicated by a series of models which are made from light foams to capture key surface strategies. Clients are typically shown four to six higher end models of which two are chosen for further development involving precise castings and in-house engineering to manage each product through to mass production. The entire process is underpinned by substantial investment in highly advanced technol-ogy including Pro-E for detail design and final definition, Computer Aided Design (CAD) tools for designing complex surfaces and solids, and the latest Computer Numerical Control (CNC) technology to rapidly realise all designs to the highest levels of accuracy possible.

Contextual Backdrop to the Case

Ireland is an advanced economy located on the western periphery of Europe with a popula-tion of 4.3 million people. As a result of its status as an island and open economy, Ireland's socio-economic development has been markedly uneven and punctuated. In the period from the mid-1990s to 2007 Ireland experienced dramatic growth, earning the label 'the Celtic Tiger' to rival the title once afforded to East Asian 'tigers' including the likes of Hong Kong, Singapore and South Korea. This period was characterised by an unprecedented require-ment for workers, rising wages and a growing reliance on immigrant labour. Yet the impact of the global recession was particularly felt in Ireland, where an overreliance on construction, and a property bubble fuelled by cheap credit, resulted in the largest compound decline in gross national product (GNP) of any industrialised economy over the 2007–2010 period

(Kinsella, 2012). Ireland once again returned to a labour surplus economy with unemployment peaking at close to 15 percent, representing a dramatic reversal of fortunes.

Key pillars of Irish industrial policy have been at the forefront of development for a long period of time, even despite such economic turbulence. This includes a long-standing investment in attracting foreign direct investment to Ireland from the early entry of Pfizer and Intel, through to the recent additions of the European headquarters of Google and LinkedIn which are housed in Dublin. The marketing of Ireland for such investment is facilitated by its high ranking on surveys exploring the ease of doing business, its low corporate tax rate, but also its geographical location and access to the European market, low inflation and stability previously provided for by social partnership agreements and, notably, a well-educated, English-speaking workforce (Harney, 2006). Ireland's key sectors are largely high-value-added, including pharmaceuticals, medical devices, social media and gaming. Indigenous firms like Kerry Group are leading players in dairy and food, whilst Ireland has strong creative sectors across the arts. As Ireland enters economic recovery it has returned to lead economic growth in Europe, while unemployment has fallen below 10 percent. The government has placed significant emphasis on human capital in rejuvenating economic fortunes. To the benefit of organisations like Creativity Co., there is also recognition that multi-national foreign direct investment needs to be appropriately balanced with attempts to grow and sustain indigenous industry. Ireland cannot succumb to an overreliance on particular sources of wealth as it has in the past.

Ireland's Knowledge-based Agenda

Since the 1960s, Ireland has invested heavily in education as a pathway to future economic and social prosperity. By the 1980s, Ireland was a pioneer in purposefully drawing on this human capital base to position itself as an attractive location for foreign direct investment. This culminated in a policy of free third level education in the 1990s. More recently, the Irish government committed to double the number of PhD students in Ireland. As captured by Irish agency Science Foundation Ireland, 'Ireland's success on the world stage cannot be based on low labour costs or mineral resources; it must be based on our human resources and our science' (Science Foundation Ireland, 2012: 8). A consequence is that Ireland has one of the most highly educated workforces in Europe. Investment in science and technology has also reaped benefit as Ireland is ranked eighth in the Global Innovation Index (2015) and holds a similar position in the EU ranking, Innovation Union Scoreboard.

The trend of investing in talent is set to continue as indicated by the government's *Enterprise 2025 Strategy*, which positions developing and attracting talent as one of four key initiatives for the 2015–2025 period. Specific efforts to foster and embed talent as outlined in this policy include:

- closer engagement between education and enterprise than ever before, to demonstrate the agility required in today's dynamic environment.
- a greater emphasis on leadership and management development, equipping more of our people with the ability and ambition to start, innovate and grow businesses.
- continuously anticipating, identifying and addressing critical skill gaps needed to deliver in our ambition for self-sustaining clusters (DJEI, 2015: 9).

Supportive of this emphasis on talent is a cultural inheritance of a creative society with a legacy of success in literature and the arts. Moreover, Ireland is generally said to have a liberal outlook, underpinned by a clear sense of social values. Notable in this respect is the introduction of a minimum wage in 2000. More recently, Ireland became the first country in the world to democratically vote for same-sex marriage to be written into law.

All the while acknowledging this beneficial policy intent, it is also important not to ignore the dramatic consequences the global recession had for Ireland, not least the dramatic pay-cuts in the public sector and mass lay-offs in the private sector (Roche, 2014). It is evident that Ireland also faces ongoing challenges. Ireland manages only European averages in terms of lifelong learning while skill shortages remain in key growth and knowledge-based sectors (Forfás, 2012). As part of her recovery Ireland has once again turned to the strong foundation of research and development and innovative capabilities, with a particular focus on indigenous organisations like Creativity Co. This renders understanding the HRM challenges of this type of organisation all the more significant.

Creativity Co.: Strategy and Key Success Factors

Creativity Co. operates in a very distinctive niche at the front end of consumer products. Creative design is a niche industry which, while global, is said to be extremely fragmented. Even leading firms tend to be relatively small in employment terms. Clients are global players with strong brand recognition, and the hub of activity is frequently San Francisco. Key factors for success hinge on reputation not only with clients but, critically, in terms of subsequent consumer sales. Creativity Co. conducts very little traditional marketing, instead relying on client referrals. Reputation and image are critical success factors in the industry and Creativity Co. strives to gain both by exceeding client expectations. As part of tendering for projects clients would frequently come in and 'eyeball' looking for 'sense of confidence and a sense of the creativity' (Mechanical Engineer).

With the exception of small *ad hoc* projects, Creativity Co. gains all of its business internationally, most notably through its ongoing relationship with Hi-tech, which accounts for over 75 percent of its current projects.[2] Demand in industrial design is turbulent. Nonetheless, unlike the consumer fashion industry, once a project is secured the cycle of creation is relatively slow. Consequently, Creativity Co. is happy to work through the 'peaks and troughs' of demand. Creativity Co.'s niche focus, coupled with its relationship with Hi-tech, provided a degree of stability and insulation from the severest aspects of recession in Ireland. Indeed, Creativity Co. is actually selective in the work it undertakes. This involves an appreciation of the nature and limits of the firm's value proposition, including the desire to remain an optimal size 'to keep control of the design'. The firm was also cognisant of not moving outside 'comfort zones'. This recognition is captured in the following quotation:

> we've been asked by clients . . . we could have a whole packaging department, graphic design department, we could have an internet user-face department, we could grow in a whole range of areas like that.
>
> (Director, Industrial Design)

While the industry awards Creativity Co. has received over the years are recognised as important, these are necessary, but not sufficient, for organisational success. Since its inception, Creativity Co. has benefited from the fact that a number of the company's designs have become market-leading products for their clients. This was judged more important than product design awards. This in turn draws attention to the importance of having an expertise base able to relate to consumers, understand and translate client demands and work as an ensemble. In essence the management of human resources is critical.

People Management at Creativity Co.

Given the nature of their business, Creativity Co. relies on extremely talented and creative individuals. Supportive of this, marketing and promotion brochures attribute Creativity Co.'s ability to 'sell creativity' to 'the calibre and motivation of our people'. This includes domain expertise which is not readily available. Specifically, the labour market in Ireland remains particularly tight for industrial designers with Pro-E skills. A critical part of providing a service to clients involves continuous interactions and personalised communication. This includes stretching client perceptions and expectations. An industrial designer noted of his role 'you go beyond the brief, you read between the lines, search and develop the unanswered questions in the mind of the client'. Overall, these conditions shape the nature of projects and the way Creativity Co. operates. The management style is informal, with partners and clients all on first name terms. Employees are granted significant autonomy as required by their creative design tasks and their ambiguous interaction with clients. The fact that projects are frequently co-designed with clients, evolving from their initial brief, means

Table 4.1 20-point profile of HRM practices at Creativity Co.

Practice	Creativity Co.
1. Cultural change programme	X
2. Devolved management	√
3. Teamworking	√
4. Performance appraisal	√
5. Mission statement	INF
6. Team briefing	√
7. Quality circles	X
8. Harmonized terms and conditions	X
9. Psychometric tests	X
10. De-layering	X
11. Increased flexibility between jobs	X
12. Customer quality schemes	INF
13. Training programmes for all employees	INF
14. Staff suggestion schemes	INF
15. Company wide meetings	√
16. Staff attitude surveys	X
17. Employee welfare and counselling	X
18. Family friendly working	X
19. Social events	X
20. Outsourced practices	X
Total	9

Legend: √= Practice utilised, INF= Practice utilised informally X= Practice not in use (Drawing from Harney and Dundon, 2006)

that there is significant ambiguity about roles, tasks and timescales. Tasks are therefore very much collaborative and non-routine.

Although Creativity Co. has a highly specialised and professional workforce its HRM practices do not necessarily match those prescribed in the literature. The term HRM is not explicitly used at Creativity Co. Likewise, rather than there being an HRM manager the task of managing people is shared across the Directors. Table 4.1 captures the nature of HRM practices evidenced at Creativity Co. Creativity Co. utilises nine specific people management practices in either a formal way or more informally whereby the company practises the policy but there is no formal documentation or procedures. Formal practices included devolved management, teamworking, team briefing, performance appraisal and company-wide meetings. More informally implemented practices included a client focused mission, training, staff suggestion schemes and customer quality schemes, all of which formed an inherent part of exceeding customer expectations. The central facet of people management at Creativity Co. involved 'nurturing talent' and 'encouraging the journey': 'we simply empower people and follow through. It's not something you can be taught . . . you learn by experience and from making mistakes' (Director of Creativity).

Recruitment at Creativity Co.

Given the nature of expertise required, Creativity Co. utilises specialist channels and occupational networks to source staff. These include online user communities associated with particular software, or simply targeting specific people, as was the case for the Industrial Design Director. Creativity Co.'s reputation and the nature of the work it conducts also mean that people proactively contacted them in search of employment. Drawing on networks of personal contacts, testimonies and portfolios were particularly important selection techniques given the amorphous nature of work tasks. The MD was cognisant of manpower planning issues, for example taking on two people with Pro-E expertise as 'back up' because he felt that in a few years one of the existing specialists might leave.

Training at Creativity Co.

Staff recruited to work at Creativity Co. were university educated and so were both highly technically competent, and immersed in the values of the profession. One consequence was that Directors felt it was not possible to 'train up guys'. Instead, training took the form of informal mentoring whereby younger recruits were placed 'under the wing' of more experienced members of staff. Although there was limited job rotation, employees were able to develop their skills through dealing with clients, and the unique nature of each project. Designers appeared content with this, and expressed reluctance in taking on any other additional tasks, especially those associated with 'management'. Indeed, the Directors also expressed reluctance at the management aspects of their roles.

Pay and Performance at Creativity Co.

Pay was relatively high at Creativity Co., while employees leveraged intrinsic satisfaction from conducting design activities followed by pride in seeing designs materialise into products. From the perspective of the Directors, nurturing talent through the 'intangible stuff' of personal recognition and affirmation that the job was good was deemed critical. Reflective of this, performance appraisals were conducted on a six-month basis and seen as something that 'half the workforce expect or need . . . especially the engineers they need to be appraised' (MD). Nonetheless, there were no formalised criteria for these appraisals. As the Creativity Director elaborated:

> because I deal with talented people, and in terms of building a relationship with people, I find it doesn't fit relevant to . . . you are trying to encourage their talent and give them criticism or feedback and in a very kind of soft, in a way that just weaves into their everyday lives . . . a mark out of ten and you're a nine or six or whatever, that for me would be too brutal and arbitrary.

The hierarchically contracted nature of the organisation also meant that traditional routes for career progression were less evident, although this did not appear to be a concern for employees.

> I couldn't care less about having a name, title, if you're in the army you want to be the general, or you know you've got a path and you can work that system . . . for a designer or for an actor or for an artist it's about just doing great work and finding ways to achieve that, and there's no . . . you can't open any book to tell you, you've got to, it's a path that *you* have to follow.
>
> (Industrial Designer)

Appraisals did not deal with issues of pay which was dealt with separately by the MD on a 'person to person basis'. While effort was made to 'distribute profits' through a bonus scheme, differentiating between employees was said to be difficult, while employees typically 'found out' what others had received.

Employee Voice at Creativity Co.

There were limited formal channels for employee voice at Creativity Co. Instead, interaction and two-way communication occurred on daily basis over coffee or simply as a result of groups working on projects together. For example, one of the workshop workers requested his own tools so that he could ensure they were kept in an appropriate condition. Others had voiced similar suggestions for how they would like things run. Employees were provided with all the information regarding budgets and timetables to ensure that they knew 'the limits and possibilities' of the project that they were working on. A more structured weekly meeting was also held among all staff on a Friday, although rather than being a strategic forum, it 'turns into a time planning meeting, a list drawing exercise of what we have to do and how far we are behind' (Industrial Designer). As a result of recruiting from a highly skilled differentiated market there was little pressure for formalised systems of interest representation, and even less perceived need for trade unions. There was some degree of working time flexibility in that if employees had worked additional hours they might be allowed to come in late, or take Monday morning off. This was supported by a clear rationale: 'we get the design right – if it costs the company a little bit more and takes an extra two days we don't penalise the designers and we don't penalise the clients' (Director, Industrial Design).

Overall, a key factor shaping the attraction and retention of workers at Creativity Co. stemmed from the interesting and challenging nature of the work. Substantial job autonomy, temporal project-based work activities and the necessity of fostering creativity led to fluid and informal HRM and loose supervision. This approach also matched the expectations and professional norms of employees and was underpinned by a degree of certainty, in terms of both the longer-term relations with projects and the ethos of the organisation: 'we're not of the sort of psyche who could say yeah we'll just take on a few and then kick them out the door because we don't have a job, we deal in the long term' (MD).

People Management Challenges at Creativity Co.

Michael, the MD of Creativity Co., faces a constant task of attempting to balance the informality conducive to creativity and innovation with the professionalism expected by clients and the rising expectations of employees. Pressure to perform at Creativity Co. came less from managerially determined rules, and more from vocational norms including the personal desire and passion to 'exceed expectations', coupled with peer pressure stemming from the interdependence and collaborative nature of projects. Industrial designers are known for their passion, drive, flashiness and even arrogance. For these professionals working on creative activities generates an immense sense of pride, while a clear sense of accomplishment ensues from seeing their visions and ideas materialise into final products. A central task for the Directors at Creativity Co. was attempting to balance the tension between individual needs for recognition while simultaneously supporting collaborative activity:

> they need to be treated as individuals, it's a bit like any of the creative industries, you know first of all it's not a job it's a vocation, and secondly each individual is different and they all feel they are special or whatever, so you've got to somehow maintain your own desires but also deliver on the desires of others, which is definitely quite tough.
>
> (Creativity Director)

A key tension in the workflow arose when work in the form of design sketches and proposed prototypes was passed on from the Industrial Designers to employees in the workshop. In particular, workshop employees felt that projects were simply 'thrown at them', frequently under very strict deadlines and without any appreciation of the existing constraints they were already under. Designers occasionally expressed frustration at the work pace and attitudes of the workshop crew, while the workshop crew exhibited a similar discontent towards the industrial engineers, labelling them 'daydreamers'.

Towards the Future

Creativity Co.'s heavy reliance on the expertise of its design professionals and engineers coupled with its significant technological investments mean that it is exemplary of the type of creative firm that is said to hold the key to the Irish government's knowledge economy agenda. Creativity Co. has been extremely successful to date, as evidenced by its award-winning designs and continuous business with key clients. In the field of industrial design traditional marketing is judged less important than company reputation and word of mouth referrals. To this end delivering on client expectations is critical. As Creativity Co. has expanded it has promoted two long-serving engineers to directorship level. The owner manager is keen that key individuals are rewarded with a financial stake in the organisation. There has also been some discussion about a sense of clearer career progression for individuals perhaps through an 'Associate' or 'Senior Engineer' status. However, there is also an acknowledgement that this might threaten the flat structure and teamworking that has been at the core of Creativity Co.'s success to date. More recently there has been evidence of some disquiet from employees in the workshop who feel they have been treated poorly and are simply thrown projects to complete. The Director is conscious of this issue and the need to smooth relations, particularly as the workshop is a critical component in terms of delivering quality designs on time. Thus while the Directors and professionals take great pride in seeing their designs make their way into mass production, and ultimately reaching the marketplace, there are challenges ahead. One of these relates to how the organisation might grow but also sustain the informal, customised way of working that has been core to its success to date. Finishing his coffee, the MD wryly notes once again 'the hangovers of success, now that's a problem I'm happy to deal with'.

Case Study Tasks

Questions for Group/Class Discussion:

1 What type of HRM practices are likely to be most appropriate in managing the type of professional workforce employed at Creativity Co.? (The 20-point profile of practices (Table 4.1) may help structure the discussion).
2 Evaluate the way Creativity Co. conducts key HRM practices of recruitment and selection, training and development, and performance management.
3 What are the challenges of implementing HRM in a smaller firm?
4 Outline the HRM implications of organisational growth and further expanding the workforce at Creativity Co.

Further Reading

Chasserio, S., & Legault, M.-J. (2009). Strategic human resources management is irrelevant when it comes to highly skilled professionals in the Canadian new economy. *International Journal of Human Resource Management*, 20(5), 1113–1131.

Goffee, R., & Jones, G. (2007). Leading clever people. *Harvard Business Review*, March, 72–79.

Greiner, L. E. (1988). Evolution and revolution as organisations grow. *Harvard Business Review*, May/June, 3–11.

Harney, B., & Dundon, T. (2006) Capturing complexity: Developing an integrated approach to analysing HRM in SMEs. *Human Resource Management Journal*, 16(1): 48–3.

Notes

1 In order to preserve anonymity the organisation is referred to by the pseudonym Creativity Co. In this context certain details concerning the organisation have also been altered and fictional names are used.
2 Pseudonym. Hi-Tech is a manufacturer of computer and video game accessories and peripherals.

References

DJEI (2015). *Enterprise 2025: Ireland's National Enterprise Policy 2015–2015*. Department of Jobs, Enterprise and Innovation, Government Offices.

Forfás (2012). Ireland's Competitiveness Scorecard 2012. Dublin: National Competitiveness Council.

Harney, B. (2006). The challenge of sustaining Ireland's economic success: Fairy tales, leprechauns and the illusive pot of gold. *International Affairs Journal*, UC Davis, 2(1), 28–34.

Harney, B. (2010). HRM in Smaller Firms: A Theoretical and Empirical Exploration of Practices, Patterns and Determinants. *Unpublished PhD Thesis*, University of Cambridge.

Harney, B., & Monks, K. (2014). *Strategic HRM: Research and Practice in Ireland*. Dublin: Blackhall/Orpen.

Kinsella, S. (2012). Is Ireland really the role model for austerity? *Cambridge Journal of Economics,* 36, 223–235.

Lepak, D. P., & Snell, S. 1999. The human resource architecture: Toward a theory of human capital allocation and development. *Academy of Management Review*, 24(1), 31–48.

Roche, W. K. (2014) 'HRM in the Recession: Managing People in the Private and Public Sectors'. Chapter 2 in Harney, B., & Monks, K. (2014). *Strategic HRM: Research and Practice in Ireland*. Dublin: Blackhall/Orpen, pp. 17–56.

Science Foundation Ireland (2012). *Agenda 2020: Excellence and Impact*. Dublin: SFI.

5

The Netherlands
HRM and Culture at RetailCo[1]

Corine Boon and Deanne N. Den Hartog

Organisational Setting and Historical Background

RetailCo is an international retail organisation, founded in the 1920s in the Netherlands. In 2007, RetailCo had more than 350 stores, mostly located in the Netherlands. RetailCo was expanding through increasing the number of stores, on average opening 30 new stores a year in the Benelux (an economic union comprising three neighbouring countries: **Bel**gium, the **Net**herlands, and **Lux**embourg). The company had approximately 10,000 employees (4,700 FTEs). In the Netherlands, RetailCo is seen as a 'typically Dutch' retail organisation, which takes good care of its employees. RetailCo has performed well and won several awards between 2004 and 2007, including prizes for logistics and marketing, and the 'best Dutch employer' award. Below, in Part I, we describe RetailCo and a take-over that took place in 2007 and how this affected HRM and culture at RetailCo in the short term. In Part II we briefly address several changes that have occurred since then.

Part I: HRM and Culture at RetailCo (2007)

RetailCo started in 1920 by providing good products for everyone, using low, uniform prices, aimed at serving both poorer and richer people. This business idea is still central to the organisation as its mission is to make daily life easier and more pleasant for people by providing a range of basic products. Convenient, practical and high quality products for daily use are sold at relatively low prices. RetailCo distinguishes itself by selling its own brand. All products are developed by the organisation itself, and represent RetailCo's vision of simplicity, surprising solutions, high quality, and low prices. Their wide assortment focuses on household products, clothing, food, but also includes other basic articles such as cosmetics, curtains and home office supplies. RetailCo's primary target customers are women between the ages of 25 and 50, though stores attract a broader group of customers; most Dutch people regularly visit a RetailCo store.

RetailCo is a centrally managed company. It consists of headquarters, the food division, a distribution centre, and the sales division (the stores). Their focus on household products, clothing, and food forms a unique combination of branches for one company to manage. This case focuses on the sales division, which is the key division of RetailCo, in which the largest part of the employees (about 85 percent) work.

Although RetailCo became part of a larger retail corporation around 2000, this did not change the firm much. In 2007, Mr. Theo De Vries, RetailCo's HRM director, signalled that the conglomerate had emphasised the culture, management and HRM practices of each separate company, aiming to preserve each company's unique identity, style, and brand. For example, RetailCo still has a unique culture and a separate collective bargaining agreement, tailored to its own needs.

The unique culture of RetailCo is explicated in seven 'culture keys', formulated by the management team, reflecting desired behaviours of employees: *client orientation, respect and trust, proactivity, results orientation, energy, working systematically, and loving the job.* Culture is seen as important as it forms the key to the success of the company; new employees should fit into the culture, and socialisation processes and promotion from within are emphasised. De Vries describes the culture in the stores as a 'family culture': 'Everyone knows everyone else in our stores; employees are very loyal towards each other as well as the organisation as a whole, which results in a pleasant atmosphere throughout our organisation.' The culture attracts many job applicants who want to be part of this family. Also, De Vries signals that employees are very loyal and committed to the organisation and most are reluctant to leave even if they have job opportunities elsewhere. Turnover is thus very low, on average 5 percent a year. At parties held when stores met their targets, De Vries always sees employees being very proud and showing this pride to others. He states: 'They really enjoy working here.'

Mr. Jan Bakker, a store manager, comments:

In selection interviews, the main selection criterion is whether the applicant fits 'the club', or in other words, the store culture. Although this culture could differ per store, we see that these values are closely linked to RetailCo's values, and this leads to people throughout the whole organisation being extremely loyal. Many like to see their colleagues and work together and therefore stay at RetailCo.

Yet, Mrs. Janneke Jansen, an HRM manager, also sees a downside of the low turnover rates as it can lead to inflexibility:

People choose for RetailCo because of the enjoyable and interesting jobs. This is also why people tend to stay here long. The disadvantage is that a large group of employees do not move to higher or other jobs anymore; the layer of middle managers forms an inflexible layer in the organisation. As a result, there are not enough positions available for young potentials who want to move up the hierarchy, as a result of which they leave.

The Operational Context in RetailCo

RetailCo's stores can be divided into five types, ranging from 250 to more than 1200 square meters (2691 and 12916,8 square feet, respectively) in size. Small stores are located in smaller villages, whereas the largest are located in the centre of large cities. Most shop floor store employees are women (87 percent), who tend to work part time. The average age is 32.

Each store has four departments: fashion, household products, food, and catering. There are no separate cashiers; all store employees work some time at the cash registers every day. The structure of the stores is simple with four job levels:

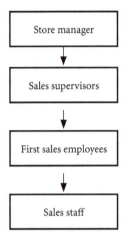

Each store has one store manager and usually four sales supervisors, one for each department, but sometimes fewer or more depending on the store size. The first sales employees are involved in day-to-day supervision and are seen as core employees. They develop work schedules, supervise work processes, and are involved in providing on-the-job training to their subordinates. In the smaller stores, there are no first sales employees and sales supervisors do the planning, supervising and training. Sales staff includes all employees working on the shop floor.

HRM in the Netherlands

Research on societal cultures shows the Netherlands to have a culture typified by strongly egalitarian (low power distance; Hofstede, 2001; House *et al.*, 2004) and individualistic as well as relatively 'feminine' and caring values.[2] The Netherlands also tends to reduce the level of uncertainty through enacting rules, laws, policies, and regulations. The content of HRM policies in Dutch firms often reflects these cultural values. Employees are typically seen as stakeholders in firms and the general agreement is that their needs should at least to some extent be taken into account. For management, maintaining good relationships with employees tends to be seen as at least as important as placing strict demands on employees' achievements. Hierarchies are not too strict and employee voice is typically encouraged. Employment security is valued; it is by law relatively difficult to fire employees. HRM in the Netherlands is characterised by a strong influence of legislation that protects conditions of employment, safety, well-being, and job security of workers. Even several so-called high performance practices are to some extent regulated. For example, a basic level of employee participation is regulated through works councils; minimum wages and set pay grades tend to be regulated at the industry level; and safety and health policies are regulated by national law. As a result, many of the so-called 'best practices' in HRM listed below (Pfeffer, 1998) are to some extent present in Dutch companies (for more information on HRM practices in the Netherlands, see Boselie, Paauwe, & Jansen, 2001):

- Employment security
- High wages
- Employee ownership
- Information sharing
- Participation
- Self-managed teams
- Training and development
- Wage compression
- Promotion from within
- Long-term orientation

Works councils and trade unions have substantial influence on HRM in Dutch companies. Most employees in the Netherlands are covered by a collective bargaining agreement for their organisation or the whole sector they work in.

The HRM Context in RetailCo

The aim of the HRM strategy is 'striving for top performance by having an enjoyable job'. HRM director De Vries describes how RetailCo is known for the social nature of its HRM policy; an important aim of this HRM policy has been to keep employees committed and satisfied and make work enjoyable, in order to increase performance. Above-average salaries and benefits and high employment security are offered. In case of necessary downsizing, RetailCo has always retained as many employees as possible with a minimal amount of compulsory redundancies. People typically choose to apply for a job at RetailCo as the salary and benefits are good, and because of RetailCo's good reputation. Jobs are diverse and working times are flexible. A full-time job is 35 hours a week, mostly scheduled in four days.

RetailCo sees that a downside of this relatively luxurious position of employees is that certain changes are more difficult to implement. The workforce is used to having extensive benefits, which reduces workers' flexibility. For example, although their formal contract states that full-time employees have the right to choose only one particular day a week off, employees often resist changes in their working hours when changes are needed in the stores, as they have traditionally had the opportunity to choose their own working hours. Also, employees are very comfortable working in specific departments and stores. HRM manager Jansen mentions:

> Contracts of employees have always included opportunities to transfer employees to a different store or department when needed, but up till a few years ago, we never made use of it. Now that we do want to make use of this opportunity, we see that people have difficulties with change. Most don't even want to work in a different department in the same store.

Recruitment, Selection, and Socialization

The 'culture keys' of RetailCo guide the content of many HRM practices such as selection, training and development, and performance appraisal.

Store managers are responsible for selecting new employees. HRM managers only assist when needed, and are involved in selecting store managers. Formal guidelines for selection and socialisation have been written up in a general booklet which is used, but De Vries sees that store managers find it even more important that people are selected who fit well into the culture and into the group already working in that store. When selecting full-time employees, RetailCo uses a future-oriented approach, selecting people with the potential to grow to higher functions within the store, and anticipating which knowledge and skills stores will need in the future.

Each new employee participates in an introduction program, which emphasises Retail-Co's culture, and desired behaviours and habits within RetailCo. New employees receive information about the culture and the type of work, products, and departments within the store from the regional HRM manager.

Training and Development

For all levels of staff, RetailCo has developed job-specific training programs. For all levels above the sales staff level, the job-specific training is compulsory; for sales staff it is voluntary as are other training programs.

The focus on employee development is strong. Employees have development opportunities linked to their specific jobs and have considerable freedom in making choices regarding their own development. RetailCo has implemented a (voluntary) development tool for employees; the development tool can be accessed through the intranet, and it lists for each type of job a range of possible ways for employees to develop themselves further. These development options are linked to the different culture keys as well. This development tool is very extensive and well-developed, but as it is voluntary, De Vries unfortunately observes that many employees do not use it.

RetailCo strongly prefers internal development and promotion of employees. As RetailCo combines different branches (fashion, household products, food, and catering) in one organisation, it is a difficult organisation for an outsider to understand. That makes it very difficult for RetailCo to hire managers, who need knowledge relating to all departments, from the outside. RetailCo's experience with hiring managers from outside is that they encounter problems with performing well in their job and are less committed to RetailCo. Jansen comments:

> RetailCo seems less complicated than it actually is. It is therefore more difficult to hire someone from outside for store manager positions. Experience shows that store managers who are selected from outside perform less and quit more often than store managers selected from inside the organisation. Therefore, we chose to select sales supervisors who have the potential to grow into store manager positions. This way, he or she starts on the work floor having close contact with other employees, and can get to know RetailCo slowly before making the next career step.

Appraisal and Rewards

Appraisal is not that strict in RetailCo, which stems from the 'social orientation' of the firm. Until recently, almost all employees were evaluated positively, without having a formal appraisal procedure. As a result, RetailCo did not have good insight into which employees were not performing well. This has changed somewhat during the last two years, as a matrix was developed providing insight into which skills and behaviours are expected in each of the different jobs in a store. Each employee's skills and behaviours are now compared with the desired skills and behaviours in the matrix. The resulting similarities and differences serve as input for the performance appraisal.

Rewards are set in the collective bargaining agreement, which includes a basic salary, and a yearly increase in salary based on tenure on the job. Only in the case of very unusual good performance are individual or store bonuses given.

The Take-over

In the last few years increasing market pressures in the Dutch retail market occurred which forced RetailCo to work more efficiently and to cut their already relatively low prices to keep profits up.

In 2007, RetailCo was taken over by a US-based investment firm with extensive experience in the US retail industry. The predominant approaches to HRM in the USA and the Netherlands differ. Typically, HRM in the USA is characterised by relatively low job security, a focus on high performance work systems, an increasing use of variable pay systems, a relatively low level of union involvement, a relatively low influence of regulations on HRM practices, and extensive outsourcing of HRM functions, contrary to Dutch HRM, which as mentioned has relatively higher job security, higher base wages with less variable pay, and attention to employee well-being. In addition to these general differences, there are also some differences specific to these two firms. The investment firm that took over RetailCo uses a shareholder approach, which focuses on increasing shareholder value instead of focusing on benefits for a range of stakeholders – such as employees, customers, etc. – as emphasised in the stakeholder model that was followed at RetailCo until the take-over (for more information on shareholder vs. stakeholder models, see e.g. Donaldson & Preston, 1995). The previous CEO of RetailCo was replaced by a new CEO who was selected by the investment firm and who was supposed to implement a new shareholder-based strategy.

The take-over further accelerated the changes that started in RetailCo as a result of the increasing market pressures. As a result of the take-over, RetailCo is now more centrally managed than before, with an even stronger focus on profits. RetailCo is more tightly managed on output, costs, and efficiency. De Vries worries about the effects these changes have on employees:

> The take-over has led to major changes in RetailCo. The approach to managing people of the investment firm is totally different from our approach. Our vision focuses on happiness, which is achieved by having an enjoyable job and performing well. The investment firm on the other hand, focuses mainly on financials, which is seen for example in their plans to introduce incentive pay.

This change is already starting to impact on RetailCo's culture; it is becoming more business-like and tougher, compared to the family-type, social culture before. Jansen also sees that the culture has hardened. 'If you don't perform well, you get fired. This compromises employees' feeling of job security and their enjoyment in the job.' De Vries also signals some positive aspects of more closely monitoring employee performance. 'In the past, people who didn't do their job well were not detected, as nearly everyone received a good appraisal each year.

The true performance and differences between employees become clear now, as we need to assess their performance more strictly.'

At management levels, the take-over led to more pressure from the top, with store managers having less freedom in managing their store. De Vries describes how the amount of control has increased: 'They focus on procedural control instead of results control; both "what" and "how" is determined by them.' Several management and HRM practices were centralised. For example, a new service philosophy and new values were introduced. The successful set of values and HRM practices that were closely aligned with each other and with the specific nature of RetailCo, were changed into the values the investment firm has successfully introduced in retail companies in the past. The new values include *passion for customers, striving for continuous improvement, fulfilling performance goals,* and *working together as a team.* These values place the customer at the centre, emphasise the serving role of employees and the importance of high performance, and expect full flexibility from employees. To achieve full flexibility, part-time workers are now often scheduled to work six days a week, a few hours a day based on busy store hours. Many part-time employees, often mothers with small children, experience difficulties arranging child care because of this high spread of working hours.

The investment firm also introduced increased control and centralisation of many HRM practices. For example, general retail training programs replaced the company-specific training programs of RetailCo, and a standard appraisal procedure and form have just been introduced, in which employees will be evaluated on competencies which are more standard in the US retail sector, but differ from the competencies employees are familiar with in RetailCo.

De Vries does not understand why a new HRM policy and values are needed:

The last couple of years, RetailCo has developed and implemented a strong, culture-driven HRM policy. The investment firm does not take this policy into consideration. Instead, they impose a different HRM policy, which in some respects is similar to our existing HRM policy. I'm sure it is a good policy, but why should I implement it when it doesn't match our values? An example is the appraisal form. The investment firm has introduced new forms to be used from now on, which are based on 6 new values they introduced, instead of the 7 culture keys of RetailCo.

Also, the role of the HRM managers is changing. Jansen signals that HRM managers used to be involved mainly in 'soft' issues. But, 'Now, HRM managers are also involved in financial figures. HR is now becoming more involved in the operation, for example by being involved in the sales figures, which determine the availability of staff.'

The Dilemma

Overall, the take-over presents a dilemma for RetailCo. The investment firm has introduced a more centralised and efficiency-driven way of managing the organisation, focused more on profits and shareholder interests than on the stakeholder model, and it uses a different management style. Both conflict with the traditional (Dutch) values of RetailCo.

As there is high resistance against the new policies of the investment firm, De Vries and Jansen are asked by the new director to submit a proposal in which they outline an HRM policy which they believe to be the most effective one for RetailCo, but which at the same time aims to increase efficiency and performance. This provides De Vries and Jansen with the opportunity to propose an HRM policy which takes into account RetailCo's and its employees' interests better. They struggle with this request. Clearly, something needs to be changed, but what exactly? How to combine RetailCo's values with increasing financial performance? Their future within RetailCo could depend on the success of their proposal . . .

Case Study Tasks – Part I

1 Describe and evaluate the HRM policies and practices *before* and *after* the take-over. What are the strong and weak points?
2 The take-over has meant the shift to a shareholder approach impacting HRM in RetailCo, which contrasts with the stakeholder focus originally used. Describe the influence of the shareholder vs. the stakeholder model on HRM in RetailCo.
3 RetailCo has a unique set HRM practices. Describe and evaluate how you think the HRM practices *before* and *after* the take-over have been influenced by

    (a) National culture?
    (b) Organisational culture?
    (c) Other organisational characteristics?

    In which areas might problems arise? Explain why.
4 Given the differences in culture and institutional context between the Netherlands and the USA, what would an ideal-type HRM system look like in the Netherlands, and in the USA? Describe the main characteristics of HRM policy and HRM practices for both countries, focusing on the following HRM practices:

    • Recruitment and selection
    • Training and development
    • Appraisal and rewards

5 'Best Practice' and 'Best Fit' models are two dominant approaches in the HRM literature that explain how HRM affects performance. Which of these two approaches do you believe to be part of the HRM policy and practices at RetailCo (a) *before* the take-over, and (b) *after* the take-over? Do you believe that the take-over has changed the overall approach used in RetailCo or not? Explain why.
6 As experts on HRM, you are to advise Mr. De Vries and Mrs. Jansen on their new HRM proposal for the CEO. What would you recommend? Present your view on what an effective HRM policy for RetailCo might look like (i.e. a full description of the HRM policy and practices) and explain why your solution should be effective for RetailCo.

Part II: HRM and Culture at RetailCo

Only one year after the take-over discussed above, the US-based investment firm sold RetailCo to a UK-based investment firm (for more information on HRM in the UK, see e.g. Guest *et al.*, 2003). This UK-based investment firm had a more long-term interest in RetailCo. Volume has become increasingly important in this competitive market to keep the purchase price of the raw materials needed to make RetailCo's products low. Thus, the UK-based investment firm decided that to increase bargaining power, RetailCo needed to grow more rapidly than before. Therefore, in the period after this second take-over, RetailCo expanded internationally at a more rapid pace than before, now opening approximately 50 new stores each year and expanding to several new countries. Currently, seven years after the second take-over, RetailCo owns over 700 stores in 10 different countries, among which are France, Spain, Hong Kong, and China.

Also, as market pressures continue to grow, it becomes increasingly important to stay ahead of the market. One big change made in response to this, for example, was the adoption of a fast fashion positioning, which required substantial changes for RetailCo in terms of product development, production and logistics.

Managers of RetailCo have noticed that the way of working of the UK-based investment firm is closer to the traditional RetailCo culture described in the first part of the case before the take-over, for example, by focusing more on long-term success than on short-term shareholder value. To make the long-term growth strategy a success in the competitive market RetailCo operates in, the investment firm made plans to improve RetailCo's performance while maintaining the RetailCo brand and culture as much as possible. In 2015, HRM manager Jansen mentions: 'We kept the RetailCo brand, and the RetailCo feeling. Right after the take-overs it was not visible how RetailCo could benefit from these developments, but now, several years later, we do see that this strategy works.'

Also, while expanding internationally, the company wants to stay typically Dutch – the products RetailCo sells are 'no-nonsense with a smile'. Again, new values were implemented by the UK-based investment firm, which aim to reflect RetailCo's heritage and guide everything RetailCo does, with the goal of creating a customer-centric culture of collaboration and cooperation. As De Vries puts it: 'Our customer first, quality in everything we do, we keep things simple, we do what we say, we win together, and every penny counts.' These new values also describe desired behaviours of RetailCo's employees. To implement these values and to decrease the distance between the Head Quarters, where new products are designed and changes are developed, and the stores of RetailCo, each year around the holidays, the headquarters employees work one day in the store that performed best that year. This is seen as a bonus for that store's employees, and the staff of headquarters see what happens on the shop floor and learn from how the best performing store is run.

To improve performance, all stores in the Netherlands were remodelled, a new range of products was introduced, and prices of various products were further reduced. This investment in the brand seems to have paid off; consumers voted RetailCo the most indispensable brand in the Netherlands eight times in a row, and RetailCo has been voted the best retail chain in the Netherlands twice during this period.

However, after seven years of rapid growth, returns decreased which led to some losses for RetailCo. HRM director De Vries therefore wonders whether RetailCo has perhaps expanded too fast, and whether the changes that have been introduced were too comprehensive and costly or the pace of change may have been too high . . .

Case Study Tasks – Part II

1 The second take-over has led to another change in the approach with which RetailCo is managed, focusing on performance improvements as well as long-term growth. Describe the change and how this change could influence culture and HRM in RetailCo.

2 Given the differences in culture and institutional context between the Netherlands and the UK, what would an ideal-type HRM system look like in the Netherlands, and in

the UK? Describe the main characteristics of HRM policy and HRM practices for both countries, focusing on the following HRM practices:

- Recruitment and selection
- Training and development
- Appraisal and rewards

3 As mentioned, 'Best Practice' and 'Best Fit' models are two dominant approaches in the HRM literature that explain how HRM affects performance. Do you believe that the second take-over will change the overall approach used in RetailCo or not? Explain why.

4 Do you think the expansion may have been too fast? Present your view on how this rapid growth may (have) affect(ed) RetailCo, and more specifically, RetailCo's culture and HRM system. What changes could be made for the years to come in order to try to increase profits again?

Notes

1 To preserve the privacy of the firm, names and other identifying information have been modified.
2 Power distance is the extent to which a society accepts that power is distributed unequally. Masculinity versus femininity refers to the distribution of roles between the genders and the dominance of assertive and competitive values versus caring and modest ones. Individualism versus collectivism reflects whether individuals are more loosely coupled or integrated into strong and cohesive groups. Uncertainty avoidance refers to a society's tolerance for uncertainty and ambiguity.

References and Further Reading

Boselie, P., Paauwe, J., & Jansen, P. (2001). Human resource management and performance: lessons from the Netherlands. *International Journal of Human Resource Management, 12*(7), 1107–1125.

Donaldson, T., & Preston, L. E. (1995). The stakeholder theory of the corporation: Concepts, evidence, and implications. *Academy of Management Review, 20*(1), 65–91.

Guest, D.E., Michie, J., Conway, N., & Sheehan, M. (2003). Human resource management and corporate performance in the UK. *British Journal of Industrial Relations, 41*(2), 291–314.

Hofstede, G. (2001). *Culture's consequences: Comparing values, behaviors, institutions, and organizations across nations.* Sage Publications.

House, R.J., Leadership, G., Hanges, P.J., Javidan, M., Dorfman, P.W., & Gupta, V. (2004). *Culture, leadership, and organizations: The GLOBE study of 62 societies.* Sage Publications.

Pfeffer, J. (1998). *The human equation: Building profits by putting people first.* Boston: Harvard Business School Press.

Part II
Scandinavia

6

Denmark

Redesigning Talent Assets: Grundfos Revisits their Talent Engine

Liza Castro Christiansen

After having developed 380 leaders, innovators, and specialists during the first six years of their talent development programme, the Danish pump manufacturer, Grundfos, takes a step back, assesses the initial results of their award winning Talent Engine,[1] revisits the programme, puts it on hold and re-aligns it with the organisation's objectives and strategies. This case describes the Grundfos Talent Engine, which ran from 2009 until January 2016; the issues that Grundfos had to consider during the introductory phase of the programme; the lessons learned, and plans on how to move forward. It illustrates how a leading multinational exercises agility to develop talents during a crisis and to keep pace with constantly changing market trends.

Introduction

In 2006, the former CEO, Carsten Bjerg, announced aggressive growth ambitions for Grundfos 2025: The innovation intent stipulated massive growth as a company from 18,000 to 75,000 employees, and, correspondingly, the need to build a very strong pipeline of talents to be able to fill all those leadership positions that would emerge out of this growth. In particular, 50 percent of the growth of Grundfos in 2025 would be coming from technology platforms that were not invented in 2007 and one-third of the turnover would be coming from products other than pumps. This innovation imperative meant that Grundfos would need to invent products that they do not even know about today. For this reason, there was a strong focus on innovation and on building innovative and specialised capabilities in the company. And it is for this same reason that one of the foundations of the first version of the Talent Engine was to produce not only leaders, but innovators, and specialists as well.

Brief Historical Background

Grundfos was established in 1945 by Poul Due Jensen under the name *Bjerringbro Pressestøberi og Maskinfabrik:* Bjerringbro Press Foundry and Machine Factory (Bjerringbro is the town where the headquarters are located) and in 1967, the firm changed its name to

Grundfos. They have production, sales, and service facilities in most of the world's most important pump markets and they wish to continue to increase their presence in new markets. Grundfos is organised in this way for two reasons: firstly, because there is a need for high-quality pumps all over the world, and secondly, because the need for consultancy service and service in general differs from country to country. Grundfos customises their solutions to meet local requirements because it is impossible to operate and manage a global organisation from one central point. Aware that this cannot be accomplished by forcing Danish culture on all their companies in other countries, or on their communities, Grundfos gives maximum freedom to the local people while at the same time harvesting efficiency gains from global alignment. By focusing on regional production facilities and a local set-up, Grundfos is able to demonstrate respect for local values, culture, social conditions, and ways of doing business.

HRM in Denmark

The practice of human resource management in Denmark is derived from its institutional roots. The Danish HRM model can be described as being collaborative with a distinctly more developmental or humanistic approach, often based on the value of the employees and their employment relation to the firm. The collaborative emphasis is characterised by efforts to create and communicate a culture of partnership between employer and employee as well as among employees (Gooderham, Nordhaug and Ringdal, 1999). It should be mentioned, however, that Denmark is the country in Europe where it is easiest to fire and hire employees, a concept, which has become known as "flexicurity"[2] (the combination of two English words "**flexi**bility" and "se**curity**"). Denmark is probably the European country with the best-established security net, in case one becomes unemployed (Larsen, 2010). The Danish model functions as a form of unwritten contract between the government and labour market partners, Danish Employers' Association and the Danish Confederation of Trade Unions. It works only with the acceptance of these three parties.

The industrial landscape of modern Denmark is made up of many small to medium-sized organisations. There are far fewer very large organisations in Denmark than in other major industrial nations in Europe with the possible exception of Spain. Danish companies have tended to specialise and Denmark is famous, not for mass-market products, but for production, which stresses creativity in design and excellence in the quality of the finished goods.

In most Danish organisations, most of the administrative functions are outsourced or executed by IT systems and the HR department still constitutes only a very small percentage of the total organisation (0–0.5 percent of the organisation's size). Denmark is also the only country in Europe where line management holds the strongest responsibility on all HR areas (e.g., compensation and benefits, recruitment and training) (Larsen 2010). Line managers are held more accountable for their HR/people management practices than HR managers are. It appears, however, that HR responsibility is slowly going back to the HR function and the HR function is beginning to develop a very strong partnership with top management. This development stems from the increasing attention that organisations give to the alignment of HR strategy and business strategy (Castro Christiansen & Higgs, 2008a; 2009). It also indicates a deeper understanding and greater need and appreciation for the role of HR (Castro Christiansen & Higgs, 2008b).

In a similar vein, HR practices, e.g., skills development and training, are planned with a view to realising the longer-term needs of the organisation. All employees receive training possibilities, although the top tier receives the first priority. The results of the most recent CRANET study show that in general, Danish organisations are still quite conservative about formalising career development schemes in terms of career plans, high-flying programmes and development centres, in which case career development through job-related learning and in collaboration with managers and colleagues is practised more (Bévort, Larsen, Hjalager and Christensen, 2014). Grundfos is among the very few huge Danish organisations, which have gone their own way, in designing career development opportunities in the form of their Talent Engine.

Background to the Case: The Starting Point

One of the means through which Grundfos tried to meet future challenges was the establishment of their Talent Engine concept, a huge step beyond the HRM activity that it used to be. Talented people at Grundfos were trained and developed in individually designed programmes within the Talent Engine on one of three routes: managers, innovators and specialists. The three main deliverables of the concept were:

1 Grundfos will be a world class place of work, also for top talents
2 Grundfos will move away from the standard talent development scheme to a more individual and personalised activity that will promote transparency for and among the talents
3 Grundfos will create a strong integration between talent development and the direct implementation of business strategy

To create an effective concept for talent development in an organisation with 18,000 employees around the world, which could function in all the different cultures, and which could engage people with diverse responsibilities, was not an easy task. Grundfos chose to apply an untraditional co-creation approach. They invited 40 carefully selected leaders from around the world to a four-day workshop with the sole purpose of designing the future concept for Grundfos' talent development. The selection of these 40 leaders, who possessed personality, drive, and enthusiasm, and who represented different departments such as sales, production, business development, and general management, was based on their passion for developing talents and their capacity as opinion leaders in their local areas.

Choosing the Cream of the Crop

To encourage ownership of the talent concept, at a meeting all the general managers received a "golden envelope" containing the guidelines for the nomination process. Thereafter, these general managers sent their lists with the names of the talents that they had spotted in their own organisations together with their HR people to the Regional HR Managers, who evaluated and challenged these lists. Encouraging the general managers to argue for their choices contributed to a sharper definition of exactly what was meant by talent at Grundfos. The result of this process was a list of 135 nominated talents from the whole world, who were chosen based on the nine-box grid in Figure 6.1. With potential and performance on the two axes, the qualified candidates eligible to enter the talent programme needed to be in the blue box, which is the "star performer box". These were the people who were believed to have the potential to advance in the organisation, who were delivering above expectations, and who could drive the strategic agenda.

The Talent Engine population

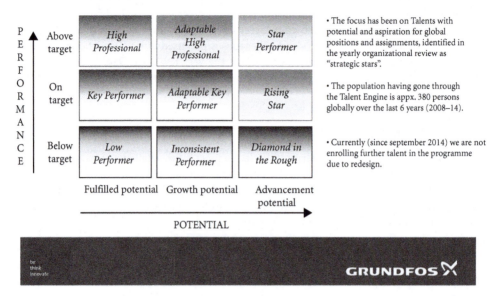

Figure 6.1 The talent engine population

The nominees went through the Talent Centre where their competencies were assessed. The Talent Centre was an important part of the concept because here the nominees were evaluated and qualified in terms of their global and local potential. All these talents were equally important to Grundfos, but it was crucial to determine where they could add most value. Out of the 135 nominees who participated in the first selection phase, 33 percent were qualified as "global talents" and the rest as "local talents". The "global talents" were those assessed to have the perspective, outlook, and mindset towards driving Grundfos globally, while the "local talents" were those who had potential, but more within a local or regional context. From 2009 until January 2016, the Talent Engine produced an average of 50 to 60 talents every year, resulting in a pool of 380 today.

The Talent Centre was a 2½-day very concentrated, focused event, where the talents were challenged extremely hard with simulation exercises. They then received detailed and fact-based feedback on which a personal development plan was based. For example, one talent whose motivation was to become a leader, but whose initial results proved less fitting to a leader profile was given the following feedback:

Areas to develop:

Inspiring Leadership: You need to demonstrate enthusiasm and passion and demonstrate your ability to lead others and take charge of the situation in a consistent way.

Business Acumen/Delivering Outstanding Results: You need to gain a greater business awareness to enable you to identify your own targets.

The assessors were General Managers and other high-level key persons, trained by an external consultancy at a tailor-made Grundfos Talent Assessor Training Programme. Six to eight talent assessors at each Talent Centre assessed between 12 and 14 talents.

Before the Talent Engine was introduced, the selection process was more a question of time, place, and network and was to a great extent, a *subjective* evaluation, which could be attributed to a widely held belief that managers' "liking" of their employees is positively related to their ratings of employees' performance – and, in Grundfos' case, further potential – which Sutton, Baldwin, Wood and Hoffman (2013) found evidence for from their research. The very structured selection process that developed afterwards enabled Grundfos to have a clear definition of what a talent is and the level of competency necessary to be able to go through the process.

The Talent Greenhouse: Where Talents Develop

When the talents were chosen, a personal development plan consisting of a series of activities targeted towards their development was designed. The personal development plan was closely linked to the talent's daily workplace, e.g., by involving people from the local HR department and the talents' own general managers. Integrating the talents' development with operational activities encouraged them to engage in a closer dialogue with their managers about their personal development plans as it gave them the possibility to get their managers' evaluation of their performance in their daily work. The personal development plan created a structure for further development through activities designed and developed, namely:

(a) The **Master Classes** from which the talents drew new knowledge for the needed competencies.
(b) **Matchmaking** in which the talents were assigned to manage and/or implement projects that would help reach the organisation's concern-wide strategy.
(c) **Membership in a network of global talents** in which they could share experiences.
(d) **Virtual Greenhouse Community**, where the talents stayed in a closed virtual room together with top management, members of whom were assigned as a mentor to each talent.

These different elements enabled the talents to prove their skills in actual business situations and to achieve accelerated learning through the combination of theory and practice. The talents took part in the activities in the Talent Greenhouse for a period of three years (see Figure 6.2).

Challenges

Through the six-year talent training and development period, Grundfos experienced a number of challenges. One was related to preparing all leaders on how to manage the talents. Although the direct leader had an opinion on the extent to which the talent's potential was fulfilled, the reason why working with talents could be difficult was that it was a novel project and there did not exist a formal procedure on how to manage them. And because it was so new, it was also difficult to determine its real effects. Another challenge for Grundfos was how to ensure the alignment of the Talent Engine with other systems and processes in the organisation. For example, it was necessary to design a compensation scheme for the talent's respective organisation in terms of "lending out" the talent to other parts of the organisation, so that their leaders would be motivated to "share" their talents and support this initiative.

Figure 6.2 Grundfos' Talent Greenhouse

A third challenge was identifying non-financial benefits. Giving the talents assignments beyond their operational duties provided the leaders with the possibility to "keep" the talents for a longer time instead of risking that they leave the organisation because of lack of opportunities for development.

One particular challenge stems from a specific Danish cultural phenomenon called 'janteloven' ("Do not think that you are better than others"), which is essentially the Danish philosophy of egalitarianism. A leader, must accept that his employees can become more competent than he is in some areas and he must let them develop themselves in other areas. It will be a waste if the talents and their potential can not be maximised because their success is dependent on others (their leaders). At Grundfos, open communication has helped alleviate the detrimental effects of *jantelov*. They now dare to say out loud that people are blessed with different kinds of talent and they dare to publicise the names of the talents with global potential in Grundfos.

Another more general challenge was encountered in obtaining a good balance of talents from important areas such as Eastern Europe, China, India, Japan, and Korea. One of the barriers was the language. Since this was a global programme, all the programme activities were run in English and some of the candidates from the Far East had difficulties in taking part in the discussions and in making presentations because of lack of language skills. Furthermore, most of the people who went through the assessment ended up in the specialist box; a few were classified as leaders and even fewer as innovators. Grundfos did not define how many they needed in each group, nor in each geographical area, but were simply guided by the ambition that there should be an even distribution across geography. "We did not make any calculations on what would be the appropriate number of talents that we would need in our talent pool if we were to meet the growth target we had at that point of time. We did not have a lot of data, nor a lot of KPIs then", explains Anne Bisbjerg Lee, then HR Global Partner, now Group Senior Director, Product Sales Capability Build-Up for Grundfos.

The Turning Point

Grundfos was not spared from the world financial crisis that started in 2008. From 2009, although the turnover increased year by year, the growth rate – and profit – were declining. This was an unfortunate situation that coincided with the start-up of the Talent Engine. The Board of Directors decided to turn this negative development around, dismissed the CEO in 2013, and established a new management team.

The new management team conducted a deep analysis of the current and future situation of Grundfos and assessed that there was a need for a much sharper focus on both market segmentation and product segmentation. They concluded that they were not going to be 75,000 people in 2025, that they needed to continue being innovative, that they still had to develop some new technologies, but new technologies within their core competencies. This is the basis of Grundfos' new strategic direction. The talent programme has a duration of three years and the last batch of talents who started in 2013 completed the programme in January 2016. The intake of new talents was put on hold in late 2015. The management team plans to resume talent development with a new innovation engine, but an engine with a clear view on nurturing and managing talent forward.

Key Lessons Learned

There are many lessons learned from the first version of the Talent Engine with the following implications:

The need to build talent where the business is and the need to use the talents' potential to the fullest. The talents were transformed and trained to solve assignments totally out of their comfort zones and in areas different from everyday life. The previous programme took a centralised approach with all initiatives being pushed by and driven from the headquarters in Bjerringbro, resulting in talent development being detached from the talents' regular business. The talents gained a lot of personal insights on their own development needs and potential, but it was difficult for them to go back to their organisation and deploy these newly gained competencies. It was also difficult for the leaders who were not involved in talent activities to support and utilise the talent.

The need for a much more decentralised and distributed model for choosing the talents. Even though 380 people sounded like a lot of people, it was also a very heavy investment in a few people. A large proportion of the HR budget was spent on talent development activities, a level of investment that could reach more people and develop more potential in the organisation. For the first three batches of the talent nomination, candidates with obvious potential were selected. Candidates for the suceeding batches were more difficult to spot, partly because the managers who nominated the talents did not have the skills and competencies to make the assessment. Thus, the latest batches of talents included some people who did not really know why they were selected. Grundfos had a situation where they had people who were not even qualified or motivated to be part of the programme.

The need to label everyone as a global talent. Everyone wanted to be classified as a "global talent", so two-thirds of the talents who were labelled "talent" were disappointed and consequently less motivated and engaged after they had gone through the assessment centre than when they were nominated to the talent pool. These findings were evident from Grundfos' motivation surveys, which also support the work of Björkman, Ehrnrooth, Mäkelä, Smale, and Sumelius (2013), who found that informing talented individuals of their "expected" status has a motivational effect.

The need to make the talents feel special also after they have gone through the programme. Grundfos did a very good job in ensuring that these talents felt special, that they received unique opportunities, but the organisation needs to help the talents see brighter career perspectives rather than see the talent programme more as a retention and recognition exercise. All these go back to the need to complete the cycle from choosing the relevant talents, developing the talent where the business is, deploying the newly acquired knowledge and competencies where their potential can be utilised best, and making the talent "feel good" about enhancing their career and contributing to the organisation.

The Way Forward

Anne Bisbjerg Lee, Group Senior Director for Product Sales Capability Build-Up at Grundfos, has lined up imperatives for the new Talent Engine:

Focus on costs. The new framework needs to be cost effective, it has to be related to the financial results and it should be for the benefit of the broader talent population. The new talent concept will, therefore, be targeted around accelerating the development of capabilities in critical segments of the new strategy, and this means a targeted population for the talent activities and a bigger pipeline of talents who can work with bigger projects. This is a totally different approach because it will exclude others. An example would be project sales in geographical segments such as China, where there are a lot of opportunities to sell big projects within water utility and water treatment. As a consequence, some people will be out of scope for talent activities during the next years.

Focus on building the succession pipeline. Whereas there was no link between the talent programme and succession mapping previously, pipelines for leadership positions will be ensured. To be able to build even stronger pipelines, the focus will be put on identifying people who could fill these positions in the longer term and then develop them towards specific types of roles.

Focus on developing tools for the organisation. A toolbox approach where easy online tutorials, training modules, templates, and questionnaires for the leaders and for the talents in different geographies, rather than running programmes from the headquarters, will be developed.

Focus on the link between talent development and talent deployment. Previously, the focus had been around developing the assessment, the mentoring, and matchmaking concepts. Questions that should dominate the talent arena are: *"How do we utilise the potential of a given talent?"* and more importantly, *"How do we ensure that we recognise their newly developed competencies and that we give them concrete challenges, assignments, and positions that match these competencies?".* A solution could be pushing out job opportunities to talents in a more structured way through the provision of available job listings that will work much more inclusively on the deployment part.

Focus on a leader-team approach supported by HR and not the other way around. Targets for the leaders will be established among the core leadership tasks in the organisation.

Ways to motivate and ensure that the leaders understand the business and the talents that they have will be provided and supported by HR, but these will have to be driven by regional/local leadership.

Amidst the forthcoming changes, and apart from the master classes, mentoring, and matchmaking, the feedback and support the talents receive from HR regarding their own career paths and the choices that they consider taking are elements that will be carried over to the new Talent Engine. Assessments both from HR and from business leaders are valuable for the talents' understanding of where they should concentrate their further development.

Case Study Tasks

1 Describe the special HRM practices that Grundfos introduced in their first Talent Engine. How do these compare with the HRM practices prescribed by theory? How do these compare with the talent management programme of your organisation or an organisation that you are familiar with?
2 Which specific aspects of Grundfos' organisational culture and the Danish national culture contributed to the development of the Talent Engine?
3 There is a need for measuring the results of talent management. Based on theory and your understanding of Grundfos' overall strategy, which measurements would you suggest that Grundfos should use in evaluating the results of their new Talent Engine?
4 Apart from the responsibilities of HRM mentioned in the case, which other roles can HRM assume in the new Talent Engine, which can add value?

Notes

1 Grundfos won the award for Talent Innovation from the HR Leadership Alliance in November 2010.
2 Flexicurity is an intergrated strategy for enhancing, at the same time, flexibility and security in the labour market. It attempts to reconcile employers' need for a flexible workforce with workers' need for security – with the confidence that they will not face long periods of unemployment (Wilthagen 1998 as cited by Bredgaard et al., 2009).

References

Bévort, F., Larsen, H.H., Hjalager, A. & Christensen, J. (2014). *HRM i Danmark: Back to square one eller fugl fønix? CRANET Undersøgelsen 2014.* Copenhagen, Denmark: Copenhagen Business School.

Björkman, I., Ehrnrooth, M., Mäkelä, K., Smale, A., & Sumelius, J. (2013). Talent or not? Employee reactions to talent identification. *Human Resource Management*, 52(2), 195–214.

Bredgaard, T., Larsen, F., Madsen, P.K., & Rasmussen, S. (2009). Flexicurity på Dansk. CARMA Research paper. *Centre for Labour Market Research.* Aalborg, Denmark: Aalborg University Press.

Castro Christiansen, L. & Higgs, M. (2008a). How the alignment of business strategy and HR strategy can impact performance. *Journal of General Management.* 33(4), 13–33.

Castro Christiansen, L. & Higgs, M. (2008b). Do HR competencies enable organisations to perform more effectively? An empirical study of HR competencies and organisational performance in Danish companies. *2008 BAM proceedings.* Leeds: British Academy of Management.

Castro Christiansen, L. & Higgs, M. (2009). HR strategy and business strategy alignment: Operationalizing the dynamics of fit. *2009 AOM proceedings.* Chicago: Academy of Management.

Gooderham, P., Nordhaug, O. & Ringdal, K. (1999). Institutional and rational determinants of organizational practices: Human resource practices in European firms. *Administrative Science Quarterly*, 44(3), 507–531.

Larsen, H. H. (2010). *Human Resource Management: License to Work.* Copenhagen, Denmark: Valmuen.

Sutton, A., Baldwin, S. Wood, L. & Hoffmann, J. (2013). A meta-analysis of the relationship between rater liking and performance ratings. *Human Performance*, 26, 409–429.

7

Finland
Implementing a Global Diversity Management Initiative in Finland

Adam Smale,[a] Ingmar Björkman,[b] Risto Säntti,[a] and Narashima Boopathi Sivasubramanian[a]

[a] *Department of Management, University of Vaasa, Finland*
[b] *Aalto University School of Business, Finland*

Introduction

Maria, the HR Manager of Petrocom[a] Finland, had been both excited and anxious when news came through from regional headquarters that Finland had been selected as one of the first to implement the new 'Global Workforce Diversity Management and Inclusiveness Initiative' (hereafter D&I Initiative). The mission of the D&I initiative was to integrate employees from a broad variety of backgrounds such as gender, race, sexual orientation, age, family status, values, beliefs, physical and mental abilities, income, education, and work experience. Maria had known that it was going to mean a lot of work and that getting local buy-in to a corporate initiative of this kind would be a huge challenge. Although she knew that there had been very few cases of harassment or discrimination, she had felt for some time now that Finland and the people at Petrocom Finland had limited experience in addressing certain areas of workforce diversity management in comparison with some of their European counterparts. Maria just hoped that her personal convictions about the business case for diversity management would be shared by others. She also knew this would mean working very closely with Ashoka, the European Diversity Management Coordinator, who had been given the task to support and monitor the implementation of the initiative in Finland. Ashoka, Indian by origin with considerable management experience in the USA, was located at the European regional headquarters. Even from the outset, he was sceptical about Petrocom Finland's ability to meet the expectations of headquarters and the strict global D&I policy guidelines. Now, five years later, Maria and Ashoka were about to sit in a D&I review meeting to reflect and evaluate the status of Petrocom's D&I Initiative in the Finnish subsidiary.

Organisational Setting

Petrocom Group, a well-known European energy firm, operates in nearly 100 countries employing more than 100,000 people. In the early 2000s the Petrocom Group initiated a significant organisational restructuring which saw the launch of its 'Global Organisation' vision – a desire to reduce the complexity of its previous conglomerate, multi-domestic approach and to adopt a matrix-type structure with fewer lines of business and standardised core processes. The restructuring was also justified as an attempt to achieve greater synergies and more organisation-wide control. The implications of the 'Global Organisation' for Petrocom Group's global HRM strategy were translated into three key objectives: (i) Greater HRM functionality in how it serves the newly defined lines of business, (ii) greater standardisation of HRM processes, and (iii) the creation of a single global HRM system.

Around the same time, Petrocom headquarters (HQ) began to develop the D&I Initiative that was presented as being an extension of their global business principles, a reinforcement of their existing core values, and a means of reaffirming Petrocom Group's commitment to sustainable development by enhancing social performance and strengthening engagement with external stakeholders. Based on the reportedly successful model of managing workforce diversity in Petrocom Group's US subsidiary, and in accordance with the 'Global Organisation' vision, Petrocom HQ developed a five-year implementation plan, which sought to integrate the principles of diversity and inclusiveness into key business and HRM practices throughout their worldwide operations. In doing so, Petrocom HQ aimed to attract and retain key global talent, to increase productivity through improved employee engagement, and to strengthen their reputation within the global community. Petrocom Group's ambitious plans and the significant amount of time and resources dedicated to the D&I Initiative led many industry peers to regard Petrocom Group as a pioneer in this area.

Representing one of the smallest of their foreign operations, Petrocom Finland was established before World War I and employed over 1,700 people across 400 service outlets at the time the D&I Initiative began. After several years of planning and development, Petrocom HQ began to launch the D&I Initiative in waves. Along with several other select European operations, Petrocom Finland was included in the first wave which began in early 2008.

Finland: Country Background

Finland is an advanced industrial economy located in Northern Europe and has a population of 5.48 million. The country has transformed its economy over the past few decades to become one of the richest and most stable societies in the world. Today, Finland is leading or near the top of many international comparisons in terms of growth and development in the economic, technological and social spheres. For instance, according to the World Economic Forum's Global Competitiveness Report (2014–15),[1] Finland has the best availability of scientists and engineers in the world and they are trained by one of the best educational systems. According to the report, Finland also ranks number one in terms of training, health and education. Indeed, Finland is one of the highest ranking countries in the world with regard to the proficiency of high-school students in science, reading and mathematics based on the PISA studies (Finnish Ministry of Education, 2012),[2] and is the world's third least corrupt country (Transparency International, 2014).[3] Taking a more comprehensive view across the different spheres of education, health, quality of life, economic competitiveness, and political environment, Finland has been ranked as the world's best place to live (Newsweek, 2010).[4] The success of the Finnish economy has been driven by the combination of economic efficiency and growth, a peaceful labour market, an egalitarian distribution of income and social cohesion, all backed up by a generous social security system. Despite changes in recent years, the Finnish economy remains heavily manufacturing based, led by engineering and high technology firms. However, the 2008 financial crisis coupled with the rapid decline of Nokia – Finland's national champion – led to a newly elected government to enact a tough programme of austerity measures. Hope for the future is increasingly being placed in non-manufacturing industries and innovative start-ups, epitomised by gaming companies such as Supercell (creators of Clash of Clans) and Rovio (creators of Angry Birds).

Managing Workforce Diversity in Finland

From a legal perspective, the cornerstone of Finnish legislation relating to workforce diversity is the 1999 revised Constitution, according to which everyone is equal before the law. In addition, there are several acts and codes that prevent discrimination in work communities based on any visible or invisible aspects of diversity (e.g. the Penal Code; the Employment Contracts Act (55/2001); the Act on Equality between Women and Men (609/1986, 2005); and the Equality Act (21/2004)).

From a cultural perspective and the attitudes of Finnish citizens, Finland could be characterised as somewhat bipolar. On the one hand, Finland is representative of a Nordic welfare state that has integrated equality legislation with a distinctively inclusive political ideology, which has served to promote with good effect certain aspects of diversity. Perhaps the best example of this is gender equality. Finland was the first country to give women equal political rights and there is evidence of its positive long-term effect in working life, despite inequalities in the upper echelons of private sector firms and in salaries of those in male- versus female-dominated professions. A testament to Finland's status regarding gender issues is its second position in the Global Gender Gap Report 2014 published by the World Economic Forum.[5]

On the other hand, the acknowledgement and inclusion of ethnic, cultural and sexual minorities remain problematic. This was apparent, for instance, in a report on Finland's working life environment conducted by the European Commission against Racism and Intolerance (ECRI).[6] According to the report, various anti-discrimination measures have had only limited impact when viewed in light of the difficulties experienced by immigrants. One of the studies comparing experiences of work harassment by different ethnic groups also found that immigrants from sub-Saharan Africa had experienced ten times more bullying and harassment than ethnic majority members in Finnish workplaces.[7] Cultural openness to different sexual orientations has changed considerably from being somewhat of a taboo subject in Finnish society to more of an open issue to express and discuss.

One possible explanation for the above is Finland's relative cultural, racial, religious and linguistic homogeneity, and thus a historical lack of exposure to certain minority groups. However, in line with similar developments in other countries this composition is in flux due to increased labour mobility. The contracting labour market has become particularly topical in Finland as the aging population is placing increasing pressure on the country's ability to attract migrants. Between 2005 and 2020, it is estimated that some 900,000 employees will leave the workforce, representing 40 percent of the total, which will take the proportion of the population over the age of 65 to 25 percent.[8] The government has recently launched a series of initiatives to attract and support immigrant workers in Finland, but multiculturalism remains relatively low. According to Statistics Finland (2014),[9] at the end of 2012 the proportion of foreign citizens living in Finland was 3.6 percent (compared to 7 percent in Sweden) which is one of the lowest percentages among the 28 EU countries. Whilst the political move to increase the number of international students and the recent mass migration from the Middle East and Africa are seen as potential means to address the looming labour market and pensions crises, these developments also represent a considerable political, economic, social and cultural challenge for a relatively young and homogenous country like Finland. At the same time, many Finnish companies are waking up to the reality that these demographic changes and related diversity management issues are now business issues.

Implementing the D&I Initiative in Petrocom Finland[b]

In 2001, 'Diversity and Inclusiveness' was adopted as one of Petrocom Group's formal, 'Global Standards', which not only meant that it was a commitment for all countries and businesses, but also that implementation would be subjected to a formal assurance auditing process (at country level) and publicly reported (at Group level). The D&I Global Standard comprised statements on the values and core commitments to diversity, laying out its intent and business case, as well as the expected organisational outcomes and individual behaviours. The European Regional Diversity Coordinator Ashoka describes Petrocom's stance regarding the Global Standard:

> We start from the point that it must be followed. Naturally, there will be some legal limitations to its application that will be considered, but otherwise we assume that the D&I Standard is translated directly and that there are no local modifications. This is necessary to create truly a global D&I Standard for Petrocom and to ensure the implementation of one of our key business principles.

During implementation a deliberate decision was made to extend the emphasis on diversity to include the notion of inclusiveness. From early on, the D&I Initiative was being perceived as an external and largely Anglo-Saxon intervention concerned only with the narrower issues of gender, nationality and the staffing of senior country positions with host-country nationals (i.e. not expatriates). Subsequently, Petrocom HQ began to promote the inclusiveness component of the initiative to make employees and managers realise that discrimination can occur in the workplace due either to visible differences between individuals (e.g. physical ability, age, language) or invisible differences (e.g. beliefs, sexual orientation, family status).

Petrocom HQ utilised a top-down Global Policy Framework to provide more detailed provisions for the attainment of the D&I Global Standard. However, in implementing the global standard there was a dilemma since not all the dimensions of diversity that HQ was including were applicable in the Finnish context. The Framework provided guidelines about, for example, the identification and monitoring of common diversity performance criteria, the setting of clear targets and plans, and the development of appropriate leadership behaviours. This meant that whilst the type of diversity management targets (e.g. proportion of women and expatriates in managerial positions), annual plans and time schedules were determined centrally and applied on a global basis, the actual targets and means of policy implementation were to be modified by the subsidiaries to reflect local legislative, demographic and business needs.

The practices associated with diversity management therefore required both globally standardised and locally customised elements depending on the issue in question. For example, when integrating the new D&I principles into existing HRM practices there was no standardised way of achieving this. The interpretation of Petrocom Finland's HR Manager Maria was that 'diversity and inclusiveness is not included in writing in HRM processes nor is written guidance given, but it is a kind of new lens within each HRM practice'. On the other hand, a much more standardised approach was evident in the launch of new globally standardised forms for conducting performance appraisals and new reward and bonus schemes, which all included a universal set of diversity criteria.

The D&I Initiative was implemented through a vast array of systems and tools (see Appendix 1). Reinforcing the diversity management philosophy, a dedicated local Diversity Coordinator was appointed instead of an expatriate from Group or Regional headquarters, which had often been the case in the past when implementing global initiatives. With full working responsibility for the implementation of D&I into the policies, practices and culture of the local subsidiary, the Finnish Diversity Coordinator was actively involved in meetings with Ashoka at Regional headquarters and with other Diversity Coordinators to update on progress, exchange ideas, and develop informal benchmarks.

Reflected in Petrocom Group's overall approach to global diversity management as a strategic business issue and to the employment of Local Coordinators, diversity and inclusiveness was not considered to be owned by HR but driven by the whole business. The aim, at least at the outset, was that since diversity work should largely take place independently from the HR function, local HR should instead 'shape' and 'support' diversity and facilitate an appropriate culture change. Accordingly, HRM practices were seen more as targets for diversity integration than the key forces behind it. The long-term plan was that Diversity Coordinators would remain in their positions until the end of the implementation process or until that time when it was considered that diversity management had become everyone's responsibility. In 2012, four years after the beginning of implementation efforts, the local Diversity Coordinator stepped down. The role of diversity management 'champion' and any remaining diversity management issues were taken on by the HR department.

All local line managers were brought to the European HQ for centrally delivered training in the form of a one-day 'awareness' session and some of the more senior managers attended a three-day intensive diversity management course. Since D&I was a Group Global Standard, Petrocom HQ had communicated from the outset that unscheduled 'spot-checks' by Diversity Auditors (where company representatives visit the unit and review diversity plans and actions and conduct interviews with key individuals) would be in force throughout the course of implementation. This assurance process also included subsidiary Presidents around the world having to sign annual Diversity Assurance Letters to confirm how far subsidiaries had come in working towards agreed regional targets.

Petrocom HQ formalised the implementation of the D&I Initiative through the operationalisation and strict application of performance measures in conjunction with organisational and individual tools of assessment. Starting from the annual regional diversity plans, diversity and inclusiveness performance criteria were formally integrated into subsidiary-level balanced scorecards and the scorecards of individual managers. This was designed to mean that diversity management was to represent a feature of subsequent decisions about individual rewards and bonuses. Furthermore, 'barometer'-type surveys were carried out both organisation-wide and on an individual basis in the form of general working environment surveys, diversity and inclusiveness surveys, leadership self-assessments and 360-degree appraisals.

While the setting of targets and the drawing up of plans were carried out by the corporate Diversity Council and Diversity Steering Group at Petrocom HQ, Petrocom Finland was granted considerable autonomy in how these were implemented.

Issues Encountered During D&I Implementation

The implementation of the D&I Initiative did not encounter any significant legal obstacles in Finland as Petrocom Finland was cautious from the outset not to violate any local laws and to allow legally obliged modifications. This was also reflected in the responses of local union representatives (who are typically quite influential in the highly unionised Finnish business environment), who remained relatively silent throughout the implementation process, despite some short-lived defensive reactions at the beginning when discussions turned to the employment of immigrants (e.g. the effect of low-cost labour on employee wage levels and rights). Instead, the biggest challenges were associated with the level of priority given to diversity management and how to introduce the issue of diversity sensitively into the workplace.

Getting the Priorities Straight

From the outset of the D&I Initiative, people within Petrocom Finland disagreed about the level of priority that should be given to diversity management issues. Some of these arguments were based on whether diversity management represents a critical business issue, some were based on its relevance in a workplace setting, and others were based on its relevance given Finland's and the Finnish unit's demographics. The newly appointed Finnish Diversity Coordinator believed the D&I Initiative was an important business issue and had come at the right time:

> Our group faces more and more challenges related to personnel. We are talking about various groups that are formed based around certain minority status. Well, not only have these groups now become a very important target for recruitment, but we also have to understand that such a variety of individuals can't be managed in the same way, so we need to adapt. I think we need to pay more attention to these groups, and consider the special needs of women, ethnic minorities and so on.

The subsidiary's CEO, however, was somewhat more sceptical about diversity management's current relevance for the unit:

> Even though diversity issues are not evidently as topical here as they are in some other areas, we have to understand our position as a member of this group and also consider the logic of Global Standards. [. . .] without doubt diversity issues will be topical here as they are elsewhere and probably sooner than we anticipate.

The CEO's perception that diversity management issues were premature, but that it was sensible to be 'proactive', was also reflected in the opinions of many shop floor employees, even several years into the implementation process. However, certain employees could still not find grounds to support the amount of effort being directed at diversity in the Finnish unit, generally describing the D&I Initiative as being an overreaction and 'like using a sledgehammer to crack a nut':

> We have been told that diversity is just about anything that distinguishes individuals from each other, like religion, culture and ethnicity, language and so on. But I still think

that here in my work it is a question of males and females being equal. [...] We haven't got any immigrants for example. In my work everybody speaks largely Finnish and English. Religion isn't visible here, why would it be? It is work, after all. [...] I guess the guys at headquarters have a point generally, and I do understand that the main issues are important at that level. A small office in Finland doesn't count for much there and thus it has to go with the flow, regardless of the local importance of these matters. [...] Suddenly we have all kinds of promotional events and training going on. I'll be retired before those things become important here.

(Petrocom Finland employee)

Both Ashoka the European Diversity Coordinator and Maria the HR Manager found it difficult to strike the right balance in delivering information about diversity to individuals. On the one hand they needed to be active in creating awareness, educating and supporting individuals to focus on the unfamiliar aspects of work and behaviours presented by the principles of D&I. On the other hand, if D&I was seen to be given more attention than key business issues, people would view it with scepticism and as a passing fad.

A particular challenge was the absence of appropriate 'hard' targets at the local subsidiary level. Although there were global targets regarding the number of expatriates in the highest management positions (within subsidiaries as well as HQ), and the proportion of women in senior executive posts, neither of these were relevant in Finland since the CEO had always been Finnish and the 'senior executive posts' on which the units were compared did not exist in the relatively small Finnish subsidiary. For this reason, Maria and the local Diversity Coordinator had to devise their own 'hard' targets which received only passive agreement from Ashoka at regional headquarters. The absence of appropriate measures thus led senior and line managers at Petrocom Finland to question why they should do anything above what was officially required by Petrocom HQ. As a result, Maria experienced difficulties in implementing their own D&I performance targets without any backing from higher up the organisation. Instead, the case for going beyond Petrocom HQ's D&I targets was presented emotively as 'the right thing to do' on a personal level.

Reflecting on the D&I Initiative, Maria put the firm's D&I Initiative in a broader context:

We are not here to change society. That's not our prime reason for being in Finland. We are here to do business. But we have to do it as a good Finnish company, as a good Finnish citizen, so that everyone who works for Petrocom can be proud of what we are doing. But I don't feel that our task is to be the one who comes and breaks the walls down.

Global Policy, Local Obstacles

At a relatively early stage in the implementation process it became apparent that the magnitude of cultural adjustments required to openly discuss diversity meant that the Finnish subsidiary considered itself insufficiently prepared to embrace everything that was being suggested by Ashoka at regional headquarters. This was especially true regarding the assumptions underlying some of the methods being promoted to raise awareness about D&I. For example, the suggested use of affinity groups was regarded as inappropriate and not used by the Finnish subsidiary. It was argued that they represented a culture-specific tool reflecting Anglo-Saxon assumptions that everybody is ready and willing to discuss issues such as religion and homosexuality with others in a group.

For employees, the introduction of sensitive and personal issues in discussions of D&I made typically reserved Finnish people feel noticeably uncomfortable. Middle managers started to voice concerns about whether these types of discussions would require them to 'reveal who we really are' to their colleagues and subordinates. The questioning of people's values and norms regarding diversity and inequality was also shown at times to be a painful experience for some. Maria recalls a certain landmark team meeting a year into the implementation process in which they discussed issues of inequality and were asked to share personal experiences: 'The atmosphere was unique. The subjects of discussion were unique. The inner dynamics of that team were discussed openly [. . .]. It had people crying. And that was certainly unique in that department!'

The perceived Anglo-Saxon approach of discussing diversity-related issues in the open in order to raise awareness and provide evidence of 'progress' did not sit comfortably with the much more modest, reserved and private nature of the Finns. Although Maria and Ashoka suspected possible traces of denial in people's attitudes to diversity, even fairly open-minded employees voiced their preferences to keep such personal matters separate from the workplace and were certainly opposed to confronting them in intimate, face-to-face settings. Maria found that:

> It may also be the Finnish way. People do feel uncomfortable when, for example, sexual orientation is brought up as a topic of discussion, and then you are given the instruction to change your behaviour, to be more open towards this. I think most people think that the best way to approach diversity is to focus on work. There, you have to cooperate and get along with everybody. One might ask why we pay so much attention to these issues. I think it is better to be open towards everything, but not pay too much attention to individual differences, because at the end of the day work is why we are here.

Another dilemma that concerned how to implement diversity management was finding the right balance between centrally and locally driven approaches. Whilst a centrally driven approach, pushed by Ashoka, was acknowledged as appropriate at the beginning in order to raise awareness, achieve buy-in, and establish a shared understanding, the weaknesses of this approach gradually became apparent to Maria as time went on. After four years of developmental activities, Maria conceded that the centrally-driven approach was becoming more of a hindrance than a help:

> One key problem we have is that our goals are set by headquarters, not us. I think that this really hinders development. I mean, it is such a huge organisation with subsidiaries operating in such different contexts. Now I would support a more locally-driven approach. [. . .] to be able to truly change the way people behave and further develop our practices more openly. We have to think about how to adapt this Standard to fit better with the Finnish context. Some measures will always be negative because we haven't got 20 per cent of applicants from a certain (ethnic) minority to recruit even if we recruited them all. We also have very low turnover, so new people arrive very seldom. And that's just one example.

What Now?

Whilst putting the final touches on the last official diversity and inclusiveness progress report for the D&I review meeting with Ashoka, Maria reflected back on how she felt when she heard about Finland's inclusion in the global D&I Initiative. She was right to have felt excited and anxious since the D&I Initiative had proven to be rewarding yet very challenging. Maria knew that Petrocom Finland had started off in a strong position in certain areas such as gender diversity and having Finnish nationals (not expatriates) in senior country positions,[10] and that position had not changed. Some progress had been made in recruiting ethnic minorities and supporting their inclusion in the workplace. However, Maria knew intuitively that the D&I Initiative had been much less effective in influencing people's attitudes and behaviours concerning the more 'invisible' aspects of diversity such as individuals' beliefs and sexual orientation. Maria felt she was at a crossroads.

With corporate expectations met and Finnish society perhaps not quite ready for it, how far should she pursue progress in these areas and what was the best way to do it? And what should she tell Ashoka? Relations between them had become quite tense and it seemed to Maria that Ashoka was still, after five long years, pretty insensitive to the Finnish setting and the reasons for not having made more progress. To make things worse, deep down Maria agreed with a lot of what Ashoka and the Petrocom Group were trying to achieve in the area of D&I. It is an area where Maria feels she can make a real difference – but where should the line be drawn?

Case Study Tasks

Questions for Group/Class Discussion

1 In your opinion, how well was the implementation of Petrocom's global D&I Initiative handled?

2 Given what you have understood about the Finnish legislative, institutional and cultural context regarding the management of workforce diversity, together with the perceptions of people at Petrocom Finland about the importance of workforce diversity issues:

   (i) How would you present the business case for diversity and inclusiveness in the Finnish subsidiary without coming across as over-sensationalising the issue?

   (ii) How might the recent demographic changes in Finland help or hinder you in the above?

3 Using Appendix 1 as a guide, what specific methods would you continue or stop using in efforts to further implement the Group's D&I Initiative whilst taking into account the cultural sensitivities of the Finnish workforce? Can you think of any alternative methods that might be effective?

4 How would you best seek to reconcile Petrocom Finland's desire for a more locally-driven approach versus Petrocom Group's 'Global Organisation' vision, strategy and Global D&I Standard?

5 'I don't feel that our task is to be the one who comes and breaks the walls down.' Where do (i) Petrocom's, (ii) Petrocom Finland's and (iii) Maria's responsibilities begin and end in terms of changing Finnish employees' attitudes and behaviours about diversity and inclusiveness?

Role-play Exercise

Maria, the HR Manager at Petrocom Finland, is convinced that workforce diversity and inclusiveness *is* a key strategic business issue – in Finland generally and for her subsidiary in particular – despite what others might think. She is also sure that any positive developments in this area will only be possible when her subsidiary starts to get more autonomy in the kinds of goals it sets and the way to go about achieving them, which reflect Finland's and her subsidiary's unique setting. However, she is painfully aware that she will need the backing of several different groups of people to make this happen.

After much thought she decides to set up a meeting with select key people to put her message across and convince them of the benefits of her approach over the current one. The key people with whom she decides to meet are:

- The Regional Diversity Coordinator, Ashoka
- Petrocom Finland's CEO
- Petrocom Finland's employee representative

Appendix 1 Diversity management implementation tools used in Petrocom Finland [11]

Through People [12]	Through Information Systems	Through Formalisation	Through Decision-Making (Centralisation)

• Local 'Diversity Coordinators'
• Benchmarking amongst Diversity Coordinators
• Diversity training courses
  - Managerial-level and regionally standardised
• 'Diversity Auditors'
• Development and appraisal discussions at managerial level
• Local voluntary workshop sessions
	• Corporate Internet
	  - Stakeholder communication
	  - D&I publications, news and progress
	• Company Intranet
	  - Evaluation tools
	  - Database of survey results
	  - E-learning material
	  - Diversity 'games' and quizzes
	• Annual corporate, regional and local diversity plans
		• D&I Standard (mission & values)
		• D&I Policy Framework
		• D&I integration into existing organisational policies (e.g. Harassment & Discrimination)
		• 'Barometer'-style survey on working environment
		• D&I-focused survey
		• Leadership self- and 360° appraisals
		• Diversity criteria on organisational and individual balanced scorecards
		• Diversity criteria added to reward and bonus schemes
		• Signing of Annual Diversity Assurance Statements
		• Diversity issues made compulsory in all meeting agendas
			• Diversity Council (corporate level)
			• Diversity Steering Group (corporate level)
			• Regional HQ
			• Local 'Diversity Coordinators'

(a) Allocate the four roles to individuals.
(b) Each individual should take 10–15 minutes to prepare the issues or arguments that are considered to be relevant to his/her role.
(c) Hold the meeting in which the HR Manager first states his/her case together with some concrete plans, then second, the other meeting participants give their reactions and concerns, and third, the parties engage in a constructive dialogue on what courses of action to take.
(d) One alternative to the above is to run each of these meetings once in front of all the other class members. The other class members can then act as commentators and share their thoughts on the meeting they just witnessed.

Acknowledgements

The authors would like to thank Aulikki Sippola and Jussi Leponiemi for their efforts in data collection and The Finnish Funding Agency for Technology and Innovation (TEKES) and Liikesivistysrahasto for funding the research.

Notes

a The authors have been granted permission to publish findings about this case. However, for confidentiality and teaching purposes, a pseudonym is used and certain details concerning the organisation's titles and activities have been altered.
b The case is partly based on the fieldwork and findings published in Sippola, A. and Smale, A. (2007). The global integration of diversity management: A longitudinal case study, *International Journal of Human Resource Management*, 18(11): 1895–1916.
1 World Economic Forum (2014–15) World Competitiveness Report. Available at: www.investinfinland.fi/why-finland/competent-professionals/152
2 PISA 2012 Science Competencies for Tomorrow's World, OECD Programme for International Student Assessment (PISA). Available at: www.minedu.fi/pisa/2012.html?lang=en
3 Corruption Perceptions Index 2014, Transparency International.
4 The World's Best Countries, Newsweek (2010). Available at: www.newsweek.com/feature/2010/the-world-s-best-countries
5 World Economic Forum. *The Global Gender Gap Report 2014*. Geneva. Available at: http://reports.weforum.org/global-gender-gap-report-2014/rankings/
6 ECRI (2013) *Report on Finland*. Council of Europe, Strasbourg. Available at: http://www.coe.int/t/dghl/monitoring/ecri/Country-by-country/Finland/FIN-CbC-IV-2013-019-ENG.pdf
7 Vartia, M., B. Bergbom, T. Giorgiani, A. Rintala-Rasmus, R. Riala & S. Salminen (2007). *Monikulttuurisuus työn arjessa* (Multiculturalism in working life). Helsinki: Finnish Institute of Occupational Health.
8 Financial Times, The (2007). Baby boom retirement aftershock looms. *Financial Times* Special Report, 4 September 2007, London (UK), pg.6.
9 Statistics of Finland (2015) Available at: http://www.stat.fi/til/vaerak/2013/02/vaerak_2013_02_2014-12-10_tie_001_en.html
10 One of Petrocom Group's D&I targets was to achieve a certain degree of coverage of senior country management positions being filled by host-country nationals (as opposed to staffing many of those positions with expatriates from the parent country which was the case in several countries, but not Finland). The idea was that this would make senior management teams and decision-making at that level more inclusive of people from different national backgrounds.
11 Taken from Sippola and Smale (2007).
12 Categorization based on Kim *et al.*'s (2003) Global Integration Modes.

8

Iceland

Merger, Culture, and HRM: The Marel and Stork Case

Ingi Runar Edvardsson and Gudrun Berta Danielsdottir

Introduction

This case focuses on the merger of Marel and Stork in 2008 and its effects on human resources. The two companies had different organizational structures, in addition to which their organizational cultures and HRM policies were quite dissimilar. Moreover, the two companies grew out of different national contexts. Marel developed in Iceland in an environment characterized by liberal labor legislation, strong optimism, informality and short-term orientation. Stork grew out of the Netherlands, with stricter labor legislation, more formality and a long-term orientation. How does one integrate such different traditions? This is the great dilemma facing the managers of the newly merged company. Which HRM policy should rule in the merged company? That of Marel or Stork? Or is there a need for an entirely new HRM policy in the united company? How will the merger affect recruitment processes, training of personnel, decision-making and the implementation of incentive schemes?

The integration of the two companies did not start immediately in May 2008. At the beginning both companies were run separately. Preparation work for the integration started soon after the acquisition, but it was delayed due to the financial crisis in October 2008. The integration work started in late 2009.

Marel is a private global market leader of advanced equipment and systems for the food processing industry. Marel is proud of its multinational heritage. The company traces its roots as far back as the 1930s and across several countries, including Iceland, Denmark, France, Germany, the Netherlands, United Kingdom and United States. The Icelandic part of the company, from which the Marel name originates, was established in Iceland in 1983 and has grown rapidly on the basis of a dynamic organizational culture and simple hierarchy. Marel has escalated its sales and revenues through the acquisition of three rival companies since 2006, one each in Denmark, the Netherlands and the UK. The focus of this case will be on the May 2008 acquisition of the Dutch company Stork Food Systems, which had been part of Stork B.V., a 132-year-old Dutch conglomerate. Both Marel and Stork were highly successful companies but the different cultures and national backgrounds made the merger challenging in many respects. The aim of Marel is to fully harness the potential synergies from the integration of the two companies and to present one common "face" to the customer.

Comparison of the Two Organizational Settings

Both companies operated in the same industry before Marel acquired Stork in May 2008. The external environment of the two companies differed due to different regulations, labor markets and national cultures. Marel's organization was based on a decentralized matrix structure where teamwork was emphasized, while Stork was more centralized with an organizational structure based on process flow. Both companies had extensive global sales networks. Marel operated subsidiaries overseas and also had a network of agents, whereas Stork operated with a network of agents.

Historical Background of Marel in Iceland

Marel was formally established in Reykjavik, Iceland, on March 17, 1983 by a group of 22 companies, mainly Icelandic fish processors. The history of Marel goes back even further, to 1977, when two engineers at the University of Iceland began to explore the possibility of developing and manufacturing scales intended to improve weighing accuracy and efficiency in the fish processing industry.[1] In the beginning, the company employed fewer than ten employees. Most came from one of the founding companies, Framleiðni hf, and from the Faculty of Science at the University of Iceland. In 1987, the number of employees had risen to around 50 but was subsequently decreased to 30 and stayed that way until 1990 when Marel began to recruit again.[2]

Early on it was recognized that the Icelandic fish industry would not suffice as the primary market for the company's products. Management therefore looked to Norway, mainly because the processing procedures there were similar to those employed in the Icelandic market. In 1983, the first Marel scale was sold to Norway through an agent and in 1985 a sales office in Canada was established. At the same time, a new product was launched—a marine scale that made on-board processing more accurate. The company also added Russia to the list of countries it sold to. Until 1992, the marine scale and graders were the main source of income for Marel but the company was close to stagnating in terms of growth. In 1992, Marel began selling flow lines to the fish industry, which revolutionized the handling of fish products.

In the late 1980s, Marel began to transfer knowledge accumulated in the fish industry to the poultry industry with the development of a concept similar to the fish industry flow lines. The research and development required for this transfer of knowledge took a few years and in 1995 the company was ready to establish a subsidiary in the US, which, at the time, was the largest market for poultry in the world. In 1996, the company took another major step when it began to sell equipment to the red meat industry. In 1997, Marel acquired the Danish company Carnitech A/S, which was comparable in size and turnover to Marel. The numbers of employees doubled to approximately 250.

Today, Marel's main product categories include weighing, grading, batching, portioning, inspection, processing lines and integrated software solutions. From early on, it was recognized that innovation and teamwork would be the driving force for Marel. The organizational matrix structure that the company has built on through the years has been characterized by a minimum level of hierarchy combined with a dynamic and creative work culture.

Historical Background of Stork

The history of Stork spans more than a century. Its formal founding date is said to be September 4, 1868 when Charles Theodor Stork moved his textile manufacturing business to Hengelo to combine the many activities under his own name. Charles Theodor Stork was an entrepreneur in more than one sense of the word. He still holds the record as the youngest entrepreneur in the Netherlands in the Guinness Book of Records. His ambition was to be a textile manufacturer and at the age of 13 he borrowed money from his father to buy three looms and established Weefgoederenfabriek C.T. Stork & Co.[3] In this case, we are focusing on Stork Food Systems, which was acquired by Marel in 2008.[4] There are three major brands within Stork Food Systems: Stork PMT, Stork Titan and Townsend.

Stork PMT

Stork became involved in the poultry processing industry back in 1963. At that time, when the company was expanding its existing production facilities in Boxmeer, it acquired a local engineering company called De Wiericke. The acquisition meant that Stork now owned this company's activities, which included poultry processing installations. This was around the time that the European poultry processing industry was on the brink of automation, so Stork seized the opportunity and a poultry division was born. The poultry sector grew rapidly. In 1975, the subsidiary became independent and was named Stork PMT (Poultry processing Machinery and Technology). A year later, Stork PMT decided to expand into the US market, by acquiring Gainesville Machine Company, which it then renamed Stork Gamco.

Stork Titan

Stork Titan's story begins at the end of the 1950s at Machinefabriek Kruijer in Amsterdam. This is where the so-called Titan machines were made for the production of meatballs. Ownership of these machines moved around in a series of acquisitions and finally ended up at Gebroeders Nijhuis, which renamed the company Titan International. By 1988, Stork had been involved in the poultry processing industry for several years and knew that there was more to poultry processing than killing, eviscerating and portioning. It acquired Titan International in order to gain an entrance into the attractive convenience food market.

All the activities of the renamed Stork Titan were transferred to Boxmeer in the Netherlands. To be able to properly accommodate Stork Titan there, Stork had to build the necessary facilities, including a production shop and a fully equipped test center. The new space was used by Stork Titan to expand its product range into the current range of forming machines, coating systems and ovens.

Before the merger, Stork PMT was a global market leader and a trend-setting company in poultry processing equipment and systems. Stork Titan is a relatively small player; however, the company has been very busy marking out a distinct profile for itself. Stork PMT and Stork Titan share the Boxmeer premises. Stork PMT also has a second site, in Dongen, where it manufactures specific parts.

Stork Townsend

Townsend, originally an American company, was founded in 1946 by Ray Townsend, who built the world's first pork skinner. The 1950s saw the introduction of the membrane skinner and the automated pork belly skinner, as well as the expansion of sales into Europe. In the 1960s, business in Europe prospered. Offices were opened in the UK and the Netherlands.

The organization developed further and expansion continued in Europe, with offices being opened in Germany, France, Italy and Spain. In the 1980s, Townsend expanded its network of agents into 35 countries in Asia, Africa and Latin America. In the 1990s, Townsend moved into Russia. Townsend Engineering was acquired by Stork Food Systems in 2006.

Historical Background to the Case

At the beginning of 2006, Marel in Iceland introduced a two-phased growth strategy designed to establish the company as the market leader over a period of 3–5 years. The goal was to first triple turnover to €500 million through strategic acquisitions. In phase two, a turnover of €1 billion was to be reached by 2015 through strong organic growth and smaller bolt-on acquisitions. When the strategy was presented at a meeting of Board of Directors in February 2006, the market was defined by a large number of competitors, none of whom had a dominant position. It was Marel's view that there would inevitably be consolidation in the industry, a natural step in the development of any industry. There were two alternative ways of achieving results: on the one hand, through economies of scale, and on the other hand, through specialization and a niche position. It was decided to aim for growth and a large market share. Economies of scale were considered necessary in order to be able to provide customers with the service they need and to be able to follow them into emerging markets in Eastern Europe, South America and Asia. Economies of scale and increased market share were achieved through strategic acquisitions of three companies: AEW Delford in UK in 2006; Scanvaegt in Denmark in 2006; and Stork Food Systems in the Netherlands in 2008. With support from shareholders, Marel completely transformed the landscape in the industry and the company's market share grew from 4 percent to 15 percent over the next four years (Marel, *Advance with Marel*, n.d.).

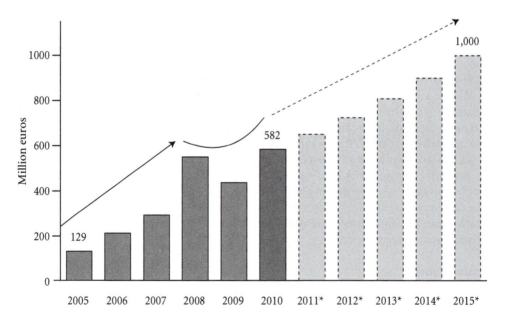

Figure 8.1 Marel expected growth

At the time that the new strategy was announced, the industry was expected to grow at an average annual rate of 5.6 percent between 2006 and 2011. The growth of Marel has been substantially higher than that and is expected to continue to exceed the growth of the market for the next few years (see Figure 8.1, Thordarson, 2006).

HRM in Iceland and the Netherlands: Historical Perspective and Current State

Labour Markets and Regulation

The Netherlands adheres to the so-called "Rhineland" model, characterized by a regulated market economy with a comprehensive system of social security. Iceland is more closely linked to the Nordic welfare model. In Europe, a corporatist cooperation between the state, employers' organizations and labor unions is common in order to secure stable economic growth and harmonization of interests. As well as being substantial employers in their own right, the European states take an active part on the labor market in the form of unemployment benefits or active labor market policies. Another core feature of European states is the legislative status and influence of unions. Most European countries have legislation requiring employers over a certain size to recognize unions for consultative purposes (Gooderham, Morley, Brewster and Mayrhofer, 2004).

There are some notable differences between the HRM practices of Iceland and the Netherlands. First, the union density in Iceland is far higher than in the Netherlands. In 2012, 82.6 percent of employees in Iceland were union members, compared to 17.7 percent in the Netherlands (OECD labor force statistics, 2015). However, the bargaining coverage (the numbers of workers that the unions negotiate for) is far higher in Holland, or 88 percent (Gooderham *et al.*, 2004). Second, employee involvement is much more widespread in the Netherlands where 91 percent of firms have works councils present (Dietz, Hoogendoorn, Kabst and Schmelter, 2004). Such employee involvement is absent in Iceland (Edvardsson, 1992). Third, the labor legislation in Iceland is far less restrictive than in the Netherlands. On a comparable scale ranging from 0–6, the "strictness of employment protection" in Iceland was 1.73 in 2013, compared to 2.82 in the Netherlands (it was 3.08 until 1998). The "strictness of employment protection" rating measures the procedures and costs involved in dismissing individuals or groups of workers and the procedures involved in hiring workers on fixed-term or temporary work agency contracts.[5] Iceland was close to the United Kingdom, which is among the lowest countries, while Indonesia was the highest in 2008 with a score of 4.24 (OECD labor force statistics, 2015).

The Netherlands is a founding member of the European Union, while Iceland has belonged to the European Economic Area since 1994. Many aspects of HRM are affected by the Social Chapter of the Maastricht Treaty, such as working hours, working conditions, consultation, equal opportunity, social security, dismissals, employee representation, etc. (European Union, 2010).

The labor markets in Iceland and the Netherlands function in many respects quite well. The employment rate, or the percentage of people between the ages of 15–64 who are employed, was 84.1 percent in Iceland in 2015 and 74.1 percent in Holland. Both are close to the high end of the spectrum in an international context. Similarly, the unemployment rate was rather low in Iceland and the Netherlands in 2015, or 4.1 percent and 6.8 percent respectively, and it grew somewhat after the financial crisis in late 2008. Part-time employment is far higher in the Netherlands than in Iceland, 57.9 percent compared to 33.6 percent (OECD labor statistics, 2015).

National HRM Practices

In general, HRM practices in Icelandic and Dutch firms are similar, according to the 2003 Cranet survey (see Table 8.1). The table reveals that the majority of firms in the survey have a written HRM policy, and HRM managers sit on the board of management and are involved in the development of corporate strategy. The only difference is that performance-related pay is far less common in Icelandic firms than in other European firms.

National Culture

National culture, or the "software of the mind" (Hofstede, 2003), affects how people relate to each other, their sense of power and equality, how they feel about competition or cooperation, and so on. National culture has, then, a direct impact on organizational cultures and management. Hofstede (2003) has identified four dimensions of culture, and his standardized measurement shows that the Netherlands and the Scandinavian countries scores similarly on these dimensions; they score low on "power distance", they score quite high on "individualism", low on "masculinity" and moderate or low on "uncertainty avoidance".

Iceland was not included in Hofstede's study, but Eyjolfsdottir and Smith (1997) did use his concepts in their analysis of Icelandic management culture. They conclude that Icelandic culture is characterized by egalitarianism, low power distance, individualism, femininity, and low uncertainty avoidance. Moreover, they argue that Icelanders have developed a strong optimism as a reaction to the adverse natural conditions of the country; they have a positive outlook, which is reflected in their happiness and lack of reliance on rules in decision-making. Eyjolfsdottir and Smith also mention the "action-poet" mentality in Iceland, a mixture of a strong intuitive or artistic inclination and a tendency to be independent, stubborn and action-oriented.

Table 8.1 HRM practices in firms in Britain, Denmark, the Netherlands, and Iceland in 2003 (%)

	Britain	Denmark	Netherlands	Iceland
Written HR policy	61.2	68.0	59.4	69.3
HR managers on the main board of management	46.0	53.0	61.0	58.0
HR managers involved in development of corporate strategy …				
• from the outset	48.7	52.3	48.3	42.6
• through consultation	30.5	28.7	36.6	28.7
• on implementation	9.0	9.5	11.1	11.7
• not consulted	11.8	9.5	4.0	17.0
Performance-related pay				
Management	45	58	45	21
Professional/technical	37	42	42	15
Clerical	32	32	35	11
Manual	25	33	36	18

Source: Bjarnadottir, Oddson, Bragason, Jónsdóttir, and Bjarnason, 2004

From the above, it is clear that the Icelandic and Dutch cultures resemble each other in many respects. The main differences are probably related to the unique features of the Icelandic culture, namely the strong optimism, the "action-poet" and "fisherman" mentalities, the focus on entrepreneurship, informality in communications and short-term orientation.

The Operational Context at Marel

Marel is today the global provider of advanced equipment, systems and services to the fish, meat, poultry and further processing industries. One of the cornerstones of Marel's success is its devotion to innovation and research and development. The company invests an average of 5–7 percent of revenues annually, approximately €25 million, in R&D (Marel, n.d., *Advance with Marel*).

When Marel in Iceland was established in 1983, a divisional structure was put in place. It wasn't until 1997 that the matrix structure, which is still in place (until the new organizational structure that has been decided upon is implemented), was introduced. On the basis of socio-technical theories such as organizational theory, Stork Food Systems has been transformed from a functional organization into a process-oriented organization, using so-called Entire Task Groups. At Stork PMT, this transformation took place from 1988 to 1991.

Both organizations have increased in size and complexity over the years. After the acquisition of Stork Food Systems, the organizational structure of Marel needed to be changed. The strategic decision was made to follow the market and to base the new structure on the four industry segments that the company specializes in – fish, meat, poultry and further processing. The new structure is based on the model of a network organization where a Board of Management has the highest authority. The Board of Management constituted three members after the merger: Theo Hoen, CEO; Erik Kaman, CFO; and Sigsteinn Gretarsson, Managing Director of Marel ehf in Iceland. In 2013 a change was made in the management of Marel and Arni Oddur Thordarson became CEO (Marel n.d.a).

The HRM Context at Marel and Stork

From the beginning, the CEO and Managing Directors of Marel in Iceland took care of all HRM issues related to their respective divisions. In early 1999, one of the directors took on the role of HRM Manager but within a few months, Marel recruited an HRM Manager from outside the organization. It was not until then that Marel introduced a formal HRM strategy, appraisal interviews and formal recruitment procedures.[6] It can be said that until 1999, Marel defined HRM issues as hiring and firing, salary processing and vacation scheduling.

Human Resources

The employees of Marel have been steadily growing in number since 1990, especially following the three acquisitions since 2006. Today, the "new" Marel employs approximately 4,000 employees worldwide, the majority of whom are located in Europe (see Figure 8.2).[7]

HRM Policy

The first formal HRM policy at Marel Iceland was introduced in late 1999. At present, its human resource mission states: "We employ competent employees and provide a supportive, ambitious work environment that motivates initiative and encourages employees to make the company vision their own."

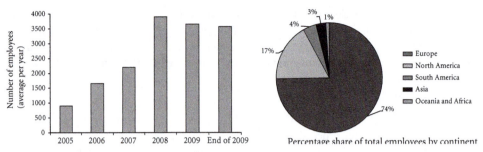

Figure 8.2 Number of Marel employees 2005–2009

Marel's strategic HRM goals and overall objectives are the following:

- We recruit competent employees, provide excellent training and offer opportunities for further education and job development.
- We maintain excellent cooperation and teamwork throughout the company.
- We respect different cultures while strengthening shared values.
- We maintain a good information flow throughout the organization, ensuring open and honest communication.
- We enable employees to have a healthy work–life balance.
- We support a creative and innovative work environment.
- Our leaders walk the talk, lead by example and are capable of guiding employees in fulfilling the corporate vision.

The objectives are very descriptive of the company culture and management style at Marel.

At Stork, a formal HRM mission statement was not defined. The company defined a set of values and issued a brochure called "Rules of conduct" which described the ethical principles that form the basis for the business conduct of all units of the company and employees. The values were: openness, trust, freedom, involvement, equality, knowledge, pleasure, dynamics and respect.

Social benefits for the employees of Stork were a precious topic for the founder, Charles Stork. In the nineteenth century, he put a social benefit structure in place. At the beginning, the focus was on benefits for industrial accidents but was soon expanded to include a cooperative society for the purchase of groceries, a health care fund, a widows' fund and a pension fund. These funds were financed by contributions from the members of the association and the company. Today, the Stork pension is still in operation and is one the oldest pension funds in the world (Stork, n.d., Social Benefits).

Organizational Culture

From the beginning, Marel has been defined as an entrepreneurial organization. This is reflected in different aspects of its organizational culture, such as risk-taking. A lot of time and capital is spent on research and development without knowing the return on investment (ROI). The acquisitions of companies that are equal or even larger in size can also be considered to be an indication of risk-taking.

The entrepreneurial nature is also reflected in another aspect of the organization culture, namely in the devotion to innovation that has made Marel into a global leader in its field. The structure implemented in the manufacturing process in 1997 was very innovative; it was based on dividing manufacturing into individual production cells. This structure is still in place at company headquarters in Gardabaer, Iceland. Still another relevant feature of Marel's culture is its competitive aggressiveness, manifested among other things in the growth strategy presented in 2006 and the acquisitions that followed after a careful analysis of about 130 companies. Finally, autonomy is highly encouraged at Marel and managers have the freedom to take independent decisions. This feature is especially encouraged among teams developing new solutions in cooperation with customers (Ólafsson and Hermannsdóttir, 2009).

Marel's employees say that the workplace atmosphere is dynamic and that they are encouraged to take the initiative and develop their ideas. In September 1999, a new project was launched at Stork Food Systems – "Chaos, Dialogue and Dolphin". The project was prompted by the feeling that although ten years of organizational restructuring in line with socio-technical theory had brought about a huge numbers of improvements, there was still a lack of initiative among employees. It was also felt that employees were too overloaded with day-to-day work and that management did not delegate enough, was too controlling, did not allow people to make mistakes and could not let go at busy times. In other words, a lot had been achieved in terms of structure but the corporate culture had not kept pace.

Socio-technical theory had brought about changes to the external aspects of the organization (structures, tasks and competences). The aim of the new project was therefore to focus on the internal aspects – people and the organization – and thus to make up for the inadequacies of the socio-technical theory introduced and to improve inefficient behavioral patterns.

This organizational modernization was ushered in using chaos theory as the basis and dialogue as the means. The aim with these two methods was to develop the culture and to obtain a joint reference framework within which ideas are given a greater chance of success, and initiative and creativity are put to better use. The organizational modernization process consisted of workshops in chaos theory, dialogue and dolphin training, and vision conferences. The ultimate aim was to stimulate a transformation of the organization, a fundamental modernization.

In short, over the past few years, Stork Food Systems invested a lot of time and energy in the process-oriented design of the departments on the basis of profit-center sectors.

The Outcomes for the Comparison Case

On HRM matters it was decided by the managers to retain management development and performance appraisal in the two companies, while other aspects of HRM should be integrated. The HRM managers of Marel – Friso Luimes, HRM Manager in Boxmeer, and Hrund Rudolfsdóttir, Corporate Director of Human Resources – are struggling with this formidable challenge. They have drawn up the HRM house in four layers to explain the practical dilemma they are facing and what is needed to complete each layer and move up to the next level. Using a house as a metaphor helps in prioritizing activities and providing internal and external stakeholders a clear overview of what needs to be done and what should be avoided (Figure 8.3).

According to the HRM managers of Marel, the foundation is the most important layer but a global market leader like Marel needs the complete house. Both Marel and Stork had moved up the different layers of the HRM house and were close to reaching the top layer when the companies were merged into one. With the merger, the "new" company found itself back in the foundation of the HRM house. Even though they needed to start building the foundation again, the HRM managers decided that the company would keep two important features of the previous HRM houses, namely management development and performance appraisal.

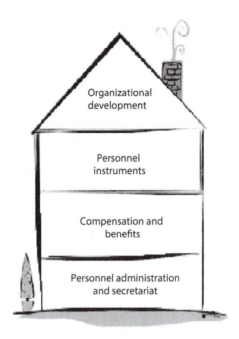

Figure 8.3 Prioritizing activities at Marel

The HRM house for the merged company has been defined and in general is as follows:

Foundation: Personnel Administration & Secretariat

- General support of HRM
- Personnel administration
- Time registration
- Organization of education programs
- Personnel care
- Requests and needs of subsidiaries
- HRM reporting (employee statistics, such as number of employees, temporary workers, sickness, etc.)
- Transition process
- Orientation

First layer: Compensation & Benefits

- Salary administration
- Salary house, reward systems and policies
- Pension
- Health insurance
- Other compensation and benefits issues

Second layer: Personnel Instruments

- Recruitment (including: trainees, internship, graduates) and labor market communications
- Purchasing temps together with purchasing department

- Personnel care (individual issues, jubilee)
- Processing appraisal policies (implementation of DEBbie)
- Competitive salary house
- Processing internal transitions
- Career and management development policy, including education policy
- Exit procedures of employees
- Health and illness management
- Contacts and meetings with working councils and unions
- Internal communications (staff newsletter, intranet, etc.)

Top layer: Organizational development

- HRM is a part of the management and process teams (innovation, sales, service and manufacturing)
- Training role vis-à-vis management
- Facilitator of team development
- Organizational development process (based on time, quality and cost); culture change and development

As can be seen from above, the practical challenges for HRM are enormous and it will undoubtedly take a few years for Marel to get to the top layer. The work has already begun and good progress has been made. HRM is optimistic that good results will be achieved within the next 36 months.

Questions

1. What are the main HRM challenges in the merger of Marel and Stork?
2. Are the managers of Marel defining the HRM challenge in the right way? Can you give alternative solutions?
3. How do labor market practices of the Iceland and Netherland have an impact on the HRM practice of the merged company?
4. Which culture do you think is more favorable for the new organization to maintain and why?
5. Given the previous history of mergers of large companies, how successful do you think the Marel-Stork merger will be in the long run?

Notes

1. All references in this section, if not otherwise stated, are based on Marel's web site: www.marel.com
2. Jon Thor Olafsson, interview, date 2010.
3. http://www.stork.nl/Stork/1208/Stork_foundation.html
4. The history of Stork is based on the introduction material "Getting to know the organisation" published by Stork in 2008, unless otherwise stated.
5. To explain the scale, for instance, individual dismissals of workers with regular contracts yields the score 0 if the dismissal period is 0–2 days, 1 if the days are fewer than 10, 2 if the days are 11–18, 3 if days are 17–26, 4 for 27–35 days, 5 for 36–45 days, and finally 6 if the dismissal days are more than 45.
6. Jakobsdottir, verbal comment April 19, 2010.
7. Marel.com (n.d.b.).

References

Dietz, B., Hoogendoorn, J., Kabst, R., and Schmelter, A. (2004). The Netherlands and Germany: flexibility or rigidity? In C. Brewster, W. Mayrhofer and M. Morley, M. (Eds.), *Human Resource Management in Europe: Evidence of Convergence?* Amsterdam: Elsevier, pp. 73–94.

Edvardsson, I. R. (1992). *Printing in Action: General Printing in Iceland and Sweden.* Lund: Lund University Press.

European Union (2010). Facts about the 'Social Chapter'. Downloaded on August 24, 2010 from http://europa.eu/rapid/pressReleasesAction.do?reference=MEMO/97/13&format=HTML&aged=0&language=EN&guiLanguage=enP.

Eyjolfsdottir, H. M., and Smith, P. B., (1997). Icelandic business and management culture. *International Studies of Management and Organization,* 26(3), 61–72.

Gooderham, P., Morley, M., Brewster, C., and Mayrhofer, W. (2004). Human Resource Management: A Universal Concept? In C. Brewster, W. Mayrhofer and M. Morley, M. (Eds.), *Human Resource Management in Europe: Evidence of Convergence?* Amsterdam: Elsevier, pp. 3–26.

Hofstede, G. (2003). *Cultures and Organizations: Intercultural cooperation and its importance for Survival.* London: Profile Books.

Marel (n.d.). *Advance with Marel.* Iceland, Gardabaer: Author. Unpublished material.

Marel.com (n.d.a) *Executive Team.* Marel. Downloaded on September 24, 2015 from http://marel.com/corporate/about-marel/governance/management

Marel.com (n.d.b.). Marel Facta Sheet. Downloaded on January 23, 2016 from http://marel.com/corporate/media/fact-sheet

OECD Labour force statistics. Data extracted on September 24, 2015 from http://www.oecd.org/employment/labour-stats/

Ólafsson, S. and Hermannsdóttir, A. (2009). *Vaxtarsaga Marel.* Downloaded on April 20, 2010 from (http://www3.hi.is/Apps/WebObjects/HI.woa/swdocument/1014597/marel_loka.pdf,2009).

Stork (n.d.) *Social Benefits.* Stork. Downloaded on April 20, 2010 from http://www.stork.nl/1206/Social_Benefits.html

Thordarson (2006). *Marel Annual Meeting 2006.* Unpublished material.

9

Norway

Comparing Internally Consistent HRM at the Airport Express Train (AET), Oslo, Norway and Southwest Airlines (SA), Dallas, USA

Bård Kuvaas and Anders Dysvik

This case study uses the backdrop of a very large, well-established, US-listed company that focuses on cost-leadership and customer service to highlight the perhaps surprisingly similar HRM characteristics of a small, relatively young, independent Norwegian company that reports to the Ministry of Trade, Industry and Fisheries, and that competes based on differentiation and customer service. The purpose of comparing the US company, Southwest Airlines (SA), with the Norwegian company, Airport Express Train (AET), is to show how companies that have very different characteristics, and operate in very different national and HRM contexts, can still both aim to achieve competitive advantage through people by implementing internally consistent HRM. Internally consistent HRM is the degree to which the various HRM practices support, complement, and reinforce each other.

Brief Historical Background of Southwest
Airlines and the Airport Express Train

2014 marked SA's forty-second consecutive year of profitability. The company was established in 1971, with three Boeing 737 aircraft, and became a major airline in 1989 when it exceeded the billion-dollar revenue mark. SA is currently the USA's most successful low-fare, high frequency, point-to-point carrier, and has more than 47,000 employees, operating more than 3,600 flights a day. The CEO of SA, Gary C. Kelly, concluded the 2014 Annual Report to Shareholders by stating:

> I am enormously proud of our People. These are truly remarkable 2014 results, and they would not have been possible without the Warrior Spirits of our People. It has been a long, decade-plus period of challenges and change. They not only survived it without resorting to bankruptcy, they also delivered Shareholder returns and built a better airline. Now, through their hard work, they have positioned Southwest stronger than ever, and with future opportunities that we believe are brighter than ever.

Clearly, the CEO of SA believes that their remarkable success stems from their employees, and how they are selected, trained, managed, and taken care of, as we will explain in this case study. SA is a widely debated and cited success story.

When first we approached the comparator case, AET, we thought it was just another company trying to benchmark 'the SA way'. Trying to imitate a successful company can be risky, as evidenced by the problems Delta experienced when implementing 'Leadership 7.5' in 1994 – an effort to reduce Delta's costs per available seat mile to match SA's 7.5 cents (Wright & Snell, 2005). However, after having interviewed Kari Skybak, the Director of HRM at AET, we learned that they knew little about SA. Instead, her inspiration with respect to HRM at AET derives from Janne Carlsson, the former CEO of Scandinavian Airlines (SAS), who transformed the company in the early 1980s by creating a business airline with exceptional customer service and punctuality. In 1982, SAS was the most punctual airline in Europe and in 1983, SAS was awarded the title 'Airline of the Year' by Air Transport World. Another inspiration, in particular with respect to the importance of nice and clean trains, is from Walt Disney's emphasis on quality and keeping their facilities clean and customer-friendly as much as possible.

AET (Flytoget, 2015) is a member of an international niche of Air Rail Links who have the dedicated task of transporting flight passengers to and from major airports. The major airport served by AET is Oslo Airport – Gardermoen, carrying more than 24.2 million passengers in 2014. In 2014, AET had approximately 330 employees (approximately 110 conductors, 160 train attendants, and 30 customer consultants). It currently has 16 trains and 218 departures every 24 hours. AET has 10-minute departures between the airport and Central Oslo, a distance of 47 kilometres, and 20-minute departures through the city into the heavily populated suburbs close to the airport. Recently, AET extended its line by another 20 kilometres westwards to the city of Drammen.

AET is a young company established in 1998 with the goal of achieving a total public transportation share for airline passengers of more than 50 percent. Encouraging people to leave their cars behind and change their travel habits drastically required a solution that was better than anything else available with respect to short travel times and comfort, reliability, and punctuality. Trains were also considered to be the best environmental solution. From the outset, the philosophy of AET has been to deliver an exceptional product down to the smallest detail. For instance, while you will often see other trains covered in graffiti, AET trains are always cleaned before they are used. The customer is the centre of attention and the train journey should be highly comfortable and easy. Accordingly, AET prides itself on effective ticketless payment solutions, good travel warranties, and effective procedures to manage disruptions, but for a price. For comparison purposes, the fare for travelling from downtown Oslo to the airport is NOK 180 (approximately USD 22) and from Drammen to the airport NOK 260. In contrast, the fares for travelling with the alternative Norwegian State Railways are NOK 90 and 210 respectively. Accordingly, AET attracts customers who are willing to pay more for a more pleasant journey.

AET's market share is currently 33.2 percent, which is among the world's highest market shares for an Air Rail Link service. AET has a 97.3 percent punctuality rate within 3 minutes and a regularity rate in comparison to planned journeys of 99.4 percent. These numbers are especially impressive when compared to trains operated by the Norwegian State Railways, which score markedly lower on the same effectiveness measures. AET has also experienced a remarkable increase in customer satisfaction ratings from 92 percent in 2001 and 2003 to 97 percent in 2014, and received several customer satisfaction and brand awards. In 2015, they were ranked third on the Norwegian Customer Satisfaction Barometer, while the Norwegian State Railways came out among the last on the list (ranked as number 161 among 186 companies). Earnings before interest, taxes, depreciation and amortisation (EBITDA) have risen from NOK 87 million in 2000 to NOK 253 million in 2014.

With respect to HRM and employees, AET was ranked top in the Great Place to Work survey in Norway in 2008, and has remained in the top ten. AET's business concept is to offer the best means of transportation to and from Oslo Airport by emphasising security, punctuality, and service. AET achieves this 'through a unique identity, the most effective solutions, and an enthusiastic staff', according to Kari Skybak. Similar to SA, AET emphasises its people, security, profitability, and the environment.

The Context for HRM in Norway

Compared to other countries, a high proportion (71.6 percent) of the adult population in Norway (5.19 million as of May 2015) is in employment (Statistics-Norway, 2015). This is mainly due to the majority of Norwegian women being in employment (68.7 percent of women and 74.4 percent of men) and the low unemployment rate. For the last eight to ten years, the unemployment rate has been around 3.5 percent, but due to declining oil prices since July 2014 and lower investments in the oil and gas industry, the unemployment rate has more recently increased to 4.3 percent (as of May 2015).

In Norway, approximately 70 percent are employed in the private sector and 30 percent in the public sector. Forty percent of employees in the private sector are members of trade unions, compared with 81 percent of employees in the public sector (Olberg, 2008). The Norwegian welfare state represents a cornerstone of Norwegian society and thus exerts considerable influence on working conditions in Norway. The fundamental principle for the Norwegian welfare state is that its citizens should contribute based on their assets, and receive according to their needs. Norwegian citizens enjoy considerable benefits 'from the cradle to the grave'. Examples of benefits provided are free health care for all, free education up to Master's level for those eligible, unemployment benefits and sickness benefits from the first day of unemployment or sickness for all, retirement pensions from the age of 67 for all, and 5 weeks of paid vacation annually for all members of the working population (Hatland, Kuhnle, & Romøren, 2001). In addition, when having children, parents are given 46 weeks of leave of absence with 100 percent pay or 56 weeks of leave of absence with 80 percent pay, and nearly all children are offered a place in a kindergarten from the age of one year. The welfare system is funded largely by taxes, and the average tax rate of Norwegian employees was 28 percent in 2013 (Statistics-Norway, 2015). These selected benefits, along with a range of others, illustrate why Norway was ranked number one on the United Nation's Human Development Index for both 2013 and 2014 (UNDP, 2015) and number one on the Trust Index in 2014 (ASEPJDS, 2015).

For the last twenty-five years, there has been a large increase in the number of people working in the service industry (currently approximately 70 percent) and in jobs with higher demands for formal education (approximately one third of all employed people in Norway have attained higher level education), whereas the number of employees working in traditional production industry has declined.

With respect to the work context in particular, the working conditions in Norway are regulated by the Working Environment Act issued by the Ministry of Labour in 1977. In section 12 of this Act, it is emphasised that jobs should provide workers with a reasonable degree of freedom, opportunities for learning and career development, varia-tion and meaningful content, recognition and social support, and they should be able to relate their work to the wider societal context. These requirements were introduced in a joint agreement between the main labour organisations in Norway representing both employers and employees (Gustavsen, 1977), and were actually based on research on Nor-wegian organisations emphasising the role of employee involvement at work (Thorsrud & Emery, 1976).

Despite labour-friendly law not guaranteeing good working conditions, Norwegian employees experience among the highest levels of satisfaction with their working conditions among European countries (Parent-Thirion *et al.*, 2007). These conditions, as perceived by employees, include job security, having good friends as colleagues at work, feeling 'at home' in their place of work, being provided with opportunities for personal development, being well paid for doing their job, and having good opportunities for career advancement. With respect to wages, the differences between hourly wages for employees in Norway are among the lowest across the 30 countries included in the Organisation for Economic Co-operation and Development (OECD). Norway has a GINI index of 0.25 compared to 0.40 in the USA (where 0 represents perfect equality and 1 implies perfect inequality) (OECD, 2015). Norway also has a relatively low income poverty score of 8.1 percent compared to 17.6 percent in the USA (OECD, 2015).

The Operational and HRM Contexts in SA and AET

Jeffrey Pfeffer (1998a) summarised high involvement, high commitment, high performance and soft HRM in a set of seven practices that characterise most organisations producing profits through people. In the following sections, AET and SA are briefly compared across these practices.

Employment Security

SA provide job security for their employees because they do not want to put their best assets, their people, in the hands of the competition. Besides, it is much easier to achieve flexibil-ity and cooperation to become more efficient and productive when promising employment security. As former CEO Herb Kelleher wrote:

> Our most important tools for building employee partnership are job security and a stimulating work environment . . . Certainly there were times when we could have made substantially more profits in the short term if we had furloughed people, but we didn't. We were looking at our employees' and our company's longer term interests . . . [A]s it turns out, providing job security imposes additional discipline, because if your goal is to avoid layoffs, then you hire very sparingly. So our commit-ment to job security has actually helped us keep our labour force smaller and more productive than our competitors.
>
> (Pfeffer, 1998b)

Even following the aftermath of 9/11, SA did not lay off a single employee despite the average reduction in flights by 20 percent and average lay-off of employees of 16 percent in the airline industry in the USA in the weeks that followed after the attack. Instead,

SA used the crisis as an opportunity to show that they were serious when they talked about 'taking care of our people'. According to Jim Parker at SA (Gittell, Cameron, Lim, & Rivas, 2006): 'We are willing to suffer some damage, even to our stock price, to protect the jobs of our people.'

According to the Director of HRM at AET, Kari Skybak, they do not have an official policy that promises job security. They have, however, never been confronted with situations where downsizing would be an option. After all, the company has grown continuously since it was established in 1998.

Selective Hiring

Organisations that promise job security and want to achieve profit through people need to ensure that they recruit the right people in the first place. This includes being an attractive employer and having a large applicant pool from which to select. In 2009, SA received 90,043 resumés and hired 831 new employees. The company spends a lot of time screening, and hires primarily for attitudinal fit with the SA values and culture (i.e. they want happy people and team workers), since skills can be learned.

Kari Skybak at AET explains that they also recruit based on attitudes that fit with the company values, which are effectiveness, innovation, and enthusiasm. In practice, they try to ensure that their employees act as ambassadors of the company. In the last round of recruitment in 2009, they received 400 resumés for twelve train attendant positions. In 2010, the company also introduced recruitment cards that their employees could distribute to former colleagues or to friends.

Self-managed Teams and Decentralisation as Basic Elements of Organisational Design

Part of SA's cost advantage comes from having people who will do what is required to achieve extremely short turnaround time (the time from when an aircraft arrives at the gate until it leaves again). Short turnaround times and being on time require teamwork among those responsible for different operations (e.g. check in, boarding, mechanical operations, cleaning the aircraft, baggage handling, and so on), and for every employee to feel responsible for almost everything. Accordingly, at SA, they typically use team goals rather than functional metrics. A Boston Consulting Group consultant noted: 'Southwest works because people pull together to do what they need to do to get a plane turned around. That is part of the Southwest culture. And if it means the pilots need to load bags, they'll do it' (O'Reilly & Pfeffer, 2000).

Also at AET, they place heavy emphasis on decentralised decision-making, as employees on the trains have the authority to solve any problem that may arise on the spot and immediately.

High Compensation Contingent on Organisational Performance

SA's compensation practices include comparatively high use of collective pay for performance (as opposed to individual), compressed pay levels, and consistent treatment, i.e. not giving executives large raises when employees are being asked to accept pay freezes. The company adopted the first profit-sharing plan in the US airline industry in 1973. Through this plan and others, employees own about 8 percent of the company stock.

In comparison, at AET, the conductors are better paid than their largest competitor, the Norwegian State Railways. Train attendants, however, have slightly lower pay levels than in the Norwegian State Railways, but higher than comparable positions in the service industry. According to the number of applicants per available position and the 'Great Place to Work' ratings, this does not seem to negatively affect the attractiveness of the company. AET does not have a collective pay-for-performance plan.

Training

Given SA's emphasis on selecting for attitude and fit and employment security, heavy investment in training becomes an important part of the package of internally consistent HRM. At SA's University for People, approximately 25,000 employees are trained each year (O'Reilly & Pfeffer, 2000). Several different training programmes are conducted, with an emphasis on content such as doing things better, faster, and cheaper, customer service, understanding other employees' work, and how to keep the culture alive and well.

As in SA, all newcomers in AET begin by attending an introduction programme. This three-day training programme includes general information about the company and its different functions and operations, training in customer service and communication, on-the-job training where newcomers follow the operations of a regular train, and visits to every train station, the head office, and the maintenance department. On the first day of the programme, the top management team, including the CEO, welcomes the newcomers. After the programme, a top management representative makes a brief speech and hands out a certificate stating that they have completed the training programme.

After the introduction programme, conductors and train attendants complete five-week programmes dedicated to their different functions, where they are trained in, for instance, security, communication, and the specific AET culture. In addition, e-learning programmes are offered that make it easier for shift workers to conduct training. Newly hired administrative employees engage in a four-week programme, during which most of the time is spent on trains and train stations in order to learn and understand the daily operations of AET. This training is also useful because the administrative staff are mobilised when incidents happen (e.g. delays and cancellations), i.e. administrative employees travel to the stations to assist customers and operational employees.

In 2009, a new training programme that educates hosts for Norway's capital, Oslo, was introduced. The programme is offered in order to provide additional developmental opportunities for the employees and at the same time increase customer service by providing employees with in depth information about Oslo. The programme is mandatory for newcomers, but optional for current employees.

Reduction of Status Differences

A fundamental premise of achieving competitive advantage through people is that companies are able to get the most and best out of all of their people. At SA, the atmosphere is extremely informal and egalitarian, and everything is done in order to highlight that every single employee is important. Compressed pay and benefits are parts of this, but the value statement from the early 1980s, the Golden Rule, sums up SA's approach: 'Above, all, employees will be provided the same concern, respect, and caring attitude within the organisation they are expected to share externally with every Southwest customer.'

AET also emphasises minimising hierarchical levels and encourages informal communication between all employees. In addition, top management is not only called upon in cases of incidents on the train or the stations, they regularly have to spend time on the trains at least once a month.

Sharing Information

Widespread sharing of information about strategy, financial performance, and operational metrics ensures that employees have the necessary information to be involved and able to contribute to doing things better, and it signals that they are trusted that they will not misuse the information. At SA, information on costs, operations, and financial data, including how SA is doing compared to its competitors, is shared among all employees.

Since AET operates almost around-the-clock, several steps have been taken to ensure sharing of information throughout the company. The main information channel is the intranet, but SMS, internal leaflets, and notice boards are also used. The intranet is used to publish information on the news of the day at AET, facts and figures, strategy and business plans, financial and operational results, work processes and regulations, employee manuals, who does what at AET (including pictures of every employee), and a calendar with important meetings, training activities and social arrangements.

Summary and Case Questions

This chapter has applied learning from the SA case, as well as the principles of high commitment HRM systems to demonstrate how AET is also able to focus on its people to achieve competitive advantage. Both SA and AET are successful companies, but learning from such success stories can be risky (Pfeffer & Sutton, 2006). As a final note, we therefore need to mention that the value of implementing this type of high commitment HRM system is also supported by research evidence. First, a meta-analysis (Combs, Liu, Hall, & Ketchen, 2006) of the relationship between HRM and organisational performance including a total of 19,319 organisations and 92 individual studies showed positive relationships for organisational performance for HRM practices such as having a strong focus on training, high compensation, widespread participation, selectivity in hiring, internal promotion, flexitime, the existence of grievance procedures, and employment security. Even more importantly, a significantly stronger relationship was found for systems of internally consistent or aligned HRM practices than for individual practices. Moreover, a meta-analysis of 35,767 firms and establishments showed a positive relationship between commitment-based HRM and performance across 29 countries (Rabl, Jayasinghe, Gerhart, & Kuhlmann, 2014), suggesting that such HRM systems may be effective across national and cultural contexts.

In addition, and at the micro level, meta-analyses suggest that important work outcomes (e.g., in-role and contextual work performance) arise from employees being empowered and provided with job autonomy (Humphrey, Nahrgang, & Morgeson, 2007), job security (Cheng & Chan, 2008; Sverke, Hellgren, & Näswall, 2002), fair treatment (Cohen-Charash & Spector, 2001), receiving support from the company (Rhoades & Eisenberger, 2002), and demonstrating effective commitment to the company (Meyer, Stanley, Herscovitch, & Topolnytsky, 2002; Riketta, 2002).

Questions

1 What are the main similarities and differences between SA and AET with respect to HRM issues?
2 SA and AET have completely different strategies, but a similar set of HRM practices. How does this observation fit with the proposed importance of establishing a match between strategy and HRM?
3 Given the different nations, their culture and labour laws, do you think it is easier or more difficult to gain competitive advantage through people in the USA than in Norway and similar countries (e.g. Sweden and Denmark)? Why?
4 AET is currently planning to expand its services from being an airport train company exclusively, to competing on other routes in the area surrounding Oslo. Will it succeed by using the same HRM strategy or should the HRM strategy be changed in order to fit with a different market segment?

References

ASEPJDS. (2015). Interpersonal trust. Retrieved from http://www.jdsurvey.net/jds/jdsurveyActualidad.jsp?Idioma=I&SeccionTexto=0404&NOID=104
Cheng, G. H.-L., & Chan, D. K.-S. (2008). Who suffers more from job insecurity? A meta-analytic review. *Applied Psychology: An International Review, 57*(2), 272–303. doi:10.1111/j.1464–0597.2007.00312.
Cohen-Charash, Y., & Spector, P. E. (2001). The role of justice in organizations: A meta-analysis. *Organizational Behavior and Human Decision Processes, 86*, 278–324.
Combs, J., Liu, Y., Hall, A., & Ketchen, D. (2006). How much do high-performance work practices matter? A meta-analysis of their effects on organizational performance. *Personnel Psychology, 59*, 501–528. doi:10.1111/j.1744–6570.2006.00045.
Delery, J. E., & Doty, D. H. (1996). Modes of theorizing in strategic human resource management: Tests of universalistic, contingency, and configural performance predictions. *Academy of Management Journal, 39*, 802–835.
Flytoget. (2015). Retrieved from http://www.flytoget.no/flytoget_eng/
Gittell, J. H., Cameron, K., Lim, S., & Rivas, V. (2006). Relationships, layoffs, and organizational resilience: Airline industry responses to September 11. *Journal of Behavioral Science, 42*(3), 300–329.
Gustavsen, B. (1977). Legislative approach to job reform in Norway. *International Labor Review, 115*(3), 263–276.
Hatland, A., Kuhnle, S., & Romøren, T. I. (2001). *The Norwegian welfare state.* Oslo: Gyldendal Akademisk.
Humphrey, S. E., Nahrgang, J. D., & Morgeson, F. P. (2007). Integrating motivational, social and contextual work design features: A meta-analytic summary and theoretical extension of the work design literature. *Journal of Applied Psychology, 92*(5), 1332–1356.
Meyer, J. P., Stanley, D. J., Herscovitch, L., & Topolnytsky, L. (2002). Affective, continuance, and normative commitment to the organization: A meta-analysis of antecedents, correlates, and consequences. *Journal of Vocational Behavior, 61*, 20–52.
O'Reilly, C. A., & Pfeffer, J. (2000). *Hidden value: How great companies achieve extraordinary results with ordinary people.* Boston, MA: Harvard Business School Press.
OECD. (2015). Inequality. Retrieved from http://www.oecd.org/social/inequality.htm
Olberg, D. (2008). *The Norwegian workforce.* Oslo: Institute for Labor and Social Research.
Paauwe, J. (2009). HRM and performance: Achievements, methodological issues and prospects. *Journal of Management Studies, 46*(1), 129–141.
Parent-Thirion, A., Macías, E. F., Hurley, J., & Vermeylen, G. (2007). Fourth European working conditions survey. European Foundation for the Improvement of Living and Working Conditions: Dublin.
Pfeffer, J. (1998a). *The human equation: Building profits by putting people first.* Boston, MA: Harvard Business School Press.
Pfeffer, J. (1998b). Seven practices of successful organizations. *California Management Review, 40*(2), 96–124.

Pfeffer, J., & Sutton, R. I. (2006). *Hard facts, dangerous half-truths, and total nonsense: Profiting from evidence-based management*. Boston, MA: Harvard Business School Press.

Rabl, T., Jayasinghe, M., Gerhart, B., & Kuhlmann, T. M. (2014). A meta-analysis of country differences in the high-performance work system-business performance relationship: The roles of national culture and managerial discretion. *Journal of Applied Psychology, 99*(6), 1011–1041. doi:10.1037/a0037712

Rhoades, L., & Eisenberger, R. (2002). Perceived organizational support: A review of the literature. *Journal of Applied Psychology, 87*(4), 698–714.

Riketta, M. (2002). Attitudinal organizational commitment and job performance. *Journal of Organizational Behavior, 23*(3), 257–266.

Statistics-Norway. (2015). Retrieved from http://www.ssb.no/en/forside;jsessionid=0B211C6A4A60B994CEBA 0B8E5EE7915E.kpld-as-prod11?hide-from-left-menu=true&language-code=en&menu-root-alternative-language=true

Sverke, M., Hellgren, J., & Näswall, K. (2002). No security: A meta-analysis and review of job insecurity and its consequences. *Journal of Occupational Health Psychology, 7*(3), 242–264.

Thorsrud, E., & Emery, F. E. (1976). *Democracy at work*. Leiden: Martinus Nijoff.

UNDP. (2015). Human development reports. Retrieved from http://hdr.undp.org/en

Wright, P. M., & Snell, S. A. (2005). Partner or guardian: HR's challenge in balancing value and values. *Human Resource Management, 44*, 177–182.

10

Sweden

At the End of the Road: The Process of Plant Closure

Magnus Hansson*

Little is known, among both scholars and practitioners, of what happens in an organisa-tion during the process of plant closure. Rather, the majority of reporting and experiences of organisational metamorphosis has focused on the causes and consequences of decline, downsizing, retrenchment and turnarounds.

Downsizing and plant closures are events that often come into practice in corporate restructurings. This is something that has been widely reported in the media especially during economic and financial turmoil. Changes in institutional structures, such as financial, envi-ronmental, political, societal, and technological conditions, can have long-term consequences for various types of business. The financial crisis that, to some extent, began with the break-down of the sub-prime loan market in the USA and escalated from 2008 onwards, produced long-term consequences not only for business in the USA, but throughout the world. Cases were widely reported in which manufacturing industries had empty order-books, which also caused various types of downsizing, including mass layoffs, as well as plant closures.

The extant and oft-cited scholarly literature on downsizing indicates that workforce reduc-tions often lead to job insecurity and negative performance outcomes. These outcomes are often manifested through and referred to as the 'survivor syndrome'. The survivor syndrome is, typically, associated with low worker commitment, centralisation of decision-making, loss of innovativeness and trust, resistance to change, lack of teamwork and leadership and decreasing morale among the employees who are left in the organisation post downsizing activities. On the other hand, scholars have reported somewhat paradoxical results, indi-cating that plant closures result in high performance outcomes and increased productivity despite the certainty of job loss.

Researchers have pointed out that during the process of plant closures certain dynamics come into play, such as: operations management diminishing; worker autonomy increasing; more space for innovation; and devolution of planning of daily operations to the workers

---

* The author has the permission to publish the Gusab Stainless case.

and informal leadership. This, together with a recorded productivity increase and a 'close-down' effect, suggests that the previously understood drivers of productivity, motivation of individuals, and small group behaviour might have to be reconsidered.

An often-applied argument for plant closure is cost reduction. This is sometimes achieved by transferring production to low-wage countries and/or reducing production capacity within the corporation, due to market saturation or decline. The latter was the case of Gusab Stainless (hereafter Gusab), a unit within the Sandvik Steel Corporation's Wire Division (hereafter Sandvik), in Sweden. In January 2002, Sandvik decided to close Gusab down. Gusab reached the end of its road on 31 August 2003.

Organisational Setting

Gusab was founded in 1876 and from 1990 was part of the Sandvik Steel Corporation, as it was acquired from Gunnebo Bruk, Sya Bruks AB. At Gusab, a range of cold heated steel wires were produced, primarily for customer-specific orders, with only a small amount of the volume produced for stock.

The average worker was about 47 years old and had been working for a little more than 20 years at Gusab, and the employee turnover rate was low (2 percent annually). The majority of workers were male (87 percent) and lived in the local community close to the plant. In production, labour was divided between those who ran the machines for the wire production and those who handled other functions, for example, providing supplies and conducting analyses on the manufactured wires.

The victims of the Gusab closure faced a local labour market that was characterised by moderate unemployment (5.5 percent compared to 5.8 percent for Sweden on average in 2003). The municipality in which Gusab was located had approximately 25,200 inhabitants (as of June 2003). The local industrial structure was characterised by relatively few manu-facturing companies located within reasonable commuting distance in other neighbouring industrial regions.

The Gusab case is interesting in several respects. Firstly, the closure period took eigh-teen months, which is a relatively long period by international standards. This facilitated the study of fluctuations in productivity and worker reactions, revealing multiple nuanced outcomes. Secondly, the relationship between management and the labour union was char-acterised as non-conflictual, and the labour union played a central role in the development of the HRM programme. Thirdly, management applied a socially responsible approach, including an extensive HRM programme including severance payments, production bonus programmes, early retirement and educational programmes. Notably, no strikes, protests or sabotages were carried out at the plant during the closure process. Fourthly, productivity increased throughout the entire closure process indicating a 'closedown' effect.

Background to the Case

Prior to the closure decision, Sandvik's management had had to address problems at Gusab. Gusab had an unfavourable production-mix for the future of wire production within Sand-vik. Over-capacity within the corporation was the major reason for decreasing the number of production units. Furthermore, the goal was to increase efficiency and adjust capacity at the remaining sites. The production sites in Brazil, Spain and the USA were seen as strategically important and therefore not real options for closure, whilst the two Swedish plants (Gusab and another Sandviken plant) were the only real alternatives. As a result, corporate management announced a decision to close down the Gusab plant.

The net-profit development of Gusab was insufficient in comparison with the other the production units within Sandvik. Some investments were made at Gusab, which during the late 1990s came to affect the result of Gusab negatively. Following 1989, Gusab had nine consecutive years of negative financial results. The workers were aware of the prevailing situation and saw it as a threat, as management repeatedly informed them about the situation. The workers did little to try to change the situation but continued work as usual. Nevertheless, Gusab was profitable over the last two years prior to the closure decision.

HRM in Sweden: Historical Perspective and Current State

Swedish HRM practices and the legislative framework that stipulates the management–worker relationship hold a rather long tradition. Labour unions are often a significant actor in negotiations with the management. The unions also have legislative rights to be represented in the board of directors in larger corporations. Labour union density is, by international standards, rather high, especially among blue collar workers. In general, many of the HRM practices in Sweden are regulated by legislative agreements between employer organisations (representing the company) and the labour unions (representing the workers).

In general, the labour market is highly regulated by collective agreements. The collective agreement is a written agreement between unions and employers' organisations or a single employer that governs wages and other employment conditions for workers.

For unions, it is usually a key objective to have as many employers as possible to conclude a collective agreement. This creates a minimum level of salaries, benefits, and employment conditions. Employers with collective agreements can always offer better terms for employees than the collective agreement provides. As many workplaces are covered by collective agreements, this can prevent salary-dumping, i.e. whereby employees are forced to compete with each other for jobs by accepting progressively lower wages and worse working conditions. The goal of the unions is that competition will take place instead in terms of skills.

For employers, collective agreements can be attractive because they offer a truce: in other words, when an agreement is in place centrally, the employer can expect to avoid strikes as long as the agreement pertains. Conversely, the collective agreement terms can be to the detriment of the employer if it were to try to employ the same staff at lower wages or other conditions. To the extent that collective agreements prevent low-wage markets, they are also potentially disadvantageous for employers.

Advance notice of termination is required by Swedish labour law, which means that an employer must warn when there is to be a large number of layoffs in the organisation, specifically if at least five workers are affected at one time, or if the employer believes that more than twenty workers will be affected during a ninety-day period. From 1 January 2008, the law has required management to inform the Employment Service if they are about to lay off employees and/or shut down a plant. In addition, collective agreements also stipulate the sequence in which employees who are dismissed must leave the company.

According to the Co-determination Act (1976), labour unions at the workplace have the right to access information and to negotiate with management about the current situation. The labour unions do not have a veto in these negotiations, but are given certain opportunities to investigate, gather information, and express their view before the decision is implemented. This is usually interpreted as the unions, for example, having the right to access all relevant financial information that serves as the basis for, and not only limited to, the closedown decision, but also other management activities such as various types of organisational change, reorganisation and downsizing.

Since the early 1990s, it has been common to have information and bargaining obligations with the unions under the Co-determination Act supplemented by direct consultation, whereby management communicates with the workers through workplace meetings and similar activities.

The Operational Context in Gusab Stainless

Following the decision to close the plant down, management were engaged in multiple activities, such as administrating the plant closure and negotiating with the different stakeholders, including the labour union, the municipality, and the country-board. (Sweden is divided into different regions/counties, each administrated by county-boards. One responsibility that these county-boards have is to administer a labour board that serves as a supportive function when a region is facing massive layoffs or closedowns of significant employers.)

Management control over daily operations diminished, providing space for the workers. Managers abolished previous requirements regarding productivity levels, expecting a downturn, but were surprised by productivity increasing throughout the plant closure process, as well as hitting a record-breaking all-time high in productivity.

At Gusab, the workers were designated to specific routine-based tasks such as wire manufacturing, warehousing, testing, and maintenance. Operations were organised in small autonomous groups that strengthened the informal groups, who had responsibility for planning and operations during the first period of the plant closure process.

The majority of workers were male and the jargon among workers somewhat manly. Evident from interviews conducted at the plant, the attitude towards work was characterised by a 'work-hard-when-in-the-plant' attitude. For the majority of interviewees, their main objective to work in the plant was primarily based on a monetary incentive. Workers had specific working hours and a time clock for registration of their attendance. The time clock was abandoned during the plant closure.

Prior to the decision to close the plant down, Sandvik corporate management had employed a rather strict management-by-objectives style, including targets for productivity levels and turnover rate. However, both the corporate and local management's control diminished and previously established objectives were abandoned during the closure period. This provided increased space and autonomy for the workers, from which informal leadership as well as spontaneous organising evolved.

The Outcomes of the Plant Closure Process

The closure decision itself became a trigger for certain activities, some critical episodes, and served as a starting-point for somewhat surprising organisational behaviour. Once employees were clear about collectively losing their jobs, they increased their efforts, conducting day-to-day rationalisations and incremental improvement. During the plant closure, productivity increased, indicating a statistically significant 'closedown' effect, recording an all-time productivity high (see: Hansson, 2015; Arman, 2014; for methodological issues regarding calculation of the statistical significance of the 'closedown' effect, see: Hansson & Wigblad, 2006).

Productivity During the Plant Closure Process

The aggregate change in productivity from January 2000 and throughout the closure period was positive. During 2000, productivity was at a relatively high level, whereas from May 2001 to January 2002, Gusab faced a decrease in productivity due to a weakening trend in their market.

Figure 10.1 represents all the changes in productivity, from January 2000 until March 2003, as required to conduct a comparison during the closure period. In Figure 10.2, a linear

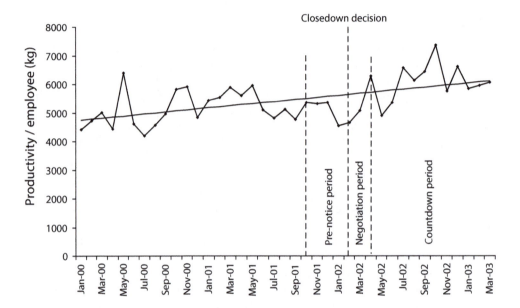

Figure 10.1 Productivity changes from January 2000 to March 2003

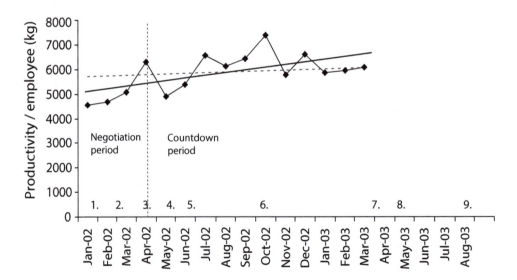

Figure 10.2 Productivity changes from January 2002 to March 2003

trend line (bold) is added for the specific closure period (January 2002–March 2003), the dotted trend line represents the aggregate change in productivity for the period January 2000–March 2003, showing a positive change in productivity for both periods. Notably, productivity had a stronger positive change during the closure period, compared to the total period of accessible data. During the closure period, the capacity utilisation increased from 87 percent (on average for January 2000 to December 2002) to 96 percent (on average for the closure period). It is also notable that during the period 2000 to 2003 there was a constant flow of orders, i.e. no market restrictions.

Turning to some critical episodes that occurred during the plant closure, these were identified as episodes with implications for productivity during the plant closure. These episodes were identified as critical, based on the empirical evidence from the interviewees, as they frequently came back to talk about these episodes, indicating empirical saturation. The critical episodes are numbered one to nine in Figure 10.3.

The schematic Figure 10.3 in conjunction with Figure 10.2 can partially describe and to some extent explain fluctuations in productivity during the plant closure process. This is somewhat similar to previous research which has indicated increased productivity during the plant closure process. Similar to other studies on plant closures, this case indicates a 'closedown' effect, through the recorded increased productivity as outlined in Figure 10.2. However, Figure 10.3, as well as previous research, is limited in its ability to analyse and identify links between explanatory factors, instead providing *ad hoc* and context-specific explanations of the increased productivity. In the next section, the nine critical episodes linked to the changes in productivity will be discussed.

Critical Episodes (CE) During the Process of Closure of Gusab

The nine critical episodes are:

1 Rumours start to spread in the organisation about a possible plant closure.
2 Closure decision is made.
3 Three-month evaluation is completed.
4 Wage-earners report is completed.
5 HRM programme is negotiated and decided.
6 All-time high in productivity achieved.
7 Agreement with the potential customer fails.
8 Workers have the opportunity to finish all orders in stock.
9 The end of the road. Closure of Gusab.

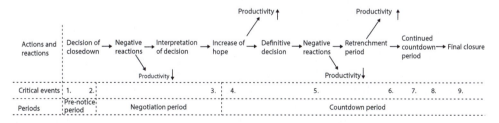

Figure 10.3 Understanding fluctuations in productivity during the plant closure process

In December 2002, rumours started to spread in Gusab that a decision to close the plant was imminent. These rumours were confirmed neither by corporate nor local management. Nevertheless, the local management knew about the closure plans already in the autumn of 2001. However, they were forbidden to inform Gusab employees of this (CE 1). As one of the interviewees put it:

> There had been rumours going on for quite some time, we were aware of them, but couldn't believe them, nor take them seriously [. . .] over the years rumours had been drifting around and we couldn't think that it was for real this time.

As the closure decision was announced (CE 2), management held a meeting for all employees, during which information on the background and the arguments for the plant closure were presented. The decision came as a shock to most of the employees, and although a few of the interviewees argued that it was expected, it was not expected at the time of the announcement.

In general, the interviewees were clear that they believed that local management did a good job before and during the plant closure process. They believed that local management took responsibility for closing the plant down, providing what the interviewees felt to be a generous HRM programme.

As the closure decision was announced, formal group leaders took responsibility together with the labour unions for handling the situation, encouraging employees to maintain production, and an attitude of leaving the organisation with pride evolved. The formal group leaders assigned to different workgroups shared information concerning the actual situation and became responsible for providing the day-to-day information to the workers. The formal leaders' attention and presence in the day-to-day activities diminished over time.

In February 2002, the formal announcement of the closure decision came. The local management objected to the decision and demanded a serious investigation, as they believed that the decision was made on erroneous grounds. The Sandvik corporate management agreed to this in accordance with Swedish legislation. Gusab had three months to prove its capability and productivity rose during that period (January–March 2002). Local management believed that this investigation would not change the decision they believed corporate management had already made. As predicted, after the three months a decision was made establishing the final date of the closure (CE 3).

A wage-earners' consultant (representing the workers) was contracted by the labour union and in April 2002 presented an alternative analysis of the arguments and economic consequences of the plant closure, countering the closure. The report stated several inaccuracies in the decision documents from Sandvik, such as the savings from closing down Gusab, costs of restructuring and education, transmission of data, and expected decreased productivity during the running-in phase for machines. The report generated arguments for a preservation strategy, but was neglected and dismissed by corporate management (CE 4).

Productivity declined in May 2002, as in the case of the formal decision. This was followed by negative reactions from the workers. At that time, there was interplay between the workers and the labour union. The workers requested the labour union to put pressure on management to take social responsibility for the decision, i.e. providing an HRM programme including both economic and future job-directed incentives for the workers. The labour union also tried to extend the life of the organisation as they argued that Gusab was an important part of the Sandvik Corporation. The willingness to understand the arguments of management was limited, and the labour union could not affect the closure decision. However, they were able to negotiate the HRM programme (CE 5).

The HRM programme was discussed and the workers found it to be a fair deal. It included a payment incentive scheme, which was based on production and the volume sold. Other components in the HRM programme were job-search aid, training in resumé writing, individually tailored educational programmes, and an early-retirement programme. The HRM programme that was established served as a foundation for managing the plant closure. The labour unions were, despite the closure decision, pleased with the retrenchment agreement in the HRM programme (CE 5).

Renewed hope came to the organisation in the autumn of 2002, as rumours started to spread about an opportunity of partial survival, as there was one customer showing interest in supply from Gusab. Out of the 108 employees, the local management calculated continued production for approximately 30 people. Due to these rumours, activities, performance, and efforts increased as some of the workers were interested in maintaining their employment. Productivity continued to increase between May and October 2002, and the plant recorded its all-time high in October that year (CE 6). As one of the interviewees stated:

> Most of us really believed that this new opportunity was going to save us, or at least provide jobs for some of us [...] several guys tried really hard to show their best side in order to be picked out for continued production, sad but true. . . the deal never came through and that's a real shame.

As the critical episodes 7 to 9 occurred, management had already abandoned the productivity measures for production. Nevertheless, the apprehension of both management and interviewees, together with evidence from participant observations being conducted, indicated that productivity remained high and did not decrease until the very end of the plant closure process.

As the negotiations with a potential new customer failed (CE 7), the interviewees claimed that the anger and frustration rose once again. This anger and frustration was aimed at top management, as the interviewees believed that corporate management had delayed the agreement-process, causing the failure.

Gusab had to continue the closure in accordance with the plan, scheduled for 31 August 2003. The production mix at Gusab changed slightly between March and August 2003 as they produced more for stock. Successively the orders decreased and the workers had an opportunity to complete all orders that were available in stock (registered in the IT-based production system). As the plant was closing down, no more orders were added post-May 2003. If they decided to complete these orders, they could have time off with full salary for the rest of the closure period. However, the workers refused this offer (CE 8), and continued production according to the scheduled plant closure process (CE 9).

Throughout the plant closure, productivity continued to increase. All of the interviewees claimed that only minor changes in routines, processes or activities were conducted; instead, they tried to work harder, as they wanted to leave the organisation with pride. In addition, the workers wanted to show corporate management that the decision was wrong and had hopes of a revised decision, which is why they were more careful about keeping the machines running, even during coffee breaks. As one of the interviewees put it: "I am keen on doing a good job [...] I have been working here for over 30 years [...] it is not an alternative to just sit [...] I want to leave this place with my head high."

The worker collective played an important role in how the rules, norms and associations with the profession as well as the organisational culture were shaped. These rules and norms went beyond the formalised and pre-defined routine descriptions and were formed by a tradition of how the work should be carried out in accordance with the tacit knowledge and craftsmanship that were a part of the job. Certain individuals' informal leadership also had a critical role to play.

It was evident that certain individuals, who were not in positions of formal leadership, took greater responsibility, going beyond their formal job description, encouraging colleagues and trying to manage the day-to-day activities during the closure period. This informal leadership was legitimised by the majority of workers. Due to the informal leaders' actions and a unanimous group decision, workers continued to carry out their work, even increasing their efforts, throughout the plant closure. However, the importance of the informal groups diminished and the workers became more individualised throughout the plant closure process. As one of the interviewees stated it: "I couldn't care less anymore [. . .] I do what I want, I say what I want to say, and don't care so much about the others."

Even though the importance of the worker collective diminished and individualisation grew stronger, spontaneous self-organising sub-groups emerged within the organisation. These sub-groups were formed primarily based on social rather than professional relationships. As one of the interviewees stated in the later interviews: "I used to, and particularly as the closure was announced, care about the others, the group – now, I don't do that anymore. I just hang out with the guys that I know best."

The following section includes a discussion of the outcomes and fluctuations in productivity during the closure process, highlighting potential explanatory factors of the "close-down" effect.

Discussion of the Outcomes and Fluctuations in Productivity During the Closure Process

Prior to the closure decision, conflict was minimal. During the pre-notice period, the level of conflict and disputes was high due to counter-arguments regarding the closure decision from the labour union, attempting to preserve the plant and its workers. Consequently, the speed of conflict resolution was low. During the negotiation period, the level of conflict remained high and the willingness to resolve conflicts low. As the countdown period started, the level of conflict decreased and when conflict arose, it was often quickly resolved.

Confidence in management is often dependent on the level of conflict and speed in conflict resolution. Multiple conflicts and a low speed of conflict resolution negatively affect employee motivation. The critical events of the Gusab plant closure process indicate how workers interpreted management actions and decision-making. For example, as the HRM programme was negotiated and later presented, workers were pleased with that deal, and conflict decreased while productivity increased. On the other hand, as the negotiations with the potential new customer failed to materialise, the level of conflict increased and productivity decreased (temporarily).

The level of confidence in management plays a significant role in how productivity develops during a closure process, given its temporal and fluctuating character. Throughout the plant closure, management control diminished whereas worker autonomy increased. Increased worker autonomy positively affected both employee motivation and work-design. The scope for autonomy provided space for the workers to initiate changes in work-design and day-to-day rationalisations. This positively affected employee motivation and acted as a driver of enhanced performance. The worker-initiated changes in work-design positively affected technical enhancements vis-à-vis productivity.

It is argued that the evolution of informal leadership can, but does not have to, create alienation and distance between management and workers, and the reliance on internal arguments, prior expectations as well as attention to dominant cues. Instead, with informal leadership comes spontaneous organising within and among informal groups, and enhanced employee motivation due to the newly achieved space and decreased levels of formalisation (Hansson, 2015).

Similar to the evolution of informal leadership, informal groups emerged and played a significant role during the initial phases of the closure. Interpretations of management decisions and actions were not only a consequence of a single individual's interpretation but were also the outcome of informal group behaviour. Mutual expectations and strong norms for social conduct generated generally accepted behaviour among the workers. This case study indicates how informal groups affect individuals in different ways, intensifying and impairing behaviour, depending on the situation and the actions and decisions that are taken (Hansson, 2015; Arman, 2014).

Individualisation grows stronger throughout the plant closure process and incentives for employee motivation change. In addition, the importance of informal groups has a temporal dimension: Informal groups that are prevalent and play a significant role in the initial stages of the plant closure and that determine the dominant level responses to a major extent can either be helpful or hinder performance. Consequently, individualisation grows stronger; workers tend to rely on internal dispositions and hypothesise the cause of their motivation.

Workers' perceptions of the threat of job loss have a certain explanatory value for the "closedown" effect. Initially, and closely related to the closure decision, the threat of job losses generates certain dynamics and positively affects workers' levels of confidence in management. The workers become successively more autonomous and individualised the closer they come to their final day of departure from the organisation. Increased worker autonomy and increased individualisation, together with the successive phase-out of employees, highlights the threat of job loss the closer individuals come to their final day at work. Workers process information and managerial actions through a filter represented by the closure decision. From this case, it is evident that worker reactions vary, depending on the prevalent situation and critical events, leading in this case to positive reactions, such as the hope for prolongation of production, and the trend of increased productivity. Negative reactions, such as when negotiations with the potentially new customer failed to materialise and the definitive closure decision was announced, tend to decrease the level of productivity. In summary, from detailed analysis it becomes clear that the interpretations, reactions and actions of the workers were directly related to fluctuations in productivity. Also, there was no clear evidence either from this reported case or in previous research on plant closures that increased up-time and enhanced resource utilisation can fully (or to a large extent) explain the appearance of the "closedown" effect. Instead, worker-initiated changes in work-design partially contribute to increased productivity.

Questions and Key Issues

1 Given the reported dynamics that come into play during a plant closure process as well as increased productivity, what can be learned from this case study and how can this knowledge be transferred to other (non-closure) contexts (such as normal operations in a manufacturing organisation)?

2 Based on the case, what are the primary reasons why productivity increases during the process of plant closure?

(a) Why are there differences in performance outcomes between downsizing events and plant closures?

3 Given the background to the Gusab case, what detailed strategies and tactics for managers can be designed to manage a plant closure process? Take into consideration the legislative conditions, institutional, and cultural contexts that this plant is facing.

(a) As a consequence of the strategies you present, suggest a timely roll-out plan for the entire plant closure process, including the following: time-frame, managerial setting, support programmes, transfer of production equipment to another production unit, switching-over logistics, etc.

References and Further Reading

Arman, R. (2014) Death metaphors and factory closure. *Culture and Organization,* 20 (1), 23–40.

Gandolfi, F and Hansson, M. (2015) A Global Perspective on the Non-financial Consequences of Downsizing. *Review of International Comparative Management,* 16 (2), 185–204.

Hansson, M. (2015) Organizational Closedown and the Process of Deconstruction and Creativity. *Culture and Organization.* DOI:10.1080/14759551.2015.1060231

Hansson, M. and Wigblad, R. (2006). Pyrrhic victories – anticipating the Closedown effect. *International Journal of Human Resource Management* 17 (5), 938–958.

Häsenen, L., Hellgren, J. and Hansson, M. (2010). Goal Setting during a Closedown Process: A longitudinal study. *Economic and Industrial Democracy* (in press).

Marks, M. L. and Vansteenkiste, R. (2008). Organizational Death: Proactive HR Engagement in an Organizational Transition. *Human Resource Management,* 47 (4), 809–827.

Sutton, R., I. (1987). The Process of Organizational Death: Disbanding and reconnecting. *Administrative Science Quarterly,* 32 (4), 542–569.

Watts, H. D., & Stafford, H. A. (1986). Plant Closure and the Multiplant Firm: Some Conceptual Issues. *Progress in Human Geography,* 10 (2), 206–227.

Part III
Central and Eastern Europe

11

Bulgaria

Telerik: Minding Your Own Business and Making Progress

Lucia F. Miree and John E. Galletly

As of May 16, 2016 Telerik operates under the Progress brand, both in Bulgaria and globally. Along with the new name, the company announced their new logo and brand, which contain a new, forward-facing symbol of transformation, and a clean typeface of the word "Progress" to reflect the company's rock-solid reputation. The bold and vibrant green in the logo represents the innovation that Telerik brought to Progress, and that Progress will bring forward.

Introduction

In late 2014, the Bulgarian software industry and region were abuzz with a story about the acquisition of the Bulgarian software development company, Telerik, by a large, global corporation.

Beginning as a small start-up with four employees in 2002, Telerik grew in only 12 years to gain the favourable attention of software conglomerate, Progress, which acquired Telerik in late 2014 for $262.5 million. By 2015, the 550 Telerik Sofia employees had become part of the 1,800-strong workforce of the global corporation. Telerik's founders joined Progress top management.

Currently, the headquarters of Telerik in Sofia, the capital city of Bulgaria, occupies four adjacent buildings, housing the typical software development environment that has come to be the norm for the industry – open spaces, playrooms, bright colours, food areas, team meeting spaces, and ever-present whiteboard graffiti. The headquarters also include the Telerik Academy, a large training facility for software developers and IT professionals, and a Kids Centre, a day-care programme for the children of employees.

The National Context – Bulgaria

Bulgaria, a former Communist country in South-East Europe, has moved from its turbulent economic and political past to its relative economic stability of 2015. After becoming a member of the European Union in 2007, many economic and social programmes were implemented, and now Bulgaria has become an upper middle-income economy of 7.2 million people with an annual per capita income of US $7,420, according to the World Bank (World Bank, 2015).

With impetus from the EU, Bulgaria has moved forward in reform, and development of its health, judicial and transportation systems. Its educational system had been a target of reform during Communist times, and has continued to be a strong part of the society. Bulgaria supports education through state funding, and requires education for all children from seven to 16 years of age. It boasts over 51 institutions of higher education offering graduate and undergraduate education, with all but a handful being state funded. In 2014, 73.8 percent of all Bulgarians had achieved an upper secondary or tertiary level of education (Eurostat, 2015). As with other post-Communist countries, there is very little difference between the genders, with men and women being equally represented in education.

In terms of linguistic skills, Bulgaria is a source of major recruitment by companies in Europe as 74 percent of young people in Bulgaria speak at least two languages in addition to Bulgarian. Of the languages, 90 percent speak English, 12.9 percent speak French, and 34.1 percent speak German (Eurostat, 2015).

While the country is stabilising, and growing economically and educationally (World Bank, 2015), it is nonetheless experiencing an ongoing population decline. In only nine years, the population has declined from 7,629,371 (2006) to 7,202,198 (2015), and it is predicted to continue in this direction without intervention (Eurostat, 2015). The decline is due to a lower birth-rate, and to the continued emigration of mainly first-degree university graduates. The change in population size and the negative migration trends certainly impact the development of industry and employment trends in Bulgaria. Due to its membership in the European Union, it is possible for workers to enter the country quite easily from other member countries. At this time, the Bulgarian government is aware of this population trend and has plans to develop and implement policies that encourage the return of citizens to their country, and that support citizens remaining in their home country and opening businesses.

The government has been very vocal and visible in its continued support of development of a countrywide software-related infrastructure that incudes educational programmes, funding for investment in the technology industry, and encouragement of Bulgarian entrepreneurship in fields related to technology. Many companies have taken advantage of this in Bulgaria, including such giants as HP, IBM and SAP.

The Global Information Technology Industry

The software development segment of the IT industry has been experiencing major growth in the past 25 years. As the accessibility to information technology continues to spread, and as more applications are identified and expanded, companies providing these services are continuing to grow in number, and to expand in services. Geographic flexibility, rapid product development and deployment cycles, and relatively low barriers to entry, in terms of regulation and capital costs, characterise the industry. Its major challenges include rapidly changing technology, global competition, and the need for knowledgeable and skilled employees who are educated, and can learn and adapt quickly. Companies and their employees, like technology itself, are related in increasingly sophisticated ways that offer opportunities, but also challenge the industry.

Worldwide, companies work closely with educational institutions to ensure a supply of highly-qualified potential employees. The "ideal" job candidates in this industry are those with high educational attainment (including solid studies in maths and computer science), and with linguistic abilities (generally with English as one of the languages). Demographically, most software developers are relatively young (average age 28.9 years), male (92.1 percent), have completed undergraduate or graduate education, have formal or continuing education, and are extremely mobile geographically (Stack Overflow, 2015). They are in high demand and, therefore, can command relatively high salaries, and competitive packages of benefits.

The Bulgarian IT Sector

In Communist times, Bulgaria was the Eastern Bloc's computer specialist country, supplying computer expertise to the Bloc's other countries. And this tradition has carried through to this day. In the succeeding 25 years since the end of Communism in Bulgaria, the Bulgarian IT sector, particularly software development, has gone from strength to strength. So much so that now Bulgaria is regarded by many as being the Silicon Valley of Europe (EDUKWEST, 2015). The IT sector has been one of the driving forces behind Bulgaria's steady economic growth over the past few years. With an average annual increase of 17 percent since 2007, IT businesses are one of the fastest growing sectors of the Bulgarian economy (Questers, 2015).

According to the Bulgarian IT industry barometer report (BASSCOM, 2015), the IT sector experienced double-digit growth for a fourth consecutive year, with 65 percent of revenues generated by export-oriented software business. The 2014 Global Services Location Index (Kearney, 2014), ranked Bulgaria ninth top country with an index of 5.62, and again the first destination in Eastern Europe for providing outsourcing activities, including IT services and support, contact centres, and back-office support. A high number of top multinational IT corporations have based themselves in Sofia. Among these are SAP, HP, IBM, Johnson Controls and VMware.

One of the really important growth factors for the Bulgarian IT sector is the supply of an IT-savvy workforce. Evidence suggests that Bulgarian universities produce over 3,000 IT graduates each year.

Working in Bulgaria: The Role of Human Resources

In the past, Bulgarian companies were described as hierarchical, managers as autocratic, employees as individualistic and unmotivated, and products and service as poor in quality. The approaches shown by organisations towards their employees reflected these beliefs, and therefore one saw human resource activities limited to transactional activities, and government and legal compliance efforts only. The focus was on work hours, payroll, overtime, on-the-job training, adherence to government programmes, and similar activities. Benefits were limited, and employee development followed only strict protocols, based primarily upon seniority. With the entry of Bulgaria into the EU, the subsequent opening of markets, and the expansion of international companies into Bulgaria, the practices have changed, and a more supportive and development-focused environment has emerged in businesses.

In the past ten years, most labour legislation has concentrated on the protection of individual employee rights, including guarantees of annual increases for years of service, labour contract wording, payments from employers and employees into social systems, and payment for overtime, travel and meals. Currently, there are glimpses of further reform as legislation about employee development programmes, educational accreditation to include more professional education, and similar "new" areas that impact the workplace are examined. At the same time, Bulgaria and the region have seen the introduction and growth of professional development programmes (including certifications), graduate education in business, and regional and international professional associations, all of which have raised the awareness of, and participation in, modern human resource practices.

While small businesses continue to be developed in Bulgaria, and alliances with global companies grow, the country continues to see two types of human resource systems working in parallel. In older, more traditional companies, one finds the traditional "Personnel Office" staffed primarily with clerks, trainers, safety specialists, and accountants. Newer companies in Bulgaria, particularly those in developing industries like software engineering, are populated in their "Human Capital Areas" with Business Partners, Talent Acquisition Managers, and On-Boarding Specialists. These are often referred to as "transaction" versus "integration" approaches in this region.

Telerik – The Company

Telerik grew from modest beginnings to become part of the global, multi-million-dollar company, Progress. In 2002, four friends decided to leave their jobs, and take a risk by setting up their own software development company, named Telerik. The focus of Telerik was the development of customisable user interface (UI) controls for applications involving the then newly-introduced Microsoft ASP.NET Framework. These UI controls are essentially software plug-ins, allowing developers, who do not have the time or expertise to develop their own UI controls, to quickly install Telerik controls in their software applications, either desktop- or Web-based.

Such was the commercial success of the initial UI control that the development of a suite of UI controls quickly followed. By 2004, Telerik had become prominent in the ASP.NET UI controls market, and by 2005, thanks to the quality of its software products, had achieved Microsoft Gold Certified Partner status.

Early on, Telerik started to grow organically by diversifying its portfolio of software products. Today as part of Progress, the product family includes leading .NET solutions (Telerik® DevCraft™ suite), popular UI tools (Telerik Kendo UI framework), innovative content management and customer analytics platforms (Telerik® Sitefinity™ CMS and Telerik® Sitefinity™ Digital Experience Cloud) and a mobile app development platform for iOS, Android and Windows Phone applications (Telerik® Platform).

In 2014, Telerik boasted a 1.7+ million-strong developer community, and over 130,000 customers. Some key customers include Microsoft, Sony, NASA, Toshiba, Merrill Lynch, Astra Zeneca, and the World Bank. Telerik's reported revenue was over $60 million for the year 2013–14.

In late 2014, Progress acquired Telerik for $262.5 million (Progress, 2014). This acquisition is the biggest software "deal" in South-East Europe, and was one of the leading economic news stories for 2014 in Bulgaria. According to one of the founders of Telerik, this was a natural, well-timed and welcomed move for the company, and represented a strong strategic alliance. Furthermore, he claims that the companies have a good cultural fit.

Over the years, Telerik has won numerous accolades and awards in various categories, such as business development, product quality and human resources. In late 2015, the number stood at over 300 awards. In 2007, Hewitt Associates named Telerik the number one employer for small and medium-sized companies in Bulgaria – the first of six such awards (Telerik AD, 2013). In 2012, Telerik received two Forbes Magazine Business Awards for "Human Resources Development" and "Community Involvement" (Telerik, 2015). Telerik continues to produce high-quality products, and to manage its company in ways that gain attention, respect, and industry awards.

The Telerik Progress office in Sofia, which is the biggest one worldwide, has become a key innovation centre, and strategic driver for the company. Since the acquisition by Progress at the end of 2014, the Sofia employee base has grown by more than 10 percent. This trend is anticipated to continue with the expectation that the Bulgarian employee footprint will grow to more than 900 employees by 2020. The company expects to continue to expand its software engineering talent as well as all other business functions in Bulgaria, including a focus on digital marketing, aligning with its overarching Digital Transformation strategy.

The office in Sofia is today a key innovation centre for Telerik Progress, who also have offices in the USA, UK, Germany, France, the Netherlands, Australia, Brazil, India and Singapore.

The software engineering teams are organised into product teams. Typically, there are four to ten people in a team (but sometimes more). Each team takes care of the execution of the complete product development lifecycle – planning, development, documentation, support, etc. There is a manager who represents the team to senior management, and is responsible for team organisation, assignments, feedback, and career growth of team members.

The engineering teams follow agile methodologies, mainly Scrum and Kanban. The majority of the teams meet every morning for about 15 minutes – the so-called "scrum" – and each reports on the previous day's activities, the plans for the current day, and any problems encountered. This is part of the on-going communication and problem-solving technique in the engineering organisation.

The engineering teams work closely with the Product Strategy organisation. There are Product Managers assigned to each product, and they keep in close contact with the customers and prospects, conduct surveys, and use other means to gather insight needed to make data-driven decisions. In this way, the company not only finds out about problems with its software, but also, through this very open dialogue, has insights into the customers' desired improvements to existing products, and their requirements for new features and products.

In addition to the product teams, Telerik also has teams responsible for sales, marketing, and graphic design. These teams ensure that software products are ready for the market, and their release is backed up by advertising campaigns, sales support, etc. Telerik also has two further teams who work on the company's infrastructure – a web team responsible for the development and maintenance of both Telerik's and Progress's websites, and an administration and IT team managing the office facilities, networks and computers respectively.

All employees interact with other employees, professional peers, customers, user groups, distributors, bloggers, and anyone else who might have information related to the company products and processes. Also, Telerik uses "viral marketing" to bond their customers and "friends" to the company, while creating excitement about the product releases.

When it comes to the physical environment, employees can be found talking with others in the hallways, consulting with other teams in their work areas, grabbing snacks and lunch from the company cafeteria, playing games of table tennis or foosball, or relaxing in the recreation areas.

Managing Human Capital at Telerik

Telerik's human resource professionals are called the Human Capital (HC) Team, a term started at its founding in 2002, and continued after its acquisition by Progress. The responsibilities of individuals in this team have always been critical in the company and continue to be of strategic importance. There are 32 people on this global team with Progress, and seven are based in Bulgaria. The HC Team consists of the following units:

- *Business Partners*: This unit has individuals who align and partner with senior leadership in a consulting capacity, aimed at providing the best human capital practices for improving organisational effectiveness and developing organisational capability.
- *Total Rewards*: Members of the unit harmonise and create cutting-edge compensation, benefits and recognition programmes which aim to attract and retain top talent across the globe. They also are responsible for talent management across the organisation.
- *Go-to-Market Team*: This team delivers operational efficiency, flawless execution of programmes, and excellence in employee and manager relations.
- *Talent Acquisition*: This group determines the unique employee value proposition, and markets Progress as a preferred destination for the best and the brightest in the global market, as well as acquiring talent.
- *Talent Development*: The focus in this team is on assessment of workforce development needs, and the translation of the needs into strategic projects and initiatives. The group manages the leadership development efforts, and coordinates job-specific learning interventions across the different organisational functions.

Telerik has a relatively low turnover rate (under 10 percent), but its expansion plans mean that it must continuously update its supply of employees. In terms of the focus of activity, the HC Team representatives speak of both the need to acquire appropriate talent in relatively effective (and quick) ways, and the need to bring them up-to-speed in a relatively short time.

Telerik recruits in the usual ways seen in the industry, using webpages, blogs, social media, professional associations, training programmes, employee referrals, friends of the company, notices, and university connections. As a company with over 550 employees in Bulgaria and more worldwide, it is using the model of on-going recruiting, or what some call the "Always Be Recruiting" approach. At the time of the case, it was attempting to fill over 30 jobs in less than three months.

The screening process consists of an on-line employee application system, and the Talent Acquisition Team likes to conclude the process within one to two weeks from application submission. Applications are initially screened by the Talent Acquisition Team for qualifications and experience as required by the particular job. Those deemed qualified at that point are interviewed by a team of three to four employees. The interviewing team usually consists of a Human Capital representative, a senior employee and the team manager. In the selection process, the team checks for "fit" with the current culture, and, after the interview, the candidate is usually given a technical task to complete. The decision to hire must be unanimous or hiring does not occur.

On-boarding is critical. During a new employee's first day, there is a presentation delivered by HC to the employees on topics such as the company history, key achievements, the product lines, the organisation and operations of the company, as well as information on benefits and policies. There is also a presentation delivered by IT covering useful information about account administration, helpdesk systems and IT-specific policies. At the end of the day there is a tour of the office space. In addition to the first day experience, the

HC team have developed the "Acceleration Program" to facilitate the integration of new employees into the company. It is a streamlined process that lasts over six months, starting with the first day of a new employee, and continuing until their sixth month of employment. Each employee is assigned a "guide" to serve as a mentor and coach for the employee. There is further in-team training, and regular "check-ins" during the entire Acceleration Program.

The Talent Development team ensures regular training and development opportunities are offered, and Telerik employees are active in pursing these opportunities. They have many professional development activities, including, technical, leadership, English, and on-demand courses, as well as professional certification.

Telerik provides a supportive environment for its employees, including its physical environment, the amenities provided in the workplace, and its benefits package. The benefits are generous and broad, including student time off, fitness and sports memberships, social programmes, childcare, and health programmes. The package includes flexible working hours and an additional medical and pension insurance plan, in addition to the government-required programmes. Of course, like other software companies, they provide the game rooms, the recreation areas and, what is more, massage onsite in the office by appointment. Their Concierge Services are one of the most popular benefits wherein they provide assistance to employees with activities that might take time away from work. These would include activities such as having automobiles repaired, and running other errands.

One of their differentiating benefits is the Kids Centre, located in an adjacent building, where parents may enrol children from three to seven years of age for day-long activities. Grandparents or nannies are welcome to accompany children from birth to three years of age, all for free. The only cost involved is for meals that are served for the children.

Teambuilding is important at Telerik. There are several company parties, and events throughout the year where the whole company gets together. There is also a teambuilding budget that teams can use to spend on teambuilding initiatives during the year.

In addition to the various benefits, there are also a number of employee recognition programmes. For example, there are "Spot Bonuses" – cash awards for employees who go above and beyond in delivering in areas of significant importance to the company, as well as for extraordinary performance and contribution outside of their job scope. Recognition awards demonstrate immediate appreciation for the exceptional contributions of individuals or teams. There are also "Night on the Town" awards, used to reward extraordinary accomplishments or performance on a project. An employee receiving such an award can spend the voucher enjoying a night on the town, for example purchasing concert tickets, going out to dinner, or any other social event. Last but not least, there is a Service Award Programme, the purpose of which is to mark key work anniversaries. Employees who reach such a milestone receive a gift card as well as an extra week's vacation time.

Welcome and exit surveys are implemented that capture employees' experience. Regular engagement surveys are also conducted with all employees to get feedback related to organisational health – collaboration, execution, company confidence, employer brand, etc.

Like other companies in the industry, Telerik continues to be concerned about an on-going supply of talent. In 2009, it opened the Telerik Academy to deal with this problem by offering a variety of training programmes – an in-house training centre for software developers and IT professionals based in Bulgaria.

Telerik Academy trains, for free, thousands of IT professionals per year, and supplies the Bulgarian software industry with highly skilled developers, QA engineers and IT professionals. Because of the competitive nature of the Academy, only those students who demonstrate consistent activity and excellent results in examinations administered during the training have the opportunity to progress.

The Academy gives Telerik the chance to hire a steady stream of promising developers each year. This is extremely important for an industry which is globally suffering from a massive shortfall of such people. Other IT firms in Bulgaria have followed suit with in-house training, although they have not reached the scope or esteem of the Telerik Academy. Today, the "tech-ed" initiative, which will remain "Telerik Academy by Progress", focuses on software engineering, digital technologies, and recently added digital marketing.

The Academy introduced two initiatives: the Telerik Kids Academy, and the Telerik School Academy. The idea behind the Kids Academy is to complement traditional IT education in schools by educating young children in the major Bulgarian cities. The School Academy is a series of free training courses for older children in order for them to absorb the basic skills and knowledge in software development and training. Both these initiatives demonstrate a new level of investing in human capital while, at the same time, showing Telerik's and Progress's commitment to community education and development.

The Future at Telerik

As Telerik continues its growth as part of Progress, it will certainly face many opportunities and challenges. The global support will be helpful as the company offers new products and services, and develops new relationships. As the company further integrates into the global network of Progress, and adapts into the corporate team, the Human Capital team will have access to, and knowledge of, more human capital practices, therefore creating greater opportunities for the employees. How this plays out in the future in terms of the "local versus global", the "small versus big", and the "them versus us" dilemmas will be of interest to those studying human resources management. There is an initiative that started just after the acquisition related to defining the ideal culture at the global company, and activating it. Innovation, collaboration, and engagement are at the heart of the company's integration, and are key to its culture transformation.

Other companies such as Google and Microsoft are noted for their open cultures, great benefits packages, and inviting physical settings. It would not be surprising to find the Telerik-type of work environment in Silicon Valley, California, or even in some places in Western Europe. However, Telerik is in Bulgaria, in Eastern Europe – a region more accustomed to structured and policy-riddled companies, forbidding environments, and autocratic and remote management.

Yet, the four founders of Telerik have established, and maintain a company that is successful, and is recognised within the industry as being innovative in both content and process – and continues to do so while being part of a larger corporation. The challenges of growth and integration lie ahead, and the key for success could be how they handle the human capital of the company.

Case Study Questions

1 Describe the two major human resource challenges being faced by Telerik as it moves into its growth and integration phases. For each, discuss the specifics of the challenge, and the various tactics tried in the past to address the challenge. Then, make recommendations for each of the challenges that will support the future of Telerik.

2 The new Human Capital Team has been organised into five different groups of people and activities. Describe what specific activities you see Telerik undertaking in each unit to meet their on-going and upcoming human resource challenges.

3 You have been asked to consult with the Human Capital Team at Telerik on the success of their Telerik Academy. Describe the aspects of the endeavour that you would examine and the process you would use to study this human capital activity. Then, describe the advantages and challenges of the Academy and make specific recommendations for its future.

4 Telerik are competing in a global environment for employees in their Bulgarian location. We know that they are facing a competitive environment in terms of software development within the company, and that they are also facing a demographic "brain drain" from the country and region. They have tried to address this by providing a "Western-like" work environment, and compensation and benefits package. Evaluate whether Telerik can reverse the brain drain from the country with this approach, and continue to attract sufficient qualified employees for their growth.

References

BASSCOM (2015). Accessed 4 March 2016. *BASSCOM Barometer Report 2015.* Accessed 4 March 2016. http://www.basscom.org/RapidASPEditor/MyUploadDocs/BASSCOM_Barometer_2015_ENG.pdf

EDUKWEST (2015) *Bulgaria is Europe's Silicon Valley.* Accessed 4 March 2016. http://edukwest.eu/bulgaria-europes-silicon-valley/

Eurostat (2015). *Europe in Figures: Eurostat Yearbook.* Accessed 26 June 2016. http://ec.europa.eu/eurostat/documents/3217494/7072644/KS-EI-15-001-EN-N.pdf/318ee884-50d6-48f0-b086-4410da85d6b6

Kearney (2014). Accessed 4 March 2016. *The 2014 A.T. Kearney Global Services Location Index.* Accessed 4 March 2016. https://www.atkearney.com/documents/10192/5082922/A+Wealth+of+Choices.pdf/61c80111-41b2-4411-ad1e-db4a3d6d5f0d

Progress (2014). *Progress Completes Acquisition of Telerik and Expands Executive Management Team.* Accessed 4 March 2016. http://www.telerik.com/company/press-releases/2014/12/02/progress-completes-acquisition-of-telerik-and-expands-executive-management-team

Questers (2015). *Why is Bulgaria the leading destination in Eastern Europe for IT?* Accessed 4 March 2016. https://www.questers.com/blog/why-bulgaria-leading-destination-eastern-europe-it

Stack Overflow (2015). *Annual Developer Survey, 2015.* Accessed 26 June 2016. https://arc.applause.com/2015/04/08/the-average-programmer-28-9-years-old-male-and-loves-swift/

Telerik AD (2013). *Telerik AD is Named "Best Employer in Bulgaria" for Sixth Consecutive Year.* Accessed 4 March 2016. http://www.telerik.com/company/awards/details/telerik-ad-is-named-best-employer-in-bulgaria-for-sixth-consecutive-year

Telerik (2015). *Telerik: A Progress Company Takes Home Three Awards at the "Forbes Business Awards 2014" in Bulgaria.* Accessed 4 March 2016. http://www.telerik.com/blogs/telerik-a-progress-company-takes-home-three-awards-at-the-business-awards-2014-in-bulgaria

World Bank (2015). Accessed 4 March 2016. http://www.worldbank.org/en/country/bulgaria/overview

12
Czech Republic
The Impact of Managerial Decisions on the Occurrence of Company Crisis

Martina Fejfarová

Organisational Setting[1]

The LIQUEUR Company was established in 1847 and it was the first company in the territory of Bohemia to produce spirits, compressed yeast and liqueurs. It witnessed its greatest boom in the 1920s and it continued to prosper until 1945 when the LIQUEUR Company passed into state administration. The year 1992 turned out to be an important milestone for the LIQUEUR Company as it regained its legal persona and was transformed into a joint stock company. The LIQUEUR Company produced dozens of standard and first-class spirits. It then went bankrupt five years later as a result of a series of managerial decisions.

Country Background

Economic, Technological, and Political Advancement of the Country

The Czech Republic is a democratic country located in Central Europe. It came into being on January 1, 1993 following the division of the Czech and Slovak Federative Republic. The Czech Republic is a country with a liberal constitution and its political system is based on the free competition of political parties and movements. It is headed by the president of the republic with the highest legislative body being the bicameral Parliament of the Czech Republic. The Czech Republic is administratively divided into 14 self-governing regions. The capital of the country is Prague. The Czech Republic is a member of the North Atlantic Treaty Organization (NATO) and the European Union (EU). It is also a member of the Visegrad Group.

The Czech Republic is a transition economy which has undergone economic transformation from a socialist system based on central planning and collective ownership to a capitalist system characterised by a market economy and private ownership. This transformation took place in the first half of the 1990s (following the 1989 Velvet Revolution) and it created the conditions for further development and economic growth. The first problems started to occur in the middle of the 1990s. Growth in productivity lagged behind the growth in wages, and a more liberal fiscal policy deepened the internal imbalance. In 1997, following a strong decrease in the exchange rate of the Czech crown, the Czech National Bank ceased to apply a fixed exchange rate and replaced it with the floating exchange rate system. The country only managed to lower inflation and restore economic growth in 1999. The newly introduced monetary policy system, i.e. inflation targeting, was reflected in the gradual lowering of inflation and its stabilisation at low levels. The growth in GDP in 1999–2006 ranged from 1.4 percent to 6.9 percent. Economic growth slowed in 2007–2008, and in 2009 economic activities experienced a 4.8 percent drop as a result of the world financial crisis. In 2010, the ongoing problems in the global and European economies prevented the rapid recovery of the national economy. The debt crisis in the Eurozone meant that economic growth in 2011 was rather slow and ended in a recession in 2012–2013, during which GDP decreased by a total of 1.4 percent. The economy only resumed its growth trend (+2 percent) in 2014. Although the increase was quite significant in comparison with the boom experienced in 2004–2008, when GDP showed an average annual growth of 5.3 percent, it was still insufficient. The Czech Republic's economy also continued to grow in 2015 and this progress was faster than in 2014 year on year (Czech National Bank, 2015).

Population Size and Homogeneity

The Czech Republic has more than 10.5 million inhabitants. Over the course of recent years, the population of the Czech Republic has increased, but it is also ageing. In 2014, the average age was 41.7. The percentage of people aged 65 and over was 17.8 percent. The number of people in the productive group (15 to 64 years of age) decreased in parallel. However, the number of children below 15 years of age also showed a growing trend. The population structure based on gender was quite balanced in general terms. At the end of 2014, the population of the Czech Republic consisted of 49.1 percent males and 50.9 percent females (Czech Statistical Office, 2015a). The number of single and divorced people is growing too. The number of immigrants exceeds the number of emigrants. The largest immigrant groups are Ukrainians, Slovaks, Vietnamese and foreigners from Russia.

Leading Industries

The positive development of the Czech economy has been significantly determined by manufacturing industries, in particular, the production of motor vehicles (excluding motorcycles), trailers and semi-trailers, other means of transport and equipment and the electrical equipment. In the long term, industry has accounted for one-third of the gross added value for the entire Czech national economy (32.4 percent in 2014). The Czech Republic remains one of the most industry-oriented countries in the European Union. According to the value added factor cost, the share of industry in the Czech business economy is the highest in comparison with all the other European Union countries (47.3 percent in 2014).

Typical Levels of Education

The level of education has been improving in the Czech Republic. The number of people with only primary education has dropped several times, whereas the number of people with all kinds of higher education has increased. In 2014, 34 percent of inhabitants in the 15+ age group had a secondary education (vocational education) without the state school leaving exam. People with a full secondary education represented the largest group (34.3 percent), whereas 17.6 percent of inhabitants had a university education. Currently, the proportion of people with only a primary education is 13.9 percent. People with no formal education at all are 0.2% (Czech Statistical Office, 2015b).

Quality of Life Indicators and Core Cultural Values

The Czech Republic ranked twenty-sixth in the Legatum Prosperity Index (Legatum Institute, 2015) which evaluates living conditions in countries around the world. It has improved its ranking by three positions since 2011; in particular, in the areas of personal freedom, education and the economy. Of the former communist bloc countries, only Slovenia (25th position) has achieved a better position than the Czech Republic. Based on the survey conducted by Prudký *et al.* (2009), the essential values in Czech society are as follows (ranked according to importance): family, friends, free time, work, politics and religion.

HRM Background

Human resource management in the Czech Republic has been determined by the historical development of the country and its transition from a centrally planned economy to a market economy. Unlike in the case of previous reforms, this does not involve improving the economic system, but its overall transformation. New legislation has been passed, rapid and massive privatisation has taken place, the country has seen restitutions, price liberalisation, currency devaluation and the liberalisation of external relationships, as well as the restoration and maintenance of the macroeconomic balance. This transition has influenced the approach to human resource management.

The legislative framework of the human resource management in the Czech Republic consists of the following documents: the Constitution of the Czech Republic, the Bills of Rights and Freedom, the Labour Code, the Employment Act and other legal regulations.

The current labour market in the Czech Republic reflects a number of significant socio-economic changes which have occurred in the past 24 years (Czech Statistical Office, 2014). After the fall of the socialist regime, the labour market remained stable until 1996. The long-term unemployment rate of 3–4 percent initially showed a slow increase, but this was later followed by more rapid growth. In 1999, unemployment first exceeded the limit of 8 percent and it further reached this limit several times in the following six years. The growing number of unemployed was caused not only by economic but also demographic developments. The first years of the new millennium brought economic recovery resulting from overall industrial restructuring, improved competitiveness and the influx of new foreign investments. This manifested itself in the labour market which showed higher employment rates and a decrease in the unemployment level to 4.4 percent in 2008. In 2009, economic productivity decreased and the unemployment rate increased as a result of the global financial crisis and the postponement of the retirement age. The unemployment rate only started to decrease in 2014 when the Czech Republic managed to overcome the recession. In comparison with other countries in the European Union, the Czech Republic has had a lower long-term unemployment rate (the lowest rate in November 2016 (Eurostat, 2016)). In 2015, labour productivity rose in the Czech Republic compared to previous years when it stagnated. A minimum number of companies in the Czech Republic offer part-time jobs. Unlike the majority of EU countries, the Czech Republic has a much higher female unemployment rate than male, whereas the number of women holding managerial positions is still rather low, despite the fact that the ratio of qualified women and men is comparable.

Even though the Czech Republic has recently undertaken a number of activities targeted at gender equality, the traditional division of roles still persists with the majority of the population. There are still differences in the remuneration of males and females. Flexible work arrangements are rarely used.

The following main problems have been identified in the area of human resource management in the Czech Republic: (1) the lower employment level of people aged 55–64 years, in particular women, (2) an ageing population, (3) insufficient offers of part-time jobs and other flexible work arrangements, (4) low work mobility and insufficient will to move to where the jobs are, (5) low investments in the active employment policy compared to the passive employment policy.

The Operational Context in the LIQUEUR Company

The LIQUEUR Company focused primarily on manufacturing alcohol, spirits, yeast and non-alcoholic drinks. It had a long tradition and employed more than 300 people. They were supervised by the company management, consisting of 21 managers. The organisational structure of the LIQUEUR Company is shown in Figure 12.1.

1993 turned out to be the beginning of the critical period. The decision was made to bottle alcoholic drinks in non-returnable bottles, to apply for the registration of a trademark for atypical non-returnable bottles and to extend the range of products. The LIQUEUR Company invested in technology, modernisation and the further automation of its bottling

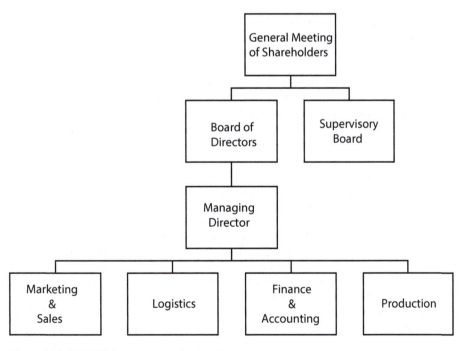

Figure 12.1 LIQUEUR Company organizational structure

lines. More money was put into promotion and the modification of the labels and the non-returnable bottles for alcoholic drinks. In the following year, these changes were reflected in a substantial price increase and sellers' demand continued to fall. A focus on exports, in particular to Russia and Germany, was thought to offer a way out of the crisis. Although the demand from these countries was growing, the LIQUEUR Company was not capable of ensuring export checks. State regulation bodies later found out that the goods had not actually crossed the country's borders according to the final customs documents. The LIQUEUR Company therefore hired a security agency to escort the goods to the border, which resulted in a further cost increase. During the course of 1994, the LIQUEUR Company was struck by a complex sales crisis which affected its economic results. This in turn led to changes in its top management and a significant reduction in staff. The intention was to trigger the positive development and the efficient operation of the LIQUEUR Company.

In 1995, the reduction of staff continued and the new employee recruitment process was improved, in particular for the Marketing and Sales Department. The production of new alcoholic drinks was launched and supported by promotional activities. As the sales of non-alcoholic drinks went into decline, attention was focussed on the manufacturing of spirits. It was decided to stop the production of yeast, which later proved to be a mistake, as the LIQUEUR Company was one of the largest producers of this commodity in the Czech Republic. The new management failed to reverse the unfavourable economic situation caused in particular by the unstable markets in Slovakia and Russia.

The negative development of the previous year also continued in 1996. One of the many problems which the LIQUEUR Company faced was a stock of eggnog containing *Bacillus cereus*. This meant that the LIQUEUR Company had its funds tied up in finished products in stock and its costs went up. After HRM changes in the top management in August 1996, the new leaders started to deal with the situation radically with the consent of the Board of Directors. There was a significant reduction in the number of staff and changes in the sales and marketing strategy were introduced. The Board of Directors considered the situation to be quite critical and proposed the following solutions:

1 To sell any movable and immovable property including inventory, with the exception of the buildings and facilities which were absolutely necessary for maintaining production, at the market price as soon as possible.
2 To efficiently lease the rest of the assets, in particular, the non-residential premises.
3 To use the yields from the sale of property and the leases to settle the LIQUEUR Company's debts towards the state.
4 To negotiate with the Inland Revenue Department on establishing the conditions for maintaining production and sales in the LIQUEUR Company.
5 To preserve the full production and sales of spirits.

The General Meeting of Shareholders did not accept this proposal to change the business plan and company asset restructuring and the following counterproposal was presented:

1 To rent the facilities and non-residential premises for at least their depreciation value.
2 To lease all equipment and rights to ensure production and sales.
3 To efficiently rent any unnecessary non-residential premises and production facilities or to use them for the LIQUEUR Company's other business activities.
4 To sell real property – the building and the plot.
5 To organise the lease as soon as possible.

The Board of Directors immediately started to implement the new business strategy (in March 1997). Production activities were fully terminated and the non-residential and warehouse premises and the production facilities were leased. The stock was sold and the rights to some trademarks were also transferred at the same time. The LIQUEUR Company also leased its other unused non-residential premises as a result of the measures taken. On the basis of the concluded contracts, the LIQUEUR Company provided the leaseholders with administration and security services, common maintenance, building and production facility repairs, transportation and warehousing. The lease of the non-residential premises became the LIQUEUR Company's main business activity.

Despite all the decisions and measures taken, the LIQUEUR Company was not able to repay its debts, in particular, its debts to the state and the banks, in real time. It was therefore decided to file a bankruptcy petition with the court of the relevant jurisdiction on grounds of insolvency due to overcapitalisation. Bankruptcy was awarded on 10 September 1997 and a trustee in bankruptcy was appointed. The lease of the non-residential premises was the main source of finances for the LIQUEUR Company and it was, therefore, capable of settling all its debts with respect to its suppliers, the health insurance and social security bodies, the Inland Revenue Department and its employees as of their maturity date and thus to ensure the flawless progression of the bankruptcy proceedings until the call for a tender for the sale of the LIQUEUR Company premises. All the employees' employment contracts were terminated. The DUAS Company won the tender and acquired the LIQUEUR Company in 1998 (Szalayova, 2007). In 2008, the DUAS Company (excluding the spirits division) was sold to a DUTCH Company. The spirits division, a subsidiary of the DUAS Company, became the DISTILLERY Company. In order to strengthen its position in the market, the owner of the DISTILLERY Company took over one of the five leading liqueur companies in the Czech Republic in 2010 and thus became a leading liqueur producer in the country, exporting goods to more than 20 countries around the world.

The HRM Context in the LIQUEUR Company

In the period after 1989, the interest in entrepreneurial activities in the Czech Republic was booming and each businessman wanted to achieve a profit in a short period of time. This trend was also followed by the managers of the LIQUEUR Company.

The general manager, who joined the LIQUEUR Company in 1992 (after its transformation into a joint stock company), applied a liberal leadership style. He did not have any impact on his subordinates' activities, his formal powers gradually weakened and the interests and ideas of his subordinates prevailed over his. He tried to avoid conflicts and unpopular solutions, refused to take any risks, willingly delegated his powers to his subordinates and let them make a number of important decisions. He pushed forward his favourites without taking their performance into account and placed their individual interests above the interests of the LIQUEUR Company. The general manager was under pressure from his subordinates, failed to monitor their activities and only set low-level and short-term goals. Thus, the General Meeting of Shareholders in 1994 decided to remove him from office and to terminate his employment contract. This was followed by changes in the top management team and a significant decrease in the number of employees which also continued throughout 1995. Despite the gradual outflow of employees, the quality of the new employee recruitment improved, in particular for the Marketing and Sales Department. The production of new alcoholic drinks was launched and supported by promotional activities. Yet despite all this, the new management failed to reverse the unfavourable economic situation.

The LIQUEUR Company had lacked a well elaborated HRM strategy since its inception. The general manager only had a general idea of recruiting and employing people he did not have the HRM strategy in place, the HRM manager and the HRM department. The LIQUEUR Company lacked clearly defined, long-term and comprehensive objectives in the area of HRM needs and the resources necessary to meet them. At the same time, no plans were made as to how to achieve the set objectives. HRM problems were dealt with on an *ad hoc* basis, no job descriptions were available that would specify the powers and responsibilities of individual employees and attention was paid solely to selected HRM activities.

After the changes made in the top management in August 1996, the new leaders started to deal with the situation radically with the consent of the Board of Directors. The newly recruited general manager, who also became a crisis manager, continued to reduce the number of employees and to centralise management. He started to use an autocratic leadership style. Despite the implementation of measures proposed to resolve the ongoing critical situation, there was no significant improvement. At that point, the LIQUEUR Company crisis had reached its acute stage. Based on the undertaken analyses, it was felt that any other measures would continue to deepen and worsen the company's situation. The General Meeting of Shareholders, therefore, recommended that the LIQUEUR Company should file for bankruptcy with the court of the relevant jurisdiction, despite all the changes which had been introduced to the management of the LIQUEUR Company. The employment relations with the 16 remaining employees were terminated.

A new management team was established in 2008 after many changes in ownership structure (from the LIQUEUR Company to the DISTILLERY Company). Due to the acquisition, investments and debt repayments, the DISTILLERY Company suffered losses in 2008–2010. In 2011, the DISTILLERY Company managed to return to the black and it achieved a profit for the first time. In 2012, it once again made a loss, in particular due to the so-called methanol affair which ended with the announcement of a prohibition by the Minister of Health following a series of poisonings by poor-quality spirits. Apart from the drop in spirit sales, this affair also had a negative impact on consumer trust. The DISTILLERY Company has been profitable again since 2013. Recent positive results have been achieved with the contribution of the following factors: a long-term plan for cost-saving measures, an active company-wide plan for growth measures, the restructuring of production, building key brands and the strengthening of their position on the market. At present, the DISTILLERY Company employs 101 employees, i.e. 69.2 percent of the staff employed in 2010. The DISTILLERY Company already has the HRM Department.

Outcomes in the Case-study Company

The following are the main conclusions arising from the above case study:

1   The changes in the entrepreneurial environment which took place in the Czech Republic in 1989 triggered a number of changes in Czech society. All the former rules ceased to be valid. The country saw the biggest shift of property from the state to private hands

in its history. Often, however, the first owners were more courageous than effective. Not all privatised companies were prosperous, work productivity was low, technologies were outdated and the prospects for future development were insecure. Thus, the majority of privatised companies found themselves in a critical situation in a short period of time due to poor managerial decisions. Only the key companies in the Czech economy, where the majority share was held by the state or by a strong strategic partner, managed to survive the crisis. More than half the companies ceased to exist, two-thirds of which were as a result of acquisitions or their division into several companies (Garnac, 2014).

2 Crises are quite natural and logical events as critical moments during attempts to regain balance and they are unavoidable in the life cycle of a company. For this reason, managers must pay attention to strategic management and especially to crisis management in order to avoid crises and subsequent bankruptcy. It is important to be prepared for a company crisis and to handle it.

3 Human resources are a company's most valuable asset. The quality of the human resources and their potential is a crucial factor for success. In the present business environment characterised by dynamic development and changes, human resources have become the main resource for achieving a competitive advantage.

Case Study Tasks

1 The LIQUEUR Company had a number of problems during its existence and operation. One of them was related to the personality of the general manager who applied a far too liberal leadership style which finally led, amongst other things, to the insufficient monitoring of subordinates. There are a wide variety of leadership styles. Discuss which one is the best and state the factors which you consider important for the change in the leadership style both on the part of the manager and his subordinates. Then determine the factors that would prevent such a change.

2 Despite all the decisions taken, the LIQUEUR Company did not manage to ward off the critical situation. State the key negative consequences of dismissing a huge number of employees, both in the short-term and in the long-term horizons.

3 One of the problems the LIQUEUR Company was dealing with was an insufficiently elaborated HRM policy. Try to develop an HRM strategy for the LIQUEUR Company as an independent advisor of the LIQUEUR Company. What are the main outcomes of the LIQUEUR Company's new HRM strategy?

4 In connection with point 3, develop a job description for the position of the HRM manager and specify his/her powers and responsibilities. Where in the organisational structure would this position be?

5 In connection with point 4, prepare an advertisement for the position of the HRM manager. What external recruiting resources would you select to publish the advertisement? Be specific and provide your reasons for your choice(s).

Role-play Exercise

One of the main mistakes made by the LIQUEUR Company was its insufficient interest in human resources. The LIQUEUR Company did not have an HRM strategy in place and the position of the HRM manager was vacant. Simulate the recruitment process based on the case study and the case study tasks. The members of the group will choose the roles according to the number of members in their team. Each group should have the following roles: the LIQUEUR Company general manager, a psychologist, an external advisor, the general manager's assistant, and at least two applicants for the job. Prepare the necessary material based on the selected role. The members of the recruitment committee should prepare individual recruitment process steps, questions for the applicants and evaluation criteria. The applicants should prepare cover letters and CVs. Then role play the recruitment and selection process and recommend the most suitable applicant for the position of the HRM manager.

Questions for Group/Class Discussion

1 Why are human resources the most valuable company asset?
2 What skills do you think an HRM manager needs to work successfully in the area of HRM?
3 Why should managers delegate? And how? What benefits does delegation bring to managers and their subordinates?

Note

1 The names have been modified to preserve the privacy of the companies.

References and Further Reading

Czech National Bank (2015). *Ekonomický vývoj na území České republiky*. Retrieved from http://www.historie.cnb.cz/cs/menova_politika/prurezova_temata_menova_politika/1_ekonomicky_vyvoj_na_uzemi_ceske_repub liky.html

Czech Statistical Office (2014). *Trh práce 1993–2013*. Retrieved from https://www.czso.cz/csu/czso/trh_prace_1993_2013_20140804

Czech Statistical Office (2015a). *Vývoj obyvatelstva České republiky—2014*. Retrieved from https://www.czso.cz/csu/czso/vyvoj-obyvatelstva-ceske-republiky-2014

Czech Statistical Office (2015b). *Za 60 let se zvýšil podíl vysokoškoláků 12krát*. Retrieved from http://www.statistikaamy.cz/2015/03/za-60-let-se-zvysil-podil-vysokoskolaku-12krat/

Eurostat (2016). *Unemployment statistics*. Retrieved from http://ec.europa.eu/eurostat/statistics-explained/index.php/Unemployment_statistics

Garnac, M. (2014). *Kuponová privatizace: Jak dopadly společnosti z kuponovky a jejich akcionáři*. Retrieved from http://www.penize.cz/rm-system/290603-kuponova-privatizace-jak-dopadly-spolecnosti-z-kuponovky-a-jejich-akcionari

Legatum Institute (2015). *Legatum Prosperity Index™*. Retrieved from http://www.li.com/activities/publications/2015-legatum-prosperity-index

Prudký, L. et al. (2009). *Inventura hodnot: výsledky sociologických výzkumů hodnot ve společnosti České republiky*. Prague: Academia.

Szalayová, M. (2007). *The Impact of Managerial Decisions on the Occurrence of Company Crises* (Bachelor Thesis). Czech University of Life Sciences Prague, Prague.

13

Hungary

An Online Game for Recruiting IT-Programmers at an American Subsidiary in Hungary[1]

Dr. József Poór,[2] **Iris Kassim,**[3] **and Dr. Lajos Reich**[4]

In January 2014, General Electric (GE) Healthcare set itself the goal of using the Industrial Internet for reforming healthcare informatics. To achieve this goal, the company needed 180 additional highly talented Java software developers in Hungary – in a country where there are 10,000 open IT job positions. GE Healthcare, therefore, in cooperation with the creative agency, Laboratory Group, launched its most ambitious recruiting campaign of the year. In the first part of the case study, we present a general picture of the socio-economic situation in Hungary. Next, we highlight the most important macro-level country characteristics (labour law, labour market dynamics and characteristics of the national culture) that affect corporate HRM practices on the micro-level. In the third part of the case study we examine the market entrance of a US subsidiary – GE – to Hungary and subsequent developmental steps undertaken by this subsidiary. The fourth part of this case deals with the presentation of the selection method by which software developers were recruited.

Socio-economic Background of Hungary

Socio-economic Environment

Before the sudden political changes in 1989, eight countries existed in this region. The political and administrative map of the region has undergone drastic changes. Besides the Eurasian region of the former Soviet Union, there are now 15 countries here with more than 200 million people (see Table 13.1). Before the political changes the whole region had been culturally treated very similarly by the Western world. These nations belonged to the communist bloc. Within the new borders, we have to recognise a historically and culturally highly diversified environment.

A noticeable trend in these countries is *privatisation*. W.I. Lenin (1966), the grandfather of the former Soviet Union, explains in his historical essay in "Against Revisionism" that the workers are holding the factories firmly in their hands, and the peasants will not return the land to the landlord. This historical proclamation is becoming more and more outdated.

Table 13.1 Hungary among Central Eastern European countries

No	Countries	Population (million people)	Size(km^2)	GDP per capita(USD)
1	Albania	2.9	28.748	4.610
2	Bosnia-Herzegovina	3.8	51.129	4.826
3	Bulgaria	7.2	110.910	5.833
4	Croatia	4.2	56.538	10.151
5	Czech Republic	10.5	78.866	14.696
6	Estonia	1.3	45.339	14.804
7	Hungary	9.9	93.000	11.888
8	Latvia	2.0	64.589	11.835
9	Lithuania	2.9	65.200	12.330
10	Macedonia	2.1	25.333	5.390
11	Poland	38.0	312.679	10.862
12	Romania	19.9	238.500	7.527
13	Serbia	7.1	77.474*	6.178
			(88.361)**	
14	Slovakia	5.4	49.035	13.885
15	Slovenia	2.1	20.253	18.074

*excluding Kosovo, **including Kosovo

Source: https://www.cia.gov/library/publications/the-world-factbook/

The share of the private sector in GDP is becoming dominant in these countries. The highest level of privatisation has been achieved in the Czech Republic, Poland and Hungary.

The transition has been overshadowed by high inflation and a drastic decrease in output performance. In the meantime, increasing numbers of countries in the region, including Hungary, have managed to change this economic trend. During the last decade, most of the countries within the region have begun to grow. Despite economic growth and the low inflation rate of many Central and Eastern European (CEE) countries, including Hungary, large GDP differences remain between the highly developed OECD and CEE countries.

Foreign Capital Involvement

According to a report on the region by UNCTAD (2014), the total stock of foreign direct investment (FDI) grew from some hundred million USD in 1988 to 100 billion by 2014. The pattern of foreign investments can be classified as follows:

- **Evolutionary or revolutionary pattern:** Many firms followed a pattern of longer, *evolutionary* growth. They obtained experience of almost all types of international business relationships before launching any form of FDI in Hungary or the rest of CEE. Besides traditional buying and selling relationships, they sold licences or established sales offices or service agencies in the CEE countries even during former socialist times. The next steps involved the establishment of joint ventures with one or several local partners. Finally, these local partners were bought out or a wholly independent company was formed.

- Since the political and economic changes in Hungary and in CEE countries, there are increasing numbers of so-called newcomer firms that are doing business in this region. These organisations have not had any prior business relationships with the firms or governments of these countries. Regardless of previous local business experiences or business relationships, their method of entry is a jump into the unknown world. This is referred to as a *revolutionary pattern* of expansion. GE, as presented in this case, has followed this pattern.
- **Growth through green-field investments or acquisitions:** Almost 90 percent of total FDI stocks are brought into the region through Western-European and North American firms. These firms adopt both forms of firm expansion, including acquisitions and green-field investments. Their Asian counterparts are fairly behind in the level of investment in this region compared to Western firms. Their general business practices prefer green-field expansion, establishing a trading outpost first. The second typical step in their expansion is in the form of strategic investment for the future. The high debt ratios of Japanese banks and firms or stability problems within the region have hampered many Japanese firms in following this pattern. There have therefore been very few large Japanese investments in this region, compared to the Korean *chaebols* (conglomerates), which are trying to profit from the European Union (EU) membership status of Hungary and several other CEE countries.

Overall, foreign firms employ almost 25 percent of the total workforce in Hungary.

Leading Industries

The main leading industries in Hungary are automotive, electronics, pharmaceutical and medical technology, information technology (IT) and food processing. The majority of R&D activities are driven by pharmaceutical and IT industries. Hungary has become a regional incubator for software development, including process control software, game programs and geographical IT, focusing on navigation systems. Hungarian software developers have achieved international success in several fields, such as virus protection, bioinformatics, and IT security. The presence and successful operation of companies such as Ericsson, GE Healthcare, Prezi and Gameloft show further evidence of the high quality of IT in Hungary.

Typical Levels of Education

Hungarian education and training programmes involve:

- Pre-school: school-based programme for children aged 3–7, including basic skills development, pre-reading, drawing, singing, and school preparation.
- Primary school: lower level general education in grades 1–4 and higher level general education in grades 5–8.
- Vocational training school programmes in grades 9–11 providing qualifications for trade, industry and similar jobs.
- General secondary education in grades 9–12 preparing students for secondary school final examination.[5]
- College, university: There are three distincti levels of these programmes including bachelor (undergraduate), master (graduate) and PhD.[6]

Core Cultural Values

Hofstede (1980) developed a universal framework for understanding cultural differences based on a worldwide survey. Power distance (PDI) shows the extent to which inequalities among people are accepted. In Hungary, PDI is quite low with a score of 46, which means power is decentralised, communication is direct, and control is disliked. Uncertainty avoidance (UAI) refers to a preference for structured versus unstructured situations. Hungary scores 82 on UAI and thus has a preference for avoiding uncertainty. Individualism–collectivism (IND) considers whether individuals are used to acting as individuals or as a part of cohesive groups. Hungary, with a score of 80, is definitely an individualist society. Masculinity–femininity (MAS) distinguishes between hard or masculine values, such as assertiveness and competition, and soft or feminine values, such as personal relations, quality of life and caring about others. Hungary scores 88 on this dimension and is thus a masculine society. Long-Term Orientation (LTO) describes how every society has to maintain some links with its own past while dealing with the challenges of the present and future. Hungary is a pragmatic country with a high score of 58 on this dimension. Indulgence (IND) is defined as the extent to which people try to control their desires and impulses, based on the way they were raised. Hungarian culture has a low score of 31 on this dimension, meaning that in Hungary people have a tendency to cynicism and pessimism and they feel restrained by social norms. These elements of national culture in Hungary compared to six other CEE countries according to Hofstede (Culture compares, 2015) appear in Table 13.2.

HRM Background in Hungary

The development of the HRM function in Hungary has roots going back to the industrial age, when labour legislation was in its infancy and employers were allowed to maintain sometimes hard working conditions (e.g. long working hours, unhealthy work conditions, starvation wages, employment of children). The first welfare officers' main focus was to act as an agent for employee wellbeing and improve the working conditions of blue-collar workers. Later, their roles were extended with other personnel activities such as recruitment, payroll and other administrative duties.

Table 13.2 National culture dimensions of Hofstede theory

No	Countries	Dimensions					
		PDI	IDV	MAS	UAI	LTO	IND
1	Croatia	73	80	40	33	58	33
2	Estonia	40	60	30	60	82	16
3	Hungary	46	80	88	82	58	31
4	Poland	93	39	36	95	38	29
5	Romania	90	30	42	90	52	20
6	Serbia	86	92	43	25	52	28
7	Slovakia	104	52	110	51	77	28

Source: The Hofstede Centre. Culture compares. http://geert-hofstede.com/countries.html (downloaded: 30 November 2015)

While in many developed countries, the administrative stage of the HRM function's development was followed by the emergence of the personnel management and later the human resource management phases, in Hungary it took another direction. After 1945, during the four-decade era of socialism, personnel-related activities were regulated by the Communist Party and were driven by solely political interests. For example, hiring decisions were not based on qualification and competence, but on the candidate's loyalty to the Communist Party. Personnel officers had to follow the regulations and execute their duties without any professional consideration. Furthermore, the traditional personnel activities, such as selection, evaluation, training and promotion were basically focused on the leadership elite and not on all employees.

Following economic and societal progression starting in 1968, three main HRM functional areas emerged. *Personnel departments*' main activities included recruitment, selection, training, and development of the leadership elite. *Labour departments* were responsible for the administrative duties related to blue-collar workers. *Welfare departments* dealt with welfare affairs including the operations of company nurseries and kindergartens, canteens, holiday centres or compulsory healthcare services. In the meantime, the first state-approved labour and later personnel and welfare educational programmes officially institutionalised the profession. After the 1990 downfall of the Communist Party and as a result of the follow-up privatisation and consequently the re-structuring and downsizing of companies, the profession experienced a temporary setback.

It was only after 2000 that the modern HRM function started to evolve in Hungary, accelerated by the appearance of multinational corporations (MNCs) which implemented their advanced HRM practices. As international HRM consulting agencies also entered the Hungarian market, they also contributed to the rapid development of the HRM function in Hungary. With the market conditions becoming more competitive and challenging, even Hungarian companies were forced to re-organise their business operations and apply more effective and up-to-date management and HRM practices.

At the same time, increasing numbers of universities started to offer high quality graduate and post-graduate HRM educational programmes. A number of non-profit organisations (e.g. the Hungarian Association of HR Professionals, the Hungarian Association of Human Resource Management, the Hungarian Society of Organization Development Professionals, the Association of Training Roundtable, etc.) also contributed to the development of the HR profession by building a community of HR professionals, offering knowledge sharing platforms (e.g. professional conferences, workshops, HRM journals, HRM awards, etc.) and executing professional and academic research.

Company Background

Market Entrance and Early Years

Tungsram, the light source producer, was founded in 1896 and has been traditionally one of the largest Hungarian manufacturing firms, with a strong presence in the European market. In 1989, General Electric (GE) acquired 50 percent plus one share of the light source producer, Tungsram, for $150 million. Later, GE made a further $500 million investment in the venture, obtaining the remainder of the shares and making it the largest US foreign investment to date in CEE. Tungsram's turnover was HUF 50 billion in 1995 and it employed ten thousand employees in eight plants with headquarters in Budapest.

The overall headcount of Tungsram had been reduced from 17,600 to 9,200 by the end of 1993. A slow increase then followed, up to the level of 10,2000 as a result of significantly increased productivity and profitability. The mix of the employment changed as well. Eliminating bureaucracy, the salaried employment ratio went down from 20 percent to 10 percent. The reduction in headcount was managed very carefully and it became a role model in Hungary. The so-called "Workforce Redeployment Programme" included attrition, job offers at other companies, early retirement, retraining courses, counselling, and partnership with Unions. In the first year of the acquisition it was extremely difficult to find good candidates for jobs specifically in marketing, finance, and HR. To ensure the right mix, several expatriates were assigned to top and mid-level managerial jobs. The number of expatriates has never exceeded thirty. Young talents were brought into the company, with the most important channel being the entry-level programme for university graduates. This programme involves two to three years on-the-job training with four to six assignments in different functional areas, possibly including an assignment abroad.

Later Years and Today

The most important drivers of the changes after the acquisition were the expatriates taking top managerial positions. The new Hungarian-born CEO created a good mix of expatriates and local top managers, and very carefully started to merge the two cultures. The appropriate selection of expatriates based on skills, cultural sensitivity and people management ensured the smooth transition and success of the first step towards the integration into GE.

There were two other groups of people who played a major role in the transition. The first group in the new generation of managers included the graduates from GE entry-level programmes. The second group to benefit from the changes was that containing the professionals and skilled workers, who gained much more responsibility and independence because of de-layering. Finally, the most important driver of the changes was the growing cross-functional and cross-country teamwork, in which the Hungarian team members had the opportunity to experience the GE culture in practice.

In 2000, Tungsram had been functionally integrated into GE Lighting Europe, headquartered in London. The integration has meant that Tungsram does not have a separate organisational structure; the whole organisational structure is established and the positions and responsibilities are allocated at a pan-European level. GE Lighting Europe as the umbrella organisation has manufacturing plants in five countries: Hungary, UK, Germany, Italy, and Turkey, as well as sales and logistics organisations throughout Europe.

> When Jack Welch, former chief executive of General Electric of the USA, spoke to an interviewer about his company's impending purchase of Hungary's light bulb maker, Tungsram, he described it as 'sailing in uncharted waters'. That was in late 1989. As it turned out, and luckily for GE, the ship's pilot knew where the reefs were hidden.
>
> (Bangert, 1994)

In 2012, GE was the largest US investor and employer (12,500 employees) and one of the biggest exporters in Hungary. GE has two major legal entities in Hungary and has 12 manufacturing plants in ten cities throughout the country. As part of GE Hungary Ltd. and its affiliates GE businesses – technology infrastructure, industrial solutions and healthcare – operate six factories (Aviation, Power & Water, Oil & Gas) in five cities, and also three regional headquarters and two technology centres in Hungary. In addition, in the framework of GE Hungary Ltd., the Europe, the Middle East and Africa (EMEA) headquarters and a global technology centre for GE Lighting are also located in Budapest. The regional headquarters operate an additional six factories in five cities of Hungary. GE Hungary Ltd. generated HUF 1,395 billion in revenue in 2012, with 98 percent exports (GE-Central-Europe, 2015).

GE Healthcare Within GE Hungary

GE Healthcare provides transformational medical technologies and services to meet the demand for increased access, enhanced quality and more affordable healthcare around the world. GE works on things that matter – great people and technologies taking on tough challenges. From medical imaging, software & IT, patient monitoring and diagnostics to drug discovery, biopharmaceutical manufacturing technologies and performance improvement solutions, GE Healthcare helps medical professionals deliver great healthcare to their patients.

GE Healthcare began operations in Hungary in 1997 as a trade representative of the local business. Today, at its regional sales and service centre for CEE, it has over 400 employees working for GE Healthcare Hungary, as part of GE Hungary Ltd. In 1999, the research and development of clinical applications began and expansion is ongoing. The world-class research and development centres in Budapest and Szeged currently employ more than 200 software engineers.

GE Healthcare's research and development centre is designed to combat cancer and cardiovascular diseases. It supports the work of medical professionals with advanced imaging software which helps doctors diagnose pathological changes more accurately at an earlier stage. Hence they can provide more effective treatment, which ultimately improves the life expectancy of patients and reduces the cost of healthcare. In addition to the fact that these products represent the highest quality in countries all over the world, in Hungary they play a particularly important role due to the cardiology, oncology and public health characteristics of the region.

GE Healthcare Hungary has in recent years evolved into a globally recognised competence centre for medical image processing algorithms and software. The more than $15 million invested here annually into research and development creates an annual value of $300 million for doctors. Throughout the world, every fourth application of patient radiology software used in diagnostics was developed by GE Healthcare Hungary.

IT-Programmer – Recruiting with an Online Game "Bitfection"

Key Stakeholders of the Project

Given this background, in January 2014 GE Healthcare set a goal to reform healthcare informatics with the help of the Industrial Internet. To achieve its goal, the company needed the best 180 Java developers of the region. GE Healthcare therefore, in cooperation with Laboratory Group creative agency, launched the largest recruitment campaign of the year.

The project was led by Dr. Lajos Reich (that time MD of GE Hungary Ltd. and CTO of GE Healthcare in Hungary), János Gyarmati (CMO of GE Healthcare in CEE), Balázs Steixner (at that time member of GE Healthcare's technical leadership programme), Sándor Haszon (creative director of Laboratory Group), Márton Tóth (digital designer at Laboratory Group),

Gábor Váradi (client service director at Laboratory Group) and Alex Szénássy (founder and managing director at Laboratory Group).

Online Game "Bitfection" for Identifying Right Programmers

It is not easy to reach the target group, as software developers typically do not read traditional media, nor do they write resumés for themselves. Many of them, however, are obsessive gamers who have lived under the spell of computer games since their childhood. Based on this understanding, GE Healthcare and Laboratory Group developed an online game that could be solved solely by the best Java developers.

The aim of the game, named Bitfection (merging "bit" and "infection"), is to find and identify ill cells, or in other words, pixel groups, in fictitious medical images created by nanorobots activated by a Java code. The shorter the time and less the energy used by successful players to solve the increasingly difficult stages, the higher the scores they receive. Gamers with the highest scores were contacted by recruitment specialists and invited for a job interview, where they could prove their suitability. Those who passed this step received a job offer from GE.

During the campaign, the attention of potential players was attracted through online advertisements, billboards, and cafeteria trays in canteens of the main competitors employing a large number of Java developers – perhaps a little unusual, but obviously only after receiving the written consent of cafeteria management.

How Was the Game Developed?

The game was prepared in just three months, including the design of online and offline advertisements. The user experience design was also created by Laboratory Group, one of the leading advertisement agencies in Hungary. The visual elements smartly mix a modern and retro look and feel, which the target group proved to buy into. The basic concept was set by the joint team of GE Healthcare and Laboratory Ideas. The software that was the basis of the game was developed by three Laboratory Group programmers under the leadership of an experienced GE engineer, for whom this project also meant credit in the technical leadership programme. The team followed lean start-up methodology during all phases of development. Instead of insisting on a fixed concept, the team reached out and involved several GE Healthcare software developers similar to the members of the target group. They served with a number of advisors who helped the team to set the appropriate difficulty level of each stage: hence the game not only attracted the best coders but it encouraged their perseverance, too. They were the ones who tested the final game as well.

It was surprising to see how quickly records were broken again and again from day one. The team realised that the game had not only created a recruitment platform, but also a highly effective crowd-sourced algorithm optimisation process. Participants inspired each other to achieve increasingly better results, finally reaching unbelievable success, beating all prior expectations. Playfully encouraging the community apparently leads to better outcomes than relying on a few experts, geniuses that they are, to work on the solution for a problem.

Feedback on Online Game from Different Stakeholders

It was amusing and at the same time instructive, to see reader comments in newsfeeds after launching the campaign. Although many started of course to argue "why Java" and "what is actually the best programming language", the most memorable comment was the following: "Smart: on the one hand they are looking for really gifted people using a gamified solution that closely resembles the real task. On the other hand, the best performing algorithm can be monetised . . ." If the medical nanorobot business had really existed, GE would have been extremely fortunate!

The development budget and marketing campaign was a fraction of what traditional headhunters would have cost. The results speak for themselves: before the campaign closure, GE Healthcare's Bitfection site had 14,000 unique visitors; more than 650 of them tried to solve the puzzle. The awareness and reputation of GE Healthcare Hungary has significantly improved: Today, GE Healthcare's development centre in Budapest is one of the most impactful global software competence centres of GE, as well as being one of the most admired and hyped research and development employer in Hungary.

Futu re Use of the Game

Although the Bitfection campaign was a single event, its platform is capable of solving other gamified challenges. The fame of the project reached India, France and the USA. Both inside and outside of GE, several locations viewed and applied it as a best practice.

Questions

1 What were the main risks for GE in regard to establishing its research and development centre in Hungary?
2 What are the main difficulties of recruiting a large number of talented Java developers in Hungary?
3 What made Bitfection popular among Java developers?
4 How did Bitfection contribute to the assessment and selection of the most talented Java developers?
5 What is the short- and long-term business impact of the Bitfection project?

Notes

1 The authors are grateful to GE Healthcare Hungary for granting permission to publish this case.
2 Professor of Management of Szent István University (Hungary) and J. Selye University (Slovakia), Director of Management and Leadership Program (Msc.), Certified Management Consultant (CMC), President of Hungarian Association of HR Professionals and HR Ambassador of Academy of Management for Hungary, poorjf@t-online.hu, +36 20 464 9168.
3 Co-founder of Society of Management Innovators, Board Member of Hungarian Association of HR Professionals, PhD candidate at Szent István University (Hungary), iris@managementinnovators.org, +36 70 275 5969
4 Currently CEO at Healcloud, previously MD at GE Hungary Ltd. and CTO at GE Healthcare Hungary, lajos.reich@healcloud.com, +36 30 391 4017.
5 In Hungary, 82 percent of adults aged 25–64 have completed upper secondary education. This is higher than the OECD average of 75 percent. Retrieved from http://www.oecdbetterlifeindex.org/countries/hungary/ (downloaded: March 13, 2015).
6 Higher education in Hungary dates back to 1367 when *Louis the Great* founded the first Hungarian university in the city of *Pécs*. Retrieved from http://www.english.ktk.pte.hu/university-of-pecs (downloaded: March 11, 2015).

References and Further Reading

Bangert, D.C. (1994). Hungary: exploring new European management challenges. (includes appendices) (Research Sites: Considering Some Less-Known Locations). *International Studies of Management & Organization*, March 22. (https://business.highbeam.com/436988/article-1G1–16678614/hungary-exploring-new-european-management-challenges, down-loaded: November 15, 2016).
Bruner, R. (1992). Tungsram's leading light. *International Management*, 47(11), 42–45.

EUGO Hungary. Main industries. Retrieved from http://eugo.gov.hu/key-facts-about-hungary/main-industries (downloaded: November 19, 2015).

GE-Central-Europe. Retrieved from http://www.ge.com/hu/en/company/ce_en.html (downloaded: November 19, 2015).

GE Reports CEE (2015). GE Healthcare Hungary Continues to be Committed to Education and Knowledge Sharing. Retrieved from http://gereportscee.com/post/129202439451/ge-healthcare-hungary-continues-to-be-com mitted-to (downloaded: September 16, 2015).

Hofstede, G. (1980). *Culture's Consequences: International Differences in Work-Related Values.* Beverly Hills, CA: Sage Publications.

Lenin, W.I (1966). *Against Revisionism.* Moscow: Progress Publishers.

OECD Better Life Index Hungary (2015). Retrieved from http://www.oecdbetterlifeindex.org/countries/hungary/ (downloaded: November 19, 2015).

The Hofstede Centre. Culture compare (2015). Retrieved from http://geert-hofstede.com/countries.html (downloaded: November 30, 2015).

The World Factbook. Retrieved from https://www.cia.gov/library/publications/the-world-factbook/ (downloaded: November 19, 2015).

UNCTAD (2014). *World Investment Report 2014.* Geneva-New York: United Nations Conference on Trade and Development (UNCTAD).

14
Poland
Reward Management in Small and Medium Enterprises on the Basis of Alfa i Omega, Głogów, Poland

Peter Odrakiewicz, Magdalena Szulc, and David Odrakiewicz

Organizational Setting

Alfa i Omega (AIO) was established in October 1991 in Głogów, Poland. Głogów is a town in southwestern Poland, in the Lower Silesian Province, with a total population of 67,953 (Central Statistical Office, 2009). Southwestern and southern Poland are both areas with high levels of investment in the steel and mining industries. Many companies from neighboring Germany, as well as many other international corporations, have opened their production plants in southwestern and in southern Poland.

AIO's main areas of interest are safety, security and health at work. AIO services a wide range of industries, including: chemical manufacturing, Polish oil and gas companies, electricity companies, coal mines, salt mines, steelworks, glassworks, food processing, general industrial, pharmaceutical and electronics manufacturing.

AIO was founded as a general partnership between two friends, Jan Nowak and Adam Kowalski, and had no other employees at that time. The partnership between the two friends lasted for nine years, but in 2000 the tension between them was so strong that they made a decision to divide the capital and end their cooperation. The main reason was a conflict of interests. Nowak wanted to expand AIO sales from regional to country-oriented and also had new ideas for gaining new working partners. In October 2000 Adam Kowalski took half of AIO's capital and left the company. Jan Nowak again formed a partnership, this time with his wife Anna Nowak. The partnership between Anna and Jan Nowak set new standards for AIO. As managers they put pressure on AIO to improve the performance and quality of products and services the company has been delivering. AIO invested in new company's facilities, employed more workers, made its own brand and increased their company's profile by expanding marketing. In addition, the company began cooperation at the international level, supplying services to manufacturers in Germany.

In recent years, AIO has been a fast-developing company because employee health and safety has become very important in Polish industries. AIO is presently recognized as one of the largest companies in Poland selling safety, security and health-at-work products.

The quality and efficiency of AIO's management system is proved and documented by the certificate ISO 9001:2008.

Historical Background of the Case

The Republic of Poland is a country in Central Europe. Poland shares borders with Germany to the west; the Czech Republic and Slovakia are to the south; Ukraine, Belarus and Lithuania are to the east; and the Baltic Sea and Kaliningrad Oblast, a Russian exclave, are to the north.

Poland is an example of a transition from a centrally planned economy to a primarily capitalistic market economy. These changes have occurred since the fall of the communist government. The development of the private sector has been possible because liberal law on establishing new firms was introduced. Restructuring and privatization of coal, steel, rail transport and energy sectors has been ongoing since 1990. Although privatization of such sectors meets very strong public criticism, nowadays Poland is struggling to fulfill all structural reforms to be able to enter into the European Single Currency (Euro). Joining the EU was extremely significant for Polish citizens. The work of importers and exporters, especially, became much easier. They no longer had to wait in queues in customs before sending or receiving their commodities. The days of paying import duties in order to import products from European Union countries have ended.

Polish Labor Law Summarized

Polish labor law is determined in the Labor Code, as well as in other laws such as: collective labor agreements, a company's labor regulations, a company's remuneration regulations and international law, including the World Labor Organization's conventions and recommendations as well as international agreements (Polish Ministry of Economic Affairs and Labor, 2015).

The Labor Code mostly contains regulations connected with contractual employment, including: entering into a contract, its termination, expiry, remuneration, hours of work and vacations. Work regulation defines the rights and duties of employers and employees connected with order in the place of work. It ensures that employees have all materials necessary for adequate safety; also they should work according to a fair and regular schedule and receive supplementary vacation time; they should receive adequate compensation for overtime, night and weekend work; finally, it is acknowledged that women who are pregnant and/or have young children have special needs and that these needs should be met.

Total Average Monthly Gross Salary in Polish Zloty, the Polish National Currency (PLN)

The average gross monthly salary has risen in recent years. For instance, between 2014 and 2015, according to the Central Statistical Office, it rose by 3.6 percent to just under 4,000 PLN per month (Central Statistical Office, 2015). This growth was observed in virtually all employment sectors (the exceptions being mining and quarrying, where salaries leveled off). For more details on these figures, see: http://stat.gov.pl/en/topics/labour-salaries/working-employed-wages-and-salaries-cost-of-labour/employment-wages-and-salaries-in-national-economy-in-1st-half-2015,1,26.html.

Types of Employment Contracts in Poland

There are four main types of employment contracts in Poland. A permanent contract is, arguably, the most favorable type of contract for an employee in that it provides maximum employment stability. However, under this contract the employer must pay compulsory social and health benefits premiums. Therefore, it may be viewed by small and medium-sized enterprises as a burden, one that potentially undermines the continuation of firms in these categories and potentially threatens the social and health stability of employees. Hence, other types of contracts have gained popularity. First, a contract of employment for a specific period of time involves the employer and employee agreeing to a contract for a specific time (one year, two years, ten years, etc.). In this case, the expiry date of the employment stated is in the contract. Secondly, a contract of mandate stipulates that the contractor (the employee) undertakes a specified task for the employer and health and social insurance premiums are the employee's responsibility. Finally, a contract for specific work may be signed when the employee agrees to perform work that is recognized as tangible under Polish law. Since this definition of tangibility is interpreted in a flexible manner, it may include such employment as construction projects or written work, as well as administrative and lecturing positions. Under the terms of this last type of contract, no health or insurance payments are required but the employee does pay income tax.

All Polish citizens have the same rights to medical care, old-age and disability pension, and also to family and sickness benefits. Nevertheless, everyone is subject to social and health insurance legislation, whether he or she is self-employed or employed by another entity. In the latter situation, the amount paid depends on each employee's amount of earnings. With respect to self-employment, one can choose from various insurance schemes. In Poland, the Ministry of Labor and Social Policy clarifies who is recognized as employed, self-employed and non-employed and outlines employees' basic rights and obligations (for a full list of these obligations, see: http://www.mpips.gov.pl/en/working-conditions/).

Basic Information on Occupational Safety and Health for Employers

In Poland, the Labor Code stipulates that the employer is responsible for following occupational safety and health (OSH) regulations. Most importantly, this code outlines the ways by which employers are obligated to protect their employees' health, provide safe conditions of work and make use of scientific and technological progress where applicable. These responsibilities include accident prevention and protection of especially vulnerable employees by adherence to OSH rules and principles; also the employer must provide necessary personal protective equipment and organize staff training sessions that facilitate the employees' knowledge of health and safety measures.

Furthermore, the format in which OSH regulations are delivered to employees is dependent on the size of the business organization. In other words, organizations with fewer than 100 employees may employ an outside entity (or an existing staff) to implement the OSH guidelines; in organizations that employ more than 100 employees, the company must establish an OSH service department that performs advisory and control functions; firms that have more than 250 employees must establish an occupational safety and health committee to act as an advisory and opinion-making body to the employer. Basic obligations of the employer are provided for in the Act of 26 June 1974 – Labor Code (Journal of Laws of 1998, No 21, item 94, as amended), mainly in its SECTION TEN, "Occupational safety and health".

The Structure of Alfa i Omega (a Detailed Description)

At present, AIO employs 22 workers. Additionally, it is outsourcing some work to external companies. Sixteen employees work at AIO's headquarters in Głogów, from 8 a.m. till 4 p.m. Six external sales representatives work in their own areas, with flexible working hours. The majority of employees live close to the company's headquarters in Głogów, except external sales managers. AIO has its external sales representatives in the areas of: Katowice, Rzeszów, Wrocław, Poznań, Warszawa and Gdańsk. Sixty percent of AIO employees are male. The average age of an AIO employee is 35. Throughout the years, the company's owners have built friendly relationships with employees. The owners and employees refer to each other by their first names, which is very unusual for Polish companies.

AIO is recognized locally. The owners have good relations with local community, as the company supports local schools, charities and sport events.

The structure of the company may be divided into five departments: administrative, accountancy, IT, sales, warehousing plus drivers and two caretakers (cleaning staff). Additionally, AIO employs extra workers for short periods of time when the company is facing a large amount of additional work.

The owners of AIO both have equal power within the company. However, to make the work easier they have divided the work. Anna Nowak is mainly responsible for sales. Therefore the sales department, warehouse and drivers are assigned to her. Anna supervises imports and sales of goods. She takes part in important sales meetings and is responsible for contact with the most important clients.

Jan Nowak is in charge of AIO's finances and is responsible for some of the human resources (HR) functions. His work is dedicated to finance and marketing. Therefore accountants, administrative workers and IT workers report to him. As far as Human Resources Management is concerned, Jan defines job descriptions, primary selection of new employees,

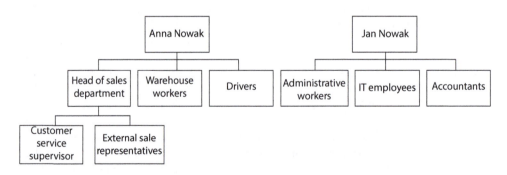

Figure 14.1 AIO's organizational structure

contracts, pay and benefits. Both owners make decisions concerning motivation and training and development.

Relations Between Importing and Selling

AIO has two sales departments, internal and external. The head of the sales department is also responsible for ordering goods from Germany. The employee doing this job at AIO is a woman in her early thirties. She is bilingual (Polish and German). The process of importing goods proceeds through several stages. Once the amount of needed goods is established, they are ordered, by an AIO employee, from a German business partner. Afterwards transport is organized to ship goods from Germany to Poland. Usually goods are transported by freight-forwarding companies. Finally, products are checked within AIO headquarters by warehouse workers and shipped to AIO's customers in Poland.

Problems Faced

Over time, the company offered new services and gained new business partners. As it grew, new challenges were identified by AIO's owners and employees. First, it was noticed that there was an insufficient and uncompetitive reward system. Second, it became clear that it would be necessary to choose an appropriate type of contract which would be profitable, motivational and fair for AIO and its employees.

Reward Management in AIO

The reward system in AIO used to be very simple and not employee-oriented. Such a reward system was very popular in Poland for many years, and is still found among many companies. At AIO as well, a salary was seen as a tool for rewarding employees for performed work. There were no motivational factors. Most employees were treated equally: all worked the same number of hours; warehouse workers earned a little bit less than office workers; there was not much distinction between an accountant and a customer service worker. But as AIO hired new employees, internal and external sales representatives, giving a similar amount of money to everyone was no longer seen as being a fair practice.

In the past, the sales department had a specific reward system. Sales groups as a whole were given a base salary plus a percentage (approximately 5 percent) of AIO's total net sales attained during each month. Sales representatives were not getting many sales, because they knew that even if they did not sell much, their colleague probably would sell something, meaning that they would still get a reward at the end of month. Moreover, after hiring two sales representatives the amount of sales did not increase. Sales representatives did not work efficiently. This situation caused communication problems and conflicts among sales department employees.

The owners were amazed that after AIO hired new employees, the company's sales were still at the same point and the sales representatives were in conflict. This was the point at which the owners decided to change the whole reward system within AIO. Hence, in 2006 the reward system underwent an enormous transformation.

Presently, the reward system is one of the most basic tools for managing employee motivation in AIO. The heads of AIO have found that rewards that are given for performance have a big impact on motivation and on the actual performance of AIO's employees. The owners share the view of Griffin (2008) about motivation and rewards – that rewards are related to motivation and to performance. As an organization, AIO wants employees to perform at relatively high levels and needs to make it worth their effort to do so.

Hence, the reward system has been changed so that members of staff in the administrative and accountancy departments get a competitive base salary. Staff in the IT and sales departments (both internal and external sales), however, receive performance-based rewards in addition to their competitive base salaries. For IT employees, these rewards are based on contributions in the areas of innovation and design and, in the case of the internal sales staff, commissions are given that are based on personal net sales. Warehouse employees and drivers, in addition to receiving competitive salaries, may receive rewards that are performance-based.

Contracts Between AIO and its Permanent Employees

When AIO hires new employees, each is given a trial period contract for three months. Up until 2006, each employee, after a three-month trial contract, was given a contract of permanent employment. Employees were sure of their position of permanence within AIO; hence, their motivation decreased. As the company expanded to new areas of Poland, the owners of the company started to search for new methods of employing workers (various contracts with different levels of basic and extended benefits, and employment security in hopes of providing additional motivation). Currently the structure of employment is characterized in the following ways. As a new employee is hired, he or she is given a three-month trial contract. This three-month period is a time for the employer to decide whether the person chosen is appropriate for this position. It is also a time for the employee to decide whether it is an appropriate job for him or her, and to see how he or she feels in AIO's working environment. Within this period, AIO covers its employees' social and health insurance costs.

If the employer is satisfied with the employee's performance after this three-month period the employee is offered a temporary contract for a specified period of time. He or she may be offered a two-year temporary contract. If an employee is doing his or her best during the two-year period he or she will be promoted with a permanent employment contract after two years. The two-year period is a time for the employee to show his or her ongoing motivation towards work and their ability to produce measurable effects. Within this period, AIO covers its employees' social and health insurance. A permanent employment contract is given to those who have worked hard, have met and exceeded all work-related requirements, for those two years. As mentioned above, the permanent contract is very profitable for the employee. Within this period, AIO covers its employees' social and health insurance.

Contracts for Seasonal Workers

AIO uses two types of contracts for seasonal workers. One is a contract for a specific work agreement, which carries specific tasks with social and health insurance premiums covered by the employer, usually without an extended benefits package. Contracts for specific work are assigned within AIO for the following jobs: hosting events during international fairs and seasonal jobs for students during holidays. The other is a contract of mandate, which is given when the outcome of the casual employee's performance is tangible, e.g. the translation of a products catalogue, building a new warehouse, etc.

Summary of the Rewards System

AIO uses three types of rewards: base salary, performance-based rewards and non-monetary rewards. Base salary is a gross income that an individual is paid each month, regardless of their performance. A performance-based reward is given to employees on the basis of the value of their contributions to the company's performance. Employees who make greater contributions are given higher pay than those who make lesser contributions. Rather than increasing the person's base salary at the end of the year, an individual instead receives 5–15 percent of their net sales in conjunction with demonstrated performance during that performance period (at the beginning of each month). This kind of reward system is very likely to be used when performance can be objectively assessed in terms of number of units of output or similar measures, rather than via a subjective assessment by a superior. Non-monetary rewards are also other ways by which AIO's employees are rewarded for their performance. In addition to monetary and non-monetary rewards, the head managers have found another way to motivate their employees. They enable their workers to set their own goals, make decisions and solve problems. This strategy applies mainly to the administrative and sales departments. What is more, AIO's owners wanted to increase the motivation of IT and accountancy workers, so they now give them the opportunity to make decisions on their own. AIO's owners are aware of the fact that motivation is important at work, although they also know how important communication in an organization is. Thus, once each month, AIO organizes whole company meetings. These meetings usually begin with a short training session for employees. During the afternoon there is a dinner in a restaurant. If possible, AIO's partners from Germany attend these meetings. As AIO's employees underline, it is much easier and more enjoyable for them to work with people they know in person, rather than working with people known only via e-mails or telephone conversations.

Class Discussion

1 Identify reward systems in "Alfa and Omega". Is the reward system used by AIO an efficient and effective way of motivating employees work according to their job requirements?
2 What motivational tools are used by AIO owners? Would you consider them as effective in a small to medium enterprise in your country? Would you recommend any changes to AIO's owners?

Role Play Exercise

A focus group has been set up to consider issues of hiring new employees and signing contracts with them. The goal of the group is to create a list of evaluation criteria for job positions and to choose appropriate types of contracts of employment for each job position.

The group should hire 5 new employees:

* a customer service supervisor,
* a translator of a new catalogue from German to Polish,
* an external sale representative,
* a part-time worker to help in a warehouse,
* a translator and an interpreter for a five-day international exhibition in Milan, Italy.

Class Discussion

- Why is it important to motivate employees? How should employers motivate their employees?
- Unlike in the old reward system, the new strategies implemented at AIO include quantitative and qualitative components. In what ways do the implemented strategies encourage employees' motivation towards work and team work?
- Consider the future effect of the introduction of the Euro as a currency in Poland on the AIO's imports from Germany.
- Consider and discuss similarities and differences in providing employment contracts and motivation systems in similar types of companies between Poland and your country.

References

Central Statistical Office (2015). Employment, wages and salaries in national economy in 1st half of 2015; accessed at http://www.stat.gov.pl/gus/5840_685_PLK_HTML.htm

Griffin, R. W. (2008). *Management* (9th edition). Boston: Houghton Mifflin Company.

Narodowy Bank Polski (National Bank of Poland). Exchange rates. (17th November 2010); accessed at http://www.nbp.pl/home.aspx?f=/kursy/kursy_archiwum.html

Narodowy Bank Polski (National Bank of Poland). Official exchange rate page; accessed on 14th October, 2015, at http://www.nbp.pl/.

Polish Ministry of Economic Affairs and Labor: Polish Labor Law (2015). http://baltic.mg.gov.pl/LabourMarket/sll (accessed 10th January, 2010).

Sejm of the Republic of Poland. Internet Legal Act System; accessed at http://isap.sejm.gov.pl/DetailsServlet?id= WDU19640160093 (accessed 15th January, 2010).

The Money Converter: website for currency conversions; accessed on 31st of October, 2015, at http://themoney converter.com/PLN/USD.aspx

The Social Insurance Institution (2010); accessed at http://www.zus.pl/default.asp?p=1&id=24

15

Romania
Employee Motivation at a Romanian Clothing Manufacturing Company

Kinga Kerekes[1]

The surrounding hills were colourfully shining in the sun on this late October morning, when Mihaela Popa was driving to her second meeting with the CEO of Textico Romania Ltd.,[2] Mr. Ionescu. During the past week she had driven this way every day and spent several hours at the company to collect data for the report she was going to present at the meeting she was heading towards.

The Company and the Challenge It Faced

Textico Romania Ltd. was established in 2006, its main activity being clothing manufacturing. The company is settled in a small town in Romania, where all activities are carried out, including production, distribution, administration and management. The main product of the company is shirts, and it operates in the following way: raw materials and designs are provided by the foreign customers, Textico workers sew the shirts, and the company transports the products weekly to Western Europe where the customers sell them in various shops. Unused materials are sent back to the customer.

The company employs 62 people: a CEO (who is the owner of the company), a technical manager, a production manager, an acquisition manager, one programmer, two production technologists, two accountants, two storekeepers, five quality inspectors, 42 seamstresses in production and four packers. Textico believes that the main asset of the company is its employees; thus management concern grew when the employee turnover rate increased in the first quarter of 2015, and employees who left were recruited by a company with a similar profile set up recently in a bigger city situated within 40 km.

As the company does not employ a human resources (HR) professional, the CEO decided to approach an HR consultant to help diagnose the source of the problem and find solutions.

Mihaela Popa, the HR consultant contracted by Textico, graduated in 2012 from the Management specialisation at the Babeş-Bolyai University Faculty of Economics and Business Administration in Cluj-Napoca, the second largest city in Romania. During her studies, she completed a 9-month internship offered by the HR department of an important multinational company with a branch in Cluj-Napoca. After graduation, she returned to her city of origin and started up her own HR consultancy.

Mihaela suggested that motivational problems lay behind the growing turnover, but Mr. Ionescu disagreed: "Our employees are happy and we take very good care of them," he said at the first encounter with the HR consultant. He continued:

> Wages at Textico are composed of fixed and variable amounts. The basic wages are calculated based on hours worked, and the gross wages are registered in the work contract. The basic wage of each worker in production equals the minimum wage established by law. Administrative staff have higher wages. This basic wage is complemented by allowances prescribed by law (for night-shift, overtime work, etc.) and length of service. The variable wage depends on performance and quality: workers who exceed the prescribed norm or make no mistakes in a batch of ten shirts, receive bonus points, which are translated into money at the end of the month. The opportunity to earn higher wages motivates employees to work faster and with greater accuracy. Negative motivation is also used: those who commit errors receive negative points, which are then translated into a wage decrease. We carefully monitor work performance; we can identify precisely who made mistakes in each phase of production. We have opted for these motivational tools because good quality products and keeping to deadlines are most important for our company. Besides the performance-related bonuses, we use other motivational tools as well, such as regular health check-ups, gifts offered for Christmas and Easter, surprises for the employees' children on International Children's Day (1st June). Workplace conditions are decent, relationships between supervisors and subordinates are friendly, and workers are praised when they perform well. So, we do everything to motivate them to work hard.

Nevertheless, the CEO approved Mihaela's request to carry out a survey among the company's employees. In the following week each of the 61 employees completed the questionnaire designed by Mihaela, so a complete picture could be drawn.

Background Information on Romania

Population Data

Romania is one of the largest countries in Central and Eastern Europe (CEE), with a territory of 238,391 km^2 and a population of 20.1 million inhabitants as registered at the Census from 2011. Around 54 percent of the population lives in the urban area (cities and towns) and the share of women within the total population is 51.4 percent. The population is aging and demographic trends are negative. In the period 2002–2011 the total population decreased by 1.6 million (7.2 percent), mostly because of emigration, but also due to natural decrease (Census, 2011). Negative natural increase and emigration has continued since 2011, thus the population further decreased to 19.9 million in 2015 (NIS, 2016). Overall life expectancy in 2014 was 75.4 years, around five years below the EU average (NIS, 2016).

The educational level of the population is unfavourable: only 15.9 percent of the 25–64-years-old population had completed tertiary education in 2014 (the lowest share among the EU countries and just above half of the EU28 average of 29.3 percent), while early leavers from education and training[3] reached 18.1 percent (Eurostat, 2016).

Economy and Business Environment

The country has changed dramatically in the last 25 years from political, social and economic viewpoints. After the fall of the communist regime in December 1989, democratic institutions were installed and the transition began from a state-controlled economy towards a capitalist free-market economy. In the first ten years of transition the economy of Romania shrank, and over 3.5 million jobs were lost. After 2000, the economy of Romania started to grow, but the global economic and financial crisis of 2008 impacted Romania severely.

According to World Economic Forum data (Schwab, 2015), Romanian GDP in 2014 was US$200 billion (representing 0.36 percent of the world total GDP) and GDP per capita reached US$10,035 (on a growing trend). Still, Romania is one of the poorest and least developed countries of the European Union (EU) and GDP per capita in Purchasing Power Standards (PPS) just exceeds half of the EU average (54 percent in 2014). Over 8.5 million people are considered to be at risk of poverty according to European standards[4] (Eurostat, 2016).

The Global Competitiveness Index for Romania in 2015–2016 was set at 53 (out of 140 economies) with a score of 4.3 (on a scale from 1 to 7), according to the World Economic Forum Global Competitiveness Report (Schwab, 2015). Romania achieved the highest scores (above 5 points) for macroeconomic environment, health and primary education, and the lowest (below 4 points) for innovation, infrastructure, institutions and business sophistication.

According to the World Bank Ease of Doing Business ranking (World Bank, 2014), in 2015 Romania occupied the 48th position out of 189 economies. The best rankings were granted for getting credit (7) and for the ease of starting a business[5] (38), and the worst, for getting electricity (171) and dealing with construction permits (140).

Labour Market

Several aspects of the Romanian labour market have been modified over the past quarter century, including the legal framework regarding employment, working age limits, ownership of enterprises, distribution of the labour force within the different professions and sectors of the economy, and geographical distribution of employment opportunities.

At present, Romania offers far fewer job opportunities and much lower wages than other countries in the European Union (EU). The employment rate among 20–64-year-olds was 65.7 percent in 2014, slowly increasing since 2010 (64.8 percent), but much below the EU28 average of 69.2 percent, while the unemployment rate of 15–74-year-olds was 6.8 percent in 2014, slightly decreasing since 2010 and lower than the average of EU28 of 10.2 percent (Eurostat, 2016).

The share of employment in agriculture and forestry in Romania is traditionally very high (29 percent in 2014), in industry it is 29 percent, while services account for 42 percent of employment (NIS, 2016). High employment in agriculture conceals hidden unemployment and a lack of alternative forms of employment. Salaried employees represent only 69.5% of the employed population, while 30.5% are self-employed. The average number of employees in 2014 was 4.5 million (NIS, 2016).

Foreign-owned companies employed fewer than 5,000 people in Romania in 1995, while this number increased to 557,000 in 2014, representing 12.4 percent of the total number of employees in the entire Romanian economy (NIS, 2016). SMEs (small and medium-sized enterprises) represent 99.6 percent of the companies in Romania, but they only account for half of the sales revenue and 66.4 percent of total employees (Eurostat, 2016).

HRM Practices

Regarding HRM practices of Romanian companies, we have to differentiate between SMEs and large companies (companies with more than 250 employees). SMEs very often do not have an HR department or employ an HR professional, and HR-related functions are undertaken by the general manager and accountant. As a general practice, HR professionals can be found in companies with over 70–100 employees. Even in large multinational companies, however, line managers make the final decision regarding most of the interventions in the key functions of HR, based usually on consultation with the HR department. Only seldom is the final decision maker the representative of the local HR department. Recruitment and health and safety are those areas where HR departments are generally in charge. External service providers are most often used for training and development, but also for recruitment and selection. Currently, Romanian HR managers consider attracting and retaining a skilled workforce the most important task they face (Kerekes *et al.*, 2015).

The labour force lacks work experience and the skills required by employers. The degree of qualification mismatch in Romania represents about 20 percent of the workforce: 7–9 percent of employees in Romania are over-qualified and about 10 percent under-qualified (IMF, 2015). Soft skills needed for the labour market, such as entrepreneurship and digital skills, are insufficiently developed and participation in adult education is the lowest in the EU (1.5 percent in 2014 compared with an EU average of 11 percent) (Eurostat, 2016). The availability of staff with key abilities was mentioned by 84 percent of managers participating in a recent survey as the main threat to company growth, but only 32 percent of the companies have a strategy in place for talent promotion (PwC Romania, 2015).

Labour productivity per hour worked in Romania in 2013 was €5.6, compared to €32.1 in the EU28 (Eurostat, 2016). Between 2009 and 2014 productivity in both the tradable and non-tradable sectors rose by 6 percent, while compensation per employee grew during the same period by 2 percent and 3 percent respectively (European Commission, 2016).

In Romania, wages are benchmarked using average gross salaries. The average monthly gross wage in Romania in 2014 was equivalent to €524 (nett wage €382), much lower than in other EU countries. The average gross hourly wage in Romania was €2, while the EU average is €19.6. Women generally earn 12.1 percent less than men. Wages differ across economic sectors: the highest wages are paid in the financial services and oil/gas extraction sectors, while the lowest are in the hospitality industry, food industry and clothing manufacturing (NIS, 2016).

Under Romania's Labour Code, the statutory minimum wage is set by government decision after consultation with trade unions and employers' organisations. The minimum wage has increased considerably over the last years: from €162 per month in 2012 to €235 per month in 2015. In relative terms, the minimum wage grew from 34 percent of the average wage in 2012 to about 43 percent in 2015. As a consequence, the share of workers earning the minimum wage increased substantially, with currently more than 30 percent of registered employees estimated to be receiving the minimum wage, compared with below 10 percent until 2012. Minimum wage earners are concentrated in specific sectors (such as hospitality services, light industry, food industry, transport and storage, construction) where cost-competitiveness issues may arise, hampering employment prospects for low-skilled workers in these sectors (European Commission, 2016). A person earning the minimum wage has to work for almost one month to earn the money the CEO of his/her company makes in one hour, according to the Economist (2013). The higher the position one occupies, the closer his/her wage is to that found in Western countries.

Tax on income in Romania is 16 percent and employment income is generally subject to social contributions. The social contribution rates paid by employers and employees apply based on certain calculations as provided by the Romanian Fiscal Code. Employers calculate and withhold social contributions when paying salaries. Tax wedge on labour for a single person earning the average wage was 25.9 percent in 2014 (European Commission, 2016).

As regards the main incentives received by employees in Romania, Casuneanu (2011) found that performance-related bonuses take first place (39.1 percent of cases), followed by bonuses unrelated to performance (holiday premiums) with a weight of 33.1 percent and short-term training courses (26.1 percent), whereas the most important motivating factors are job authority, responsibility and autonomy, job stability and professional development.

Results of the Employee Satisfaction Survey Carried Out at Textico Romania Ltd.

In Textico Romania Ltd., an overwhelming majority of the employees are women (72 percent) and most of them work in production (sewing). Male employees work mainly in the administration (accountancy and acquisition departments), management and technical fields. Administrative tasks are carried out by 11 percent of the employees, while 89 percent work directly in production.

The mean age of the employees is 42 years. Regarding the age structure of the employees, the highest percentage (43 percent) are 41–50 years old, 34 percent are between 31 and 40, 15 percent are 51–65, and only 8 percent are below 30 years of age (the low share of young workers is explained partly by the fact that the company believes that the productivity of the employees with vast work experience is higher and also the desire to move to another workplace is lower at older ages).

Employees without qualifications and work experience earn less than nett 750 RON[6]/month (around 15 percent). Around 66 percent of the employees earn between 750–1200 RON; the wages of the administrative staff (8 percent) are between 1200–1500 RON/month (8 percent) and over 1500 RON (11 percent), depending on their position.

Several employees have been working in the company since the beginning; one third of the employees have 6–9 years in service, another 33 percent 3–5 years, and the rest have been working for the company for less than 3 years.

Regarding education, 11 percent of employees have a university degree, 44 percent graduated high school, 31 percent graduated apprentice professional school, and 13 percent completed only lower secondary school (eight years).

Mihaela wanted to find out how the employees perceived the motivational tools used by Textico and what other motivational tools might be considered important to them. The questionnaire contained a list of tools and the employees had to choose those that they would like the company to offer. They could opt for as many tools as they wanted, without any limitation. Results are shown in Table 15.1.

Mihaela concluded from the answers that an overall wage increase is the preferred motivational tool for an overwhelming majority (82 percent) of the employees, and the second option is a performance-based bonus system (52 percent). Other material benefits, such as meal tickets and money for clothing, were chosen by 39 percent of respondents. Considering that the wage level adopted by the company is rather low (close to the statutory minimum wage), it is understandable that the main concern of the employees is to increase their income.

More than half of the employees would appreciate a flexible work schedule, which would enable them to carry out family responsibilities or, eventually, take up a second job. Thus,

Table 15.1 Motivational tools preferred by Textico employees

Motivational tools	Respondents	
	Number	%
Annual percent of wage increase, irrespective of individual performance	50	82%
Performance-based bonus system	31	53%
Career development within the company, new tasks and responsibilities	10	16%
Regular feedback from the supervisor (praise in case of success)	10	16%
Flexible work schedule	31	51%
Contribution to a private pension scheme	10	16%
Increase of personal security (life insurance, accident insurance, travel insurance)	19	31%
Financial support (for travel, for dislocation, company discount)	12	20%
Other benefits (meal tickets, money for clothing)	24	39%

Source: survey carried out at Textico Romania Ltd., questionnaire developed based on Klein (2009)

besides a better work–life balance, a flexible work schedule would offer opportunities to save costs or to increase income.

Only 16 percent of the employees are motivated by the opportunity of career development, or new tasks and responsibilities; they are the better educated and younger ones, as Mihaela discovered after analysing the questionnaire in greater detail.

Self-actualisation turned out to be an important issue for most of the employees. Independent work is considered to be very important by 71 percent of the employees and only 5 percent consider it unimportant, while personal autonomy is very important to 66 percent and no-one thinks it is unimportant.

Table 15.2 presents average employee satisfaction with the main indicators as identified by Mihaela based on HRM literature and the interviews she carried out prior to the survey.

Regarding workplace conditions, we can see that workers are least satisfied with the climate (temperature, humidity, ventilation, pressure) and noise, while satisfaction is rather high regarding the security of machines and tools. There is room for improvement also with respect to the tidiness and cleanliness of the work premises, which depends very much on the workers' involvement.

Satisfaction with opportunities for career development is above average. The least satisfied are the young and educated employees, who could best be motivated by these opportunities and who believe that management is not open to their innovative ideas.

Indicators of material and moral recognition score rather low: satisfaction with the wage and benefits only receive 3.30 and 2.95 points, respectively, on a five-point scale. This, combined with the previous results regarding a preference for materialistic motivational tools, explains at least partly the growing turnover.

High team cohesion and good cooperation between colleagues could be important for retention, but Textico employees are not very satisfied with these aspects of their work.

Table 15.2 Average employee satisfaction by components

Employee satisfaction indicators	Average score (1 – not at all satisfied to 5 – totally satisfied)
1. Workplace conditions	
Light	4.16
Colours	3.98
Climate (temperature, humidity, ventilation, pressure)	2.95
Noise	3.18
Security of machines and tools	4.28
Condition of order, tidiness, cleanliness at the work premises	3.90
2. Opportunities for career development	
Training opportunities	3.75
Advancement opportunities	3.62
Professional challenges in the present position	3.84
Reception of innovative ideas by the management	3.46
3. Self-realisation	
Independent work	4.03
Personal autonomy	3.79
Job enrichment, higher responsibility	3.54
4. Material and moral recognition	
Wage	3.30
Benefits (meal tickets, bonuses)	2.95
Moral recognition of the work by management	3.56
Moral recognition of the work by colleagues	3.39
5. Relationship needs	
Team cohesion, professional community	3.56
Direct relationship with the direct supervisor	3.92
Cooperation between colleagues	3.36
Helpfulness of colleagues	3.52
Professional reliability of colleagues	3.82
6. Work–private life balance	
Work-related stress	3.30
Free time	3.36
Possibility of working time reorganisation (change of shifts, different starting and leaving time)	3.80
Overall satisfaction index	**3.61**

Source: survey carried out at Textico Romania Ltd., questionnaire developed based on Klein (2009)

Respondents are also rather dissatisfied with work-related stress, but Mihaela could not identify the main factors of stress despite her attempts to discuss this subject with a group of selected workers. Probably they do not trust an "outsider" enough, she concluded.

The overall satisfaction index (calculated as the average of individual satisfaction levels) is 3.61, which shows that the employees are relatively satisfied with the working conditions offered by the company, but there is much room for improvement.

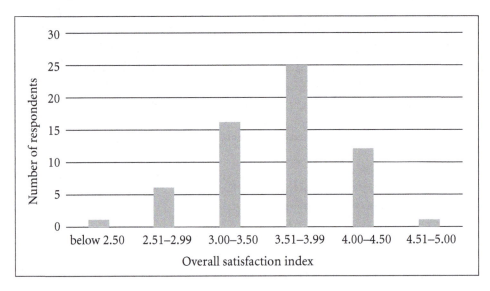

Figure 15.1 Distribution of Textico employees according to their level of work satisfaction

Source: survey carried out at Textico Romania Ltd.

As Figure 15.1 shows, the satisfaction level of the majority of the respondents is above average: 55 persons (90.2 percent) have an average score over 3.00 on a 1 to 5 scale. Mihaela was curious about how age is related to work satisfaction and calculated the correlation coefficient between the two variables. The result shows a weak negative correlation, indicating that older employees are a little less satisfied with their work than younger employees.

Recommendations: An Employee Retaining Strategy for Textico Romania Ltd.

At their first meeting, Mr. Ionescu made it clear to Mihaela that retaining the well-performing workers is the main concern of the company. Both theory and the results of the company-level survey suggested that in order to achieve this aim, the company should take measures to increase the level of satisfaction and motivation of the employees. Mihaela was also aware that competition in the clothing manufacturing sector was harsh and thus Textico could not afford to raise its costs too much without endangering its profitability. Therefore, she tried to focus on possible steps the company could implement on a short-term basis and sustain in the long run.

In her report Mihaela proposed the following solutions:

1 Introduce the "Employee of the month" award, which means that in each month the best performing worker would receive a bonus for a limited period of time (3 to 6 months). This would answer the need for higher income and for performance-recognition expressed by the workers. As this bonus payment would be offered to only a small number of the employees, the costs of this measure would be much lower than an overall increase in wages, but it would motivate employees to perform better.

2 Wherever possible, delegate more responsibility to employees, and leave room for decision-making at each level of the organisational hierarchy.

3 Develop personal autonomy mechanisms, with the involvement of employees carrying out the different tasks. Thus the amount of control from the direct supervisor could be reduced and workers would feel more responsible for their results.

4 Discuss the question of work–life balance in each department and find ways of introducing some flexibility in the work schedule, without disturbing the production process. Take into account individual needs in planning shifts and holidays, as well as extra working hours.

5 Discuss the working conditions in each department and make improvements whenever possible, with a special attention to air conditioning.

6 Offer training opportunities to those employees who would like to advance in their career or to enrich their job.

7 The CEO should be in personal contact with each employee regularly and praise them as often as possible, assuring them that they are important to the company.

8 Organise a party at least once every year when family members are also invited and the achievements of the company are celebrated.

Mihaela Popa was pleased with the outcomes of her report and, on her way to the Textico Romania Ltd. headquarters, she was hoping that her proposals would be well received by Mr. Ionescu, the CEO of the company, and that she would be appointed to lead the changes she had proposed.

Discussion Questions

1 What are the main differences between labour market conditions in Romania and your own home country? How do these conditions influence HRM practices?

2 How do the wages paid at Textico Romania Ltd. compare with wages in other Romanian companies, or to wages in your home country?

3 Which of the proposals presented by Mihaela Popa would you accept if you were the CEO of Textico Romania Ltd.?

4 What do you expect the impact of the "Employee of the month" award on employee motivation to be compared to a general wage increase?

5 Which other (financial or non-financial) measures could Textico Romania Ltd. introduce in order to increase employee motivation?

6 Discuss the influence of age and education on the preferences for motivational tools, as well as on employee satisfaction.

Notes

1 PhD, associate professor at Babeş-Bolyai University, Faculty of Economics and Business Administration from Cluj-Napoca, Romania. E-mail: kinga.kerekes@econ.ubbcluj.ro

2 Although the presented case is based on real data, Textico Romania Ltd. is a fictional name and some company-related data and characters have been altered. Acknowledgments to Éva Serilla, who collected the original data at the company for her BA thesis.

3 Early leavers from education and training represent the percentage of population aged 18–24 with at most lower secondary education and not in further education or training.

4 With an income below the risk-of-poverty threshold, which is set at 60 percent of the national median income.
5 Starting a business in Romania requires 5 procedures, takes 8 days, costs 2.1 percent of income per capita and requires a paid-in minimum capital of 0.7 percent of income per capita (World Bank, 2014).
6 Average exchange rate in 2014 was 1 US$ = 3.3492 RON and €1 = 4.4446 RON (Romanian Lei), according to the National Bank of Romania (www.bnr.ro, accessed on 5/12/2015).

References

Casuneanu, C. (2011). The Romanian employee motivation system: an empirical analysis. *International Journal of Mathematical Models and Methods in Applied Sciences* 5(5), 931–938.
Census (2011). http://www.recensamantromania.ro/rezultate-2/. Accessed 21/11/2015.
Economist (2013). *A week's wages.* http://www.economist.com/blogs/graphicdetail/2013/06/daily-chart-6. Accessed 20/11/2015.
European Commission (2016). *Country Report Romania* 2016. http://ec.europa.eu/europe2020/pdf/csr2016/cr2016_romania_en.pdf. Accessed 30/03/2016.
Eurostat (2016). http://ec.europa.eu/eurostat. Accessed 22/11/2015 and 30/03/2016.
IMF (2015). *Country Report No. 15/80: Romania.* Washington, DC: International Monetary Fund.
Kerekes, K., Zaharie, M., Poór, J. & Kovács, I. É. (2015). Romania. In: Poór, J., Engle, A. D., Szlávicz, Á., Kerekes, K., Szabó, K., Kovács, I. É. & Józsa, I. (eds.): *Human Resource Management issues and challenges in foreign owned companies: Central and Eastern Europe (2011–2013).* Komárno: J. Selye University Faculty of Economics.
Klein, S. (2009). *Vezetés- és szervezetpszichológia (Psychology of leadership and organizations – in Hungarian).* Budapest: Edge 2000.
NIS (2016). http://www.insse.ro/cms/en. Accessed 22/11/2015 and 30/03/2016.
PwC Romania (2015). *Global CEO Survey.* http://www.pwc.ro/ceosurvey2015. Accessed 25/11/2015.
Schwab, K. (ed.) (2015). *The Global Competitiveness Report 2015–2016.* Geneva: World Economic Forum.
World Bank (2014). *Doing Business 2015: Going Beyond Efficiency.* Washington, DC: World Bank Group.

16

Russia

Succession Planning at Eldorado

Anna Gryaznova

In 2008 Ruslan Ilyasov (46) was excited about joining Eldorado, the largest Russian electronics retailer, as its Human Resources Vice President. Since 2000, the company had been growing aggressively, benefitting from the booming Russian consumption market. The number of stores had skyrocketed from just 62 in 2000 to 1,064 at the beginning of 2007. Eldorado was worth more than USD 5 billion (Adelaja, 2007) in 2007 and was the only company not dependent on primary resources among the ten largest Russian private companies.

Eldorado had direct distribution contracts with Bosch, Philips, Samsung, Sony, Panasonic, LG, HP, Nokia and other leading global brands, and offered customers a wide range of electronics and domestic appliances. The company's strategic objective was to become consumers' retailer of choice by being closer to the customers, increasing the quality of its services and offering the products that gave the best value for the money.

2008, a difficult year for Russian retailers, started badly for Eldorado. A criminal investigation into alleged nonpayment of about USD 300 million in taxes was launched against Eldorado's General Director. These allegations provoked a chain reaction: banks began requesting repayment of loans and suppliers began cutting supplies. The successful resolution of the tax dispute coincided with two new developments: the beginning of the global economic downturn, which had a significant effect on Russian consumption, and a change in Eldorado's ownership and management structure. In 2008, the Czech investment group PPF offered Igor Yakovlev, Eldorado's sole shareholder, a way out of the company's liquidity crisis. PPF would pay off USD 400 million of Eldorado's debt in exchange for a 50 percent plus 1 share stake in the company. Yakovlev accepted.

Organizational Setting and Historical Background

Russia is an important country in the world economy. It is the largest country in terms of land area, the ninth-largest country in terms of population and the seventh-largest in terms of GDP (World Factbook, 2016). Russia's global ranking as 79th in terms of per capita GDP means that its consumer and retail market are very attractive from both the short-term and long-term perspectives. In 2004, the value of the overall retail market in Russia was estimated at USD 200 billion, of which the electronics market was valued at USD 5.6 billion. At that time, Eldorado was the largest electronics retailer with control of about 20 percent of the electronics market. The electronics market grew at an annual rate of 15–25 percent from 2000 to 2008, and was very attractive for both Russian and foreign retailers. However, for some reason, western chains delayed their entry into Russia. By the time MediaMarkt (Germany) made it into the Russian market in 2006, three major domestic chains (Eldorado, M.Video, Technosila) were already operating on the national level.

Unlike many other Russian retailers, Eldorado first targeted the peripheral regions and then slowly moved into the lucrative Moscow market, albeit later than many of its competitors. The first Eldorado store was opened in 1994 in Samara, which was shortly followed by a second store in Kazan. When the first Eldorado outlet was opened in Moscow near the end of 2001, the company already operated 255 other outlets across Russia, and was the most recognized electronics and domestic appliances retailer in most regions (Figure 16.1). This was a significant achievement. Given the dramatically unequal regional development in Russia, numerous local administrative barriers, and significant time differences (Russia covers 10 time zones from GMT+2 to GMT+12), Russian and western retailers had been wary about moving into the regions, preferring instead to concentrate their commercial activities in Moscow and St Petersburg – two of Russia's primary industrial and

Figure 16.1 Eldorado operations – geographical overview*

*4 regions, 18 divisions, 350 outlets, 400 franchisee shops in 775 Russian cities; each outlet (400–4,000 m²) employs 20–100 sales personnel

Source: company data as of April 2010

commercial centers. Having established a strong presence in the regions, Eldorado was prepared for quick expansion in Moscow. In 2002, the company opened 15 new outlets in Moscow and set a 20 percent market share target for Moscow. "We are serious about coming to Moscow and we are here to stay," commented Igor Yakovlev in a rare interview (*The Moscow Times*, 2002).

Drastically growing sales however, do not always mean growing profits. Eldorado's management traditionally saw a market leadership position as more important than operational efficiency. However, the new shareholders had a different view and insisted on the addition of efficient asset management to the company's agenda and an increase in Eldorado's operational efficiency. Therefore, a large-scale reorganization was launched, and the company went through a period of massive layoffs and payroll cuts.

HRM in Russia: Past and Present

Labor in Russia

Russia benefitted from the availability of a relatively inexpensive labor force throughout the 1990s and into the beginning of the 2000s. The main features of Russia's labor market are the high elasticity of remuneration, rather than the high elasticity of working time, and the very low elasticity of employment (Kapelyushnikov, 2003).

Despite the deep transformational economic decline experienced during the period of profound market reforms (1990s), Russia managed to keep unemployment at an impressively low level. The labor market adjusted to the new economic conditions through a significant decrease in remuneration and, to a lesser degree, through staff optimization. Russian employees tend to easily adapt to salary decreases, which partially reflects institutional aspects of the Russian economy and partially reflects psychological factors evident during periods of transitional reform.

During the 1990s economic crisis, many formal institutions, including labor law, stopped functioning. The state itself was the first to break the rules by delaying salaries for periods of six months and, more implicitly, allowing the private sector to do the same. The Russian labor code was and remains relatively tough and is extremely employee friendly. It is almost impossible to terminate a labor contract, and the use of fixed-duration employment contracts is strictly limited to cases defined in the labor code. As employers were unable to fire unnecessary employees, employees and employers had to find ways of informally adjusting to changing conditions. Another, more psychological, reason for the ease of adjustment was fear among employees of losing their jobs. During periods of uneasy or turbulent reforms, employees tend to consent to significant salary decreases and delays in payment, as well as to voluntary unpaid leaves of absence. Widespread media coverage of "massive unemployment" in Russia strengthened the trend and contributed to an even greater decline in salaries and to employee demoralization. The fear of unemployment became the strongest social regulator, and, along with the new system of informal relations between employees and employers, helped to prevent a large-scale social crisis. As a result, the labor force remained relatively inexpensive and employers were able to keep extra staff until the early 2000s.

Growth in commodity markets in the 2000s (oil and metals are two major Russian exports) significantly lifted domestic consumption and compensation. At the same time, income differentiation on the regional level increased, while central industrial and commercial centers (Moscow and St Petersburg) quickly became richer.

The market boom coincided with the first managerial staff shortages and the beginning of true competition for talent. The retention of staff became expensive: in the absence of a strong work ethic and a strong corporate culture, employees were willing to opportunistically leave companies for the promise of extra money elsewhere. Fast-moving consumer goods (FMCG) companies and other consumer goods companies were forced to offer annual salaries increases of up to 15–28 percent (while inflation was at 12–15 percent), and sometimes up to 40 percent. However, although salaries grew significantly, they were often starting from a low base. Larger Russian and, later, international companies started hiring the best Russian staff at 25–100 percent above market rates (Neuman International, 2010).

Although the global financial crisis put on pause the competition on the entry and middle management levels, top management remuneration was only selectively affected. While compensation of many top managers in telecommunications, construction and real estate development suffered a substantial decrease (of up to 37 percent), annual compensation for top managers in the oil and gas, and retail industries continued to rise, even at the height of the crisis in 2009.

Top managers' remuneration levels reflected the scarcity of highly qualified managers in the market on both the top and middle levels. The Soviet educational system had supplied the economy with qualified, highly professional personnel, especially in the areas of science, mathematics and related disciplines. Furthermore, having completed a rigorous, disciplined education, aimed at the development of superior intellectual and analytical skills, Russian personnel used to be very advanced in general culture and liberal arts. However, in the early 2000s, employers began complaining about the deterioration in the quality of recent graduates as a result of widespread failures in the educational system, which was undergoing a long and profound crisis (Neuman International, 2010).

Work Attitudes and Ethics

In an interview, Eldorado's founder, Igor Yakovlev, mentioned that Russians do not believe in the "American dream": they do not believe that honest work can allow them to improve their life (Romanova, 2008). Indeed, a certain "laziness" among Russians in relation to work and their tendency to avoid hard work are often mentioned by western employers. Of the many possible explanations for this behavior, two culture-related features of Russian labor relations are notable: collective forms of incentive-based compensation systems, which were common during the Soviet period, and excessive regulation.

Incentive-based compensation systems were used in former Soviet companies and are common in modern Russian companies, but they are implemented in a way that means that most bonuses are distributed equally across the company or across a particular group (Fey et al., 2004). Remuneration, in fact, traditionally consisted of a constant part, fixed in the contract, and seniority premiums and other diverse bonuses not prescribed in the contract and related to achievement of company's objectives. One illustration of this practice is the "13th salary" – a bonus equal to a typical month's reimbursement that many employees receive at the end of the year. As a result, employees view incentives as part of the normal routine rather than as rewards for good performance (Puffer & Shekshnia, 1996). Furthermore, the homogeneous incentive system, which was equally applicable to everyone, had no effect on individual motivation and performance. Retail and sales were the first to introduce individual performance-dependent incentives.

Western employers in Russia are often struck by the high power distance in working relations and the excessive regulation. Strict regulations ("bureaupathology") were meant to reduce the angst and unpredictability of life under the Soviet regime. However, they served as demotivators of positive, constructive working behaviors, discouraged experimentation and promoted a formally strict type of discipline (Astakhova *et al.*, 2010, Kets de Vries *et al.*, 2004). Instead of reducing uncertainty through the acceptance of informal communication channels, companies introduced plenty of new instructions to regulate everyday activities. In turn, this excessive bureaucracy, combined with a cultural preference for strong, authoritative leadership, hinders participation, group work and the delegation of responsibility (the latter is often perceived as reflecting insufficient control of subordinates). However, despite the strict formal regulations, people were always able to find subtle ways to counteract regulations. This behavior, in turn, developed into a system of double morals and the total separation of employees from the managerial bodies.

Another feature of working relations in Russia, which is often attributed to the Soviet past, is the tendency to maintain unnecessary and unjustified secrecy and confidentiality in horizontal and vertical communications. Information is viewed as power. In this respect, managers prefer to keep their power to themselves and to restrict the flow of information to a circle of chosen confidants. At the same time, employees are discouraged from sharing or communicating bad news or concerns, and they are encouraged to formally obey instructions coming from the top. "Initiative should be punished," a phrase from the Soviet period, remains relevant for many Russian employees, who prefer to keep a low profile in a culture that has a low tolerance for mistakes. The strong desire to avoid mistakes and the general lack of accountability might also be traced back to a time when the risk of making a mistake was perceived as so high that it could have a profound impact on one's life and career (May & Ledgerwood, 2007).

Leadership Issues

In times characterized by rapid economic development, deterioration of the educational system and a highly mobile opportunistic labor market, many companies encounter leadership issues. It is expensive to keep the right people and to hire new ones.

One cultural challenge faced by many Russian and foreign companies is the very low prestige associated with simple jobs. Recent graduates are too ambitious and want "to be a CEO in six months". According to a survey by KMS Group, a Moscow-based employment agency, the desired monthly salary of Moscow-based graduates (undergraduate degree) in 2009 was USD 2,230–3,250, while the minimum acceptable salary was USD 1,370–1,630 – well above the amount the majority of employers were ready to pay for entry-level positions (Target Top Twenty, 2010). In addition, graduates expected a salary increase at the end of the first six months of employment. Opportunities for rapid promotion and rapid salary growth were ranked as the primary considerations in job selection among such graduates, as were the company's dynamic development in Russia and abroad.

On a more general level, Russia has a culturally specific management style that differs in several respects from commonly accepted leadership styles in other countries. The results of a comparative study of culturally endorsed management practices in Russia, the US and China is presented in Table 16.1.

Russia scores very high on charismatic leadership style, which reflects the ability of leaders to inspire and motivate others on the basis of firmly held core values. It scores

Table 16.1 Culturally endorsed leadership styles in three countries*

Leadership Style	Russia Eastern Europe	US Anglo	China Confucian
Charismatic	5.66	6.12	5.56
Team-oriented	5.63	5.80	5.57
Participative	4.67	5.93	5.04
Humane	4.08	5.21	5.19
Autonomous	4.63	5.75	3.80
Self-protective	3.69	3.15	3.80

*Minimum of 1, maximum of 7.

Source: GLOBE Study

very low on humane leadership, which would require supportive and compassionate leadership. The line between charismatic and humane leadership is, indeed, blurred. While Russians seem to prefer explicit, formal motivation and reward systems, in actuality much depends on personal relations and on the ability of a supervisor to establish informal links with employees.

In the beginning of the transition from the Soviet planned system to the market economy, many companies uncritically adopted imported HRM solutions (Jackson, 2002). Eldorado was among these companies. It blindly adopted standard working procedures (SWP) in 2006, which seemingly fit the cultural norm of obedience to authorities and solutions imposed from above. However, the imported SWP failed to take into account the subtle complexities of Russian work ethics, work attitudes and the post-Soviet organizational environment, which was more "humanistic" (Jackson, 2002) in nature and relied on "favor-based" relations. As a result, imported SWP were received skeptically by sales personnel, who viewed them as overwhelmingly simplified job instructions. Their introduction, therefore, failed. Eldorado has since revised its SWP and introduced a new version.

Eldorado's HR Context

Human resources management and, more generally, a strong corporate culture, can serve as powerful means for increasing company competitiveness and reducing operational costs. This vital function was neglected throughout the high-paced development of Russian companies in the 2000s. At that point, the main focus was on increasing market share and gaining market leadership, so that asset-management issues, including HR functions, were not a priority for owners and top managers. Often, companies perceived HR as a compliance or bookkeeping function that existed only for the purpose of filling out forms and handling administrative work. This neglect of the HR function originated in Soviet times when industrial relations were regulated through local Communist party bureaus and trade unions, and the personnel function was limited to paperwork and personnel-related accounting. However, the assignment of progressive and strategic functions to HR usually comes with change in majority stakeholders or the introduction of new shareholders interested in optimization and the better use of assets. In that respect, as soon as HR issues are placed on the board's agenda, qualified HR managers are needed to handle them.

Eldorado experienced a strategic shift in its HR activities from serving as a mere administrative function to becoming a more strategic tool. Throughout its development from a small company in 1994 to a giant employer of 31,000 people in 2008, Eldorado's HRM practices were rudimentary. Its main workforce consisted of sales personnel in sales outlets. These jobs are often held by inexperienced students looking for extra money. Eldorado, along with other Russian companies, focused on hiring young, less-experienced sales employees, who were assumed to be more open-minded. The company viewed the need to train these employees and provide them with the necessary skills as far easier to fulfill than the need to change the possibly negative working attitudes of more-experienced staff. As a result, the average age of the sales force at Eldorado was 20–30, while the average age of stores managers was 30–40. Annual turnover among employees was over 100 percent.

As a result of the high turnover, the company was forced to invest significant amounts in training. Sales people came with diverse educational and professional backgrounds, and they needed formal training in basic skills. For those who enjoyed being a part of the company and expected to stay longer, training provided implicit "proof" that the company took them seriously and was investing in their career development. When the training and development expenditures were cut as part of the cost-saving, anti-crisis campaign in 2009, employees reacted immediately and negatively, as reflected in the low work-satisfaction figures. Furthermore, as training was provided locally and out of a strategic context, it failed to have a positive impact on retention.

Recruiting from within is an efficient, lessexpensive practice than external recruiting, and almost always results in a better fit. Internal recruiting also helps to strengthen the corporate culture and promote corporate values. Eldorado historically focused on finding its first-line managers (store supervisors and managers) from within, believing that a good sales assistant might easily become a supervisor and/or an outlet manager. Promotion decisions were traditionally made by upper-level regional managers without the input of Eldorado's HR department. Sales personnel were slated for promotion on the basis of their past sales performance and on the basis of the subjective judgments of regional managers. However, as qualified and successful sales professionals, those promoted often lacked the necessary management skills, competencies and leadership/people management abilities. Furthermore, Eldorado did not provide sufficiently extensive adaptation periods, so that success depended on the new managers' abilities to cope when they suddenly found themselves managing former colleagues and friends. Furthermore, the working schedule of a manager differed from that of a sales employee. Rather than working only 8-hour shifts, new managers quickly found themselves deep into 14–15-hour working days. Finally, there were no role models for newly appointed managers to observe or follow.

The spontaneous, subjective selection of managers resulted in high turnover of first-line management personnel of 67 percent per year, with an average period-of-service in new positions of less than 11 months.

Problems and Issues

Ruslan, an experienced, western-educated professional, had matured professionally through a number of assignments with several of the largest Russian and multinational companies (Alcoa Russia, Yukos Oil Company, The Coca-Cola Company). After completing a quick audit of HR functions at Eldorado, Ruslan knew that the high turnover of first-line managers was one of the weakest characteristics of this rapidly developing company. Instead of

Table 16.2 Responsibilities of outlet managers and supervisors

Outlet manager	Outlet supervisor
• Operational management of the outlet • Control of sales, merchandising and service standards • Sales volume control • Organization and control of personnel • Introduction and implementation of standard work procedures • Selection, adaptation and training of personnel • Control technical maintenance of the outlet, and appearance of sales area and windows • Maintaince of outlet's warehouses • Contact with landlords • Contact with various public authorities	• Coordination of sales personnel • Participation in adaptation and training processes • Ensure order and cleanliness of shopping area • Assist in resolution of complex issues related to the shopping area

Source: company data

capitalizing on the existing knowledge of its managers, Eldorado had to invest in the training and development of entry-level newcomers.

In fact, Ruslan knew that first-level line managers (store managers) were responsible for a range of HR functions (Table 16.2) and that they often substituted formal HR practices with informal processes. They diffused the company's values and mission, established appropriate behavior norms, shared information and encouraged responses to challenges through their routine daily contact with employees (Fey, 2004). He was also aware that high managerial turnover has a negative effect on important "ingredients of success" in developing companies, such as belief systems, boundary systems, and interactive control systems, which help make management development more successful (Fey, 2004). In the Russian context, these "ingredients of success" would help reduce the feelings of uncertainty and insecurity that normally arose hand-in-hand with any quick organizational development and transformation.

Ruslan decided to focus the attention of Eldorado's management on freezing the excessive turnover among first-line managers in order to develop and strengthen the continuity of managerial competencies on the shop floor level. The HR department launched a comprehensive assessment of store managers and supervisors, as the latter position often served as a transition job for future store managers. Nine hundred people went through the comprehensive assessment, which was designed to evaluate their managerial potential through group discussions, case interviews, 360° evaluations and tests of business process knowledge (Table 16.3).

The comprehensive assessment project ended with the selection of 118 candidates to participate in a succession-planning program. The objectives of the program were to extend the duration of store managers' service from 11 months to 3–5 years, and to strengthen positive working attitudes among managers. Candidates were split into groups of three, and each group was assigned a coach – an experienced store manager – who was tasked with assisting group members during a one-year transition period to a managerial position. The one-year training program included two introduction weeks with the coach (one week with the employee shadowing the coach and one week in which the roles were reversed),

Table 16.3 Components of the comprehensive assessment procedure

Assessment instrument	Focus of assessment	Weight
Face-to-face meeting with HR manager	Quarterly performance results and budgetary indicators	40%
Assessment	Managerial competencies • Customer orientation • Leadership • Influence and persuasion • Goal orientation	25%
Professional test	Business process knowledge	20%
360° evaluation	Self-assessment, and assessment by a direct supervisor, colleagues and subordinates	15%

Source: company data

four mandatory training sessions of three to four days each for both candidates and their coaches, and four annual group meetings with upper management.

Mentoring is one skill that develops with experience but it is a skill that is not generally favored in Russian culture. To overcome this culturally based neglect of mentoring behavior, the company decided to look for coaching candidates with proven success stories, developed communication skills and a strongly pronounced motive to train people. As one of the young managers (26 years old, three years as an outlet manager) and successful mentors put it: "One of the major motives for me is to be able to communicate with people and to learn through them."

The company also introduced financial incentives for both candidates and their mentors. Successful candidates would receive a regionally dependent bonus of RUB 200,000 to RUB 300,000 (approximately USD 7,000–10,000; roughly equivalent to one quarter's salary) after completing their first year as an outlet manager. Mentors would receive a bonus of RUB 50,000 to RUB 75,000 (USD 1,700–2,500) for each of the assigned candidates who successfully completed one year in the new position.

The HR department also insisted on the revision of procedures for appointments and terminations. All managerial job assignments, which had previously been handled spontaneously and subjectively by division managers, had to go through a procedure of a double approval by the vice-presidents of both human resources and sales.

The immediate results of the program were promising. The annual turnover among store managers turnover fell from 67 percent to 28 percent. The program also succeeded in promoting horizontal networking between experienced and newly assigned store managers, and providing the latter with transition guidance.

Groups Assignments and Case Discussion Questions

1 List and discuss the advantages and potential drawbacks of the new succession planning program.
2 Design a training program for newly appointed outlet managers. Take into consideration not only the specific skills they need to acquire but also the new positioning of Eldorado and new composition of the company's board.
3 What risks (organizational, cultural, etc.) might Ruslan have come across when implementing the new succession planning system?

4 What risks might be associated with the payment of a financial bonus after completion of the first year on the job?

5 Given the predominantly charismatic, team-oriented leadership style in Russia (Table 16.1) and the managerial competencies required for the job (Table 16.3), design a profile of the most desirable store manager candidate. Using the profile, conduct short assessment interviews in your small group to identify potential candidates for a job as an Eldorado outlet manager.

6 If you were in charge of human resource management at Eldorado, how would you increase the prestige of sales positions?

7 What kind of changes in HR policy do you forecast based on the growing importance of online-based sales?

References

Adelaja, T. (2007). U.K. Store Ditches Its Plans For Russia. *The Moscow Times*, June 6.

Astakhova, M., DuBois, C., and Hogue, M. (2010). A Typology of Middle Managers in Modern Russia: an Intracultural Puzzle. *International Journal of Intercultural Relations* (in press).

Fey, C., Pavlovskaya, A., and Tang, N. (2004). Does One Shoe Fit Everyone? A Comparison of Human Resource Management in Russia, China, and Finland. *Organizational Dynamics*, 33(1), 79–97.

Jackson, T. (2002) The Management of People Across Cultures: Valuing People Differently. *Human Resource Management*, 41(4), 455–475.

Kapelyushnikov, R. (2003). Mekhanismy formirovaniya zarabotnoy platy v Rossii. *GU-HSE*.

Kets de Vries, M., Shekshnia, S., Korotov, K., and Florent-Treacy, E. (2004). The New Global Russian Business Leaders. (New Horizons in Leadership Studies Series). Cheltenham/Northampton: Edward Elgar.

May, R., and Ledgerwood, P.E. (2007). One Step Forward, Two Steps Back: Negative Consequences of National Policy on Human Resource Management Practices in Russia. In Domsch, M.E., and Lidokhover, T., *Human Resource Management in Russia (Contemporary Employment Relations Series)*. Ashgate Publishing Limited, pp. 25–42.

Neuman International AG. Human Resources in Russia. www.neumann-compensation.com, retrieved on 01 June 2010.

Puffer, S.M., and Shekshnia, S.V. (1996). The fit between Russian culture and compensation. *The International Executive*, 38(2), 217–241.

Romanova, T. (2008). Our objective is to become an international corporation, an interview with Eldorado's owner Igor Yakovlev. *Vedomost*, February 11. www.vedomosti.ru, retrieved on 30 November, 2016.

Target Top Twenty: Annual Rating of Graduate Employers. http://target.egraduate.ru, retrieved on 1 June 2010.

The Moscow Times (2002). October 11.

The World Factbook. www.cia.gov, retrieved on 7 March 2016.

17

Slovenia

On Becoming a Truly Global Player: The Global Talent Management Challenge at Trimo

Robert Kaše

The sun was just setting behind the Burj Al Arab, when Sonja Klopčič, Competencies Development Manager at Trimo, was taking off from Dubai airport. Admiring the intense golden colour of the glowing desert below her she was still thinking about the events of the last couple of days in Trimo's subsidiary in Fujairah, United Arab Emirates (UAE) and about a phone call she received earlier today from the company headquarters in Trebnje, Slovenia.

The world city of Dubai was a venue for an important step in Trimo's continuous internationalization process. Just hours before heading back home, Sonja had finalised all the arrangements and formalities to hire Šenaj Avdić as the first third-country national (TCN) ever to head a subsidiary in Trimo's international network. The appointment of the new Managing Director of Trimo's United Arab Emirates subsidiary was a result of an intense recruiting and selection process which unfolded for several months and had come to a close over the last three days. One evening after a hard day of interviewing while Sonja was still weighing the pros and cons of hiring a TCN, she was interrupted by a phone call from Marta Strmec, Director of HRM and General Affairs at Trimo. Marta informed her that Trimo had a big new business in India and that Tatjana Fink, Trimo's General Manager, was planning a meeting on Monday to discuss this further. She asked her to think about the situation and prepare a short proposal on how to staff operations in India, where Trimo was not present.

Sonja had about eight more hours of flying and a weekend before the meeting, so enough time to draft a couple of initial ideas and suggestions. However, she was not really sure if she could prepare a good proposal by Monday. There were simply too many challenges related to the global talent management at Trimo that had surfaced also during the last couple of days in the UAE. What could an ambitious MNC from a small country do to successfully compete on the global expatriate market? What makes companies like Trimo attractive to international talent? Is a small MNC capable of retaining its expatriates? Is there a difference if they are TCNs? Does the composition of human resources and organization of the company's international operations reflect its ambitions? Can it be compared to similar foreign multinationals? Is it possible to run a global MNC from a small town in Slovenia?

She was playing with the idea of starting a broader discussion about IHRM and global talent management at Trimo at the meeting on Monday rather than just putting together a couple of ideas for staffing operations in India, when a flight attendant interrupted her: "Pasta or chicken?"

Historical Background – From a Local Manufacturer to an International Complete Solutions Provider

Trimo, a joint-stock company, is one of the leading European providers of original and complete solutions in pre-fabricated steel buildings, roofs, façades, steel constructions, and containers. Examples of its solutions include buildings such as (see Exhibit 17.1): Heathrow airport terminal 3 (London, UK), IKEA shopping centres (Bursa, Turkey; Sevilla, Spain; Shanghai, China; Dhahran, Saudi Arabia) a Porsche car showroom (Amsterdam, The Netherlands) the Airbus A380 Paint Shop (Hamburg, Germany), Astana Arena sport stadium (Astana, Kazakhstan), Xpand 6D cinema and entertainment centre (Ljubljana, Slovenia), and a Mercedes production facility (Vitoria, Spain).

The early days of the company go back to 1961, when its first major predecessor *Kovinsko podjetje Trebnje* was founded, and 1971, when several local manufacturers of metal elements and stainless steel equipment joined in to establish Trimo. In 1991 when Slovenia became independent the company lost its established former Yugoslav markets and was exposed to a transition from a socialist to a capitalist socio-economic system. In the following years Trimo went through a complete restructuring including ownership change, products redefinition, market reorientation, optimization of technological processes, organizational structure redesign, and a profound change in management philosophy. The most important change agent was the newly appointed top management team led by the General Manager Tatjana Fink, who has been leading the company since 1992. Amongst the novelties that Mrs Fink and her team introduced were the annual mottoes, which described the general motivation and direction of the company for the coming year.

The first yearly motto for 1992, "*Satisfied customers generate the highest profit*", indicated Trimo's strong determination to move away from its prevailing manufacturing mentality and adopt a customer orientation. This fundamental change went hand in hand with management and employee development, streamlining of their operations, and the increasing role of a continuous improvement process allowing Trimo to start closing the gap between them and their foreign competitors. In 1997 the motto "*Trimo Business Excellence is our common goal*" showed that Trimo wanted to expand excellence to all areas of the business. At the same time they introduced a new line for continuous production of light construction panels, which positioned the quality of Trimo's products in line with their competitors and fulfilled technological conditions for further internationalization. By 2001 Trimo felt strong enough to formalize their ambition and new business model into a redefined vision: "We will become the leading European company offering complete solutions in the area of steel buildings."

Their *complete solutions* business model relates to the broad range of products they produce and an entire spectrum of services they offer (see Figure 17.1). In contrast to competitors such as Paroc (Finland), Kingspan (UK), Thyssenkrupp Hoesch Bausysteme (Germany),

Figure 17.1 Trimo's complete solutions operations

Pflaum & Söhne (Austria), and Astron Building (Luxemburg), who are all manufacturers with relatively focused production programs, Trimo provides its customers with complete customized solutions from rough ideas to finished buildings. Pursuing this business model enabled Trimo to establish long term relationships with well-known clients such as IKEA and Tesco.

The year 2001 brought another turning point for Trimo as they opened the first production site outside Slovenia in Kovrov (Russia) along with several sales subsidiaries across Europe. Whereas internationalization of the company in terms of exports has been rising since the beginning of the 1990s, these developments accounted for an important leap in foreign assets and foreign employment of the company. At the same time international talent management became an important issue for them.

The next years (2003–2007) were dominated by Trimo's ambition to become the most innovative company in the industry by following the principles of a learning organization, investing heavily in competencies and product development, and adopting open-innovation principles. One of their goals was to make 30 percent of annual revenues in sales of new products (i.e., products that have been on the market for three years or less). This orientation resulted in a portfolio of highly innovative panels such as the photovoltaic roof panel EcoSolar PV, the completely customizable MultiVario façade panel, the Red Dot awarded ArtMe panel, and the highly aesthetic modular façade system Qbiss.

Over the next few years Trimo became one of the leading top European players in their business with strong emphasis on knowledge, innovation and sustainable development. The company and its employees received a lot of recognition for their solutions and business excellence from domestic and international stakeholders, including several important international awards (e.g., EFQM prize winner for leadership). The company accomplished its vision and faced new challenges. How to grow further and become a truly global player amidst the financial crisis? How to fight the stagnation of the construction business and looming global sustainability issues? Trimo's determination to address these challenges successfully was reflected in their 2009 motto "*Just do it. The best you can.*"

Internationalization of Trimo

Trimo gained initial international experience by exporting metals for large infrastructure projects in the Third World before the 1990s. After 1991, the loss of the Yugoslav market and the (small) scale of the new Slovenian domestic market demanded quick and intense internationalization. The expansion started with exporting to Western European markets, especially to Germany, and emerging East European markets. By the late 1990s Trimo had already created between 40 and 50 percent of their revenues in 30, predominantly European, countries. In 2009 Trimo's solutions were exported to 45 countries around the world creating 77 percent of all revenues abroad (see Figure 17.2). Slovenia, as the domestic market, remained the largest individual market. Other important markets included Russia, Great Britain, Germany, the Netherlands, Hungary, Croatia, and Serbia.

At the outset, Trimo was entering foreign markets through sales representatives and sales subsidiaries, later also by means of joint ventures and subsidiaries with manufacturing facilities. In 2009 Trimo was directly present in 27 countries. The majority of the company's more recent internationalization efforts were aimed at strengthening the sales network and establishing subsidiaries with manufacturing facilities in order to enlarge the radius of their potential business activity (transportation costs are an important factor in the industry and determine the radius within which companies can service the market). Whereas sales subsidiaries were strongly dependent on the parent company, subsidiaries with production plants had more autonomy. Above and beyond formal reporting mechanisms, there were also more subtle integration mechanisms such as jointly organized external training and symposia, a common Trimonet web portal along with the Annual Sales Network Meeting and Trimo Group Strategic Conference.

In addition, Trimo were very active in non-contractual modes of international cooperation, which was consistent with their stakeholder and open-innovation approaches. They cooperated with foreign architects, engineers, designers and researchers on multinational R&D projects, facilitated formal networks of their suppliers and business partners and trained them, and organized open-ended international competitions in relevant research areas and design.

Although a vibrant international company with numerous foreign collaborators, Trimo remained headquartered in a small town in one of the greenest regions of Slovenia, where most of the key employees came from. Trimo's top management team was composed only of

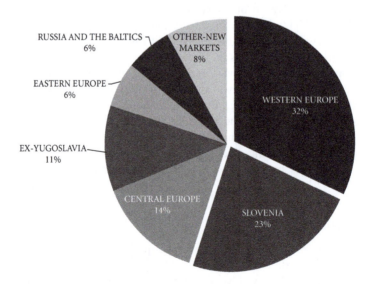

Figure 17.2 Trimo's regional sales structure in 2009

parent country nationals (PCNs). One of their more recent annual reports even emphasized that all members of the top management team were locals.

Employees and HRM Practices at Trimo

Their philosophy of managing people is described as the Trimo Way and follows the corporate values: reliability, responsibility, innovativeness, passion, partnership, and trust. It is founded on the awareness that teams, not individuals, are the key to company's success. The company formalized it by defining a true Trimo employee and setting the Trimo standards.

In 2009 Trimo employed 522 employees in the parent company and 1,213 in the whole Trimo Group. Figure 17.3 clearly shows that due to expanding foreign operations, foreign employment fuelled total employment growth. To characterize their workforce further, 85 percent of employees were employed permanently and full-time, 47 percent had a college or university degree and 70 percent of their workforce was male. Interestingly, in the management structure the percentage of women was higher. The average age of employees was 40. In 2009 staff turnover in the parent company was around 9.2 percent, whereas it amounted to 19.5 percent in affiliated companies.

Designing the HRM practices Trimo tried to strike a balance between career aspirations of individuals and strategic goals of the company. Therefore, they regularly monitored HRM effectiveness by measuring employee satisfaction, turnover of key employees, value added to cost per employee ratio, absenteeism, and competency development. New approaches to

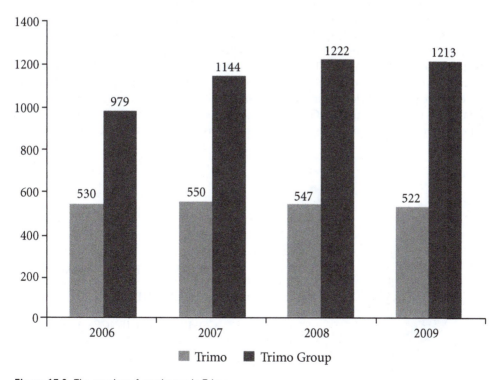

Figure 17.3 The number of employees in Trimo

managing people were usually developed in the parent company and after a period of successful implementation they were disseminated to affiliated companies.

When recruiting Trimo benefited from a strong employer brand in Slovenia and more broadly in south-eastern Europe, whereas it was still working on its recognition on the global talent/expatriate markets. In the focal period the company was paying particular attention to developers, managers of engineering projects, and international salesmen.

Amongst the most important long-term recruitment sources were international competitions and scholarships. International competitions for best research theses (annual Trimo Research Awards), architectural solutions (biannual Trimo Architectural Awards), and urban space visions (Trimo Urban Clash) served as opportunities for identifying future employees and collaborators, and as a means of strengthening ties with relevant research and professional institutions. Specifically, until 2009 the company awarded almost 300 individuals, which resulted in fruitful collaborations with almost one quarter of them.

Further, Trimo's scholarships attracted the best undergraduate and graduate students from various disciplines (see Figure 17.4). The scholarship included company-specific summer training, mentoring for student papers, and language courses to facilitate their international orientation. In 2009, Trimo supported some 30 students in their scholarship system.

The company combined traditional and new media to recruit applicants for open positions. Apart from occasional ads in printed media, they created a career leaflet *Creating a global story together* and a special section *Why Trimo* on their corporate web page. They also used employment portals, career-oriented social networking sites, and presentation videos on YouTube to attract candidates. In some cases head-hunters and direct personal search were employed. Trimo's experts were frequently keynote speakers at professional and networking events, guest speakers at universities, and distinguished members of professional associations, which enabled them to spot talent and build an effective employer brand.

Their employee selection procedure started with a purely informative interview conducted by an HRM specialist. The process continued by panel interviews led by an HRM specialist and the head of department searching for a new employee, as well as the existing employees. When selecting individuals for key positions, psychometric testing of candidates was performed, and the General Manager was present at the final interview round. Throughout the selection process, candidates were assessed on their specialist knowledge

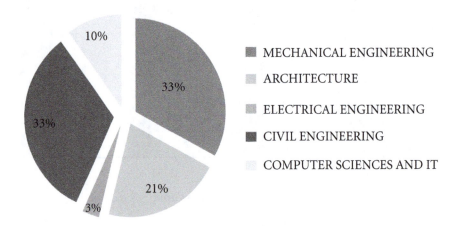

Figure 17.4 Scholarships by area

and accomplishments, their preparedness to accept international assignments, and their fit with the corporate culture.

Development of employees was based on a company-specific competency model and a developmental appraisal process – *The Trimo Dialogue*. The process was not only about mastering expert knowledge, but also about developing corporate values, and emphasizing individuals' responsibility for their personal and professional development. Every employee was involved in an annual discussion with his/her department head about their performance, goals, development of competencies, and career opportunities. Based on this discussion employee development was facilitated by offering additional training, mentoring and coaching, and providing increasingly demanding career opportunities. Formal promotions were based on their achievements, expressed ambition, and energy invested in developing their career path in areas of interest to Trimo.

Trimo provided extensive training opportunities to all their employees. Over 94 percent of training was organized on-site with internal or external trainers. Two training programs were especially important: (1) the 2-year leadership development program *Five Steps* and (2) *Trimo's Sales Academy*. The former was designed for developing leadership competencies of 50 top managers from headquarters and subsidiaries and was expected to have strong spill-over effects. The latter was a highly intensive program for developing sales competencies of about 40 employees from headquarters and the sales network. Both training programs included a follow-up in internal management school and sales coaching respectively. In recent years Trimo has also introduced a standardized orientation week for new employees.

Finally, as far as compensation is concerned Trimo's base pay was above the industry and regional average. In addition, beside base pay, employees could also receive individual pay for performance (up to 30 percent), thirteenth salary (if the profit levels were about a threshold), rewards for extra project work, a Boldest idea award and a holiday allowance. The competition and prize for the *Boldest idea award* was particularly attractive. Besides broad recognition the winners took part in an adventure such as driving a Formula 1 car, experiencing freefall, submerging in a nuclear submarine etc. Each year on average 20 percent of employees were given a raise as a result of promotion.

The HRM Context of Slovenian MNCs

Trimo is headquartered in Slovenia, a small European country (2 million inhabitants; 20,273 sq. km) situated in Central Europe, touching the Alps and bordering the Mediterranean. Slovenia is a parliamentary republic and gained its independence in 1991 after splitting from Yugoslavia. Since 2004 the country has been a member of the European Union and NATO. It is a part of the Eurozone (since 2007) and the OECD (since 2010).

Because of its small domestic market, Slovenia has always been outward-oriented. Exports amount to around 60 percent of the country's Gross Domestic Product. The country's export structure is highly diverse (Slovenia ranks 12th in the world on the Economic Complexity Index), with packaged medicaments, tourism, motor vehicles and vehicles parts, electric and electronic equipment, machinery, and refined fuels representing the largest shares of the country's exports. Slovenia's economy features several important regional MNCs, some niche global leaders, a strongly internationalized SME sector, and a vibrant start-up community. The foreign direct investment (FDI) in Slovenia has been relatively weak in comparison to other East European countries.

The institutional HRM context of the country has been characterized by a very low income inequality (Slovenia's after-tax Gini coefficient is among the lowest in the world), highly protective employment legislation (especially in terms of difficulty and costs of firing), low workforce diversity (about 85 percent of the population is ethnically homogenous), reliance on social dialogue in industrial relations, strong unions in manufacturing and in the public sector, and a relatively high tax on the incomes of higher-earning individuals. Higher taxes go hand in hand with a generous welfare state; however, the sustainability of pension, healthcare, and social security systems in the long run has been put under question recently.

Such a context is challenging for adopting a strategic approach to HRM because the above-mentioned institutional factors importantly constrain leeway for making strategic decisions about people. Historically, the personnel function in Slovenia was completely redefined in the early 1990s, when the country transitioned from the previous workers' self-management system to capitalism. The function changed gradually from being purely administrative, aimed at facilitating employee participation and well-being, towards a more business-oriented function (see Zupan & Kaše, 2005 for more). HRM as a professional area has developed considerably since then, especially in terms of better access to the HRM knowledge base, a stronger and more internationally connected professional community, and a more profound business understanding by HRM managers. Still, the function struggles to have the same strategic role and impact as some other business functions. There are notable exceptions, however, where HRM is considered strategic: strongly internationalized companies are among those companies that are most successful in instilling strategic HRM.

Slovenian national culture has changed somewhat after the big political and institutional changes in the 1990s, but has preserved the emphasis on hard work and a preference for equality. The only official data for Hofstede's cultural dimensions go back to the years when Slovenia was still part of Yugoslavia and report moderately high power distance, low individualism and masculinity, and very high uncertainty avoidance. A more recent replication of the study claims that individualism has increased, power distance has decreased considerably, and masculinity has decreased further.

Consistently with the inward-oriented privatization and low FDI levels MNCs headquartered in Slovenia usually have Slovenian ownership. They are either regional players operating in a specific region of Europe (especially in southeast Europe and Russia) or global market niche leaders. One of the greatest obstacles to further internationalization of these companies is a lack of parent country nationals (PCNs) that are available, capable and willing to accept long-term international assignments. The reasons are multifaceted. First, it is in Slovene national culture to avoid uncertainty, which could be a major issue that discourages international assignments. Second, the absolute number of potential Slovenian PCNs is small due to the size of the country and limited labour market mobility. Next, approximately 90 percent of Slovenians own their apartments or houses – a consequence of the traditional style of living and the approach used in the real-estate privatization process in the early 1990s – which creates high opportunity costs for potential expatriates. Further, Slovenian MNCs most frequently offer expatriate assignments in south-eastern Europe, which for Slovenians is still considered a less attractive region (or even a hardship post). Moreover, Slovenians generally believe that the quality of living in the country is still considerably better than at other locations for which expatriate posts are offered. To support this argument, Slovenia features a lot of landscape diversity in a very small area along with an attractive combination of (sub)urban and countryside life experience. As a final point, Slovenian MNCs often lack experience for effective expatriate management and sometimes show limited capacity to facilitate one of the obvious alternatives of PCN expatriation: assigning TCNs and inpatriates.

An often agreed compromise between Slovenian MNCs and international assignees is the use of international commuter assignment, where assignees still reside at home but drive (or fly) on a weekly or fortnightly basis to affiliated companies. Prospects for building an international assignee pool in the future seem better. A high percentage of Slovenian students going abroad for a study exchange and increasing numbers of students from abroad who study in Slovenia, might improve the situation. However, there are also fears that these developments could make the situation even worse due to a more intense brain drain. How this unfolds might also depend on the effectiveness of repatriation practices in Slovenian companies: potential candidates for expatriate assignments have to see directly how much this career path is realistically worth pursuing.

The Search for Expatriates . . .

Trimo is at a cross-roads, where it has to decide whether the company wants to stay focused on the European market or take the next step and go truly global. The business opportunity in India is a real challenge (i.e., a new continent, large cultural differences, big emerging market) and is timely for Trimo because of the business situation in Europe and Slovenia in 2009 (see Exhibits 2 and 3). It can be seen as a window of opportunity – featuring all possible potential benefits and risks – to take the next step.

To make this next step a success, the company will have to solve the international talent management puzzle. Currently, Trimo supports its internationalization efforts by working intensively with host country nationals (they run many of Trimo's sale subsidiaries), finding suitable TCNs on the global expatriate markets when needed (e.g., UAE subsidiary), offering international commuter arrangements to PCNs where applicable (e.g., director of Italian sales subsidiary), and having traditional PCN expatriates where absolutely necessary (e.g., Russia). Working with HCNs in the sales network the company relies on its strong corporate culture as a means of integration and building commitment to the company. They have been very resourceful in spreading and strengthening corporate values, but often unable to use effectively the strongest possible medium for spreading corporate culture – everyday role modeling by a PCN expatriate. Trimo also put a lot of effort into establishing a strong employer brand in the broader region to attract potential expatriates (as inpatriates) from a larger human capital pool in the long term.

To go truly global and solve the international talent management puzzle the company might have to go beyond its traditional labour markets and approaches. Can Trimo make this step with the current HR composition and organization of its international operations, or does this require a more fundamental change that will certainly be challenged by several dimensions of Slovenian national culture and embeddedness in the local social and institutional environment?

Case Questions and Tasks

Introductory question: Should Trimo internationalize further (i.e., expand to new continents) and go for being truly global or stay as it is?

1 Prepare a proposal on how to staff operations in India for a Monday meeting. Suggest approach and process for staffing forthcoming Indian operations. Consider the whole team. What kind of international assignment is most appropriate? What kind

of expatriate profiles do you plan to assign? You are free to make assumptions about Trimo's potential entry mode.

2   How should Trimo approach their global talent management in the long term? How should they build and sustain a pool of expatriates? Design a system and discuss its features, advantages and possible threats.

3   Discuss any necessary people-related changes in the parent company to enable smoother further internationalization. What kind of talent management system would be most appropriate to address this challenge?

Role play: One participant will assume Sonja's role interviewing a TCN for the open management position in Trimo's forthcoming Indian subsidiary. The second participant will play the role of a TCN inquiring about the position, subsidiary–headquarters relations and the possibility of being promoted to the company executive management level.

Web action (information gathering): Sonja asked you to prepare a report on cultural and institutional differences between Slovenia and India to provide support for her staffing decisions. She complained that she has very few resources to share with you but that she is sure there is a lot of material on-line.

Broader discussion: One of the factors that a potential international assignee considers when exploring a tentative destination is "the quality of life/living". What is "quality of life" and "what is quality of living"? Discuss the interrelatedness of quality of life perception and national culture. Evaluate extant measures of "Quality of living" (e.g., annual Mercer's study) from your institutional and cultural perspective.

Case follow-up: Discuss the impact of the financial crisis in 2008/2009 and the collapse of the construction market for Trimo's internationalization and its demand for expatriates.

Acknowledgments

The author would like to thank Trimo (http://www.trimo.eu) for their willingness to reveal information for this case study. Specifically, the author would like to thank Sonja Klopčič and Aleš Por for their help and support in preparing this case study. The author would also like to thank Darja Peljhan and Nada Zupan, who recently worked on this case study and have made the analysis of secondary sources much easier. Some of the situations in this case study have been changed to facilitate learning process and do not completely reflect reality.

References and Further Reading

Jazbec, M. (2007) Slovenian national culture and cross-cultural training of managers. In Prašnikar, J. and Cirman, A. (eds.) *New Emerging Economies and their Culture*. New York: Nova Science Publishers.

Peljhan, D. (2005) Management control systems for organisational performance management: The case of a Slovenian company. Unpublished doctoral dissertation. Ljubljana: Faculty of Economics.

Tekavčič, M., Dimovski, V., Peljhan, D., & Škerlavaj, M. (2010) Cultural differences and homogeneity in strategic alliances: the case of Trimo Trebnje (Slovenia) and Trimo VSK (Russia). In Uljin, J., Duysters, G., and Meijer, E. (eds.) *Strategic Alliances, Mergers and Acquisitions: The Influence of Culture on successful Cooperation*. Cheltenham: Edward Elgar.

Zupan, N. & Kaše, R. (2005): Strategic human resource management in European transition economies: The case of Slovenia. *International Journal of Human Resource Management*, 16(6), 882–906.

Zupan, N. & Rejc, A. (2005) Growing through the HRM Strategies – Trimo Trebnje. In Prašnikar, J. (ed.) *Medium-sized Firms and Economic Growth*. New York: Nova Science Publishers.

Exhibit 1 Examples of Trimo's solutions

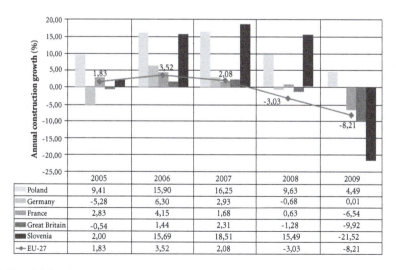

	2005	2006	2007	2008	2009
Poland	9,41	15,90	16,25	9,63	4,49
Germany	-5,28	6,30	2,93	-0,68	0,01
France	2,83	4,15	1,68	0,63	-6,54
Great Britain	-0,54	1,44	2,31	-1,28	-9,92
Slovenia	2,00	15,69	18,51	15,49	-21,52
EU-27	1,83	3,52	2,08	-3,03	-8,21

Exhibit 2 The pitfalls of the deteriorating construction market

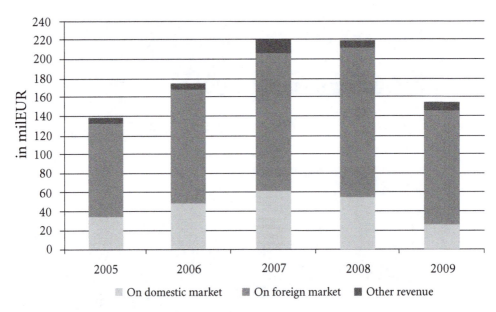

Figure E3.1 The structure of Trimo Group's total revenues

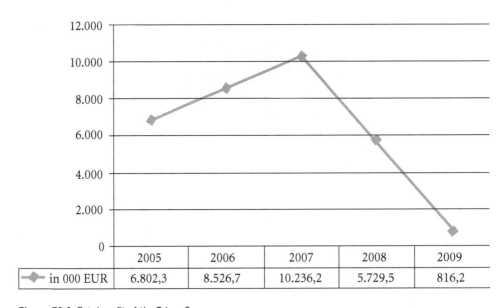

	2005	2006	2007	2008	2009
in 000 EUR	6.802,3	8.526,7	10.236,2	5.729,5	816,2

Figure E3.2 Total profit of the Trimo Group

Exhibit 3 Trends of selected business indicators for Trimo

Part IV
Mediterranean, Middle East, and Africa

18

Azerbaijan
Developing HRM Specialists in Azerbaijan: A University/Industry Collaboration

Dave Doughty, Helen Shipton and Veronica Lin

Introduction

In this case study, we demonstrate HR specialists' and line managers' perceptions of the effectiveness of a Chartered Institute of Personnel and Development (CIPD: the professional body representing HR professionals in the UK[1]) training programme delivered by a British university – Nottingham Trent University (NTU) – to an Azerbaijani subsidiary of a large multinational corporation – British Petroleum (hereafter named BP). Azerbaijan is a developing country undergoing significant transformations. As a consequence, there is lack of clarity in the role of HR specialists in this country. This provides a unique opportunity for training to effect changes and shape the HRM practices in this context. Second, the unique culture in Azerbaijan means that training programmes developed outside of this country may have to be adapted to facilitate local learning. Features and principles of the training that contributed to the training (in)effectiveness are discussed. Conclusions from this study therefore have implications for effective cross-national training.

Context of Azerbaijan

Oil-rich Azerbaijan gained independence from the Soviet Union in 1991 amid political turmoil and against a backdrop of violence in the Nagorno-Karabakh region where it continues to have an ongoing dispute with Armenia. It has been famed for its oil springs and natural gas sources since ancient times and by the beginning of the twentieth century Azerbaijan was supplying almost half of the world's oil. In 1994, Azerbaijan signed an oil contract worth $7.4 billion with a Western consortium. Since then Western companies have invested millions in the development of the country's oil and gas reserves. Caspian oil is now flowing through a pipeline running from Baku through Georgia to the Turkish port of Ceyhan providing Western countries with ready access to a vast new source of supply. Azerbaijan has huge reserves of gas and in September 2014 BP began construction of the Southern Gas corridor to supply Europe directly by 2019, bypassing Russia.

Despite the generation of massive revenues from the oil and gas reserves the general populace have not benefited as hoped. Additionally the continuing reliance on oil and gas has created major problems with the significant decline in the price of crude oil. Also, despite its wealth and increasing influence in the wider region, poverty and corruption continue to overshadow the country's development.

Whilst the political environment remains very stable with weak opposition, serious issues remain regarding the disparity of wealth and human rights issues within the country. To the "outside world" a positive image is portrayed of a nation developing its global significance illustrated by hosting the European Games in Baku in 2015. In keeping with a number of developing economies Azerbaijan has had in place a nationalisation (localisation of employment) agenda and the case study developed here is based upon the premise that the appropriate function to facilitate this development is the human resource management (HRM) function. In order for the HRM function to be effective, however, members need to develop sufficient influence and credibility to impact on the organisation's strategic decision-making.

HRM in Azerbaijan

In common with many former Soviet states the focus on people issues in Azerbaijan has tended to remain at an administrative level with little engagement with strategic business considerations. Since independence, increasing numbers of international organisations have been operating in Azerbaijan and most have brought with them different approaches to people management. This has helped to create a new perspective although many of the national companies and governmental departments have continued to operate with more traditional people management policies and procedures. The need to modernise management processes (including people management) has been recognised by both government and industry and has led to Azerbaijani universities developing new programmes as well as to significant funding for Azerbaijanis to study management programmes (undergraduate through to doctorate level) in Western Europe and the USA, to support the development of new skills within its younger generation. In some ways, developing the impact and influence of HRM in Azerbaijan is similar to problems faced elsewhere in the world as the profession remains somewhat embryonic. The work with BP in Azerbaijan therefore provided both a challenge and an opportunity.

Background to the Collaboration

There was a view from both NTU and BP that the introduction of a professional HR training/development programme would be beneficial to BP and its HR employees. A series of training sessions were organised that aimed to lead to advanced qualifications of the participants. The goal of the CIPD advanced qualifications is to enable participants to "learn how to develop and implement creative and strategic HR solutions that drive organizational performance" (CIPD). The participants taking an advanced qualifications course are also expected to "be able to develop understanding of organizations and the external context within which HR operates" (CIPD).

Prior to the start of the training, an HRM master class was held to illustrate the learning environment/style that participants would be required to engage in and sufficient interest was stimulated to ensure a postgraduate HRM programme with professional (CIPD) accreditation would be viable and welcomed. Informal discussions ensued between an expatriate member of BP's HR department and NTU. The overriding consideration on how to deliver this programme from both sides' perspectives was to ensure international standards were maintained. This was reinforced by an assessment regime that is demanded by both organisations.

Two cohorts of trainees were recruited, with eighteen in cohort 1 and sixteen in cohort 2. Training to cohort 1 was delivered in 2007 and to cohort 2 in 2008. The overall objective of the programme was to develop HR professionals who are able to make an effective contribution to the business. A range of specific objectives were applied to individual modules within the programme, which included focusing on the business context, personal and professional development and research methods, as well as the more substantive HRM activities of resourcing, learning and talent development, performance management and employment relations.

An important factor driving the introduction of this programme was the Azerbaijani government and its major localisation (i.e., nationalisation) of the employment agenda. Azerbaijan was very much at the forefront of the nationalisation movement since when many countries in the Middle East, for example, have followed suit: Emiratisation, Omanisation, Qatarisation, Saudi-isation and such. Part of the purpose of presenting this case is to examine whether the programme delivered in Azerbaijan could be adopted by countries in the Middle East and elsewhere where HR is at a similar stage of development.

Principles of the Training Programme

The Postgraduate Diploma in HRM is a qualification of NTU which has also been approved by CIPD as meeting the knowledge requirements for Chartered Membership of the Institute. The CIPD forms policy and strategies for the profession and encourages the development of HR professionals by establishing and maintaining high educational standards and professional performance, initiating research and promoting good practice.

In order to maximise the likelihood of success of this programme, considerable attention was paid to the selection of its participants. The desire and demand from the HR team in Azerbaijan was very high primarily reflecting the motivation, aspirations and the general thirst for knowledge amongst this group of Azerbaijanis. The achievement of such a qualification was viewed as a massive opportunity to enhance personal credibility and career advancement. As such it was important that the selection criteria enabled a view to be taken of both the intellectual capabilities and the commitment required to achieve success through a part-time study mode whilst continuing in a demanding work environment, added to family commitments, which the Azeri culture recognises as being of primary importance. This had particular consequences for the female applicants who operate within what continues to be a male-dominated society. To select the trainees, all applicants submitted a diagnostic essay which was used to help identify a potential student's commitment to the programme and their analytical abilities. As shown later in the discussion section, this proved critical for success on the programme.

Learning materials for this programme were developed to reflect the local context. The course leader had significant previous experience in Azerbaijan so was able to develop a number of relevant case studies with support from local Azerbaijanis he had previously worked with.

An induction to the programme was seen as critical for establishing an appropriate learning contract. Of particular significance in the induction was the emphasis on the learning approach that would be adopted. The age profile of the first cohort varied from late twenties to forties, meaning the previous learning experiences for most of the group were under the old Soviet style. Whilst most of the group had been exposed to a Western approach in training programmes within BP, the course team were conscious of the need to encourage a much more participative/interactive approach to the learning. The induction was critical in introducing a range of activities, such as role playing, use of interactive case studies – written and via DVD, self-analysis and group discussions to supplement any formal lecture style inputs. This was achieved very successfully: for example, the first four-day workshop culminated in groups being required to deliver a key HRM theme in a memorable and creative manner. The variety of approaches delivered included: a role play in which students represented line managers; employees and HR specialists having to resolve employment relations issues; a TV quiz around the contribution of HR to the business; and a "rap song" about gaining employment engagement. The concerns from staff not having taught in this part of the world that NTU's learning approach would be alien to the participants proved to be unfounded but again, support given from experienced faculty was invaluable.

As well as the learning approach, guidelines were also established for expected behaviour – from both students and staff. This included allowing all colleagues to express their views, including rotation of group membership and leading of plenary sessions. From the staff viewpoint, instructors made (and kept) promises on regular feedback and support whilst back in the UK.

To evaluate the effectiveness of the training programme and the changes in the work of HR, and to identify the factors that contributed to the (in)effectiveness of the training, two focus groups were conducted with the trainees and one focus group with the line managers. Five HR specialists were in each focus group for the trainees. Four line managers participated in the focus group, with two local line managers and two expatriates. The two expatriates had varying levels of experience in Azerbaijan. The focus groups with the HR specialists and those with the line managers were separated to ensure that genuine evaluation was obtained. Each focus group lasted two hours. Notes were taken to record the interviews. The data was analysed and findings are presented below. In addition, the HR Vice President for BP Azerbaijan was interviewed on completion of both cohorts and discussions also included any proposed changes for future cohorts.

Evaluation of Outcomes

A number of positive outcomes were identified from the key stakeholders (trainees; HR specialists; line managers; senior management) and are presented in more detail here.

Boosted Self-Confidence and Credibility of HR

Focus groups with the HR specialists suggest that the training has been positively received. It has significantly boosted the HR specialists' self-confidence. This comes, on one hand, from enhanced understanding of HR-specific knowledge. For example, a trainee from cohort 1 said: "I now have confidence as I've learned theory which gives me greater credibility with my line managers, especially as an HR Advisor who had little previous information/ knowledge to understand why HR decisions were made!" A trainee from cohort 2 stated: "The course helps develop confidence and increases credibility. Interesting to learn the theory and how it can be implemented." Another trainee from cohort 2 stated: "The programme has totally changed my understanding of my work – before I was just automatically doing things without understanding why. I now have a much deeper understanding of the cause and effect of different options and recognise there is not 'only one way of doing it' . . . the course has given me a tremendous boost to my confidence."

The enhanced confidence comes, on the other hand, from deeper understanding of the business context. The trainees from cohort 2 stated: "My language has changed and I can present HR problems within the broader business context", and "The assignments linked HR to the business and were very helpful."

The confidence enhancement was also attributed to the perception that line managers now regard the trainees as more professional and credible than before and HR specialists have gained a higher status in the organisation. "The course has given me a tremendous boost to my confidence and you know that you are now regarded as a professional (by clients and colleagues)" (trainee from cohort 2). Many trainees have mentioned that the training has added to their knowledge and increased their credibility. This perception is cross-validated by the interviews with the line managers. They appraised the HR specialists as more professional and cooperative than before the training. Line manager 1 who has eight years' experience considers the relationship between HR and the line managers to have become much stronger. To him, HR used to be "remote" but is now much more pre-pared to meet with the line managers and to offer relevant HR training. Line manager 2 has two years' experience during which time there has been significant organisational change. He has seen very positive change in the interface with HR and considers it to exhibit much better understanding of operations and the relevant competencies required for hiring and much better understanding of respective roles in the process. He sees a "big difference in the two years" and can "see a change now". Line manager 4 also believes that HR is now much more professional, as "non-qualified" people in HR have now left, leaving "really professional HR advisors".

The comments from the HR Vice President were also very positive. From a BP perspective there has been a significant cost saving with expatriates being replaced by local staff:

> The CIPD programme, with its focus on international standard HR professionals, has been a key contributor to this change because it has increased the confidence and competence of the HR team. This has translated into the team having high credibility with the line. There was a time when senior line managers preferred to be assigned an expatriate HR tag. Now, the same managers (expatriate and local) tell me that their Azerbaijani HR advisors are among the best they have ever worked with.
>
> (VP HR, BP Azerbaijan)

Of particular significance in the Azerbaijani context is that the barriers to facilitating this change were considerable, such as: the poor image of HR impacting on its low status; self-fulfilling beliefs from HR employees that they would not be able to impact on organisational strategy; and the historical view of HR being very much an administrative/record-keeping role. The fact that this change was driven by senior managers in a Western organisation, who themselves had to struggle to gain greater recognition and impact during their previous employment within the UK and USA, played a key role in the success of the programme and raises the question of the likelihood of increasing the impact of HR within Azerbaijani organisations. Evidence suggests that change is underway, in part by virtue of the development of an HR community. It will be interesting to see how such developments continue; at least one Azerbaijani University is now offering an HR Masters programme and NTU have been requested to participate in a joint HR Masters programme by the leading Azerbaijani university.

Influence on Organisational Decision-Making

Due to these changes, HR specialists were involved more often than before in the business decisions or joint decisions with line managers. Line manager 3 observed that "There was a time when ex-pats were reluctant to get HR involved. There was a lack of confidence in the support you'd get from HR. Now having HR engagement at the beginning is critical to effective HR and impact of 'fairness and equity' for all." A trainee from cohort 2 also observed that since the trust of line managers in HR's quality has increased, HR specialists are more likely to exert influence on long-term plans:

> Reaction of line managers has been great since we've been on the programme – their whole demeanour to us has changed – psychologically they now view us as having professional qualities that enable us to make a major contribution to long term plans. There is an impressive commitment that is apparent within business managers to incorporate our views.

Another trainee from cohort 1 acknowledged that "There are more opportunities now to make suggestions to improve processes, e.g., the resourcing process. The organisation (senior management) supports individuals/HR advisors in being more innovative." This provided evidence that the credibility and professionalism of HR influenced the degree to which the HR function was recognised by the line management and was involved in their decision-making.

The line managers, however, also revealed that as HR specialists were becoming involved in decision-making, different understandings of who should do what were also appearing. There was concern among the line managers about the recruitment system, which they described as a mess. Line managers believed "HR should be the driver" in recruitment and line managers provide information on the number of recruits required. Now line managers were taking the lead "who need more support". This issue, however, did not emerge in the focus group with the HR specialists. It is likely that the HR specialists were not aware of this expectation of the line managers.

Contributors to Training Effectiveness

The training was delivered by the UK-based NTU to local Azerbaijani employees in BP, an MNC, which invokes the question whether a UK-centric course can be well received. As with any learning experience, to be successful there needs to be an understanding of the most appropriate learning approach taking account of, amongst other aspects, the background of the participants and avoidance of stereotyping dominant learning approaches in different cultural contexts. Many of the initial schooling experiences of the students had been within a Soviet-style approach with little interaction and participation – very different to the approach adopted with the CIPD programme. However, many of the participants had been exposed to Western styles of learning through internal programmes of the MNC, so the use of highly interactive learning processes was well accepted and appreciated by the participants.

For the NTU tutors having this knowledge was critical to avoid false assumptions with consequential impact on their credibility occurring. The trainees commented that "The format of the programme with emphasis on the workshop has worked brilliantly. There has been a focus on impact on the business and the interaction with peers and introduction to different learning styles with lots of relevant personal examples being discussed by all." For older trainees who had received Soviet education, the experience was also valuable. One trainee stated that "It is very different to the 'Soviet education' many of us experienced and we have a wonderful opportunity to make use of our knowledge." Certainly, the international experience of the tutors also contributed to the training effectiveness, as it is recognised that "There is excellent international, world experience amongst the tutors." Therefore, although some trainees felt that the assessments were too many, in general, they viewed the organisation of the training in a positive light. One trainee mentioned that "Whilst the course is UK-centric it is really useful for benchmarking processes and really does help us understand 'foreign employees'."

While following the CIPD principles of course design and delivery described earlier and having experienced tutors definitely contributed to the effectiveness of the training, attention was also given to the local context in developing cases for class discussions. Cases reflecting the local business context were developed. For example, one of the cases described an American MNC setting up a hotel in Azerbaijan and facing various issues and problems in this process. The context in this case was similar to that in which BP operates its business. The trainees were asked to discuss what HRM solutions could be developed to solve these problems and to support the organisational strategy. This enabled the trainees to see the link between the training and their work and apply the knowledge they had learned.

In addition, local culture was attended to in order to cultivate an encouraging learning environment. Most participants in this training were female. On commencement of the first programme the dominant male role was challenged with the need to support their partner in sharing household and childcare duties. To guarantee the time commitment to the course, all candidates were interviewed before the commencement of the course to ensure they were aware of the time required outside of the workshops for successful completion of the programmes. It was interesting to witness the pride in the males when their partners graduated. This also recognises the changing nature of the culture with the current generation.

Another key feature of the culture in Azerbaijan is to be respectful of status and be deferential to age. Tutors from NTU had to encourage the students to challenge and question, which did not necessarily come easily to the students. The induction and relationship building between tutors and students was a critical factor in creating a successful learning environment. Whilst the assumption is that former Soviet states continue to have a strong collectivist identity (Hofstede, 1980), experience of the students did recognise that although they enjoyed group activity, they actually had a strong preference for individual assessments.

The effectiveness of the training was also a result of the strong motivation of the participants to develop themselves. Participants viewed this qualification course as a valuable opportunity to increase their marketability and chance of promotion. Trainees stated: "I feel more professional which also makes me more marketable and increases my career prospects"; "Personal credibility and marketability are big opportunities provided and this also adds to self-confidence." In fact, quite a few participants from cohort 1 have been promoted after receiving the training. This has made the training highly visible within the organisation and added to the motivation of cohort 2 participants.

Case Study Tasks

Questions for Group Discussion

1 The general view presented in the case is of the successful development of HR specialists for BP in Azerbaijan. Would you support this view and if so how would you convince senior BP (non-HR) management of the benefits?
2 Discuss the key features that contributed to the success of this programme in Azerbaijan.
3 HR was certainly an embryonic profession at the commencement of this programme in Azerbaijan. How might this case be of benefit to HR specialists in countries like those in the Middle East where HR remains an embryonic profession?
4 How can the organisation benefit globally from the outcomes of the programme based in Azerbaijan?

Role-play Activity

The CEO of the company (based in the UK) has heard very positive comments regarding movements towards meeting the nationalisation requirements of the company in Azerbaijan (90 percent of employees need to be nationals within the next three years). A lot of credit for this is being attributed the local HR capability with special recognition of the impact of the professional development (CIPD) programme that local HR specialists participated in.

Given the above there is discussion about delivering the University/CIPD programme across other regions in the organisation's global business. The CEO has called a meeting for further discussions and the following key participants have been asked to attend:

1 The lead (course leader) Professor from Nottingham Business School (part of NTU) who developed and helped in delivery of the programme.
2 The Vice President (VP) for HR in the company's Azerbaijan operation.
3 An Azerbaijani graduate, and now senior HR manager in the company's Head Office in the UK.

There are four roles to be allocated with the CEO chairing the meeting and adopting a neutral stance in gathering sufficient information to gain greater understanding of the programme in order to gauge its worthwhileness for "rolling out" across other global locations within the company's international operations. The three other attendees will be generally positive about the benefits and will thus be looking to be persuasive (whilst also realistic) in the discussion with the CEO. There is sufficient in these roles to feed in any particular bias that the instructor should wish to introduce.

Other class members can be asked to review the meeting and make a decision as to:

(a) The likelihood of adopting such a programme across the company's global operations (if so why?)

Or

(b) Deciding not to proceed with this programme globally (if not why not?)

Or

(c) Modifying the programme or adopting in some (not all) global operations (why?)

Note

1 The CIPD is Europe's largest HR and development professional body. It is a globally recognised brand with over 135,000 members and prides itself on supporting and developing those responsible for the management and development of people within organisations. The CIPD's aim is to drive sustained organisation performance through HRM, shape thinking, lead practice and build capability within the profession.

References and Further Reading

Black, J. S., & Mendenhall, M. (1991). The U-curve adjustment hypothesis revisited: A review and theoretical framework. *Journal of International Business Studies, 22*(2), 225–247.

Combs, J., Liu, Y., Hall, A., & Ketchen, D. (2006). How much do high-performance work practices matter? A meta-analysis of their effects on organizational performance. *Personnel Psychology, 59*(3), 501–528.

Greenhaus, J. H., Collins, K. M., & Shaw, J. D. (2003). The relation between work–family balance and quality of life. *Journal of Vocational Behavior, 63*(3), 510–531.

Gröpel, P., & Kuhl, J. (2009). Work–life balance and subjective well-being: The mediating role of need fulfilment. *British Journal of Psychology, 100*(2), 365–375.

Hofstede, G. (1980). *Culture's consequences: International differences in work-related values.* Beverly Hills, CA: Sage.

Lengnick-Hall, M. L., & Lengnick-Hall, C. A. (1999). Expanding customer orientation in the HR function. *Human Resource Management, 38*(3), 201–214.

Shenkar, O. (2001). Cultural distance revisited: Towards a more rigorous conceptualization and measurement of cultural differences. *Journal of International Business Studies, 32*(3), 519–535.

Subramony, M. (2009). A meta-analytic investigation of the relationship between HRM bundles and firm performance. *Human Resource Management, 48*(5), 745–768.

Ulrich, D. (1997). *Human Resource Champions: The Next Agenda for Adding Value and Delivering Results.* Boston, MA: Harvard Business School Press.

Vosburgh, R. M. (2007). The evolution of HR: Developing HR as an internal consulting organization. *Human Resource Planning, 30*(3), 11–23.

Wilensky, H. L. (1964). The professionalization of everyone? *American Journal of Sociology, 70*(2), 137–158.

19
Botswana
Diversity Management: The Case of Managing International Staff and Exchange Students in an Institute of Higher Learning in Botswana[1]

Dorothy Mpabanga

Introduction

The Department of Human Resource Management (HRM) at the University of Botswana (UB) is responsible for the recruitment, selection, induction and placement of local and international staff. The department is mandated with the duty of ensuring that it attracts and retains the best employees. It has to ensure that international workers are taken care of from the recruitment stage up to their arrival in Botswana so that they can adapt smoothly into the local environment. The Office of International Education and Partnerships administers and manages exchange students and visiting scholars. The office liaises with the HRM department in order to ensure that all international staff and exchange students have the necessary permits to stay in Botswana. The university has developed and designed policies and programmes that guide the recruitment and employment of international staff including administration of visiting scholars and exchange students. In addition to existing policies, managers in the human resource management department and the international office use government laws and regulations which were designed to guide the employment and engagement of foreign staff and students.

Bonolo,[2] the human resource manager, is tasked with the implementing and monitoring of the recruitment, selection and induction policies of the university. To ensure the recruitment of foreign staff with the best qualifications and experience, Bonolo is guided by various employment regulations and policies. For instance she would use the act that regulates the employment of non-citizens and the university's employment policies and conditions of service.

Thuto[3] is a manager in the Office of International Education and Partnerships and she is tasked with the responsibility of ensuring that visiting scholars and exchange students have the required documentation and permits to enter and stay in the country. In addition, Thuto has to ensure that students and staff from the University of Botswana who visit other institutions of higher learning as exchange and visiting scholars have the necessary documentation and permits to enter and stay in foreign countries; she also takes care of logistical arrangements for their journey to those countries. In order to fulfil her mandate, Thuto uses various university policies and guidelines in addition to existing national employment laws and regulations. For example, Thuto has to use the university's internationalization policy, the teaching and learning policy and the Employment of Non-citizens Act. The two managers (Bonolo and Thuto) have to work as a team when managing and administering international staff and exchange students. It is against this backdrop that this paper reports on a case study that explored diversity management at the University of Botswana in order to assess the effectiveness of diversity management policies and challenges faced during implementation. The paper concludes by suggesting ways to enhance the implementation of diversity management policies and ends with a role play exercise for students.

Organizational Setting: The University of Botswana

The University of Botswana was established in 1982, and it was the first institute of higher education in the country, although it dates back to 1964 when it was first established as part of the University of Botswana, Basutoland and Swaziland (UBBS) before it changed to the University of Botswana, Lesotho and Swaziland (UBLS) in 1966 (University of Botswana, 2012/2013a). The University of Botswana was established by an Act of Parliament after the University of Botswana, Lesotho and Swaziland (UBLS) broke into three separate universities. Since its establishment the university has expanded its programmes. In 2013 its student population stood at 18,716 students (University of Botswana, 2013/2014). The university has nine faculties and offers undergraduate, graduate and post-graduate programs in business, education, humanities, engineering and technology, medicine, social sciences, health and natural sciences (University of Botswana, 2012). A strategic plan has been developed in the six major fields entailing extending access and participation, providing relevant and high quality programmes, intensifying research performance, strengthening engagement, improving students' experience and enhancing human resources for excellence in delivery (University of Botswana, 2008).

The university strives to realize its vision and achieve the above six key strategic areas through rigorous recruitment of highly qualified academic and support staff (University of Botswana, 2012/2013). The university has a total of approximately 2,417 employees, out of which 62 percent a support and 38 percent academic staff (University of Botswana, 2013/2014). Members of the support staff perform the university's administrative responsibilities, while academic staff are responsible for the teaching and delivery of academic programmes at undergraduate, graduate and post-graduate levels. In addition, academic staff are responsible for research, engaging with external stakeholders and offering professional and community services.

The university workers comprise citizen and non-citizens employees. Academic staff constitute 72 percent local and 28 percent non-citizens staff (University of Botswana, 2013/2014). There are also staff members who are on an exchange programme or on visiting scholarships. The students comprise national, international and exchange students from different parts of the world. For example, during the 2012/13 academic year the university had 388 students from countries in the Southern African region (2.1 percent), while 490 students (2.6 percent) were from the rest of the world (University of Botswana, 2012/2013). Out of the 490 students from the rest of the world, 145 were exchange students from Europe, North America, Japan and Australia. In addition during the 2012/13 academic year out of a total of 18,717 students in the university, 10,546 (56 percent) were female while 8,171 (44 percent) were male students (University of Botswana, 2012/2013). This enrolment declined to 18,176 due to competition for students in the tertiary education market (University of Botswana, 2013/2014). This shows that the university has a diverse population comprising staff and students from different countries and backgrounds.

The University uses the general conditions of service policy to administer and manage staff and these were prescribed by provisions of Section II of the University's Act and Statutes (University of Botswana, 2013/2014). The general conditions of service are mostly in line with the constitution and the Employment Act which guide employment policies in organizations and are included in the employment contract between the employer and an employee. The Employment Act includes clauses on diversity management as it states that there should be no discrimination amongst employees on the basis of marital status, gender, religion, race, ethnicity and political beliefs (Republic of Botswana 1966, amended 2002). It is worth noting that generally an employment contract has to be signed by employees when they accept employment and indicate that they agree to comply with the conditions of service. At the University of Botswana the HRM department is responsible for the implementation and monitoring of the general conditions of service and the department guides managers in its implementation, including the international office. The following sections give a contextual background on diversity management in Botswana, commencing with a brief discussion of the economy, employment laws and regulations.

National Setting: Botswana

Botswana is a landlocked country situated in the Southern part of Africa. It shares borders with South Africa, Namibia, Zimbabwe and Zambia. The country is vast but has a very small population of about 2 million people, the majority of whom are young (Statistics Botswana, 2015). Botswana is a large and relatively flat country which has an area of 582,000 square kilometres (roughly the size of France), with a semi-arid climate (Republic of Botswana, 2003). Botswana gained independence from the British colonial government in 1966, and is one of the longest surviving democracies in Africa (Molomo, 1998). The country has enjoyed a stable political and economic environment and has experienced one of the highest growth rates in the 1980s after the discovery of diamonds in the 1970s (Salkin *et al.*, 1997). This has led to the country accumulating foreign reserves of approximately P87.8 billion (USD 7.5 billion) as of August 2015 (Botswana Government, 2015). Though recently the economy has not grown as much as it did in the 1980s and 1990s, it has maintained steady growth rates. For example, in 2014 the GDP grew by 4.4 percent compared to 9.3 percent in 2013. This was mainly due to decreased growth in the mining sector (ibid.). Botswana is also well known for having established one of the best and most successful private–public partnerships (PPP) in the continent, by partnering with the DeBeers diamond mining company, a model which has worked well for the country. The partnership has facilitated the economic growth and development of Botswana. The government used the mineral revenue to develop the education, health, social and economic sectors of the economy.

Although Botswana has been considered one of the best countries in Africa in terms of political stability and good macro-economic management policies, which have enabled the country to achieve sustained economic development and growth through the use of diamond revenue, the country has had some challenges. The biggest challenges include high rates of unemployment, particularly amongst the youth, high rates of HIV/AIDS infections, high levels of poverty, particularly in female-headed households, and high rates of income inequalities (Bank of Botswana, 2014). The unemployment rate has averaged about 17 percent in the last 20 years and is currently at 18.7 percent (Botswana Government, 2015). In addition, the country has a very weak private sector which is highly dependent on government for business, and is unable to grow and create economic and employment opportunities for the people. The small population, and hence the small domestic market, makes doing business in Botswana challenging. The government has developed policies to address these challenges, and they include continued attempts to attract foreign direct investment (FDI), diversify the economy away from mining, and develop programmes to empower citizens. The programmes are targeted specifically to women and the youth to help them establish their own businesses. The national internship programmes are used to address skills shortages by developing those skills required by industry (Botswana Government, 2015).

Diversity Management in Botswana

Diversity management in Botswana is implemented through the Employment Act and the Employment of Non-Citizens legislation. The payment structure of international staff is guided by the National Policy on Incomes, Employment, Prices and Profits. The inclusiveness of work practices is contained in the country's constitution. The employment of non-citizens legislation is implemented by the Ministry of Labour and Home Affairs. Botswana has a diverse population comprising different cohorts with diverse national and internal cultural values, norms and beliefs.

Training and Localization Policy of the 1970s

The country inherited a colonial administration from the British colonial government after gaining independence in 1966 and also a workforce mainly composed of expatriates. According to the Botswana Government (1973), there were very few locals with professional, technical and managerial skills to manage the public service. The government introduced a training and localization policy in the 1970s to educate and train citizens so that they could gradually take over positions occupied by colonial administrative staff. The government used the diamond revenue to invest in human capital development, and by the 1980s and 1990s, the country had many citizens with educational qualifications in the areas of social sciences, business and technical skills. The country experiences shortages of trained and experienced workforce in the engineering, health, medicine and natural sciences, hence the employment of non-citizens.

The Employment Act CAP 47:01 of 1982 (revised 2003)

The Employment Act of 1982 was introduced to guide the employment policy and regulate the employment relations between the employer and employee, including regulating the employment of females, people with disabilities and under-aged children. The Employment Act and regulations are enforced by the Department of Labour and Social Security under the Ministry of Labour and Home Affairs. The Employment Act of 1982 was arguably introduced to guide the management of a diverse workforce in terms of gender, age, disability, sexual orientation and was revised to include ability/disability and sexual orientation (Republic of Botswana, 2003).

Employment of Non-Citizens Act, CAP 47:02 (1982, revised 2002, 2005)

The Employment of Non-Citizens Act regulates and guides the employment of foreign, expatriate or international staff and is administered by the Department of Labour and Social

Table 19.1 Employees' average monthly cash earnings by sector and citizenship

Origin	2001	2005	2009	2010	2011
Citizens	Botswana Pula*				
Parastals and private	1414	2141	3287	3728	4392
Local government	1948	2362	3700	4678	4478
Central government	2232	3335	5230	4344	5992
Non-Citizens					
Parastals and private	2865	6764	9344	9754	12275
Local government	6018	7532	14633	17596	17221
Central government	5907	7838	10806	11092	11758

*Exchange rate: USD$1=Pula 11.43 (www.oanda.com)

Source: Bank of Botswana, 2010 & 2012, page S-27.

Security. This is guided by the National Policy on Incomes, Employment, Prices and Profits of 1980 (revised in 2010). The national policy on income falls under the responsibility of Ministry of Finance and Development Planning.

The Employment of Non-Citizens Act is the third piece of legislation introduced to guide employment relations that specifically addressed regulating the employment of non-citizens. The Act regulates various aspects of employment policies and practices. For example, the Act stipulates that recruitment should start by first sourcing within the country before recruiting external human resources and that local staff possessing the required qualifications and experience should be given priority over foreign nationals. Organizations are required to report the composition of their workforce to the Department of Labour and Social Security on an annual basis. Non-complying organizations are liable to a fine. The Employment of Non-Citizens Act also outlines conditions of service, including salaries and benefits paid to international staff. As shown in Table 19.1 above, non-citizen workers' salaries are higher than citizen staff salaries in order to attract and retain them.

The National Policy on Incomes, Employment, Prices and Profits of 1980 (revised 2010).

The national policy on incomes, which was developed to moderate wage growth, alleviate poverty and create employment, also guides the pay structure of international staff (Republic of Botswana, 2003). The following section explores challenges faced in managing international workers in an academic setting.

Implementing Diversity Management Laws and Policies at the University of Botswana

There are multiple challenges faced by the human resource management office at the University of Botswana when administering and managing foreign workers. One of the biggest challenges is the lengthy processing of work and residence permits. As pointed out earlier, all international workers and visitors to Botswana require permits or visas to enter the country for purposes of visiting or working. These permits are processed and issued by the government through the Departments of Immigration and Citizenship and Labour and Social Security. A permit to enter the country has to be applied for in advance before travelling to Botswana. The purpose of this case study is to explore challenges faced by the Department of Human Resource Management at the University of Botswana in their recruitment of international staff and exchange students. The following section discusses findings from the survey conducted at the University through semi-structured interviews with Bonolo in the human resource department and Thuto at the international office.

Managing International Staff and Exchange Students

According to Bonolo, the University recruits international staff using government laws and regulations as contained in the Employment of Non-Citizens Act. She indicated the University used to be exempted from applying for work and residence permits. However, this waiver was lifted in 2010 when all international staff intending to work for the University had to apply for residence and work permits before entering the country. In addition, the Employment Act requires that the recruitment start by recruiting locally. If the University cannot identify suitable candidates locally it is allowed to recruit outside the country.

Once the candidate has agreed to take up employment with the University, the HRM department commences the process of applying for work and residence permits on behalf of the staff member. When the permission to work and reside in Botswana has been granted by the labour and immigration departments, the HRM department sends these documents to the international staff member to commence their journey to Botswana. The HRM department is required by law to facilitate international staff travel to Botswana, including assistance with logistical arrangements such as securing accommodation and other amenities, and including induction once they have arrived in the country. The following section discusses findings on challenges encountered when implementing diversity laws and policies at the University of Botswana.

Issues Encountered During the Implementation of Laws and Policies in the Management of Foreign Staff, Exchange Students and Visiting Scholars

Lengthy Processing of Approving Work and Residence Permits

According to Bonolo in the HRM office, one of the major challenges of managing international workers is the lengthy application process for residence and work permits. This lengthy process in some cases results in international staff not being able to join the University as they have accepted offers from other universities while the University is waiting for approval from the government. This denies the University an opportunity to benefit from external staff who may have a wealth of experience or expertise.

Having to Deal With Different Officers

The second challenge relates to dealing with different officers at the immigration and labour offices every time the University follows up on applications for residence and work permits. This causes delays as the HRM officer has to explain the application process from the first date of application, and enquire multiple times before receiving assistance from a different government officer. As pointed out earlier, by the time the permits are issued, some candidates would have secured employment elsewhere, and the University loses out and has to start the recruitment process all over again.

Lack of Appreciation of Diversity Management by the University Community

There is general lack of appreciation of the urgency of preparing in advance for international staff and exchange students by academic and support departments, and the community needs to be made aware of this to ensure that residence and work permits are secured before international staff and exchange students travel to Botswana.

Approval of Applications of Entry Permits for Academic Institutions

Thuto observed that the majority of applications by non-citizen academic staff, exchange students and visiting scholars are generally approved by the government.

Improving the Implementation of Diversity Management Laws and Policies in an Academic Institution

Having an Immigration Officer as a Point of Contact for Academic Staff

The delays experienced in the processing of work and residence permits when recruiting international staff could be improved by the government employing a dedicated officer at the Department of Immigration and Citizenship and the Department of Labour and Social Security. This officer would specifically deal with or facilitate the processing of permits for foreign staff in academia. This would solve the problem of having to deal with a different officer each time one needs help from the two departments.

Develop Innovative Ways to Improve Processing of Residence and Work Permits

Stakeholders consisting of national institutes of higher education and the government should develop innovative ways to reduce the lengthy processing of work and residence permits. Improving ways to process applications for visas, work and residence permits would help speed up the approval process.

Review Immigration Laws to Enhance Internationalization of Education

The recruitment of international academic professionals is important in promoting diversity in teaching and learning. Employment laws and regulations need to be reviewed to accommodate international staff and student exchanges because education has no boundaries.

Enhance Consultation Between All Stakeholders

Thuto suggested that having consultative meetings and building partnerships to discuss matters and trends of internationalization and its impact on national policies would enhance the implementation of diversity management policies in Botswana. She further suggested consultation between government and the Botswana Education Hub on regulations and policies that affect education, and they should engage each other on the implications of immigration and labour laws on higher education and come up with innovative and progressive laws.

Involve Trade Unions in Immigration Matters

Regarding the implementation of diversity management laws and policies, Thuto was of the view that consultations, involvement and capacity building of trade unions were important in managing diversity.

Acknowledge Diverse Cultures

When implementing diversity management laws and policies the University should recognize and acknowledge cultural differences. This would help national and international staff to easily acclimatize and accept their differences.

The University Should Establish a One-stop Service to Assist International Staff and Students

The University should establish a one-stop service point to facilitate the acclimatization of international staff and exchange students. In addition the one-stop office should have an officer responsible for monitoring and evaluating progress made in the implementation of diversity management laws and policies, including the University's internationalization policy.

The University Should Enhance the Implementation, Monitoring and Evaluation of Diversity Management Laws and Policies

Thuto suggested the University should enhance the implementation and monitoring of policies and programmes designed to manage international staff and students by assigning an HRM officer who would be responsible for this purpose exclusively.

Enhance the University's Visibility Through Diverse HRM and Internationalization Policies

Thuto was of the view that the University must develop progressive diversity management laws and policies and be responsive to the needs of potential international staff and students. This could be achieved by having an officer in the HRM department to specifically deal with international staff and partners. In addition the University should use its diversity management and internationalization policies as an opportunity to enhance and increase the university's visibility globally.

Motivate the University Community to Appreciate a Diverse Workforce

Thuto in the international office made the following additional suggestions.

(a) The University's community needs to be made aware of the value of existing diversity management laws and policies, and of the importance of international partnerships established by the University as these promote its visibility in the global arena of higher education.

(b) There is need for the University community to support and commit to international partnerships as these partnerships promote the University in particular and the country's higher education's sector globally.

(c) The University community should be encouraged to appreciate and value international partnerships established by the University.

(d) The University community should be motivated to act swiftly on requests to establish these partnerships to maximize the University's benefits from such, in terms of diversity in teaching, learning and research.

The following section explains steps for the role play exercise that has to be performed by students in a group. The role play commences with students acting out the role of managers in the HRM department and the international office when they recruit international staff, visiting scholars and exchange students for the University of Botswana. The section briefly gives background about tasks of the two managers, provides guidelines for the stakeholder meeting, what the rest of the class should do and provides issues for class discussion after the role play.

Role Play Tasks

Background for role play and class discussion

Bonolo, in the HRM department and Thuto in the international office would like to improve the administration and management of international staff and exchange students at the University of Botswana. The two managers value the strategic importance of diversity management in helping the University achieve its strategic goal of producing quality and employable students, and to attract and retain international staff and students. This goal can be achieved through implementation of recruitment and retention policies, guided by national laws and regulations. These managers appreciate the challenges and constraints encountered when dealing with their everyday responsibilities of managing human resources, including the recruitment of international staff and students. In an effort to fulfil their responsibilities, the HRM manager and the international office have to perform the following duties.

(a) Identify vacant positions and prepare for the advertisement to attract, recruit and select academic staff, visiting scholars and students in the national and international market.

(b) Apply for residence and work permits for foreign staff and exchange students once they have agreed to join the university.

(c) Organize the induction of foreign staff and exchange students in order to help them acclimatize in a different environment and culture.

(d) Assist expatriate staff and students with securing accommodation, transport, medical aid and other amenities such as furniture, telephone, water and electricity to help them settle at the University and in Botswana.

Stakeholder Meeting

In order to ensure a smooth transition of international staff and students from their home countries into Botswana, Bonolo, from the HRM department and Thuto from the International Office decided to arrange a meeting with the following stakeholders in order to address issues affecting their duties, and to suggest ways to enhance the implementation of existing diversity management laws and policies.

(a) HRM Manager (Recruitment), from the HRM Department, University of Botswana.
(b) International Liaison Officer (Visiting Scholars and Exchange/international students), from the International Office, University of Botswana.
(c) Government Labour Officer (Work and residence permits), from the Department of Labour and Social Security.
(d) Government Immigration Officer (visa/entry permit), from the Department of Immigration and Citizenship.
(e) Government Official (Foreign Affairs), from the Ministry of Foreign Affairs and International Cooperation.

Role Play Exercise

(a) The instructor has to allocate the above roles (a–e) to students.
(b) Students should be allowed 10–15 minutes to prepare for the meeting.
(c) The stakeholders consisting of (a–e) above should hold the meeting.

Class Discussion

(a) The group debates issues presented and discussed and suggest possible solutions.
(b) Class members observe deliberations of the meeting, share ideas on how the meeting was conducted, for example observe and comment on:

- Presentations,
- Responses,
- Discussions and
- Suggested solutions.

Notes

* The Author is grateful to the University of Botswana for granting permission to publish this case.
** Secondary data was collected from published and non-confidential documented sources from the University of Botswana.
***Primary data was collected from the two officers as they had agreed to be interviewed and agreed for the interview material to be used in this case study.
****The names of the HRM manager and the manager in the International Office used in the case study are fictitious/not real.

Notes

1 The Author is grateful to the University of Botswana for granting permission to publish this case. The views expressed in the case study are those of the participants/respondents and are not the views and/or opinions of the University of Botswana.
2 Fictitious name: translates to Politeness in Setswana.
3 Fictitious name: translates to Education in Setswana.

References

Bank of Botswana (2010, 2012 and 2014). Annual Report, Gaborone.
Botswana Government. (2015). *Budget Speech*, Ministry of Finance and Development Planning, Gaborone.
Botswana Government. (1973, 2003 and 2010). *National Development Plan*, Ministry of Finance and Development Planning, Gaborone.
Molomo, M. G. (1998), 'The role and responsibilities of members of parliament in facilitating good governance and democracy'. In Edge, W A, and Lekorwe, M. H (eds.). Botswana politics and society. J. L. Schaik, Pretoria.

Republic of Botswana (1966, 2002), Botswana Constitution, Government Printer.

Republic of Botswana (2003a) Employment Act, CAP 476:01, Government Printer.

Republic of Botswana (1998) General Orders: Directorate of Public Service Management, Government Printer.

Republic of Botswana (1996, Amended in 2008) Public Service Act. Directorate of Public Service Management, Government Printer.

Republic of Botswana (2003b) Trade Disputes Act, Industrial Court Section 15 of the Disputes Act, Government Printer.

Republic of Botswana, Employment of Non-Citizens Act, CAP 47:02. Republic of Botswana, The National Policy on Incomes, Employment, Prices and Profits, and the Manpower Development, Training and Localization Policy, Government Printer.

Republic of Botswana (1998) Workers Compensation Act No. 2 Government Printer.

Salkin, J., Mpabanga, D, Selwe, J. and Wright, M. (eds.) (1997) *Aspects of the Botswana economy: Selected papers.* Gaborone: Lentswe la Lesedi.

Statistics Botswana (2015) Botswana population projections: 2011–2026. http://www.cso.gov.bw / http://www.stats bots.org.bw accessed 11 December, 2015.

University of Botswana (2013/14). *Annual Report.* University of Botswana, Gaborone http://www.ub.bw accessed 29 March, 2016.

University of Botswana (2012/13). *Annual Report.* University of Botswana, Gaborone http://www.ub.bw accessed 15 November, 2015.

University of Botswana (2012/2013a) Undergraduate academic calendar. University of Botswana, Gaborone.

University of Botswana (2008) Strategy for Excellence: 2016 and Beyond. University of Botswana, Gaborone.

20

Cyprus

People Management in Academia: Anna-Maria Harilaou's Story[1] Revisited

Eleni Stavrou and Nicoleta Nicolaou Pissarides

After 19 years in the Department of Law at Zenon University, now the departmental Chair, Anna-Maria Harilaou thinks back at her career progression in the department trying to make peace with the difficulties encountered in her getting tenure and figuring out how to improve her department's culture and HRM practice.

Organizational Setting

Zenon University is a state university in Cyprus. It was founded in 1987 in Larnaka, one of the smaller cities of Cyprus. It has nine Schools, 302 academic staff and 227 teaching staff in total (Table 20.1). Universities are a novelty in Cyprus but by now, three state and five private universities have been created.

Cypriots are very proud of this University. It took its name from Zenon, a Cypriot philosopher and founder of Stoicism who identifies with the city. The name Zenon comes from the name Zeus, who was the head of all Olympian Gods in ancient Greece. To be hired as academic staff at the University, one needs to have a Ph.D. degree from an accredited university. Then, based on university regulations and depending on qualifications, someone may be hired in one of the following positions: Lecturer, Assistant Professor, Associate Professor and Professor. The first two positions are on tenure-track contract while the last two are permanent (tenured) positions (see Figure 20.1).

For the first two positions, the process of hiring and promotion involves: (a) an interview by an Evaluation Committee of five academics in a rank two levels higher from the candidate, three from the relevant Department and two from outside the University (from two different countries other than Cyprus) who do not know the candidate personally; (b) evaluations from three internationally renowned academics (chosen by the Evaluation Committee) who do not know the candidate personally. The candidate has no input – other than submitting an updated CV and requesting three recommendations from colleagues of his/her choice – during the process, and has a maximum of two chances to be granted promotion to the Assistant or Associate Professor levels, otherwise (s)he has to leave the

Table 20.1 Academic and teaching staff at Zenon University

	Male	Female	Total
Professor	80	10	**90**
Associate Professor	71	39	**110**
Assistant Professor	48	28	**76**
Lecturer	20	6	**26**
Special Teaching Staff	21	35	**56**
Special Scientists (Teaching Staff)	88	83	**171**
	328	**201**	**529**

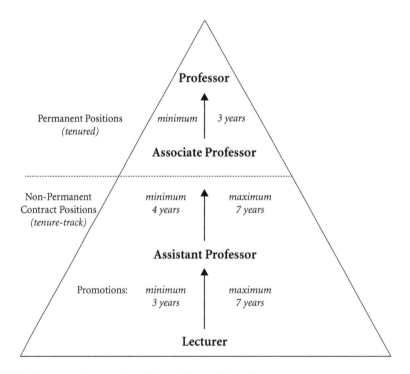

Figure 20.1 Hierarchy of academic positions at Zenon University

university. For the last two positions (to Associate Professor and Professor), the process is very similar: The only difference is in the Evaluation Committee's structure, which includes two internal Professors and three external Professors. Furthermore, Associate Professors are already considered tenured and thus, cannot be dismissed.

The official university regulations point out three broad areas for evaluation, in no particular order of importance: research, teaching, and service to the university and the local community. Other than these regulations, most Schools and Departments within the University do not have well-specified criteria, such as number or type of publications, quality of teaching or level of service for example. However, in practice, only research and specifically, only publications in highly ranked journals count for promotion in the Department of Law, as will be demonstrated below.

Historical Background

The Law Department offers both undergraduate and graduate programs in various subject areas of Law and is part of the School of Social Sciences. It consists of 10 colleagues, all relatively young (age range 35–55) and mostly males (8/10), in the various fields of Law. Due to this very small number, and in order to meet high teaching needs, the department hires external teaching staff on a per course basis.

Anna-Maria finished all her studies in very competitive universities in the USA on an earned scholarship. She joined Zenon University first as visiting faculty in 1997 and then was hired directly as Assistant Professor in 1998. She has been very active in teaching and supervising students at both the undergraduate and graduate levels. In addition, she has been the main person in charge of maintaining the Department's undergraduate and graduate programs in Business Law. At the same time, she has been a serious researcher, working on intricate research questions, creating a solid publication record over the years.

She was evaluated for tenure for the first time in 2006 but did not succeed. The committee's report noted that, while she met (even exceeded) all other criteria, she did not have the highly regarded publications the Department wanted (those considered top publications in the USA), but rather she had more specialised, but very good, publications. It was clear from the report that nothing else mattered in this case other than the top publications. A very similar situation took place with one of her male colleagues in the Department, Peter, who specialised in European Law. A third male colleague, John, did receive tenure at the same time because he did have two of the top publications considered key.

This was the first time that the Department revealed explicitly that only 'top' publications count for tenure. Not too long ago, most colleagues in the Department would get tenure, even Professorship, without such publications. Additionally, this requirement was never formally communicated to the School (Promotion and Tenure Committee) or the rest of the University (Senate, Council).

It all started towards the end of 2004, when the then Chair of the Department took the liberty of creating a list of 16 publications that through his own investigations he found to be of a high standard for each major field of Law. Three of those in each major field were marked as 'top' publications. It was a trend in those days when journal rankings were first introduced to certain schools (Sangster, 2015) and were used in career-defining decisions (Tourish and Wilmott, 2015). Even though other colleagues disagreed with this idea, some even in writing, he and two other colleagues managed to pass it through the Department Council with the explicit note that this list was only indicative.

Nevertheless, the list was used as a condition in the tenure interviews of Anna-Maria, Peter and John a year or so later. Soon after tenure was refused to the two colleagues, and after much discussion, the list was formally abolished. Those in favour of keeping the list rationalized that 'at least now colleagues know what is expected of them even without the list there.' The terms of the psychological contract were established (Rousseau, 1998).

Three years passed quickly and Anna-Maria's tenure process first, and Peter's soon after, began. They knew this was their last chance. Anna-Maria spoke with 'senior' (Professors and Associate Professors) colleagues in the Department who seemed positive. Some even clarified an unofficial 'gentlemen's agreement' (male gender in the wording is purposeful) quite widespread through the grapevine for the past three years: 'high flyers' who have (two of) the revered 'top' journal publications will be granted tenure the first time; hard workers who have a solid academic record and a portfolio of respectable publications will be granted tenure the second time; those who do not have a portfolio of solid publications will be weeded out. This became part of the psychological contract (Rousseau, 1998) between 'the Department leadership' and tenure-track faculty.

Unfortunately, even though Anna-Maria had the solid record, once more she was not recommended for tenure. Everyone in the Department (except the Committee members of course) was surprised by this outcome. Furthermore, colleagues lost their trust in the 'system' and did not know what or who to believe any more. Even the relatively new departmental psychological contract was breached: The feeling was that the department's leadership did not keep their part of the contract.

This perceived violation of the psychological contract created unprecedented friction, high insecurity and dissatisfaction among colleagues in the Department. Both overt and covert conflict was characteristic of daily interactions while many discussions took place in small groups behind closed doors: Transparency, collaboration and free academic spirit had all been buried under the fear of separation, punishment and reprimand (Harvey, 1988). All this upheaval succeeded in leading the School Promotion and Tenure Committee's majority vote (5 to 3) in favour of Anna-Maria receiving tenure. In a similar manner, colleagues in the Senate two months later voted (21 to 2) in her support. Against voted a member of Anna-Maria's Evaluation Committee and the ex-chairman who had come up with the idea of a journal list. After this, Anna-Maria made tenure! In turn, the road was paved for Peter's tenure procedure a year later.

The story does not end here however. In 2011, two other colleagues, Dora and Michael, were going up for tenure for their first time around. Each had one of the desirable top publications. So the grapevine flourished again: The discussions in the hallways centred on whether these publications would be enough or whether these colleagues would have to wait another round for their tenure. Would the psychological contract change again? The two colleagues were highly stressed, not knowing where to turn for advice. In fact, no one was willing to advise, not even their internal committee members. As it turned out, Dora and Michael's tenure process had a happy ending the first time around, updating the psychological contract once again.

Contextualising the Situation: Institutions, Culture and People Management in Cyprus

Cyprus, with a population approaching 900,000 inhabitants, is a small island country in the south-eastern Mediterranean basin experiencing much political conflict over its 8000-year-old history. It became a republic for the first time in 1960, but it still has a pending serious political problem, partly because of the Turkish invasion and subsequent occupation of a large part of the island since 1974. In addition to the political situation, due to a plethora of bad decisions over the long run and lack of strategic planning at national, sectoral and firm level, the Cypriot economy entered a recession in late 2009, as the economy shrank by 1.67 percent. By 2012, the public debt had risen to 80 percent of GDP and in June of that year Cyprus became the fifth country of the Eurozone (after Greece, Ireland, Portugal and Spain) to request financial aid from 'The Troika' in an effort to recapitalize its largest banks as well as its public sector.

In addition to the financial problems, Cyprus shares much in common with the other southern European Union (EU) countries, such as its institutional environment, its cultural values and the role of people management (Papalexandris and Stavrou-Costea, 2004). Specifically, the institutional environment in Cyprus provides high employment protection and moderate social protection for particular occupational groups such as civil servants but provides little social safety for the long-term unemployed, newcomers to the labour market, workers in the black economy or immigrants. The underground economy is dominant and trust in public institutions is consistently low. The most important institution is still the family: for catering to family members in need, for child or elderly care, unemployment or other assistance and housing. Much of the child or elderly care is expected from the female family members without pay. Despite efforts at EU level, the male bread-winner model persists even though women may be just as educated and qualified as, if not more so than, their male counterparts (Stavrou and Papalexandris, 2016).

In line with the institutional context, cultural issues of very high uncertainty avoidance (Cyprus UAI score 115) promote a system of high formalization and hierarchy, while the high power distance (Cyprus PDI score 75) promotes a gap between the powerful and the not: Those with high positions of power want to keep the power to themselves rather than share it with the rest; those with low power accept it. At the same time, the Cypriot culture, even though shifting towards individualism, is still more collective (IDV score 42); therefore people tend not to want to deviate from group norms. In-groups and out-groups abound and, in combination with the high power distance, among the powerful, the in-group is favoured. Furthermore, few are the women in high-powered positions in Cyprus including tenured women at Zenon University compared to their male counterparts (39 Associate Professors and 10 Professors among 302 tenured faculty; see Table 20.1), reinforcing the Cypriot masculine culture (MAS score 58). Finally, Cypriot culture is more long term oriented (LTO score 59), valuing traditions, life-time employment and looking into future wellbeing rather than immediate results (Stavrou and Eisenberg, 2006). In turn, performance orientation takes the second row. While all other values are in line with Anna-Maria's departmental culture, this last cultural value comes into conflict with it. Or was the performance orientation towards top-tier journals merely an excuse to suppress a different underlying issue?

Within the above context, people management at Zenon University and among Cypriot organizations at large is not strategic. In addition, it is often handled by non-HRM people. As Walker (1999) would conclude, policies may exist on paper or in principle, but may not be integrated into the organizational strategy and planning. Further, the orientation of HRM in Cyprus has remained stagnant in past practices and traditions. To illustrate, the most common hiring practice is still the interview, often non-structured. Quite often, 'who' you know is a more important criterion than 'what' you know. Also, while Cypriot organizations take pride in the emphasis they place on staff training and development, serious questions are raised as to the monitoring and effectiveness of such efforts or to their connection to training needs. Training needs analyses are not common. Further, few organizations have linked their training and development practices to management or career advancement. In addition, while most large organizations have performance management systems, these systems in many places and certainly in the wider public sector are linked directly to promotions, resulting in everyone being rated as excellent. Such practices are an indication that managing people has a long way to go before becoming a change agent or even being taken seriously among many Cypriot organizations.

Differently though from most of southern Europe, academic tradition on the island is absent. The average Cypriot cannot distinguish between the role and work of an academic and that of a high school teacher. The concept of 'research' and 'academic publications' is practically unknown. Nevertheless, there is high regard for academics and academic institutions in general, and Zenon in particular, due to the fact that acquiring tertiary education is very important to the vast majority of Cypriots.

Is the Concept of 'People Management' Applicable for Academics?

When we discuss different people management issues, we often refer to companies; sometimes, we may even refer to the not-for-profit or the wider public sector. However, we rarely, if ever, think or talk about managing academics requisitely. Nevertheless, academics need to be trained and developed (i.e. through seminars, conferences, workshops), to have transparent, (relatively) clear evaluation criteria and career paths, and to be evaluated fairly on their performance. In academic institutions with a long academic tradition, such issues have been addressed somehow, tested throughout the years and even somewhat resolved: This process usually evolves within a cultural and institutional context over a long period of time. Some of these institutions have moved from the collegial way to the more managerial HRM.

Applying the professional HRM practices in academia involves recognizing and openly discussing a number of dilemmas: (a) transparency vs. autonomy, (b) equality vs. homogeneity (c) accountability vs. academic freedom and (d) HRM managers vs. academics being in charge of the hiring and promotion process (van den Brink, Fruytier and Thunnissen, 2013). The more transparent (and thus, more accountable) the processes become, the more they are deemed time-consuming and disruptive to academic freedom. In turn, key performance indicators are often dismissed and academics prefer to stick to their collegial system. The committees involved, and the one in Anna-Maria's case is no exception, are of the persuasion that increasing the transparency and formalization of procedures will end in 'rigid' decision-making mechanisms. As a result, administrative HRM departments in universities are involved mainly in paper-pushing activities, lacking the power to ensure that hiring and promotion committees manage procedures requisitely. Academic professors tend to think they are the best qualified to identify a candidate's merits and no HRM professional is needed to advise on job profiles, evaluation criteria, performance appraisals, recruitment and selection processes (e.g., structure interviews, chair the interviewing panel, compile the report and help focus on other qualities in the academics than those purely research-related, etc.). Furthermore, academics high up in their field's scientific hierarchy exercise considerable power over the standards that govern their fields (van den Brink, Fruytier and Thunnissen, 2013) and often are positively biased towards people very similar to themselves, demonstrating an underlying tendency for 'cloning' (Essed, 2004). Hence, homogeneity in gender, age and religion strongly influences decisions in academia. The status quo is not to be disrupted, equality is *not* a priority! Or is it?

In the Cypriot context, these issues have not been resolved; they have not even been addressed. Before even getting to these intricate dilemmas, more basic matters need immediate attention. These include, but are not limited to, strategic goals at university and in turn department levels derived from the university's vision and mission; measurable criteria for achieving them; incentives and rewards; and implications if not achieved. Partly due to the inexperience of running such institutions on the island and thus the lack of such context diachronically, and partly due to the Cypriot culture of which Cypriot academics are no exception, academic institutions lag behind in establishing requisite management systems for their administrative much less for their academic staff.

And to make matters even more complex, academic institutions worldwide are nowadays being pressured into proving that academic research has an economic, societal and/or cultural impact (Gruber, 2014), in addition to the academic impact as disputably measured by citation counts and journal rankings (Sangster, 2015). This in turn, puts even more pressure on all academic institutions, including Zenon University, in establishing measurable performance indicators for all types of impact.

In the Department of Law at Zenon University, given its structure, culture and short history, Professors hold the ultimate power. They are the gate keepers and the mind guards of the Department. And quite often, they disagree with each other. Furthermore, the rest of faculty have been expected to agree with and follow their decisions: as a result, often they need to choose with whom to side, if any. Many have been the times when in staff meetings decisions have been reached in the absence of some Professors, only to be refuted and overturned in future staff meetings when these Professors were present. As younger colleagues have moved to higher ranks, this culture is slowly starting to change. But it is not uncommon for the lower levels of faculty to still experience, in silence, aggressive overt disagreements among Professors, or even to be the recipients of such aggression. In many ways, the University is true to its name, 'Zenon', where the pecking order of the ancient Greek Gods with all its consequences is alive and thriving.

Within this masculine, high-power-distance context, little mentoring takes place in the department from 'senior' to 'junior' colleagues unless an in-group is in place; research assistance is not widely available yet; and few are the synergies among colleagues. Training and development is left almost entirely to the incumbent: Colleagues may attend conferences and seminars at their discretion, but at the end of the day, as Anna-Maria realized the hard way, only publications in 'top' academic journals count. So, academic colleagues are advised to 'spend their time wisely'. This one-dimensional criterion, according to Anna-Maria, might have been acceptable in a large university abroad, where academic institutions abound, research support is open-handed, graduate programs thrive, colleagues within have shared interests, and resources are at colleagues' feet. Or, if this criterion was communicated explicitly upon hiring a colleague at the Law Department of Zenon University, then expectations, fair or not, would have been clear from the start.

But before these expectations are communicated, should not department colleagues first collectively make a strategic decision about what these expectations should be? It is clear that research comes first. Is academic impact the absolute goal in the Cypriot context? If yes, should it continue to count for 100 percent or will teaching and service also bear any weight? If so, how much weight? And after answering these questions, a whole set of other questions will need to be addressed so that the department will have a well thought out strategic HRM plan that will lead them successfully into the future.

Conclusion

The economic difficulties of the Cypriot economy and the increased competitiveness at both national and international level for the higher educational sector have led to a much needed reform. Zenon University being a public sector university needs to consider the fact that a better investment allocation system will quite likely be adopted by the government due to the critical state of its finances. The tightening of public funds means that their allocation may be based on a performance-based ranking among institutions operating in the same sector. Thus, actual performance measurement tools could be employed in a proper, transparent and consistent manner.

As Chair of the Department of Law, Anna-Maria was contemplating how her Department should build constructively on University regulations to approach this whole issue of hiring, developing, evaluating and rewarding academic colleagues fairly and strategically. She could not stop wondering what the value of teaching, service and research should be in a country like Cyprus: Should context matter or should only one best academic model exist? And if the latter, which one is it? If context does matter, where should she begin? Should the measures applied be strict or allow for academic freedom? Will the incorporation of guidelines and transparent procedures increase bureaucracy? How will equality flourish when excluding dissimilar people is the norm? Should she disrupt the status quo and promote more equitable and transparent processes? Should journal rankings be used as a performance indicator? Should she also try to incorporate indicators to assess the economic, societal or cultural impact of research in her department? And if so, which ones? Should the HRM-related procedures involve a professional HRM advisor at all stages or do the academic professors know better? All these questions were spinning in Anna-Maria's mind as she contemplated how to approach the matter in a strategic and fair way for her department.

Case Study Tasks (*address individually or in small groups*)

1 What are the main people management issues of this study?
2 How does the Cypriot context affect these issues at Zenon University? (You may need to read more about Cyprus or the southern European institutional context and culture to be able to address this question adequately.)
3 What are the constraints and opportunities, from a people management perspective, for Anna-Maria taking action now that she is department chair?
4 If you were a management consultant, in your opinion, what needs to be done differently in relation to the hiring, development and evaluation of academics at Zenon?

    (a) Provide a specific plan of action and its implications.
    (b) How are your recommendations influenced by your cultural background?

5 Draw up a list of generic competencies that, based on your research, would be important for an Associate Professor and Professor within a context similar to that of Zenon University.

Note

1 To preserve the privacy of the organization discussed, all names, dates and other identifying information have been modified.

References and Further Reading

Essed, P. (2004). Cloning amongst professors: normativities and imagined homogeneities. *NORA – Nordic Journal of Feminist and Gender Research*, 12(2): 113–122.
Gruber, T. (2014). Academic sell-out: how an obsession with metrics and rankings is damaging academia. *Journal of Marketing for Higher Education*, 24(2): 165–177.

Harvey, J.B. (1988). *The Abilene Paradox and Other Meditations on Management*. Lexington, MA: Lexington Books.

Hofstede, G. (2001). *Culture's Consequences: Comparing Values, Behaviors, Institutions, and Organizations across nations* (2nd edition). Sage Publications.

Papalexandris, N. and Stavrou-Costea, E. (2004). 'Human Resource Management in the Southeastern Mediterranean Corner of Europe: The case of Italy, Greece and Cyprus'. Chapter 10 in Brewster, Mayrhofer and Morley (eds) *Convergence and Divergence in European HRM* (Burlington, MA: Elsevier/Butterworth-Heinemann), pp. 189 –230.

Rousseau, D.M. (1998). The Psychological Contract at Work. *Journal of Organizational Behavior*, 19: 665–671.

Sangster, A. (2015). You Cannot Judge a Book by Its Cover: The Problems with Journal Rankings. *Accounting Education*, 24(3): 175–186.

Stavrou, E. and Eisenberg, J. (2006). 'Mapping Cyprus' Cultural Dimensions: Comparing Hofstede and Schwartz's values Frameworks', 18th International Congress of the International Association of Cross-Cultural Psychology (IACCP, Greece, July).

Stavrou, E. and Papalexandris, N. (2016). Chapter 4, 'Mediterranean HRM – Key Trends and Challenges' in Michael Dickmann, Chris Brewster, and Paul Sparrow (eds), *International Human Resource Management: Contemporary HR Issues in Europe* (3rd edition). Abingdon: Routledge/Taylor & Francis Group.

Tourish, D. and Willmott, H. (2015). In defiance of folly: Journal rankings, mindless measures and the ABS guide. *Critical Perspectives on Accounting*, 26(1): 37–46.

van den Brink, M., Fruytier, B. and Thunnissen, M. (2013). Talent management in academia: performance systems and HRM policies. *Human Resource Management Journal*, 23(2): 180–195.

Walker, J.W. (1999). What Makes a Great Human Resource Strategy? *Human Resource Planning*, 22(1): 11–14.

21

Israel

Implementing New Production Design and Reward System

Michal Biron

Organisational Setting

Foodco is one of the largest food corporations in Israel. It was founded in the early 1940s and now has nine manufacturing facilities in Israel, producing over 1000 products. Foodco exports its products to other countries as well, primarily in Europe. The corporation's products constantly face competition from both locally produced and imported products. Foodco became a public company in 1992 (with 25 percent of its shares traded in the Tel Aviv Stock Market). Starting in 1995, Netfood, a large, multinational corporation, has gradually increased its holdings in Foodco, and now has a holding rate of 64 percent.

The partnership with Netfood set new standards of quality and excellence and instituted advanced work procedures. The partnership afforded Foodco increased knowledge in a variety of relevant areas such as advanced technologies, management, finances, and marketing. At the same time, Netfood's management has increasingly put pressure on Foodco to improve performance. A special team of experts and consultants from Netfood ('target setting team'), designed to handle the challenges posed by the acquisition of Foodco, visited all production facilities in Israel and gave specific recommendations.

One of Foodco's biggest production facilities is Bamco. Established in 1974, the plant produced mainly pasta products. Gradually over the years its scope of activities broadened. The plant, located in Northern Israel, doubled in size due to extensions in 1997 and again in 2005; several baking production lines were installed and it became the baking centre of Foodco. Following the visit of Netfood's target setting team to Bamco, two problems have been identified whose solution may help increase the productivity of the plant. The first has to do with the structure of the production unit, and the second has to do with the reward system. This case study focuses on both issues and how they relate to the changing labour relationships in Israel as well as to globalisation processes affecting the Israeli economy.

Background to the Case

HRM in Israel: Historical Perspective and Current State[1]

From its establishment in 1948, the union movement was a dominant power in Israel, with the major trade union, the Histadrut, having strong economic and political power. Socialism was the leading socio-economic ideology during the first decades of Israel's existence, generating a strong sense of cohesion in the country and enabling it to cope with enormous difficulties such as security (which, albeit to a lesser extent, remains an issue today) and the heterogeneity of its population caused by a number of waves of mass immigration from various countries. The Histadrut represented more than 80 percent of all wage earners, while at the same time it was also one of the largest employers in Israel. Thus, the Israeli industrial relations system was highly corporatist in nature (Haberfeld, 1995). It owned the country's largest steel, chemistry and construction industries, as well as many other basic industries. As a major employer, and the sole trade union, the Histadrut had a tremendous influence on the HRM function. Labour relations were a major HRM activity, dictated mainly by a very powerful union and supported by legislation and regulations. Consequently, the HRM function during this era held a lowly, administrative position (emphasis was on recruitment, record keeping, seniority-based promotions, procedures and regulation) and had minimal influence on strategic matters.

Things began to change in the late 1970s. Global and local recessions as well as high inflation rates considerably slowed Israel's economic growth. The HRM function was facing issues of layoffs and complex compensation management, while simultaneously coping with issues of changing industrial environment, the introduction of multinationals, and a shift to private industry dominance. In particular, at the beginning of the 1980s a rapid growth in the high-tech industry occurred. This was mainly due to the availability of a high-level technical workforce, resulting from the downsizing of technical professions in the defence industry and the immigration of many scientists from the former Soviet Union. This process, together with a sharp decline in union membership between 1990 and 2010, followed by an increase in unionisation rates that is attributed to the 2011 Israeli social justice protests, had a major impact on HRM. The position of the HRM function within the organisation has changed, facing new challenges of managing a multi-cultural, highly educated, strongly socially aware workforce in large and complex organisational settings, exposed to growing national and international competition. In line with these changing demands, HRM professionals are viewed more as strategic partners contributing to the development and the accomplishment of the organisation-wide business plan and objectives, and also key players in enhancing the quality of work life, promoting work–life balance and strengthening partnerships with local communities.

Industrial Relations in Bamco

Bamco employs nearly 370 non-exempt employees, most of whom live in the nearby city. The plant is involved in local community life through such activities as supporting local schools and institutes for the elderly. The plant has enjoyed good relationships with its employees for many years. The last labour dispute took place in 1995, and concerned the introduction of a temporary (i.e., trial) contract for new employees (see below). Labour relationships at Bamco are based upon three elements:

1 Employees being affiliated to a recognised trade union.
2 A reward system graded by level and tenure, with a productivity bonus paid upon meeting quantity targets (see criteria below – sub-section on 'Reward system') and with overtime working limited to 15 hours per week.
3 Nationally agreed terms and conditions of employment determined by the joint industrial council for food workers, covering all companies in this industry.

The Production Process at Bamco

The company has two production departments: baking and pasta. Each department makes several products. Work in the production area is organised on the basis of product lines. While there are few unique production elements (for specific products), generally there are three main stages for production. The first stage involves the blending of ingredients and flavourings to form a uniform mass. This is done within the computer-controlled preparation area, where all the ingredients required for a batch are mixed according to the specification produced by the works-order program. The mixture is then mechanically formed into various shapes (based on the product line) and placed onto a belt carrying them to the cooking area. The second stage involves baking or frying, and – for some products – coating (chocolate, salt, etc.). From the cooking area, products are again automatically placed on a belt, which transfers them to the packing area. In this final stage, products are packed in single units (auto-packing). Packed units are then manually inserted into boxes/plastic bags.

Sixty four percent of the manufacturing personnel at Bamco (which composes about 70 percent of the entire workforce of the plant) are males, most are married (84 percent), and the mean age is 42. Work is organised in shifts, including nights and excluding Saturdays (Sabbath) and public holidays. Work schedules are organised with two days off per week. There are six to seven product lines operating simultaneously on each shift, led by foremen (one foreman per two to three product lines). The managers of the two production departments are usually in the plant during morning shifts only. They report to the plant manager.

Most production jobs are highly standardised. Four employees are assigned to each production line: one employee in the blending area, checking for and fixing problems with the mixture,

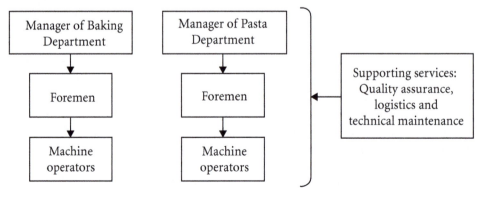

Figure 21.1 Structure of the production unit at Bamco

cleaning, etc.; one employee in the cooking area, checking for and removing defective products, cleaning, etc.; and two employees in the packing area. In addition there is a supporting staff which provides services to all production lines in a given shift: two employees assist with more general tasks such as transporting boxes, loading ingredients into the mixer, etc.; routine quality tests (mixture, cooked products, etc.) are performed by two members of the quality assurance department; and finally, two technicians handle mechanical problems and perform system maintenance. The structure of the production unit at Bamco is shown in Figure 21.1.

Problems Facing Productivity

Two problem areas were identified by Netfood's target setting team in 2004: inefficient structure of the production unit and an uncompetitive reward system.

Structure of the Production Unit

The design of the production unit often resulted in conflicts and communication problems. Department managers need to be able to change specifications during production in order to adjust to excessive demands, unexpected failures or dynamic priority setting. However, foremen are primarily concerned with meeting performance targets and maintaining production schedules – for those product lines for which they are responsible. Such a design often discourages cooperation across product lines, not to mention across departments. Further, foremen have limited authority to make adjustments during the production process, and are thus allowed to apply only partial/temporal solutions to operational problems in the absence of the department manager. In sum, the current design of manufacturing at Bamco is very inflexible, lacking a broad, system-wide perspective for managing the shop floor.

Netfood's target setting team recommended changing the structure of the production unit to 'simplify communication channels, grow employees from within by providing opportunities to take more responsibilities, and improve work processes in order to increase the plant's profitability'. To do so, the number of foremen per shift was reduced to one (instead of three), and their job description was changed to 'shift managers', responsible for the entire plant's operation during their shift. This change required extensive training, which was mainly provided by department managers, and included issues such as anticipating and responding to operational problems, over/under staffing, etc. Within this new structure, the role of department managers has shifted from administrative monitoring and technical operation (now part of the shift managers' job description) and towards coaching and training. Moreover, after the change is implemented, the plan is that department managers become more involved in strategic planning (e.g., new products), contributing their expertise and experience in relevant matters.

Finally, most production workers (machine operators) would have more power and responsibilities following the proposed change. In fact, given that there would only be one shift manager per shift, some of the tasks that were previously performed by the foremen (e.g., temperature checks) were now included in the job description of production workers. On the one hand this would increase employee sense of worth and control. On the other hand, it also involves higher workload and the need to coordinate efforts across product lines. As one employee described what happened when the change eventually went into effect: 'They expect more of us now. I like it that I don't have to stand by the machine all day . . . but I'm much more exhausted at the end of the day. I barely have a minute to just sit and relax.'

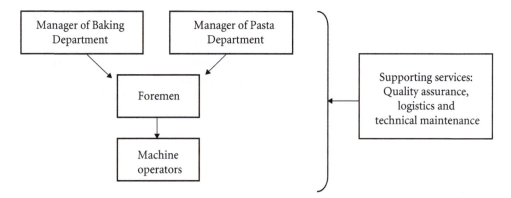

Figure 21.2 New structure of the production unit at Bamco

Reward System

Until 1995, new employees, upon recruitment, joined the recognised trade unions and were covered by the collective agreement. Since 1995, new employees have been employed on a temporary (i.e., trial) basis for the first 24 months of employment. This contract entails fewer benefits, for example, lower premiums and lower overtime work wage. After two years they move to a permanent employment contract.

Traditionally, rewards at Bamco were based on seniority increments and shift premiums (for second and night shifts). Pay also partly varied as a function of performance. The single parameter upon which performance was evaluated was quantity: specific targets were set for each production line (i.e., number of units to be produced per hour), and premiums were allocated upon meeting these targets.

Rewards at Bamco have always been considered above average compared to other firms in the Israeli food industry. Yet HRM surveys from recent years indicated that employees were unhappy with their pay. In addition, while the existing reward scheme seemed to enhance employee efforts and productivity, quality of production did not improve. To address these issues, and in line with the recommendations made by Netfood's target setting team, a new reward plan was introduced in 2005. This plan was based on the following three criteria (all of which being of equal weight):

1   Performance: an index based on the difference between the actual total time for completing all tasks in a given product line and a set criterion (i.e., standard), taking into account planned breaks, for maintenance, cleaning, etc. Performance may be increased by minimising unplanned breaks (e.g., errors) and by taking more efficient (and thus shorter) planned breaks.
2   Efficiency: an index based on the difference between the actual number of units packed and a set criterion. Efficiency may be increased by minimising unplanned breaks and working at a standard pace.
3   Quality: an index referring to the number of units produced without failures, out of all units produced in a given product line. Quality may be increased by specialising and minimising failures.

The Role of the HRM Department

Theo is the manager of the HRM department at Bamco. He was externally recruited for this job in 2000. Theo is well experienced with the challenges involved in globalisation processes in the form of mergers and acquisitions. In his former job as the HR manager of a steel production company, the company went into a merger with a Chinese firm. Theo is aware of the extensive planning and training needed for successfully implementing and surviving such processes – for both managers and employees. He has firm views about the ways in which employees should be managed under the new circumstances. In particular, he believes that instead of the rigid, repetitive tasks and traditional supervisory systems in operation, employees at Bamco should work in small, adaptable teams with rotating tasks within each team. The new reward scheme not only fosters this model, but also enhances perceptions of equity.

Zachary, Bamco's plant manager, has much trust and confidence in Theo. Theo and two other senior members of the HRM department ('the HR change management team') were given the task of leading the structural change as well as the change in the reward system. To this end, they had to work closely with the HRM functions at Foodco and Netfood to coordinate efforts from all aspects of the changes and develop relevant supporting policies and programmes. For example, they developed a training programme aimed at improving the technical and managerial skills of shift managers and a 2-day seminar for employees at all levels intended to introduce and discuss normative issues (including such topics as teamwork, communication, the global marketplace, etc.). Similarly, together with the managers of the two production departments at Bamco, the HR change management team was also responsible for developing and validating the standards for the new reward system.

Creating the Proper Climate for Union Cooperation

Given that nearly 80 percent of Bamco's workforce is unionised, the recognised trade union traditionally had much say in organisational change processes, and was involved in the planning and implementation stages of such processes. Working with the union was more complicated this time. Netfood's growing impact in recent years (in terms of share holdings) allowed for more direct, explicit pressures. The managements of Bamco and Foodco realised that, in order to enhance productivity and survive the increasing competition, Bamco would have to quickly adopt the changes recommended by Netfood's target setting team. While Theo had previous experience dealing with unions and generally preferred working through dialogue-enabled rather than unidirectional solutions, the tight schedule for administrating the current changes allowed for only little time to consult the union.

On the evening after Zachary and Theo announced the changes about to take place, the leaders of the trade union have called for a special, urgent meeting. They are disappointed by the way decisions were made, with Bamco's management neglecting employee rights and needs, particularly in light of the long-lasting legacy of collaboration. Two main areas of concern were discussed: (1) the new production design, in particular with respect to increasing job demands and changing job descriptions; and (2) the ability of the new reward system to accurately capture employee efforts and take into account extra job demands/responsibilities. At the end of the meeting, members have unanimously agreed to announce a labour dispute. Theo and Zachary realise they must resolve this matter quickly, overcoming concrete issues as well as emotional biases in employee beliefs and actions. Netfood's management expects to see some positive results already by the second quarter of next year.

Case Study Tasks

1 You are an independent consultant to Bamco's management. Prepare a report or a verbal presentation for the management about the implementation of the structural change. Refer to the HRM implications for each of the following areas in both the short and long term, taking into account the changes in HRM in Israel:

(a) work design and job descriptions for machine operators
(b) role and tasks of supervisors (shift managers, department managers)
(c) training (technical and normative elements)
(d) evaluation criteria underlying the reward system, as supporting the structural change
(e) trade union relationships

2 How might the changes recommended by Netfood's target setting team be more clearly communicated to employees? In particular, think about issues/concerns that might arise from the point of view of the individual employee, and how they might be prevented or overcome.

3 In 2014, a new HR manager was appointed at Bamco (as Theo moved to another position at Foodco's headquarters). The new manager, David, wishes to further refine the reward system. His vision is that each employee receives a detailed, annual compensation report, allowing employees to better understand the structure of their compensation package, including the monetary value of the various components. In addition to the 'obvious', traditional components (hourly income, overtime), what other components can be included in the report? What are the potential benefits and drawbacks of providing employees with such a report? Can it help to create a tighter link between rewards and performance and a stronger sense of equity (e.g., increase pay transparency)?

Role-play Exercise

A focus group has been set up to consider issues concerning the introduction of the new reward plan. The ultimate goal of the group is to put forward a list of recommendations about the evaluation criteria (quantity/quality, weight of each criterion, taking other possible elements into account, such as job grade and seniority). The group consists of the following five members:

- a trade union representative
- an experienced machine operator
- a shift manager
- a quality inspector
- an independent consultant

(a) Allocate a role to each person in the group (use name and role tags visible to all group members). The role of the independent consultant is to facilitate the discussion and make sure that all views are heard, in addition to contributing his/her own expertise.
(b) Each individual should take 5–10 minutes to list issues relevant to their own role. Consider questions such as: What concerns might the people I represent have about

the new reward system? How could these be addressed? Are there potential benefits involved for the people I represent?

(c) Hold the meeting for a set time (suggested 35–40 minutes). Suggested steps for the meeting are:

- Allow each member to introduce his/her issues.
- Prioritise and select five to seven key issues (try to identify mutual concerns).
- For each key issue, generate as many solutions as possible.

Questions for Group/Class Discussion

1 Why is it important to provide normative training in addition to technical training? In particular, in what ways do the recommended changes impose and encourage teamwork?

2 Unlike the old reward scheme, the new scheme emphasises qualitative as well as quantitative elements. How might this influence the plant's productivity? Why might this criterion be more complicated? Can you think of better quality-focused criteria within the new production design?

3 What type of problems might result from the new structure of the production unit? Give your recommendations about how these might be dealt with.

4 List the reasons for union resistance (concrete and psychological issues). Give your recommendations about how to overcome resistance.

5 Consider the effect of globalisation on Bamco's decision making. In particular, list (potential) positive and negative issues related to the need to adapt to external, global requirements posed from Netfood.

Note

1 This section is based on Tzafrir, Baruch, & Meshoulam (2007).

References and Further Reading

Haberfeld, Y. (1995). Why do workers join unions? The case of Israel. *Industrial and Labour Relations Review, 48,* 656–670.

Harel, G., Tzafrir, S.S., & Bamberger, P. (2000). Institutional change and union membership: A longitudinal analysis of union membership determinants in Israel. *Industrial Relations, 39,* 460–485.

Pindek, S., Weisberg, J., & Koslowsky, M. (2010). Human resource management in Israel: A multi-faceted perspective. *Human Resource Management Review, 20,* 173–175.

Sagie, A., & Weisberg, J. (2001). The transformation in human resource management in Israel. *International Journal of Manpower, 22,* 226–234.

Tzafrir, S.S., Baruch, Y., & Meshoulam, I. (2007). HRM in Israel: New challenges. *International Journal of Human Resource Management, 18,* 114–131.

Weisberg, J. (2010). "Evolutionary" and "revolutionary" events affecting HRM in Israel: 1948–2008. *Human Resource Management Review, 20,* 176–185.

22
Jordan
The Jordan Company of Hospitality Education (JCHE)

Muhsen Makhamreh

Introduction

In today's organizations, the function of human resource management (HRM) occupies centre stage among the various managerial functions. This importance stems from the fact that the management of human beings is the most difficult factor of production to manage in the organization. Organizations that lack qualified and motivated employees will be doomed to failure. After all, you need those individuals to use resources and operating systems effectively and efficiently in organizations. Performing HRM functions and dealing with human issues such as performance evaluation, turnover, and absenteeism in a professional and scientific manner is a recipe for success in today's organizations.

Using cases in management education in general, and in HRM in particular, has become increasingly important among faculty members. Writers in the literature have acknowledged their wide use and value to students and practitioners in a class setting. Argyris pointed out the advantages of case analysis in promoting discussion among participants of actual problems facing organizations (quoted in: Romm & Mahler, 1991). Cases use complex realistic problems as a focus to challenge and develop skills that are needed in a manager's future career (Maxwell *et al.*, 2006).

Managing turnover successfully among top management (the focus of this case) is a crucial issue that organizations have to deal with to ensure progress and success are sustainable (Makhamreh, 1985).

Organizational Setting

In 1980, the government of the Hashemite Kingdom of Jordan, with the technical and financial support of the International Labour Organization (ILO) and the World Bank (WB), established the Ammon Hospitality College (AHC), the first of its kind in Jordan to start hospitality education programmes in the Kingdom. AHC was established to offer two levels of hospitality education, a secondary level hospitality education (grades eleven and twelve) and diploma level (for two years after high school). The objective of AHC was to provide for the Jordanian hospitality sector's growing need of qualified employees. The late 1970s had brought a boom in the tourism sector, which created an increase in the demand for skilled employees in the hospitality sector.

AHC passed through different stages in its operations. In the beginning it was under the auspices of the Ministry of Tourism and Archaeology (MoTA). The responsibility then transferred to the Ministry of Education (MoE). MoE continued managing AHC until 1994 when it ceased operation due to the negligence associated with financial losses, which led to the deterioration of the facilities of AHC to the point that it ceased operations in 1994.

In 1996, hotel owners in Jordan stepped in and formed The Jordan Company for Hospitality Education (JCHE) as an outcome of the privatization process, to take over AHC and revive its mission to continue developing hospitality education in Jordan. They leased AHC facilities from the government for thirty years for minimal fees and started to renovate and upgrade the facilities for its new revived role and mission. In 2004, AHC changed its name to the Jordan Applied University College of Hospitality and Tourism Education (JAU) and started to offer its bachelor's programme.

Since 1996, JCHE has undergone turbulent changes leading to instability of operations and contradictions in managerial and academic policies in the various units of JCHE. In 2005, consultants were brought in to investigate and recommend solutions to the situation, and they found two major issues facing JCHE: high turnover among the managing directors of JCHE and the dean position at JAU. First, there was a high turnover in the top positions had resulted in employee turnover in both entities. Moreover, a lack of structure at various units of JCHE led to contradictory academic and managerial policies which in turn led to low employee morale and consequently higher turnover.

This case study focuses on these issues and how they relate to the human resource management (HRM) policies in Jordan. Furthermore, this case is real and unique in its nature because it combines different organizational settings. In particular, it focuses on how to manage a business entity, Century Park Hotel (CPH), in an educational environment (Jordan Applied University College of Hospitality and Tourism Education – JAU).

Jordan: Background Information

Jordan is located in the centre of the unstable Middle East. It occupies an area of approximately 90,000 square kilometres, between Syria to the north, Iraq to the east, Saudi Arabia to the south and Israel and Palestine to the west. Jordan's official population is approximately seven million, but the actual number living in Jordan is now around eleven million due to the inflow of refugees from the neighbouring countries over recent years.

Jordan is an emerging knowledge economy. The main obstacles to Jordan's economy are scarce water supplies, complete reliance on oil imports for energy, and regional instability. Just over 10 percent of its land is arable and rainfall is low and highly variable (World Factbook, 2008).

Jordan's economic base centres on phosphate, potash, tourism, overseas remittances and foreign aid as a major source of hard currency (World Factbook, 2008). Jordan is classified by the World Bank as an upper-middle-income country. It is also classified as the third freest economy in the Middle East and North Africa and thirty-second freest in the world (World Factbook, 2008).

Jordan is a service oriented economy; services contribute approximately 67 percent to the gross domestic product (GDP), while industry contributes 29 percent and agriculture 4 percent (World Factbook, 2015). This economic orientation is also reflected in labour distribution in the economy. The service sector employs 77 percent of the labour force while industry employs 20 percent and agriculture 3 percent (World Factbook, 2015).

Education in Jordan is widely spread and in high demand by Jordanians. School enrolment is 98 percent of those who are eligible for school and the literacy rate is approximately 96 percent among Jordanians. There are 28 universities (public and private) with a total enrolment of 280,000 students (MoHE, 2014). Ninety-five percent of high school graduates normally enrol in universities inside and outside of Jordan, one of the highest percentages in the world. Jordanians are very keen on education as a means to find a good job and good salary and ultimately a secure career. Jordanian graduates are in high demand in the Arab Gulf States as well as inside Jordan. This is why education in Jordan is a source of good living in a country that has a limited resource base. In spite of the demand from organizations, the supply is still greater, explaining why unemployment is very high among university graduates (MoHE, 2014).

Jordan's culture is based on Arabic and Islamic cultures with significant Western influence. Jordan has always been at the intersection of three continents of the ancient world, having some form of diversity at any given point due to its location. People in Jordan are very warm, friendly and hospitable especially to foreigners and guests. Approximately 92 percent of Jordanians are Sunni Muslims and approximately 6 percent are Christians (World Factbook, 2008). The spirit of tolerance and appreciation is one of the central elements contributing to the stable and peaceful culture flourishing in Jordan. The family is of central importance to Jordanian life. Village life revolves around the extended family, agriculture and hospitality. Modernity exists in urban centres especially in the capital, Amman, where all aspects of modern Western life exist. Art, music, sports, shopping malls, hotels, and restaurants from all over the world exist in Amman, which can be considered a large sophisticated cosmopolitan centre.

Employment Law in Jordan

The Jordanian Constitution establishes a number of workers' rights, including equitable working conditions, limited working hours per week, weekly and annual paid vacation/rest days, special compensation given to workers supporting families, and on dismissal, illness, old age and emergencies arising from the nature of the work. Special conditions are enforced for the employment of women and juveniles, and equal pay for equal work (ILO, 2015).

The employment law spells out all the labour constitutional rights. The employment contract between the employer and the employee states the conditions of employment between the two parties, including the time period of the contract, the probation period for the employee, the supervision of employment contract, hours of work and leave entitlements, paid leave, maternity leave and protection and pay issues. The employment contract is normally set, managed and executed by the HRM department in the organization.

Human Resource Management in Jordan

HRM practices in any country are influenced by the national context, comprising the labour market, economic forces, socio-political and cultural factors, state regulations and legislation, labour organizations and organizational characteristics. In Jordan, the basic HRM practices are similar to those applied in advanced countries. Each organization in the private sector has its own HRM system. This system is based on the top management strategy and their outlook on human resources in their organization. All HRM systems and their bylaws are in line with the employment law. Large organizations (measured by the number of employees) normally have elaborate and detailed systems that specify the role and position of the employee along his career path in the organization. HRM systems in small organizations are not that elaborate and mostly depend on the perception of top management about human resources.

A typical HRM system in Jordan includes all the regular functions of an HRM department, such as recruitment and selection, performance appraisal, training and development, compensation and benefits, and monitoring attendance, absenteeism, and sick leave. The size of these functions depends on the size of the organization and the skills and knowledge of the HRM director and his/her immediate subordinates, in addition to the sector of operation. HRM in the service sector, for example, is more advanced, and plays a more important role in the life of the organization than in other sectors (Makhamreh, 1993a).

Generally speaking, the HRM units in Jordanian firms play a moderate role in formulating HRM policies. Top management normally takes the lead and often intervenes in HRM decisions especially related to hiring and firing employees. This intervention is related to the social system of relations in Jordan, which respects the opinion of senior leaders in the hierarchy. Jordan is a relational society, in which family is the most important unit in the life of the individual. Members of the family are obliged to help and support each other in any issue that requires group support and intervention on their behalf with others. This support is exemplified in the case of employment of individuals, whereby influential persons from the family intervene with those who have the authority to employ and to give preferential treatment to a particular person.

Since 1990 Jordan has witnessed a high level of unemployment due to the Jordanian returnees from Kuwait and the Gulf State as a consequence of the first Gulf War. During recent years, and due to the additional influx of refugees from Iraq and Syria, the unemployment situation has been exacerbated, with the unofficial unemployment rate rising to more than 30 percent, with the majority of those able to find work being university graduates.

This high level of unemployment during the last 20 years has put pressure on individuals and families to find employment opportunities for their unemployed relatives. This social pressure has contributed to the increase of nepotism (*wasta*), favouring unqualified individuals to take on a job for which they are not fit. Management changes normally bring with them layoffs of employees, and new hires for the new management with the same criteria and norms. This is reflected in low job performance and high turnover rate in most Jordanian firms.

The Role of Labour Unions in HRM in Jordan

Unionization in Jordan has been legalized since 1953, but the union's role in the industrial relations system in the country has been below average in terms of defending workers' rights, developing legislation to protect workers, and achieving better work conditions and higher wages. This below-average role is attributed to the limited power given to them by the law and their low level of membership. Unionization has been low over the years due to the fact that unionization was and still is associated with the socialist political parties that were banned in Jordan before 1989. The rate of unionization is approximately 20 percent of the total labour force in the country, declining over time, previously 23 percent in 1989 (Makhamreh, 1993b; Makhamreh & Alomian, 1991).

The impact of labour unions on HRM practices is limited. Although labour unions in Jordan have the right to represent labour and defend their rights including the right to strike, this right is rarely used. The Jordanian employment law identifies three stages of disputes resolution. There are the conciliation officers at the Ministry of labour, who are trained employees assigned the task of facilitating negotiation between the disputant parties. If the conciliation officers fail to reach a settlement, the dispute goes to a conciliation board, which consists of a neutral chairperson and equal membership from the disputants' parties (management and labour). The role of the conciliation board is stronger in resolving disputes in terms of process and authority, but it has no power to force a settlement. If the conciliation board fails to reach a settlement, the dispute goes to the industrial court, which is part of the Jordanian judicial system. The decision of the court is final and binding. So technically labour unions in Jordan have the right to strike to defend their rights, but the dispute settlement system does not allow the strike in practice. This situation limits union power and influence over employment conditions in the work place.

Moreover, Article 31 of the Jordanian employment law allows companies to lay off employees due to restructuring conditions with limited penalties. This Article has allowed many companies to lay off employees legally when business is slow and even for other non-business issues that the organization finds convenient to facilitate its operations and sometimes to remove employees who are not cooperative or who are problematic in the work place.

The Case: JCHE

JCHE is a private company, with 70 percent private sector ownership, and 30 percent public sector ownership. Although JCHE is a private company, it has no profit orientation. Its mission is to educate students theoretically and practically to obtain the required skills that enable them to work in the hospitality sector. JCHE owns three entities, The Jordan Applied University College of Hospitality and Tourism Education (JAU – formerly AHC), the Jordan Hotel School (JHS), and the Century Park Hotel (CPH). JCHE is managed by a managing director and reports directly to the JCHE board of directors. JCHE is not unionized and employees' rights and duties are specified as per Jordanian employment law.

JAU is a university level college specialized in hospitality education. It offers two programmes in hotel management and tourism management. Both programmes offer two degrees: a bachelor degree (four years) and a diploma programme (two years). Since it was founded in 1980, AHC has been offering the diploma programme. In 2004 AHC changed its name to JAU and started to offer the bachelor programme. JAU is managed by a Dean who is appointed by the Ministry of Higher Education and Scientific Research based on the recommendations of the Board of Trustees. The JAU Dean reports to the board of trustees and is responsible for all academic, managerial and financial matters related to JAU. The JAU Dean works in coordination with the managing director of JCHE.

JHS is an eleven and twelve grade high school in Hotel management. It is managed by the school principal who reports to a managing director. Most JHS graduates join JAU programmes after they pass the general secondary examination.

CPH is a four-star hotel business entity. It is open for business and serves as a training hotel for JAU and JHS students. It is managed by a manager who reports to the managing director. It has 54 rooms plus the facilities for all types of events such as conferences, training workshops, and weddings.

The Management Process at JCHE

JCHE started its operations in 1998 with the appointment of a new board chairman and managing director. This person was a well known hotelier, and his family had been involved in the hospitality industry in Jordan for a long period of time. He studied hotel management and practised it; he established the foundations of AHC in terms of its programmes and practical orientation. In 2000, he left the JCHE managing director position, but remained a Board member. After that time, JCHE witnessed what could be described as chaotic operations with contradictory managerial practices in the management of JCHE due to top management turnover. Between 2000 and 2005, JCHE was managed by eight different managing directors. The average length of stay of each director was less than a year (seven and a half months). During this time, AHC was managed by four deans.

This high turnover among the top management of the two units led to continuous changes in policies and practices, which in turn led to instability of operations and considerable turnover of employees at JCHE and AHC. A lack of structure and role identification led to contradictory decisions and interference by JCHE management in AHC operations. The managing directors of JCHE arguably lacked the knowledge required to manage an academic entity. This led to professional failure and frustration on the part of AHC management and employees, which resulted in many qualified individuals leaving AHC. In addition, AHC's management was insufficiently qualified to manage its own operations, let alone to stand up to the interference of JCHE management.

The situation at JCHE can be described during this period as volatile with no clear direction. Things were managed on a daily basis without a clear strategic plan to guide the operations of the two entities, especially the understanding of the importance of the academic requirements that were needed to achieve the basic objectives of JCHE.

This issue was clear in daily operations by the joint units serving the two entities. Units such as human resources, procurement, finance, maintenance, security, etc., are centralized to provide services for all JCHE units. In practice these units used to give priority to the Century Park Hotel. Due to this, services at AHC were delayed and that sometimes led to an inability to meet the requirements of the education process.

The Human Resource Manager at JCHE since 1998 lived through the volatile period and summarized the major issues facing JCHE in general, and the HR department in particular, which consequently led to turnover problems. The major issues included:

1 The non-existence of clear points of reference for departments and divisions, i.e. a lack of organizational structure with specified job descriptions for all employees.
2 JCHE's structure, which consisted of three units that are very different from each other in terms of operation, regulations and requirements for labour and management.
3 The lack of qualified labour to work in the hospitality sector.
4 The role of 'wasta' and the personal interest of managers in the hiring of unqualified people sometimes.

5 The issue facing employees in the central units, which offer their services to all units at JCHE, receiving instructions from all units at the same time, and each one wanting its job to be finished first, which made them sometimes unable to function properly.
6 A lack of appropriate incentives for employees in terms of rewards, career paths, and social activities.

In 2004, AHC was upgraded to a university level college, licensed by the Ministry of Higher Education to grant a bachelor degree. Its name changed to the Jordan Applied University College of Hospitality and Tourism Education (JAU). This new development created more managerial complications because the new JAU is governed by a comprehensive set of academic and managerial rules and regulations established by the Ministry of Higher Education in Jordan. Unfortunately, the deanship and management of the JCHE at the time were not qualified to deal with this new development. In spite of the fact that a British Advisor was hired for JAU to assist in that respect, there was no tangible improvement to the situation.

The chairman of JCHE's Board, a well known hotelier and a very successful businessman dedicated to developing and promoting hospitality education in Jordan, realized the importance of change at this stage and the need to bring in qualified individuals to manage JCHE and JAU.

Further Developments

Due to the problems facing JCHE, a new managing director was appointed in 2005. The new managing director had very good experience and knowledge of the hospitality sector. He was a successful businessman and a member of the board of directors. Nevertheless, JAU's problems regarding academic and managerial requirements remained. Four months after the appointment of the new managing director, a Lebanese company specializing in hospitality management was brought in to manage JAU. There were high expectations of them to develop JAU and integrate it as an academic unit with the rest of the JCHE units.

Unfortunately, the Lebanese company failed to introduce any academic changes or to integrate JAU's operations with the other JCHE units. On the contrary, they tried to isolate JAU from the rest of JCHE units. After nine months, the JCHE Board of Directors decided to terminate their contract, and asked them to leave JAU after a painful dispute.

In 2006, and immediately after the termination of the Lebanese company contract, a new Dean was appointed. The regulations of the Ministry of Higher Education required that a dean should be a full professor. JCHE hired a professor of business management and a former dean of the business school at the University of Jordan, the oldest and most distinguished university in Jordan. This professor combined academic and managerial capabilities and had a success record at the University of Jordan. He was also a member of the board of trustees of JAU.

The new Dean started to work on the academic as well as the managerial issues. He found the academic plans old and out-of-date. Changes included a new academic plan, and changing the instructional language from Arabic to English. A new and intensive English programme was developed to meet the new changes. A new, unified internship system was applied to all students in the Century Park Hotel, where all operations in the hotel were executed by JAU students under the supervisors of the hotel. All regulations and procedures needed for these academic development changes were set and approved by the Board of Trustees.

Along with these academic developments, the Dean and the managing directors cooperated well to identify problems in all units and find a solution for them. Their cooperation and coordination led to stability of operations in all JCHE units as an outcome of this policy. They set a policy that only qualified individuals were eligible to be hired, and there should be no role for 'wasta' in employment. Turnover declined by almost 70 percent in all units and employees and staff are managed through an established system and structure. A new structure was developed for JCHE and JAU as presented in Figures 22.1 and 22.2.

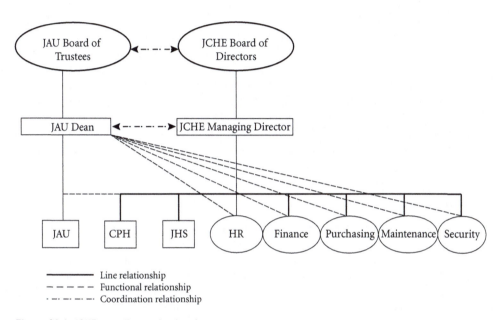

Figure 22.1 JCHE overall organizational structure

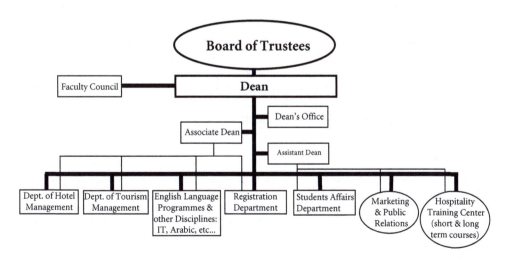

Figure 22.2 JAU organizational structure

224 • Muhsen Makhamreh

Epilogue

After four years of operation under the new top management of JCHE and JAU, JCHE management is well positioned and cooperating successfully with the JAU Deanship. Managerial as well as HRM systems are in place and developing continuously to meet the challenges facing employment in the hospitality sector. Operations at Century Park Hotel are progressing successfully and it is performing its role as a training hotel quite successfully.

The HR manager, with the policies set by top management at JCHE and JAU, developed an HRM system that defines clearly the procedures and regulations for HRM functions. He developed a job description framework for jobs at JCHE, performance evaluation programmes and an elaborate recruitment and selection process, in addition to other HRM issues. This helped in stabilizing operations and reducing many contradictory issues that had prevailed previously in the HRM operations and also led to decreased employee turnover.

JAU has come a long way. The academic system in place is unique and has comparative advantages over other similar institutions in Jordan. The academic mix of theoretical and practical aspects of the curriculum and the introduction of the English language as a means of instruction gave JAU this comparative advantage which led the Accreditation Commission of higher education institutions to adopt the JAU model for other universities to implement and to be accredited on this framework.

Case Questions

In spite of this success at both JCHE and JAU, there are still some challenges for the future:

1   What major issues do you believe will need to be dealt with to stabilize and improve the operations of JCHE and JAU, ultimately leading to decreased turnover in both entities?
2   What issues do you think need to be addressed by the Board of JCHE to be in line with the Ministry of Higher Education educational requirements?
3   Turnover is associated with employee incentives. Do you think that the management of JCHE should work on this issue? If so what types of incentives should be addressed?
4   Given the success, so far, of JCHE and JAU during the last four years, what safeguards should be provided to ensure the continuity of success?
5   If the Dean or the managing director were to leave their position, what would be the outcome and what would you recommend to ensure sustainability of progress?
6   If you were in the place of either the JCHE director or the Dean of JAU, also given an increasing level of unemployment in Jordan, how would you handle the social pressure of 'wasta' in hiring employees? Do you think that they both have to resist the social pressure of wasta, and if so, how should they do this?

References

ILO (2015). *Jordan National Labour Profile*. http://www.ilo.org/ifpdial/information-resources/national-labour-law-profiles/WCMS_158905/lang-en/index.htm.

Makhamreh, M. (1985). Determinants of absenteeism and turnover in Jordan business firms. *Dirasat*, 227–234.

Makhamreh, M., & Alomian, M. (1991). The state of labour unions and their role in industrial relations in Jordan. *Dirasat*, 18: 77–103.

Makhamreh, M. (1993a). The practices of human resource management in an Arab Country: An exploratory study of the case of Jordan. Proceedings from *Management in Commodity Driven Societies: A Middle East Perspective*, 109–118.

Makhamreh, M. (1993b). Industrial Relations in Jordan. In M. Rothman, *et al.* (eds), *Industrial Relations in the World*, pp. 80–88. Walter de Gruyter.

Maxwell, J. Maxwell, J., Gliberti, A. & Murpinga, D. (2006). Use of case study methods in human resource management. *Management. Development and Training Courses: Strategies and Techniques.* James Maxwell.

MoHE (2014). Ministry of Higher Education Report.

Romm, T., & Mahler, S. (1991). The case study challenge: A new approach to an old method. *Management Education and Development*, 22: 4.

World Factbook (2008, 2015) *CIA World Factbook: Jordan a Country Study.* US Department of State. https://www.cia.gov/library/publications/the-world-factbook/geos/jo.html, accessed November 2015.

23

Uganda

HRM Strategic Alignment and Visibility in Uganda

John C. Munene and Florence Nansubuga

Human resources management is in its infancy in Uganda despite the high demand created by the rapidly changing business environment which requires an adaptable, innovative and constantly learning labour force. To deal with these challenges, the HR function of NBL Uganda, a subsidiary of SABMiller, strategically aligned employees to cope with stiff competition. It embraced as its own line (functional HRM) strategy five corporate values, namely valuing people as the enduring advantage, making accountability clear and personal, working and winning as a team, understanding customers and consumers, and a shared reputation, embraced by all. It tracked them through a cultural audit referred to as the Organisational Effectiveness Survey in SABMiller/NBL. Using the People Balance Sheet to segment its labour force and track the bench strength, the department was able to identify a gap in its artisan level and locally designed, conducted and evaluated a remedial programme which generated a 25.75 percent return on investment. Using these strategies the department was able to mobilise and steer all activities to face in the same direction while making HRM visible by providing solutions to support the production manager to meet production targets. We explore how all this was made possible below.

General Background

Uganda has the world's youngest population with over 78 percent of its people below the age of 30. With about 8 million youth aged between 15–30, the country also has one of the highest youth unemployment rates in Sub-Saharan Africa and at an average annual growth rate of 3.03 percent, Uganda's population is projected to increase to 47.4 million in 2025 (UBOS, 2015). Coupled with the high level of fertility in the country (6.2 children per nuclear family), the youthfulness of the population creates a very high youth dependency ratio (World Bank, 2011). On top of these, youth unemployment in Uganda stands at 32 percent as against 4.8 percent of Ugandan adults. More significantly, that of the graduates stands at 36 percent (UBOS, 2012). These demographics perhaps explain the decidedly low quality of life found in Uganda (World Bank, 2014). That is, very low on purchasing power and consumer price index (23 and 25 respectively), low on health care index (38) and rather moderate on the safety index (42) (World Bank, 2014).

Uganda, nevertheless, has substantial natural resources, including fertile soils, regular rainfall, deposits of copper, gold, and other minerals, and recently discovered oil. Currently, agriculture is the most important sector of the economy, employing over 80 percent of the workforce. In this respect the country is also a leading producer of coffee and bananas and a major producer of tea, organic cotton, tobacco, flowers; it is making inroads in sericulture. Opportunities in the agribusiness sector include commercial farming and value addition. Other opportunities are found in the country's growing fish farming and processing sector with an expanding market in Europe for Uganda's fish recently estimated at approximately US$146 million annually. Uganda also possesses a rich tropical forest vegetation of over 4.9 million hectares with opportunities in afforestation and reforestation especially of medicinal trees and plants, and soft wood plantations for timber, pulp and poles.

Tourism is perhaps Uganda's most untapped natural and renewable resource. The distinctive attraction of Uganda as a tourist destination arises from the variety of game stock and its unspoiled scenic beauty. Within a relatively limited space of just over 240,000 square kilometres, Uganda offers an interesting contrast ranging from the wide East African plains and expansive savannah grasslands to the impenetrable mountain rainforests, home to gorillas, and snow-peaked mountains in the south-western parts of the country. The country also boasts a wide range of bird species for viewing in addition to numerous sporting opportunities such as mountain climbing and water sports including white-water rafting.

In terms of cultural diversity, Uganda is home to up to 56 tribes with varying dialects and distinctive languages as well as cultures, providing a significant challenge in diversity management. Laws to tackle this issue have been made although implementation remains a challenge. There are also affirmative action programmes especially relating to gender diversity management. In terms of global cultural values, Uganda cultures would be categorised as high on embeddedness, low on egalitarianism and high on environmental exploitation (Munene, Schwartz, and Smith, 2000).

HRM in Uganda: A Background

Human Resources Management (HRM) in Uganda has for decades centred on two functions, namely administration and welfare. The situation however is slowly changing with the entry into the economy of competitive industry such as mobile telecommunication and a revamping of the other fast moving goods companies, such as Coca Cola and Pepsi Cola, that had deteriorated during a period of political anarchy and economic mismanagement (1971–1986).

In Uganda economic mismanagement was kick-started by the expulsion of Asians who had dominated the artisan labour market, worsened by the 1973 fuel crisis and compounded by civil wars (1971–1979 and 1981–1986). This environment led to colossal loss of human capital quality accumulation, directly through expulsion of the Asians, a brain drain through fear of personal safety, and indirectly through the deterioration of educational institutions and general infrastructure, rated as among the best in Africa at the time (Wiegratz, 2009). Recovery in labour productivity has been slow and elusive even after economic stabilisation and structural adjustment interventions by IMF and the World Bank (1986–1997). For instance Uganda has the lowest labour productivity in Sub-Saharan

Africa, behind Kenya, Zambia and Tanzania in the sub region (World Bank, 2004 quoted from Wiegratz, 2009).

The World Bank report referred to above put forward reasons for the low productivity. It identified the general health of the population, formal and informal training through learning on the job. With regards to health Uganda has a relatively high level of HIV/AIDS infection in global terms, ranging from 6 percent to 13 percent (depending on the age group) of the productive age range (15–45-year-olds). This has affected labour productivity significantly through sick leave, and taking off time to attend burial services.

Until two decades ago training in HRM was identified with Social Work and Social Administration, Political Science and Public Administration undergraduate degrees found at Makerere University and the post-graduate diploma in Human Resources Management offered at Uganda Management Institute, designed for the Uganda Public Service administrators. At Makerere University a single course unit focusing on personnel matters such as staffing was the only source available for human resources practitioners. Uganda Management Institute was slow at revising its syllabus which until recently reflected the British personnel management training of the 1950s. All this changed in 1997 with the introduction of a Master's degree in Industrial and Organisational Psychology, followed five years later by a Bachelor's degree in Industrial Psychology at Makerere University and a Bachelor of Human Resources in Makerere University Business School seven years later. This was in addition to the founding of the Uganda Human Resources Managers' Association in 2005 by the Federation of Uganda Employers.

Despite these advances, this short history serves to confirm that human resources management is in its infancy in Uganda even though there is high demand created by the rapidly changing business environment, which requires adaptable, innovative and a constantly learning labour force. It is against this background that the Federation of Uganda Employers instituted the Employer of the Year Award and created the Uganda Human Resources Managers' Association to accelerate the modernisation of human resources management in the country.

The Federation of Uganda's Employer of the Year Award

The Employer of the Year Survey and Award (EYA) is a major activity carried out biannually by the Federation of Uganda Employers (FUE) since the year 2001. FUE is a national organisation that was instituted to represent the interests of Ugandan employers in matters dealing with employment and people management. Since its inception the EYA has recognised winners and runners-up. It also acknowledges best practice in a number of key HR functions. Most importantly, EYA provides a structured forum for employers to reflect on their employment and people management practices and how these may impact on their business goals.

Early survey awards were based on overall performance on the HR function and strategic salience. More recent winners' awards are based on efforts to transform HR into an externally oriented function by aligning it with the expectations of the stakeholders including customers, shareholders, donors, investors, and employees through proactively partnering with line departments that have a direct impact on economic and public value creation. Following recent practice, the overall winners in 2009 were based on the theme of the year namely 'HR Strategic Alignment and Visibility: Links that Unlock Enterprise Performance'. For the purpose of the survey the operational description of the subject matter was given as reflecting the essence of the business through people and/or mobilising and steering all activities to face in the same direction.

HR Visibility and Strategic Alignment

General Introduction

Human resources as human beings operate in a paradoxical environment. They need freedom to do 'their own thing' but they also need guidance on how to do it! Human resources management is the profession and practice of creating a proper balance between assisting employees to do their work and giving them the social, psychological and professional freedom to do it. Alignment, the process of ensuring that everyone pulls in one agreed direction, is a generic strategy that can simultaneously guide employees and give them the freedom they need to perform their work related responsibilities. Alignment is routinely implied in recruitment and selection where an individual is selected according to a given job description. It is also assumed that job descriptions are designed to contribute to an agreed strategy and/or mission of an organisation. This is a routine and quite often a passive form of alignment. It is alignment on 'automatic pilot' where once instruments have been set up and activated, then the pilot can take a nap or take a walk around the passenger cabin! The Human Resources Manual found in many organisations and the standard operating procedures (SOPs) found in government-oriented organisations and agencies are archetypical examples of alignment on 'automatic pilot'. For alignment to be effective in Uganda, it must be made active and kept dynamic. The 'pilot' must be on manual instruments. EYA 2009 focused on the active dynamic alignment.

Relatively recent work indicates that alignment may be most effective in four areas (Bourdreau & Ramstad, 2007; Ulrich, Brockband, Johnson, Sandholtz & Younger, 2008). The first area and the one from which alignment centrally derives its description (pulling in one direction), is strategy. It may be understood as the general business direction a corporation has set out to pursue such as brewing and marketing alcoholic and non-alcoholic beverages. The others are: articulated leadership proposition (where leaders need to focus their quality time), employee value proposition (that which an organisation promises its workers) and lastly the company's perceived strategic resource such as a brand or people (Ulrich *et al.*, 2008). In this second edition of the Casebook, we present the case of Nile Breweries Uganda, an organisation that took part in EYA 2009, and examine the various ways it tried to achieve HR alignment and visibility.

Alignment and Visibility at Nile Breweries Limited

The following case tries to show that at the time of taking part in the EYA competition, Nile Breweries Uganda Limited (NBL) centrally relied on strategy and strategic resource as alignment and visibility instruments while experimenting with the employee value proposition.

NBL Uganda is a subsidiary of SABMiller, a multinational brewing company operating on six continents and managed under regions, namely Africa, Asia Pacific, Europe, Latin America, and North America. With 28 percent net producer revenue, Africa is the largest among the regions and the second (29 percent) among the regions after Latin America (34 percent) in terms of the EBITA[1] index. Strategy ensures that an organisation will meet its objectives by revealing the business or programme direction to be shared and adopted by all internal and external stakeholders including shareholders, donors, customers, employees, and the community. Using a strategy lens the HRM function gets its most important clue on how to adopt or adapt organisational processes and structures and how to identify, deploy, motivate and retain the people resources (Ulrich *et al.*, 2008). Nile Breweries Limited (NBL) was one of the corporations from the survey that clearly demonstrated alignment through one or more of these lenses.

Alignment Through Strategy Lenses in NBL

In EYA 2009, data from competitive firms suggested that keeping focus on the strategy could be tracked through soft measures reflecting organisational or corporate values. NBL has five corporate values that the HR Department embraced as its own line (functional HRM) strategy. They include valuing people as the enduring advantage, making accountability clear and personal, working and winning as a team, understanding customers and consumers, and an undisputed reputation. These values are annually tracked through a cultural audit referred to as the Organisational Effectiveness Survey in SABMiller/NBL. The values are tracked through perceptions on management practices, performance management processes, self-management, leadership, performance management practices, employment conditions, commitment, work environment, training and development, and talent management (see Table 23.1).

Data collected in 2007 and 2009 indicated that NBL was leading the African SABMiller Group in all measures of these values, providing reasonable evidence that NBL is focusing on SABMiller Group strategy more than any other member of the group including the Hub (South Africa). The score also indirectly gave credence to the potential correlation between performance and the strategy lens since the Africa region, of which NBL was the leader at the time of the survey, was also leading in one key performance indicator in the Group and was second in another as shown in Table 3.1. In Figure 23.1, we examine the efforts

Table 23.1 Tracking strategy through cultural survey

	2 Jan Smuts (Hub) – 2007	2 Jan Smuts (Hub) – 2009	Ghana – 2007	Ghana – 2009	Mozambique – 2007	Mozambique – 2009	Uganda – 2007	Uganda – 2009
Sample Size	54	45	231	248	511	363	219	223
Total Organisational Effectiveness Score	69	69	68	60	64	61	**73**	77
Self-Management Practices	79	76	79	73	79	76	**84**	81
Performance Management Process	73	71	67	60	58	60	**76**	75
Conditions of Employment	71	74	63	52	55	57	**66**	70
Commitment	70	71	66	56	62	58	**69**	73
Work Environment	70	71	69	58	58	56	**72**	75
Leadership	65	68	66	58	60	56	**69**	73
Training and Development	61	59	65	53	61	61	**74**	77
Talent Management	53	55	61	51	56	51	**64**	67

that NBL made in aligning the HRM function through people as their most important strategic resource.

Alignment Through the Strategic Resources Lenses

Another area is in aligning using an organisation's strategic resource. This is the single resource that distinguishes one organisation from its competitors or collaborators. It may be a brand, a niche, a mandate or people. A clear articulation of this resource provides a strong basis for determining and maintaining a human resources function including structures and processes. Through two examples we demonstrate below how NBL goes about the alignment process using this lens or instrument. The first is the People Balance Sheet by which NBL segments its labour force in terms of potential and actual productivity while the second shows the efforts NBL goes through to sharpen talent through controlled and contextualised learning.

NBL uses the People Balance Sheet (PBS) to keep tabs on the people who matter in the identified pivotal positions. NBL's People Balance Sheet divides the labour force into ten cells based on the intersection between performance and potential (see also Berger, 2004). The segment referred to as Vexation indicates an individual who has high potential but fails to perform according to expectation. Another category is titled Major Leaguer, composed of those who are above average on potential as well as performance. Another category is that of High Flier with outstanding potential and outstanding performance. Other categories include 'Passive, Performer, Achiever, Negatively Plateaued, Positively Plateaued, and Solid Achiever' (See Figure 23.1 for descriptions of each segment.)

NBL uses the People Balance Sheet to review its workforce every month to track potential gaps and action points. For instance when an employee has been in the bottom left hand cell and has been classified as negatively 'plateaued', he or she is given about two chances for poor ratings after which the process of gently edging him/her out begins. It also aims to keep approximately 70 percent of the labour force in the Performer and Achiever cells. NBL believes that there are three cardinal reasons why organisations must conduct talent audits, namely to mitigate transition risks, enable staff to grow and develop, and curb succession risks. The People Balance Sheet is one way of achieving these objectives.

The second example is a training initiative that was prompted by stiff competition from the industry. An HRM response to competition was to upgrade the skills of workers on the factory floor, specifically the packing and packaging line. The perceived strategic mission or intent of the initiative was to eliminate wastage at the packaging line and increase speed, quality and accuracy. Through a needs assessment, operational competence gaps were identified in machining, fitting, electricity, and pumping. Personal and team competence gaps were identified in team work, ability to work independently from the supervisor, low problem solving skills and poor attitude to work. The available training within the Group, accessible outside Uganda would cost NBL over $40,000, well above the allocated training budget for the Artisan level. The HRM Director decided to bring the training to Uganda by partnering with Nakawa Vocational Institute, a government institution that trains artisan level technicians in various skills such as electronics, electrical machining and fitting, motor vehicles, woodworking, sheet metal and plumbing, among others. The Institute was assessed for capacity to conduct the required training with the help of the Parent Company Artisan Competence Training Guide. Any necessary upgrades to the Institute's own curricula were

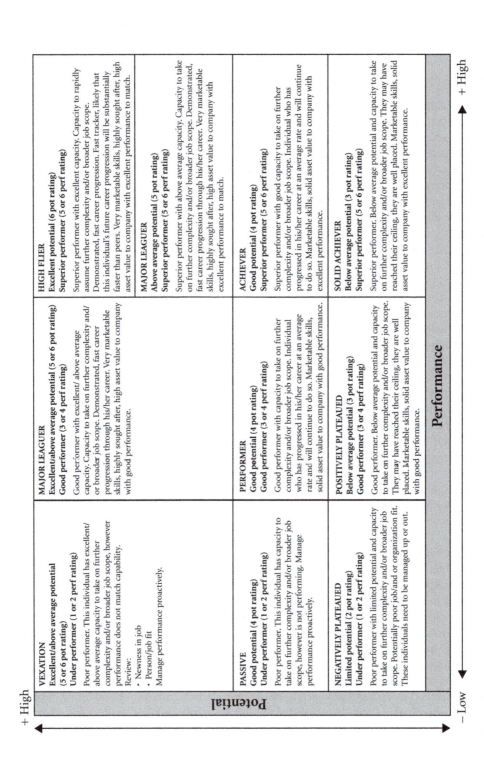

+ High

Potential

VEXATION **Excellent/above average potential (5 or 6 pot rating)** **Under performer (1 or 2 perf rating)** Poor performer. This individual has excellent/above average capacity to take on further complexity and/or broader job scope, however performance does not match capability. Review: • Newness in job • Person/job fit Manage performance proactively.	**MAJOR LEAGUER** **Excellent/above average potential (5 or 6 pot rating)** **Good performer (3 or 4 perf rating)** Good performer with excellent/ above average capacity. Capacity to take on further complexity and/or broader job scope. Demonstrated, fast career progression through his/her career. Very marketable skills, highly sought after, high asset value to company with good performance.	**HIGH FLIER** **Excellent potential (6 pot rating)** **Superior performer (5 or 6 perf rating)** Superior performer with excellent capacity. Capacity to rapidly assume further complexity and/or broader job scope. Demonstrated, fast career progression. Fast tracker, likely that this individual's future career progression will be substantially faster than peers. Very marketable skills, highly sought after, high asset value to company with excellent performance to match. **MAJOR LEAGUER** **Above average potential (5 pot rating)** **Superior performer (5 or 6 perf rating)** Superior performer with above average capacity. Capacity to take on further complexity and/or broader job scope. Demonstrated, fast career progression through his/her career. Very marketable skills, highly sought after, high asset value to company with excellent performance to match.
PASSIVE **Good potential (4 pot rating)** **Under performer (1 or 2 perf rating)** Poor performer. This individual has capacity to take on further complexity and/or broader job scope, however is not performing. Manage performance proactively.	**PERFORMER** **Good potential (4 pot rating)** **Good performer (3 or 4 perf rating)** Good performer with capacity to take on further complexity and/or broader job scope. Individual who has progressed in his/her career at an average rate and will continue to do so. Marketable skills, solid asset value to company with good performance.	**ACHIEVER** **Good potential (4 pot rating)** **Superior performer (5 or 6 perf rating)** Superior performer with good capacity to take on further complexity and/or broader job scope. Individual who has progressed in his/her career at an average rate and will continue to do so. Marketable skills, solid asset value to company with excellent performance.
NEGATIVELY PLATEAUED **Limited potential (2 pot rating)** **Under performer (1 or 2 perf rating)** Poor performer with limited potential and capacity to take on further complexity and/or broader job scope. Potentially poor job/and or organization fit. These individuals need to be managed up or out.	**POSITIVELY PLATEAUED** **Below average potential (3 pot rating)** **Good performer (3 or 4 perf rating)** Good performer. Below average potential and capacity to take on further complexity and/or broader job scope. They may have reached their ceiling, they are well placed. Marketable skills, solid asset value to company with good performance.	**SOLID ACHIEVER** **Below average potential (3 pot rating)** **Superior performer (5 or 6 perf rating)** Superior performer. Below average potential and capacity to take on further complexity and/or broader job scope. They may have reached their ceiling, they are well placed. Marketable skills, solid asset value to company with excellent performance.

Performance

− Low ◄ ────────── ► + High

Figure 23.1 The People Balance Sheet

made with the collaboration of the Institute and the training of the artisans was undertaken at a cost of $16,010, which was within the budget.

A careful design of the training as a strategic initiative enabled NBL to measure the progress of the delegates/trainees at the beginning, in the middle and at the end of the training. It also enabled the company, led by the HRM Director, his team and line managers to calculate the changes and gains in package line efficiency (Key Performance Indicator [KPI] for the initiative) and the Return on Investment. The results were as interesting as the carefully laid out initiative. Thus as a result of the training the artisans were able to get the packaging line to produce an additional 604.75 cases per week translating into $1,513.34. In addition, over the 40-week period designated to measure the effect of the training, there was an increase of 138 cases per week representing a factory efficiency gain in US dollars of $503.13 and an actual gain of $20,125 over the 40-week period. This represented a Return on Investment of ($20,125 – $16,010) $4115 or 25.75 percent.

The above initiative had some unanticipated multiplier effects. Through the hard work described above the HRM Director won a Practice Award from the America Society of Training and Development (ASTD), the second on the African Continent. The successful initiative attracted members of the Group from China, Mozambique and Tanzania who came on a study tour. This increased the prominence of HRM not only in NBL Uganda but throughout the SABMiller Group. Moreover, SABMiller rolled the initiative out in two other countries with their franchise. Lastly the HRM initiative demonstrated a successful Public Private Partnership since the Institution incorporated the upgraded and retooled institutional capacity in its regular curricula and NBL continues to send its artisans for training whenever necessary.

Lastly, NBL was the only company in the EYA 2009 that was close to openly declaring its intentions in relation to its workforce. Such an intention is now captured through the Employee Value Proposition. It publicly declares what the organisation wants from its employees and what they will offer in return for what they get.

Our Total Employment Offering: NBL offers a competitive salary and benefit package in the Uganda labour market. We aim to make our financial offering as attractive and equitable as possible which enables us to attract and retain the highest quality people and to motivate and reward high performance. We understand that money isn't everything. Our total employment offering combines the opportunity for exciting development within SABMiller with a chance to work with great brands, strong leadership and bright motivated colleagues.

In NBL there was evidence that the employment relationship was attractive in a different way from many of the organisations that took part in EYA 2009. There was evidence that its policies ensured that employees who voluntarily leave tend to return. For instance, by the time of the EYA Survey, the Manufacturing Development Manager, the Quality Assurance Manager, the Services Engineer, the Utilities Manager, the Credit Controller and the Local Raw Materials Development Manager had left and returned within the last four years!

Conclusion

The case provides anecdotal as well as hard evidence that the HRM function can be aligned successfully to play a strategic role in the realisation of business objectives and that with carefully crafted practices this role can be measured satisfactorily. According to the HRM Director of NBL, Kenneth Wanyoto, this is a result of introducing innovative HRM initiatives and actively steering the workforce to remain focused on the business strategy. NBL through its HRM Director and the solid support from the Managing Director was also not shy to apply apparently 'academic' concepts successfully and turn them into transformational alignment initiatives. We witnessed the effort to calculate the return on investment as a good example, which also won NBL an award and significant visibility for its HRM as well as for the company.

HRM strategic alignment and visibility experiences can be perceived in different ways. Essentially organisations reflect on their core business by evaluating the competences and motivation levels of employees as well as the organisational structure and organisational core processes and how they address the achievement of the business goals. Practically, HRM strategic alignment means mobilising and steering all activities to face in the same direction while HRM visibility refers to HR's ability to provide solutions that will empower managers to redeploy and develop talents that support the evolving business needs and achieve employee alignment.

Through the annual EYA surveys, it has been noted that organisational operations are consistently changing as a result of competition/market share challenges and the general national economic regulations. These factors have required employers to adopt new business models such as mergers and acquisitions, divestitures, expansion, and contraction. Whatever the model is, the EYA has demonstrated that HRM must play the principal role to realign the workforce with the overall goals of the changing business strategy or else the required adaptation is delayed, putting the competitiveness of organisations at significant risk. The case above demonstrates how NBL was strategically aligning its employees to deal with the demands of the changing business. It kept the focus on its business strategy by aligning its corporate values to employee performance measures as well as artisan reskilling in order to increase its returns on investment and remain a centre of excellence.

Case Study Questions

1 What is HRM alignment? Based on the NBL case, outline the efforts the Department of Human Resources should apply to align people with the business strategy.
2 Visibility remains a challenge to many HRM departments in Uganda. Trace the initiatives NBL has introduced to become and remain visible.
3 What is the role of the Chief Executive Officer in making HRM visible? Describe the CEO's role in enhancing the visibility of the HRM function in NBL.
4 Outline the areas on which organisations may focus when aligning resources to the business.

Note

1 Earnings before interest, taxes, and amortization.

References

Berger, L.A. (2004). Creating a Talent Management System for Organisation Excellence: Connecting the Dots. In Berger, L.A. and Berger, D.R. (eds) *The Talent Management Handbook: Creating Organisational Excellence by Identifying, Developing, and Promoting Your Best People*. New York: McGraw Hill.

Boudreau, J.W. and Ramstad, P.M. (2007). *Beyond HR: The New Science of Human Capital*. Boston, MA: Harvard Business School. nc.

Munene, J.C., Schwartz, S.H. and Smith, P.B. (2000). Development in Sub-Saharan Africa: Cultural Influences and Manager's Decision Behaviour. *Public Administration and Development*, 20, 339–351.

Uganda Bureau of Statistics (UBOS), Statistical abstract 2011.n.c.

Uganda Bureau of Statistics (UBOS), Statistical abstract 2012.

Uganda Bureau of Statistics (UBOS), Statistical abstract 2015.

Ulrich, D., Brockbank, W., Johnson, D., Sandholtz, K., and Younger, J. (2008). *HR Competencies: Mastery at the Intersection of People and Business*. Alexandria, VA: Society for Human Resources Management.

Wiegratz, F. (2009). *Uganda's Human Resource Challenge. Training, Business Culture and Economic Development*. Kampala: Fountain Publishers.

World Bank (2004). Competing in the Global Economy: An Investment Climate Assessment for Uganda. Washington DC.

World Bank. (2011). World Development Report 2011: Conflict, Security, and Development. World Bank. © World Bank. https://openknowledge.worldbank.org/handle/10986/4389. License: CC BY 3.0 IGO."

World Bank. (2014). World Development Report 2014: Poverty and prosperity. worldbank.org/ file:////Downloads/WB%20Annual%20Report%202014_EN.pdf

24
UAE
Training and Development at United Bank: What Do the Employees Think?

Scott L. Martin, Zainab Habeeb Abdulla, and Hashil Abdalla Zamzam

United Bank is a private bank that was established in 1972 in Abu Dhabi, which is the capital of the United Arab Emirates (UAE).[1] The bank was one of the first in the region and played a formative role in building the nation's financial system. Today, it has nearly 6,000 employees and operates 125 branches across 15 countries. United Bank is one of the largest banks in the UAE and has a reputation for providing superior customer service. The bank values its employees and prides itself on providing them with competitive compensation and excellent career opportunities.

The UAE has experienced rapid growth over the last few decades, and this has put pressure on the government to put policies in place to support the development of UAE Nationals. Accordingly, all banks in the UAE have a strict quota regarding the hiring and retention of UAE Nationals. To help meet these quotas and develop UAE Nationals, United Bank has implemented significant learning and development initiatives. This case study examines the effectiveness of these learning and development activities from the perspective of UAE Nationals.

Historical Background[2]

The UAE was established in 1971. Living conditions up through the 1960s were rather primitive with a heavy reliance on fishing, pearling, farming, and trading for income and survival. Oil was discovered in 1960 off the coast of Abu Dhabi, and the UAE began to receive significant revenue from oil exports in the 1970s. The UAE has nearly 10 percent of the world's known petroleum reserves.

The UAE government had to develop the oil fields and build the supporting infrastructure. This work required expertise that was not available within the UAE, so the government needed to rely on international organizations to achieve its objectives. This resulted in a major influx of expatriate labour. Among the current UAE population of about eight million, it is estimated that 80 percent are expatriates.

The UAE is governed by hereditary rule, and the rulers or Sheikhs retain a great deal of power. For instance, unions and collective bargaining do not currently exist in the UAE. However, the rulers tend to be paternalistic and humane (Muna, 1980). The UAE government has been rather generous in distributing its wealth among UAE citizens. During the initial years of growth, UAE nationals were often placed into government organizations. The employment terms in the public sector were rather attractive including, for instance, relaxed performance standards, high compensation, short working hours, and generous amounts of leave time (Al-Ali, 2008). UAE citizens also enjoy a variety of other benefits such as no taxation along with essentially free health care, university education, and utilities. Thus, the discovery of oil has led to a dramatic improvement in UAE lifestyle over a relatively short period of time. The UAE has a modern infrastructure, and disposable income is among the highest in the world.

A recent strategic goal for the UAE has been to diversify the economy to reduce its reliance on petroleum. During the early years, the petroleum industry accounted for about 90 percent of GDP and this has now been reduced to 30 percent. Other major industries include banking, insurance, construction, and general trade.

Despite the rather successful diversification efforts, the UAE is still quite dependent on oil exports. From 2014 to 2015, the price of oil dropped from more than $100 per barrel to around $30 per barrel. The government depends on oil revenue to fund more than 60 percent of its federal budget. In addition, lower oil prices have placed pressure on the entire economy. For instance, banks are facing a difficult situation as loan growth has been cut in half. The government has significant financial reserves and the economy is still growing, so there is no need for serious concern. However, the dramatic drop in oil prices highlights the fact that the UAE must continue to diversify its economy.

Human Resource Background

Despite the benefits associated with rapid economic growth, there are also major challenges. The heavy use of an expatriate labour force places tremendous political and social pressure on the UAE government and its citizens. In essence, the nation is not able to independently manage its own affairs and future (Rees, Mamman & Braik, 2007). UAE citizens do not possess the knowledge and skills needed to perform much of the nation's work. This is not sustainable from strategic, economic, or social perspectives. As a result, a major human resource challenge for the UAE is to develop its own citizens.

Unfortunately, government organizations have now become saturated and cannot accommodate additional employees (Forstenlechner, 2008). Budget constraints, due to the lower oil prices, make it difficult to expand the size of government. To make matters worse, the UAE population continues to grow. The only viable solution is to place UAE Nationals in the private sector. This is challenging for UAE Nationals as they must now compete with an international labour force and the employment terms are far less attractive than those offered in the public sector.

Given the country's rapid growth, the educational systems have not been competitive with those in most industrialized nations. UAE Nationals often lack the skills needed to succeed in the private sector (Al-Ali, 2008). Skill deficiencies tend to revolve around critical thinking, mathematical reasoning, and writing. On the positive side, there are clear signs of improvement. It is estimated that the percentage of secondary school graduates who are prepared to enter University has increased from about 10 percent to 40 percent during the last ten years.

UAE Nationals are also generally unprepared for the levels of motivation and discipline that are required in the private sector (Al-Ali, 2008). The previous cohort experienced fairly relaxed working conditions in the public sector. As a result, young adults have little prior experience with the demands of a global economy when it comes to attendance, punctuality, and long hours. In addition, UAE Nationals tend to have negative attitudes toward engaging in manual labour (Al-Ali, 2008; Suliman, 2006). Such negative perceptions often extend to many lower level positions, and any routine or non-intellectual work. This is likely due, at least in part, to the fact that the UAE, along with many other Middle Eastern countries, is considered a "high power distance" culture (Carl, Gupta, & Javidan, 2004; Hofstede, 2001). In such cultures, leaders are expected to make all major decisions and maintain a degree of distance from followers. UAE Nationals risk losing status or prestige if they engage in work that is typically conducted by those at lower levels of society.

In sum, moving large numbers of UAE Nationals into the private sector is a significant challenge, and requires action on a number of fronts. In terms of selection, the government has introduced formal hiring quotas, along with a variety of informal mechanisms, to increase the hiring of UAE Nationals. For example, in 2005, hiring quotas were introduced in the banking industry. All banks were required to increase the percentage of UAE Nationals by 4 percent per year. Today, leading banks, including United Bank, have about 40 percent UAE Nationals on their payrolls.

The government has also placed tremendous emphasis on the role of training and development to support the transition of UAE Nationals into the private sector (Suliman, 2006). This is consistent with the paternal leadership style, as a reliance on training and development implies that employees have the underlying capabilities and motivation and only need the requisite knowledge and skills to be successful. This emphasis on training and development appears to carry over into the private sector, and this is likely due to cultural expectations and skill deficiencies. Private organizations tend to devote significant resources to training and development initiatives, at least with respect to UAE Nationals.

As implied above, there has been less emphasis on motivational interventions. For example, there are laws that make it rather difficult to terminate UAE Nationals. In terms of compensation, to meet hiring quotas and citizen expectations, UAE Nationals are often paid significantly more than their expatriate counterparts. Pay-for-performance is also less common for UAE Nationals. This may be due to the already elevated salaries as well as cultural values. The UAE tends to be a collective culture (Carl, Gupta, & Javidan, 2004; Hofstede, 2001), which encourages group cohesion and discourages the recognition and punishment of individuals. When government organizations decide to provide pay increases, it is common to grant a shared, common, across-the-board increase to all employees.

There has been significant progress in moving UAE Nationals into the private sector. But, at this point only 4 percent of all private sector jobs in Abu Dhabi are held by UAE Nationals. This is despite unemployment rates among UAE Nationals that are estimated to be in double digits. There have been calls to reduce benefits and increase work demands in the public sector, but this is obviously a delicate matter particularly given the paternalistic leadership style.

Formal Training Programs at United Bank

This case focuses on the training and development initiatives in the Customer Service function at United Bank. It examines jobs such as Director of Key Clients, Manager of Customer Support, and Customer Service Representative. In general, the service employees are quite satisfied with their jobs and working conditions. The bank values the service function and this appears to be appreciated by the service employees. The employees believe they are able to perform their jobs in an effective manner. The only issue that raises some concern is the level of compensation. Although United Bank pays more than most other banks in the UAE, the compensation levels are below those in the public sector and the employees are well aware of this discrepancy.

United Bank is making significant investments in a host of formal training programs. There are programs specific to the banking sector and United Bank's specific products such as Introduction to Finance, Investments, and Credit Card Products. There are also a variety of general courses such as Providing Effective Customer Service, Bring Your Heart to Work, and Writing Professional Emails. The quality of these programs is generally quite good, and includes a mix of techniques such as role-play, case analysis, fun competitions, and on-line quizzes. Employees are also allowed to attend external seminars and courses provided they are relevant to current or future job responsibilities.

Senior management views these formal training programs as critical to individual and organizational success. Once employees are nominated to attend a training program, based on the position or a leader's recommendation, attendance is generally required. Some courses are required to assume additional job responsibilities, and may even include a final exam. For example, Administrative Assistants must complete a formal Oracle course before they can request office supplies.

Leaders are flexible in allowing employees to take time off work to attend training programs. For instance, one employee, an Assistant Manager of Customer Service, was allowed to take one year of leave time to attend a course to prepare for the Chartered Financial Analyst (CFA) exam. The employees also value the courses. Training certificates are proudly displayed in many offices.

Despite the wealth of formal training options, employees were quick to identify a few problems. In general, the training programs were often taken or assigned on a somewhat *ad hoc* basis, and were not always linked to the job or employees' specific needs. Senior management and human resources often required courses for a group of employees. Sometimes the courses were perceived as too basic. For instance, an employee with five years of sales experience complained he had to take an introductory course on Retail Credit Products. Sometimes the courses were repetitive. A Customer Service Representative said she had to take the same customer service course three times. There were also scheduling conflicts as employees were required to attend training courses, but had to complete formal job responsibilities at the same time. This was stressful as employees had to balance the bank's policies regarding attendance versus job responsibilities that often involved important customer service issues. Employees also felt there were some gaps in the course offerings. One service representative noted "there are no courses for writing in English even though English is a second language for most UAE Nationals".

On-the-Job Training and Development

Turning to on-the-job training (OJT), a number of employees recognized the importance of OJT as compared to formal training programs. The employees were generally satisfied with the support received by the immediate manager. One service representative said "my manager was very patient in giving me enough time to learn the job". Leaders also appear to be effective in providing stretch assignments. One of the marketing employees told her manager she was getting bored with her job. Later that month, the bank introduced a new product. So the manager gave the marketing employee an advertising budget and a specific sales target for the quarter. The manager also provided systematic guidance. The employee said "the assignment was very hard at first, but I was ultimately successful in reaching the sales goal".

Employees were also quite positive regarding the developmental support they received from peers. One service representative said she learned to write memos from one of her peers. Interestingly, there did not appear to be any conflict or issues between UAE Nationals and expatriates. This is noteworthy given the clear inequities between local and non-local employees.

With that said, when considering training and development in general, employees still placed more emphasis on the formal training programs as compared to OJT. There was the general sense that many leaders tended to react to specific requests or issues, and were not particularly proactive or strategic in developing subordinates. A few employees indicated that leaders were supportive during the orientation process, and helpful in providing stretch assignments, but provided less systematic guidance between these two periods (e.g., after the first month but before 18 months). Also, the leaders mentioned that they received little support from HR in terms of OJT.

Career Development

With respect to long-term career development, the employees were generally satisfied with their career progression, and this was even true for lower level employees who were in the same job for many years. The bank is rather flexible in offering employees the option of many different jobs. For example, one of the Administrative Assistants was offered a position as either a Customer Service Representative or Teller. Not surprisingly, she chose the Customer Service position as it is more prestigious than the Teller position. Employees also reported that managers have regular career discussions with them and they believe the quality of these discussions is quite good. Employees felt that managers were generally candid and accurate in discussing employee strengths and limitations. One employee was quite complimentary in indicating that her leader was correct in recognizing that she had to develop her communication and negotiation skills, and was candid in indicating that she had to develop these skills to be eligible for promotion. But, the leader did not stop there. He provided specific, weekly goals for the employee. The employee said she was often unable to reach the goals, but she felt the goals were fair and the entire process built her skills and self-confidence.

The leaders highlighted a few suggestions to improve career development processes. One leader was surprised that HR did not offer structured career paths, along with the corresponding skill requirements. She said "we are really left to our own when it comes to career coaching". Related to this, another leader wondered if the organization was providing UAE Nationals with too many career options. For example, given the choice between a corporate office position and Teller position, few would chose to be a Teller even though this is an excellent foundation for learning banking operations and building a range of important skills such as attention to detail, handling stress, and dealing with customers.

The Manager of Customer Support mentioned that it is also important to recognize that promotions generally require that a position be open. Although the bank has been flexible with creating positions and offering some "in place" promotions, it is also important that leaders and employees come to terms with the realities of managing headcount and budgets. Finally, one leader noted that UAE National leaders are naturally supportive of other UAE Nationals, and devote less attention to the development of expatriates. She went on to say: "This is understandable, but we have to be careful as preferential treatment can lead to conflict among employees. This does not appear to be a problem at the moment, but this should be managed over time".

Reflection

United Bank's emphasis on training and development is consistent with UAE culture and the government's focus on developing its citizens. Based on employee perceptions, this strategy appears to be reasonably effective. Leaders seem to be satisfied with employee performance, and employees are generally satisfied with their jobs, developmental opportunities, and rate of career progression. And if United Bank were to adopt some of the suggestions offered by the employees the training and development initiatives might even be more effective. Interestingly, this heavy reliance on training and development contrasts with Western HRM practices, which generally place more emphasis on rigorous selection processes and motivational interventions such as pay-for-performance. This provides additional evidence suggesting that best practices in HRM may be contingent on broader cultural dynamics.

Questions

1 What are the strengths of United Bank's training and development initiatives? How about the weaknesses?
2 How might the human resource function be more helpful regarding the banks' training and development activities?
3 How might the leaders be more effective in developing employees? How could employees play a more active role?
4 What cultural characteristics appear to be influencing, for better or worse, the training and development processes?
5 This case examines training and development from the employees' perspective. What other perspectives might be considered, and what issues might be most important to these stakeholders?

Notes

1 The name of the organization has been changed.
2 Sections of the background material have been reproduced from Martin and Solomon (2012), a case from the first edition of this Casebook that was also set in the UAE.

References

Al-Ali, J. (2008). Emiratisation: Drawing UAE nationals into their surging economy. *International Journal of Sociology and Social Policy*, 28(9/10), 365–379.

Blanchard, P.N., & Thacker, J.W. (2012). *Effective training: Systems, strategies, and practices*. Upper Saddle River, NJ: Prentice Hall.

Carl, D., Gupta, V., & Javidan, M. (2004). Power distance. In R.J. House, P.J. Hanges, M. Javidan, P.W. Dorfman, & V. Gupta (Eds.), *Culture, leadership, and organizations: The GLOBE study of 62 societies* (pp. 513–563). Thousand Oaks, CA: Sage Publications.

Forstenlechner, I. (2008). Workforce nationalization in the UAE: Image versus integration. *Education, Business and Society: Contemporary Middle Eastern Issues, 1*(2), 82–91.

Hofstede, G. (2001). *Culture's consequences: Comparing values, behaviors, institutions, and organizations across nations.* Thousand Oaks, CA: Sage Publications.

Martin, S.L., & Solomon, W.M. (2012). Developing the local workforce in a rapidly growing economy. In J.C. Hayton, M. Biron, L.C. Christiansen, & B. Kuvaas (Eds.), *Global Human Resource Management Casebook* (pp. 242–249). New York: Routledge.

Muna, F.A. (1980). *The Arab executive.* London: The Macmillan Press.

Rees, C.J., Mamman, A., & Braik, A.B. (2007). Emiratization as a strategic HRM change initiative: Case study evidence from a UAE petroleum company. *International Journal of Human Resource Management, 18*(1), 33–53.

Suliman, A.M.T. (2006). Human resource management in the United Arab Emirates. In P.S. Budhwar & K. Mellahi (Eds.), *Managing human resources in the Middle East* (pp. 59–78). London: Routledge.

Part V
Asia and the Pacific Rim

25

China

Using Human Resource Management to Reshape the Labour Relations Structure at a Chinese Automobile Manufacturer

Shiyong Xu, Huan Wang, Ning Li, and Lihua Zhang

Mr Sun is the head of the human resources department at Jiangsu.[1] DL Automobile (Group) Co. Ltd. is one of the largest automobile manufacturers in China, and owns fifteen plants globally, 45 production lines, sells 3.5 million vehicles annually, has net assets of 27 billion USD, and employs 95,000 employees worldwide. Jiangsu is the group's subsidiary located in Jiangsu province. Jiangsu has sold over 1 million no-frills vehicles since it was founded in 2003, and currently employs over 2,300 workers. At the end of 2014, forecasts showed Jiangsu could expect a 26.6 percent decline in annual production in 2015 due to reduced market demand for no-frills vehicles. The senior managers at Jiangsu, including Mr Sun, were called to a meeting to identify symptoms of the slump and voice their suggestion to counter it.

Regarding human resource management (HRM), the consensus indicated that there were four major challenges: first, the Jiangsu provincial government launched a strategic initiative to attract automobile manufacturers, which meant there were now seven rival brands in the region, making it extremely competitive to attract suitable research and design (R&D) talent; second, compare to other subsidiaries, Jiangsu has a lower than average educational background (i.e. 58.21 percent holding a bachelor's degree and above, compared to 97.11 percent of workers at the Beijing subsidiary), putting it at a disadvantage when acquiring resources from the corporate headquarters; third, the 11 percent wage increase the factory had offered over the recent years is lower than the provincial average, which made it harder for them to attract good new employees; finally, a complex labour relations structure that includes contract workers, dispatch workers, and outsourced workers has proven to be the biggest challenge because for every HRM practice, Jiangsu had to launch three separate standards. Acknowledging the various challenges, the senior management decided to tackle the labour relations structure problem first.

Labour Relations Structures in China

The labour relations structure refers to the co-existence of contract workers, dispatch workers, and outsourced workers. Contract workers are known as 'formal workers' in China. Besides the contract to guarantee their legal rights, a contract worker has a certain social status because this was the successor of the now extinct 'regular worker'. When China was operating under a planned economy, jobs were distributed and set for life. Workers with permanent jobs were called 'regular workers' and it was considered an honour. The situation changed when the Chinese government introduced two regulations on 12 July 1986: *Provisional Rules for Implementing Contract Works at State Owned Enterprises* and *Provisional Rules for State Owned Enterprises to Recruit*. While regular worker status remained on the books, all new workers 'formally' hired by a business thereafter (not limited to state-owned enterprises) are considered a 'contract worker'. When a worker has a contract with Jiangsu, the company is responsible for their wages and welfare expenses. At the end of 2014, contract workers accounted for 65 percent of Jiangsu's workforce.

Dispatch and outsourced workers are mostly referred to as 'informal workers'. Though outsourced workers are a sub-category of dispatch workers, the fundamental difference is that dispatch workers are managed by Jiangsu itself, although the worker signs a labour contract and receives income from the dispatch company. In comparison, the outsourced worker operates on Jiangsu production lines, but the entire production line has been outsourced and is being managed solely by the outsourcing company. Due to the similarities, we will refer to both further as dispatch workers and only distinguish outsourced workers when necessary. Dispatch and outsource workers accounted for 35 percent of Jiangsu's workforce at the end of 2014.

National Setting

China, with a population of 1.3 billion and the second largest economy in the world (International Monetary Fund, 2015), is currently striving to achieve its target of 7 percent increase in GDP set for 2015. Since the Deng Xiaoping administration initiated the market reform in 1978, the theme for Chinese economic development has been public ownership being the main body, and developing multiple forms of ownership simultaneously. Because China has a socialist market economy, public ownership is interchangeable with state-owned.

State-owned enterprises (SOE) in China serve to generate economic profit, with a workforce of 36.98 million as of 2013 (*People's Daily*, 2014). They also have political duties to maintain social stability. Therefore, SOEs in China are not as flexible as their private sector counterparts. Until now, there have been two major reforms for Chinese SOEs. The first reform occurred in the 1990s when the government deregulated many industries and as a result, millions of workers faced 'xiagang' (Chinese for 'lay-off' but this only applies when the person exits an SOE).

The birth of the dispatch system in China can be attributed to foreign entities. In the 1970s, because foreign agencies and companies could not legally hire Chinese citizens, the government issued a regulation to allow Chinese dispatch agencies to fulfil the demand. However, the flourish of dispatch agencies is a direct result from the first SOE reform, when a large number of 'xiagang' workers had to change career. In an interview conducted by Guo and Chang (2005: 97), one worker noted:

> The factory once used 11 buses to drive 3,000 people to the labour fair, and said there are thousands of jobs waiting for us, the city told the factory to take us. 11 buses made 3 trips, you tell me how many people (went there)? With all these people, for an entire morning, in the end only 3 registered. People look at your education, you are not qualified; your age is close to retirement, you are not qualified. The jobs are good, but when it comes down to actually hiring people, the companies hesitated. What skills do you

have? What education do you have? How old are you? How about your health? Aren't all these hard questions?

(source: yhsq2004fm)

To quickly reallocate labour forces to the more viable free-market, the Chinese government at the time not only encouraged non-government organisations to participate in career management, including referral, consulting, and training, but also took a step further to subsidise SOEs with large reallocation numbers to establish their own dispatch agencies. In Hofstede *et al's* (2010) cultural study 'Cultures and Organizations: Software of the Mind', China is considered a high power distance culture, in which people are more susceptible to hierarchical treatment. It was the combination of government actions and, more importantly, the sacrifices made by millions of Chinese 'xiagang' workers, which cultivated the economic boom in the following 20 years.

With the Chinese economy showing signs of slowing down, SOEs in China underwent the second major wave of national SOE reform. As part of the reform, which directly affects the labour relations structure, the Ministry of Human Resources and Social Security issued a regulation on 24 January 2014 to limit the percentage of dispatch, including outsourced, workers to a maximum of 10 percent, and set the deadline to reach this target by 1 March 2016.

The Rise of the Mixed Labour Relations Structure at Jiangsu

Jiangsu was founded almost 20 years after the first SOE reform. Over these 20 years, dispatch services in China had grown substantially. The All-China Federation of Labour estimated that there were 25 million dispatch workers in 2006, and 37 million in 2011 (13.3 percent of the entire workforce). In 2010, the Chinese automobile market sold 18.06 million vehicles, three times more than the USA, with 5.77 million (Sina Auto, 2011).

In 2005, to meet the ever-growing demand for their vehicles, Jiangsu made a request to DL headquarters for permission to bring in outside workers. Jiangsu made it very clear to the headquarters that they would only involve dispatch companies in three areas: non-core, auxiliary, and seasonal workers. Non-core means the dispatch services are not allowed into any research and development (R&D), accounting, and human resources departments; auxiliary means dispatch workers can only work on labour-intensive parts of the assembly line, such as painting but not colour mixing; finally, for seasonal workers, summer is always the busiest and winter the lowest season for the automobile industry, and was especially so for welding, painting and punching lines. In the end, in an attempt to capture the booming market opportunity, the DL headquarters gave Jiangsu the green light to bring in dispatch workers.

Bringing in Dispatch Workers

From the very beginning, different levels of management at Jiangsu were involved with dispatch services: the top management were in charge of the key issues, i.e. which part of the operation is open to dispatch, how much funding should be provided, and what standards were to be developed to choose dispatch companies. All department heads were involved in evaluating the dispatch services to ensure successful implementation.

Two key issues were quickly identified. First, some managers were not too happy at including dispatch workers on their team. First, these managers did not trust dispatch workers' ability and worried that they might jeopardise their group performance bonuses. To ease their concerns, management at both Jiangsu and the dispatch company allowed managers to participate in the initial interviews before workers were hired by the dispatch service. After five or six interviews, both the dispatch company and team leader were able to familiarise themselves with each other's preferences. The second problem was that the level of collaboration among formal Jiangsu workers was low with dispatch workers, mainly because of the feeling their jobs might be in contention. To promote teamwork, Jiangsu started training the workers together, and because the workload was so high when dispatch workers were first brought in, as time passed, the resistance from formal workers decreased. There were also certain perks, such as dental insurance, that were exclusively available to formal workers, which also helped to maintain their 'formal' status. On the other hand, an unlimited number of dispatch workers could become formal workers at Jiangsu, but to qualify, their peer-rated job performance had to pass 60 percent. Overall, by including both the supervisors and team members in the transition process, dispatch workers quickly started to fit in at Jiangsu. When asked about the benefits of bringing in dispatch workers in 2005, it was the best of both worlds for Sun: lower cost and less hassle. On the production side, as the dispatch services became more effectively embedded with Jiangsu's production, team leaders started to see the benefits: 'Most of the time, the orders come in in the afternoon, and we can call LR [the outsource company for painting], tell them we need ten people as soon as possible. Next morning, these ten people show up at work' (Jiang, line manager).

The Fall of the Mixed Labour Relations Structure at Jiangsu

A Chinese proverb says: there is an ebb and flow for everything. Just as people at Jiangsu were getting used to breaking the sales record on an annual basis, the subprime crisis originating from the USA hit China. It marked the end to the over 20 percent annual increase era for the Chinese automobile market and Jiangsu started to suffer in both manufacturing and sales units (see Figure 25.1).

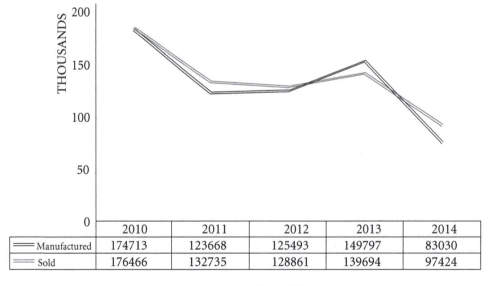

	2010	2011	2012	2013	2014
Manufactured	174713	123668	125493	149797	83030
Sold	176466	132735	128861	139694	97424

Figure 25.1 Units manufactured and sold between 2010 and 2014 at Jiangsu DL

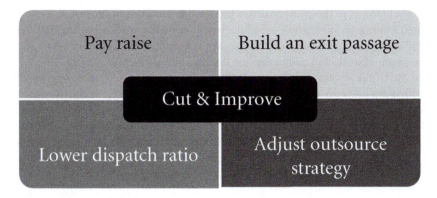

Figure 25.2 Cut and Improve at Jiangsu DL

Another major event contributing to the fall of the labour relations structure at Jiangsu happened 1900 km away on 17 May 2010, when the workers at a subsidiary of a Japanese automaker went on strike. It was one of the first publicly reported labour disputes in China. The event was ignited by differences in pay between Chinese and Japanese workers. In reaction, the government started to focus on improving workplace equity by launching the movement called 'same work same pay'. On 28 December 2012, the Chinese government issued its 'Decision to Modify Labour Contract Law', of which the main focus was to provide equal pay to dispatch workers.

With strict law and legislation to protect the interests of dispatch workers, Jiangsu was facing the difficult question of what they should do to move forward: should they relinquish the benefits of dispatch workers by staying in the legally safe zone, or continue to employ dispatch workers in large numbers but risk labour disputes?

These two questions were raised at the meeting mentioned at the very beginning of this case. At the end of the meeting, Sun and the management at Jiangsu decided to launch an initiative called 'Cut and Improve', which included four specific measures: increasing pay, building an exit strategy, lowering the dispatch worker ratio, and amending the outsourcing strategy (see Figure 25.2).

Pay Raise Versus Pay Cut

To defeat the enemy without combat is a benevolent act.

Sun Tzu, *Art of War*

Jiangsu knew their biggest enemy was the slowing market, and the strict legislation was just a growing pain. Contrary to the traditional approach used to deal with declining demand, namely pay cuts, Jiangsu decided to give all workers a pay raise to motivate them. Specifically, Jiangsu raised the monthly base wage for everyone working on the production line from 1800 RMB to 2000 RMB (around 282 USD to 313 USD), or an 11 percent increase. More importantly, to clarify values for each job position and promote organisational fairness on the production lines, Jiangsu built a six-level compensation framework from a minimum of 50 RMB to a maximum of 300 RMB based on job importance and labour intensity; the average gain from this framework was 212 RMB.

The development of the compensation framework consisted of four steps. First, Jiangsu conducted a thorough job analysis for all the positions on the production line. Each post was measured on three dimensions, which also gave three points to each dimension: the workload, the length of work, and work intensity. For example, a forklift driver has a job value of 5, while an electronic testing and debugging engineer has a value of 8. Second, based on the analysis, Jiangsu drew up a matrix to fit 43 different jobs consisting of the four production lines and four levels of job importance (allowing multiple job values to co-exist in one level so that the line managers also had some flexibility to adjust compensation pay-out on special occasions). Third, Jiangsu specified the compensation amount for each class value and job value. Finally, the company announced the compensation procedure to the workers, asked for feedback, made adjustments and reinforced the compensation framework.

Building an Exit Strategy

Victory is the most valuable aspect of war; Long lasting is the least valuable aspect.

Sun Tzu, *Art of War*

As a state-owned enterprise, the formal jobs at Jiangsu were referred to as iron bowl in the planned economy era. Although less secure in more recent times, it was still very unusual to see contracted workers being fired at Jiangsu. To Mr Sun, the problem with this lack of an exit channel was twofold. First, because Jiangsu did not have a tradition of firing people, the existing workers did not have a sense of urgency to meet work standards. As for the lack of tradition of firing contracted workers, Sun explained:

Some of their families have been with the company for 2–3 generations, and people like that also know each other very well so we know if we push too hard, they may stand together against us. So for us, even for those who had unreasonable requests to skip work or had a higher default rate, we would not go too hard on them. Besides, we need them sometimes to regulate the work climate with the locals; one manager alone sometimes cannot manage everyone on the line.

After the meeting with management, Mr Sun asked the HRM department to analyse the situation regarding some of the most troublesome workers:

One worker always said he had lung problems because he worked for us back in 2006 for 3 months, and he had been on our paid medical leave for years. On the other hand, we know he drives a taxi in town. Every time we tried to get his contract terminated, he and his family would come to the front gate, use big banners to block our gate, saying we did him wrong, but refused when we tried to take him to the hospital.

The HRM department identified four types of workers that required special attention, and decided on an appropriate strategy (see Figure 25.3): first, long-time non-working and non-qualified workers would be terminated regardless of the cost; second, workers with low performance and a temporary contract would not be renewed; third, low-performance workers would be rotated to other positions until there was no other option than terminating their contract; finally, contracts would be terminated for those committing gross misconduct, such as having a record of stealing or fighting.

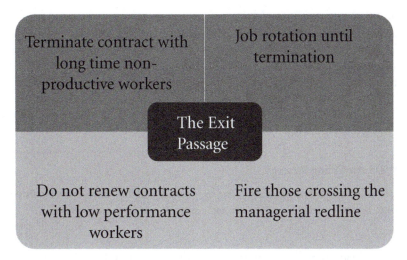

Figure 25.3 Exit passage for four types of workers

Unlike previous attempts, Jiangsu dedicated January 2015 as 'dispute resolution month' to exclusively reach deals with the long-term non-productive workers. Jiangsu drew up a plan for each of these workers based on their unique situation. They then reported to the government that there might be more than ten but fewer than 50 workers being terminated according to company policy and labour law. Jiangsu appointed the head of legal, the corresponding manager and Sun to sit in the same office every other day to deal with these long-term non-productive workers one at a time. To ensure the rights of the workers, they also invited city labour dispute officers to sit in and allowed the workers to bring a legal consultant. Some negotiations lasted for an entire day and were occasionally heated, but since the top management was present, most cases ended promptly, with a few exceptions going into legal process. As of November 2015, Jiangsu had terminated contracts with 26 employees.

Lower Dispatch Ratio

Good commanders are flexible like a snake. Attack the head, the tail will strike; attack the tail, the head will strike; attack the middle, both head and tail will strike.

Sun Tzu, *Art of War*

For Jiangsu, they had both efficiency and legal reasons to lower the ratio of dispatch workers. At the beginning of 2014, dispatch workers accounted for 35 percent of the workforce. To achieve the 10 percent target set by the government, Jiangsu decided to employ a threefold strategy. First, they sought out high performance dispatch workers, and signed them over to Jiangsu as officially contracted workers. This gesture not only showed dispatch workers that Jiangsu was a fair company that appreciated everyone's work, but it also surprised management to see formal Jiangsu workers starting to act in a more friendly way towards dispatch workers, and being more willing to collaborate with them, because they did not know who would become their next long-term co-worker. For 2014, some 200 previously dispatch workers were contracted. Second, Mr Sun started to send Jiangsu in-house HRM staff to colleges to hire qualified workers. This channel was used to replace the vacancies created from voluntary turnover or dispatch workers whose contract had come to an end. Overall, 30 students were contracted in 2015. Finally, for those low performing, low education and low attitude dispatch workers, there were six involuntary lay-offs.

As a result, from the three channels to lower the dispatch ratio, in September 2015, the ratio of dispatch workers at Jiangsu had decreased from 35 percent at the beginning of 2014 to 20 percent, or a total of 280 dispatch workers, and was on track to meet the national legal standard by December 2015.

Amend the Outsourcing Strategy

Highest level of warfare uses strategy, next level uses diplomacy, and implement large army after that, the lowest level is to siege, whereby siege should be the last resort.

Sun Tzu, *Art of War*

So far, Jiangsu had been extremely successful with its 'Cut and Improve' initiative, more specifically the 'cut' part. However, improving the labour relations structure had proven to be a challenging task. Outsourcing was successful because it was outsourced: Jiangsu did not have to directly manage the outsourced employees. So, after deliberating plans between renegotiating costs, replacing outsourced workers with dispatch workers, or layingoff some of the outsourced workers, Jiangsu decided it was time to progressively reduce outsourcing by instilling control into the process.

The first decision Jiangsu made after the meeting was to become involved in managing the outsourcing, and named it 'synchronising management'. To improve quality consistency, Jiangsu started to insert their own team leaders into all outsourced lines and directly manage the outsourced employees. In total, they inserted 37 team leaders in punching, welding and painting lines, and after two months, they had already reduced the quality problem that could be attributed to poor management by 10 percent.

When the market was booming, the most effective outsourcing payment strategy was to pay by the unit. It allowed the outsourcing company to boost bonuses for their workers and led to increased production. In addition, it was an outsourcing company's market at the time, so Jiangsu also had to set a minimum quantity pay-out, i.e. should vehicle quantity be below a certain threshold, Jiangsu would still pay for that quantity. This was never an issue until the market started to slow and the minimum pay-out became a problem, not only because of the unprocessed units that cost Jiangsu money, but also because the car prices were declining while the unit price associated with a minimum quantity had been set in 2010, at the peak of the market price.

In May 2015, with Mr Sun from the HRM department, joined by managers from legal, the corresponding department, and finance, Jiangsu commissioned a team to renegotiate the deal with the outsourcing company. In the end, Jiangsu would no longer pay outsourcing companies by the unit but by the number of workers they sent.

Finally, to implement lean production, the technical department, logistics and HRM jointly formed another team to conduct 165 job analyses on punching, welding and painting, including job timing, and deconstruction and integration of processes. With the information they gathered, they were able to re-balance the workload, improve processes and standardise worker requirements, and arranged with the outsourcing company to provide them with monthly worker requirements on the 15th of each month. The number of outsourced workers declined significantly over 2015 at Jiangsu (see Figure 25.4).

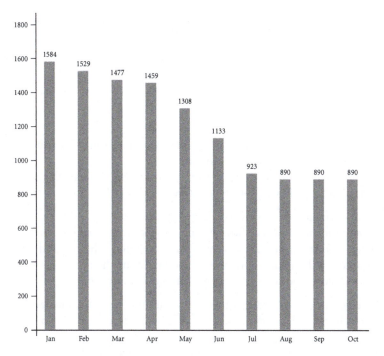

Figure 25.4 Trend for outsource workers at Jiangsu DL

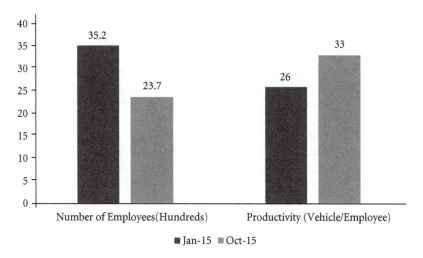

Figure 25.5 Results from Cut and Improve initiative

Closing Comments from Mr Sun (see Figure 25.5)

In 2015, there were a lot of workers we let go but our production and sales were not affected as much. When the managers said 'cut and improve', I figured I am responsible for executing the 'cut' side, but it turned out that I felt more involved being on the team responsible for improvement. It feels good to know you have motivated people here at Jiangsu, and now we are more confident to ride through whatever that is coming at us.

(Sun)

Case Study Tasks

Questions for Group/Class Discussion

1 Do you think the 'Cut and Improve' initiative was successful at Jiangsu? Are there measures you would have taken to improve it?
2 Given the information provided on China, how do you evaluate the measures Jiangsu had taken on the following four types of workers and why?

(a) Long-term non-productive workers;
(b) Low performing workers whose contract was about to end;
(c) Low performing workers whose contract was valid, who received rotation opportunities until no other option remained but to fire them;
(d) Firing those who commit gross misconduct (e.g. stealing).

2 How do you interpret 'to defeat the enemy without combat is a benevolent act' in the pay raise situation? Do you think a pay raise would be effective in your country/company?
3 Given the current shifting legislature and market circumstances in China, assume your company has a subsidiary in China and you are the HR manager: how would you determine the number of workers and the labour relations structure/ratio at your subsidiary?

Role-play Exercise

Mr Sun, the head of the HRM department at Jiangsu, was given the authority to lead the negotiation team with the outsourcing company LS. LS had collaborated with Jiangsu since 2005 when they won the outsourcing contract for three out of five painting lines. To Sun, LS is actually one of the better outsourcing companies; beside occasional minor quality control problems, Jiangsu and LS had been happy with each other.

Now it had come to the point at which the contract, which was renewed in 2013 and still had more years to go, was less advantageous to Jiangsu. The internal meeting at Jiangsu accepted a maximum compensation of half a million RMB to LS but would like to keep it to a minimum. With the heads of legal, painting, and finance on the negotiation team, Sun is determined to reach a new agreement with LS, for which the new terms would include two key features:

1 Change the payment arrangement from vehicle unit-based to being based on the number of outsourced employees.
2 Send new worker requirements to LS each month.

(a) Allocate roles to five individuals: Mr Sun (A), legal manager (B), painting department manager (C), financial manager (D) and manager of LS (E).
(b) Each individual should take 10–15 minutes to prepare the issues or arguments that are considered to be relevant to his/her role.

(c) Hold a meeting at which A first states his/her negotiation strategy with B, C and D; second, B, C and D give their feedback based on their departmental concern; and third, the parties A, B, C, D and E engage in a constructive dialogue on terms of the deal.

Note

1 The authors have been granted permission to publish findings about this case. However, at the request of the company, company name, location, employee names, numerical figures have been altered.

References

Guo, Y., & Chang, A. (2005). Life Cycle and Social Security: A Sociological Exploratory Study on the Life Cycle of Layoff Workers. *Social Sciences in China* (5), 93–107(in Chinese).

Hofstede, G., Hofstede, G. J., & Minkov, M. (2010). *Cultures and Organizations: Software of the Mind*, (Third Edition). Boston, MA: McGraw-Hill Education.

International Monetary Fund. (2015). *Report for Selected Countries and Subjects*. Retrieved Nov. 13, 2015, from http://www.imf.org/

People's Daily. (2014). *Statistics of State-owned Enterprises Making Its Debut*. Retrieved Nov. 14, 2015, from http://paper.people.com.cn/rmrbhwb/html/2014–07/29/content_1458453.htm

Sina Auto. (2011). *Chinese Automobile Market in 2010*. Retrieved Nov. 14, 2015, from http://auto.sina.com.cn/csgc/c1014/

26

Hong Kong

Engaging the Next Generation of Leaders at
MostClean Hong Kong[i]

Christina Sue-Chan[a] and Clara To[b]

Organisational Setting

MostClean Ltd. is a USA-headquartered, global leader in water, hygiene and energy technologies and services. In 2014, the company employed over 45,000 people and operated in approximately 170 countries. Over half of the company's net sales of over US$14 billion in 2014, was generated in the United States and Canada. Countries in Latin America, Europe, Middle East, Africa, and the Asia Pacific region generated the remaining sales. Hong Kong, a Special Administrative Region of the People's Republic of China (PRC) since 1997, is part of MostClean Ltd.'s emerging Asia Pacific region, which also includes India, Australia, New Zealand, and the PRC. This region accounted for 12 percent of the company's sales in 2014.

The company is currently organised into three segments globally, Global Industrial, Global Institutional, and Global Energy, around the "lines of business" principle. Global Industrial delivers solutions, such as water treatment, mainly to large industrial clients within the pulp and paper, manufacturing, commercial laundry, chemical, food and beverage processing, mining and primary metals, and power generation industries. Global Institutional offers specialised cleaning and sanitising products to the retail, healthcare, education, government, food service, hospitality, and lodging industries. Global Energy supplies the water treatment and process chemical needs of the global petrochemical and petroleum industries. A fourth segment, 'Other', comprises fee-for-services pest elimination and equipment care businesses.

MostClean Hong Kong has played a key role in the global growth of the company since 2008. In 2008, the Asia Pacific region accounted for only 9 percent of the company's sales, and globally, MostClean Ltd. employed only 55 percent of its current number of employees and had 41 percent of its current net sales. Talent development has figured prominently in the growth of MostClean Ltd. since 2008. Developing talent in MostClean Hong Kong was particularly challenging.

i The names of company and all individuals associated with the company have been changed to preserve anonymity. The authors are grateful to the company for granting permission to publish this case.

In Hong Kong, the three key lines of business are Pest Elimination, Food and Beverage Processing, and Institutional. The Pest Elimination business uses scientifically developed protocols to eliminate pests in institutional/commercial market segments. The Food and Beverage business provides critical environment sanitation products and systems for the dairy, food and beverage processing, agricultural and pharmaceutical markets. The Institutional business offers cleaning and sanitation products, programs and services to customers in a variety of industries.

Sales in Hong Kong have been significant since MostClean Ltd. acquired full interests in its Hong Kong joint venture in 1984. By 2008, MostClean Hong Kong was experiencing double-digit sales growth. This growth was achieved by approximately 200 employees employed in the Hong Kong business units (BU) and supporting departments which include Finance and Accounting, Human Resources, Information Technology, Law and Regulatory, and Marketing. Figure 26.1 shows the organisational structure of each BU.

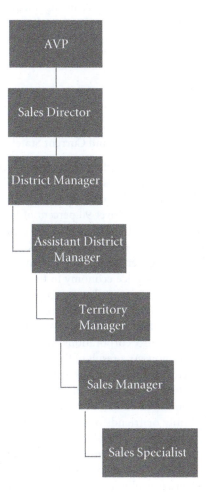

Figure 26.1 Structure of each business unit

Note: AVP = Assistant Vice-President

The key corporate account management concept for clients of MostClean Ltd. is based on the concept of bundling services for customers around the globe. As such, cross-BU synergy (i.e., Pest Elimination, Food and Beverage, and Institutional) is encouraged in order to serve key accounts around the globe. In the Asia Pacific Region International Operations, the Hong Kong office has long been serving as a role model for this concept and is a pioneer in developing cross-BU service programs for customers. This means that MostClean Ltd. differentiates itself from competitors by providing customer-focused sanitisation service and solutions rather than generic commodities to its clients.

As a contributor to the global growth of MostClean Ltd. and a pioneer in developing cross-BU services for customers, the Hong Kong office possesses a strong team work culture and positive morale. For example, cross-BUs readily support and leverage resources among themselves to work with customers, and managers are active in field work with their teams if needed. The challenges of being a growth- and service-oriented company competing in commodities industries, however, mean that the HRM challenges confronting the Hong Kong office are twofold. First, executives in the Hong Kong office need to further enhance their professional maturity and leadership competence in alignment with the global, ecologically friendly service values of the company. Second, HRM needs to engage existing managers and new employees. These twin challenges need to be met in a context where the professionalism and expertise of the HRM function in Hong Kong as well as its role as a business partner are still being developed.

Historical Background to the Case

HRM in Hong Kong: Historical Perspective and Current State[1]

Situated in the southeastern corner of the PRC, Hong Kong is enclosed by the Pearl River Delta and South China Sea. Hong Kong has economic, judicial and political systems that are different from those of the PRC. It is one of the world's leading international financial centres with a capitalist service economy (over 90 percent of Hong Kong's Gross Domestic Product, HK$2,144.6 billion (US$276.7 billion) in 2014 was generated by the service sector). Unlike citizens of the PRC, the 7 million residents of Hong Kong enjoy relatively low income taxation, free trade, and minimum government intervention.

Before its transformation into a service economy in the 1980s, Hong Kong had thrived initially as an entrepôt of the British Empire. The end of World War II and the continuing civil war in China were accompanied by an influx of unskilled migrants from China. The victory of the Communist Party in that civil war in 1949 not only saw even more migrants entering British-Hong Kong but also corporations, which relocated from Communist-controlled Shanghai and Guangzhou. As a result of this influx, Hong Kong rapidly industrialised as a textile and manufacturing hub driven by exports.

The HRM practices in the typically small, family-owned businesses that made up these low-technology, low-skill, labour-intensive industries were relatively unsophisticated. Recruitment was through family or friends of existing employees or labour contractors, all of whom received bonuses for their referrals. Selection criteria, such as physical ability, willingness to work hard and loyalty, were implicit rather than explicit. In brief, manufacturing employees were low-cost commodities who were easily replaceable. Whether these employees invested themselves physically, cognitively and emotionally in their work role performance,[2] that is, whether they were engaged with their work, seemed to matter little to employers who were only concerned about meeting production targets at the lowest cost possible. Hong Kong employees reciprocated their treatment as commodities by leaving their employers when they were able to obtain higher-paying jobs with another company.

With the implementation of the PRC's open-door policy in 1979, Hong Kong's advantage in low-cost manufacturing began to erode as even lower-cost facilities were relocated across the border and in other international locations (e.g., Vietnam, Thailand, Bangladesh) throughout the 1980s, 1990s, and first decade of the twenty-first century. Recognising that Hong Kong had to become a supplier of more value-added services to drive economic growth, the government of Hong Kong implemented policies to help Hong Kong employees and employers increase their skill levels.

Government training and re-training agencies were created, established colleges (Hong Kong Baptist and Lingnan) and polytechnics (Hong Kong Polytechnic University) were granted full university status while a new, research-oriented university (Hong Kong University of Science and Technology) and another polytechnic were founded. The latter was then transformed into a degree-granting university (City University of Hong Kong) specialising in professional education. These institutions focused on equipping high school graduates with the knowledge, skills, and abilities to perform service sectors jobs in finance, marketing, logistics, shipping, aviation, tourism, and human resource management. Beyond formal education provided by tertiary institutions in Hong Kong, however, there is little evidence that Hong Kong-owned companies value the development of their employees. This is unfortunate since employee development is one of the lynchpins of employee engagement.

Employee Engagement in HK

Engagement refers to the physical, cognitive and emotional investment of employees in the performance of their work roles.[2] Engagement is beneficial because engaged employees are proactive, motivated employees who can impact profits, sales, customer ratings, accidents, and turnover. Iconic companies in Hong Kong, such as its leading provider of public transportation (MTR Corporation) and largest financial institution (HSBC), have invested considerable human and financial resources to employ and develop workforces that proudly advocates on behalf of their companies, voluntarily performs extra work to help their companies achieve their objectives, and expresses satisfaction, commitment and pride in working for their companies. In these companies, employee engagement is considered critical to the recruitment, development, and retention of future leaders.

An employee engagement survey conducted by management professors in the Department of Management, City University of Hong Kong in 2010 found that one of the most important reasons for employees' sense of engagement is the availability of developmental opportunities in their current firms; however, employees reported in the survey that their companies did not develop them. Knowing how performance is measured was also frequently mentioned as an important reason for being engaged in their jobs. These results are consistent with those found in surveys conducted by global consulting firms, such as BlessingWhite.[3] The two reasons are complementary since communicating to employees what they are expected to do on the job provides vital clues about whether employees have the knowledge and skills to accomplish what is expected of them and whether they require training to develop knowledge and skills they may lack. While a survey of training needs conducted by the Hong Kong Institute of Human Resources Management in 2006 revealed that 80 percent of responding companies reported that they had a training and development policy, the 2010 City University of Hong Kong engagement survey suggests that HK employees desire more training than is being offered by their companies. When training is provided, only a select few appear to benefit – managers at senior and junior levels tend to be the beneficiaries while unskilled workers are not.

Surveys[4] of on-the-job training offered by companies in Hong Kong indicate that local firms lag behind non-Asian MNCs in providing training to their employees. The insufficient amount of development offered to non-managerial employees relative to the employee demand for such development creates an imbalance in local Hong Kong firms. The implication is that in Hong Kong companies, if employees want to develop their competencies, they need to do so without company support. Once they have acquired new skills, unsurprisingly, employees seek higher paying employment elsewhere to recoup their personal investment in their development.

Employee Engagement in MostClean Hong Kong

MostClean Hong Kong shares the same concerns about engaging its employees as the two iconic firms in Hong Kong, the MTR Corporation and HSBC. Several of its core HRM functions are involved in efforts to recruit, develop and retain future leaders in the company. These are aimed at aligning the values of employees at all levels with those of the organisation; ensuring that employees, particularly those with leadership potential, are knowledgeable about how their performance is measured; and providing learning and development opportunities to employees. By so doing, MostClean addresses the most important reason reported by HK employees in the 2010 engagement survey for their sense of engagement – having similar values to the organisation.

Recruitment and selection are performed to identify people with similar values. As a service-oriented company, employees in MostClean Hong Kong are heavily involved in labour-intensive hands-on field work with their customers, even at odd hours of the day. The company looks for talent who possess personal qualities that are in alignment with their value proposition of helping customers around the globe reduce their own impact on the Earth by conserving resources, improving safety and reducing waste. Employees need to be (a) strong in execution, (b) team players, (c) customer-oriented, and (d) have the potential to advance in leadership. Although it is a Fortune 500 company, it is always challenging for the company to identify the right talent because of the nature of the job and the qualities and values of the people required.

Induction, orientation, and socialisation function to teach employees what the values of the company are. How this is done depends on the level of the employee involved.

- Entry-level employees are given product and service training programs to make them familiar with the company's service portfolio;
- Mid-level managers are mentored by their line manager and encouraged to build strong relationships and obtain support from their peers across functions;
- Senior executives are sent to the HQ in the USA for on-boarding induction and organisation culture immersion.

To further orient executives, HRM acts as the business partner to the BUs to facilitate the integration of executives by leveraging relevant programs or resources locally.

On-the-job coaching and performance appraisal are used to educate employees on what the company's performance criteria are. To ensure that those with leadership potential are well informed about how performance is measured, MostClean Ltd. has a leadership pipeline model with clear benchmarks at each level to evaluate its talent management efforts:

- A six-level (L1 from the top to L6 at the bottom) leadership pipeline model gauges talent management efforts, including selection, development, and performance management, alongside business results (and related key performance indicators (KPI));
- Employees are well aware of the leadership level they are benchmarked against. At each leadership level, there are six KPIs to be evaluated: Leadership, Thinking & Decision Making, Achievement, Interpersonal Relationships, Work Management, and Self-Management.

Learning chances, including executive coaching, training, and developmental assignments, are identified as part of the annual review of the company's talent pipeline. Nominated executives at the L3 level and above will be put through leadership development assessment programs to identify their key strengths and development opportunities. For executives undergoing major transitions to new and/or expanded roles, executive coaching support may be provided to facilitate their ultimate effectiveness.

Problems and Issues

Although MostClean Hong Kong has in place many practices to recruit, develop and retain key leadership talent, there are still problems in the execution of these key practices. Of particular concern is the focus of its on-the-job coaching and the frequency with which learning chances are provided to recognised talent.

On-the-job coaching is not systematic and is geared towards company products, services and solutions. Over-emphasis on business results may have resulted in the six KPIs being overlooked. The senior management of MostClean Ltd. is especially concerned that *Leadership* and in particular, effective delegation and empowerment, as well as *Work Management* related to priority setting (urgency vs. importance) and action planning (depth vs. breadth) are skills that are not being fully developed among the managers of MostClean Hong Kong.

In addition, while learning chances are available and generally supported, there is no structured process to monitor and review who is undertaking the learning opportunities or what benefits are being derived by those who have received executive coaching, training, and developmental assignments. The HRM Director in MostClean Hong Kong is concerned that managers are not particularly motivated to initiate their own learning as the priority communicated to them by senior management is to drive results rather than develop their leadership skills.

Anson Lee's situation is typical of this conflict experienced by managers. Anson was recently promoted to the District Manager role of the Food and Beverage BU. Three months after his promotion, he finds himself with increased responsibility for supervising others, and is unsure about how to adapt from being an independent contributor to being a team leader. He is struggling to find the balance between how to get things done by himself as opposed to through others. Relying on himself prevents him from communicating with subordinates and his counterparts in other BUs and is a source of frustration because he does not see himself growing through the promotion. Yet, he finds that it is time consuming to ensure that others understand what should be done in the right way. At the same time, he has to deal with constant demands from above to attain sales targets. This inevitably drags much of his attention back to daily operational details, which he performs himself, such as client visits, follow-up on contracts, and so on. Consequently, Anson sees that he is valuable to the company because he can generate business but has started to question whether MostClean Hong Kong is committed to helping him achieve his broader leadership and career development goals.

Overall, even though managers at MostClean Hong Kong show a strong willingness to enhance their leadership and decision-making skills by working closely with HRM, the majority of the senior executives (L1 & L2) who have been with the company for a relatively long time are not as supportive in putting talent development as the priority and allocating necessary resources for HRM to drive and execute related initiatives. This is because these senior executives had advanced to leadership roles from entry positions in Sales without the benefits of talent management processes in the company. When they rose through the company in the 1980s and 1990s, the HRM function they were familiar with was one that was purely an administrative function that took orders from rather than worked in partnership with BU managers. During this time, most of the HRM practices were to accomplish mundane personnel matters, such as payroll and benefits administration and processing employment contracts of employees hired by managers, at the local level. It was not until the past decade that MostClean Hong Kong gained access to leverage and benchmark talent management approaches and processes from headquarters. With access, came opportunity and responsibility for using these company-wide talent management tools to develop local managers, and a new, strategic, value-added role for HRM that was, heretofore, unknown to the senior executives.

Jason Wong is the AVP of the Institutional BU; he exemplifies the career track of senior executives in MostClean Hong Kong. Jason progressively advanced to the AVP position because of his strong sales track record. As he joined the company in the 1980s, he is regarded and respected as one of the founding employees of the Hong Kong office. He takes pride in his success in developing new business as well as expanding business among key customer accounts. Jason has developed into a senior leader through hard work and working together with his Sales team without much supervisory support or external guidance. Drawing from his experience of self-developing into his leadership roles, he believes that he only needs to give his team appropriate support for their development in order for the team to become a higher performing team. Without the benefit of formal development or systematic training in strategic leadership as he assumed increasingly senior leadership roles, Jason is inclined to fire-fight when identifying solutions and driving results. For example, he will arrange regular sales team meetings to review and set action plans. Yet, these tend to be tactical rather than strategic in nature and Jason will typically dominate the discussion to come up with actions that he thinks would be feasible based upon his rich sales experience.

The limited functional focus of the senior executives in MostClean Hong Kong has not enabled them to broaden their thinking capacity to be able to plan strategically and execute necessary actions in a systematic manner. Yet, it is this strategic thinking that is now required to recruit, develop, and retain the leadership potential of less experienced young managers in MostClean Hong Kong.

Priscilla Cheung, the HRM Director of MostClean Hong Kong, is considering the task ahead of her. She has to implement the directive from the US headquarters to develop talent globally. Talent development practices were already in place in Hong Kong and employees who would benefit were in favour of a more systematic approach to developing their leadership and soft skills; but these development practices were not being implemented effectively. A more frustrating problem for Priscilla was that the senior executives in MostClean Hong Kong did not see the need to systematically develop leadership talent in the company and did not have high regard for HRM as a business partner. As they had, these senior executives expected the next generation of leaders to emerge from among the sales specialists who were the best at delivering business results. Priscilla knew that other companies in Hong Kong were losing their best young managers and were grappling with the problem of how to keep their talented employees engaged. She feared that if she could not win senior executive support for more systematic talent development in MostClean Hong Kong, the company would also start to lose its most promising managers, like Anson Lee. Similar to many HRM departments in Hong Kong-based companies, she has a very slim team of only one assistant to help her implement this global initiative.

Case Study Tasks

1 Assume you are Priscilla Cheung, the HRM Director of MostClean Hong Kong. What steps would you take to implement MostClean Ltd.'s global initiative of developing talent globally? How would you do this if you could not leverage relevant programs or resources locally? If you could employ locally available resources (e.g., external consultants), what type of consultants would you employ and what would you ask them to do?

2 *Role play exercise*: A focus group has been set up to consider issues concerning how to develop and engage talent in MostClean Hong Kong. The ultimate goal of the group is to develop a systematic plan for talent development. The group consists of the following 4 members:

- Mr. Anson Lee, District Manager – Food and Beverage BU
- Mr. Jason Wong, AVP – Institutional BU
- Ms. Priscilla Cheung, HRM Director
- Mr. Michael Poon, independent consultant

    (a) Allocate a role to each person in the group (use visible role tags). The role of the independent consultant is to facilitate the discussion and make sure that all members voice their concerns.

    (b) Each individual should take 5–10 minutes to list issues relevant to their own role. Consider questions such as: what concerns might I have about talent development and engagement? How could these be addressed? Are there potential benefits involved that may compensate for the possible drawbacks?

    (c) Hold the meeting for about 40 minutes. All members should introduce their issues, and then the group should prioritise 5 key issues (those with mutual concerns) and consider possible solutions.

3 *Questions for group/class discussion:*

- Why is it important to engage employees and develop talent?
- What type of problems might result from the implementation of a systematic talent development and engagement program at MostClean Hong Kong? How would you solve these problems?

Notes

a Department of Management, City University of Hong Kong, Tat Chee Avenue, Kowloon, Hong Kong, S.A.R.
b Founding Director and Principal Consultant, TalentLink Global Limited. Unit 23, 3/F, Block B, Hi-Tech Industrial Centre, 491–501 Castle Peak Road, Tsuen Wan, Hong Kong. Former Vice-President and Managing Director, Mobley Group Pacific, Hong Kong.

References

1 Tsui, A. P. Y., Lai, K. T., & Wong, I. H. M. (2009). The development and current state of HRM in Hong Kong. In A. P. Y Tsui & K. T. Lai (Eds.), *Professional practices of human resource management in Hong Kong: Linking HRM to organizational success*, pp. 1–26. Hong Kong: Hong Kong University Press.

Tsui, A. P. Y., & Lai, K. T. (2009). Conclusion: Future prospects for HRM in Hong Kong. In A. P. Y. Tsui & K. T. Lai (Eds.), *Professional practices of human resource management in Hong Kong: Linking HRM to organizational success*, pp. 281–291. Hong Kong: Hong Kong University Press.

2 Kahn, W. A. (1990). Psychological conditions of personal engagement and disengagement at work. *Academy of Management Journal, 33*, 692–724.

3 BlessingWhite (2013, January). *Employee engagement research update*. Princeton, NJ: BlessingWhite, a Division of GP Strategies.

4 Au, A. K. M., Altman, Y., & Roussel, J. (2008.) Employee training needs and perceived value of training in the Pearl River Delta of China: A human capital development approach. *Journal of European Industrial Training, 32*, 19–31.

Chen, E. (1983). *Multinational corporations, technology and employment*. London: Macmillan.

Zheng, C., Hyland, P., & Soosay, C. (2007). Training practices of multinational companies in Asia. *Journal of European Industrial Training, 31*, 472–494.

Further Readings

Evans, P., Pucik, V., & Bjorkman, I. (2011). *The global challenge: International human resource management* (2nd ed.). New York: McGraw-Hill Irwin.

Federman, B. (2009). *Employee engagement: A roadmap for creating profits, optimizing performance, and increasing loyalty*. San Francisco: Jossey-Bass.

Latham, G. P., & Sue-Chan, C. (2014). Motivational tactics. In B. Schneider and K. Barbera (eds.), *Oxford Handbook of Climate and Culture* (pp. 65–78) London: Oxford University Press.

Tsang, S. Y-S. (2004). *A modern history of Hong Kong*. New York: I. B. Tauris.

Varma, A., Budhwar, P. S., & DeNisi, A. (Eds.). (2008). *Performance management systems: A global perspective*. New York: Routledge.

27

India

Propelling Growth Engine for ICICI Bank, India: Woman Leadership, Gender Equity or Paradigm Shift?

Radha R. Sharma and Sonam Chawla

As Chanda Kochcar, MD and CEO of ICICI Bank, India, received the 'Asia Game Changer Award, 2015' for 'making a positive contribution to the future of Asia', her modest, calm yet resplendent presence resonated with the audience when she acknowledged ICICI as a workplace without glass ceiling that facilitated her journey from a management trainee to the top. Kochhar is one of the distinguished Indian women to appear as '100 Most Influential People in the world' in TIME magazine (Time, 2015) as also in Forbes' list (http://techstory. in/indian-women-in-forbes/ Feb, 2016); which is astonishing given India's gender gap index of 108 out of 145 countries in World Economic Forum Report, 2015.[1] Kochhar took tough decisions and calculated risks during the global financial crisis and her difficult choices were behind her when she declared that ICICI Bank stood no risk from the Greek financial crisis of 2015.

Organisational Setting

ICICI Bank is India's largest private sector bank in assets (USD 103 billion) and the third in market capitalisation a with network of 4,050 branches (as of 31 March 2015) operating in 17 countries. Across India 101 branches provide 'Touch Banking' services leveraging technology for consumers' convenience, and about 13,082 automated teller machines (ATMs) across India (ICICI Bank, 2015). The bank serves over 52 million customers with a range of financial services and products using a variety of delivery channels, specialised subsidiaries and affiliates in the areas of investment banking, life and non-life insurance, venture capital and asset management to serve the corporate and retail customers.

ICICI Bank was formed in 1994 as a subsidiary of the Industrial Credit and Investment Corporation of India Limited (ICICI), which was incorporated at the initiative of World Bank, the Government of India and representatives of Indian industry in 1955, to create a development financial institution for providing medium-term and long-term project financing to Indian businesses. Once established, ICICI undertook normal banking operations, i.e., mobilising deposits, offering credit cards, car loans, and other bank products.

After a series of mergers (with Bank of Madura) and a reverse merger with ICICI, the bank transformed ICICI from an industrial project finance institution into India's most comprehensive financial services powerhouse with interests in retail banking, insurance, online trading and BPO among others, thereby transforming the Indian banking industry. ICICI Bank's equity shares are listed on Indian stock exchanges at Chennai, Delhi, Kolkata and Vadodara, the Bombay stock exchange, and the National Stock Exchange of India Limited and its American Depositary Receipts (ADRs) are listed on the New York Stock Exchange (NYSE).

Background to the Case

India is the largest democracy and the second largest country in the world with 1.21 billion population (comprises over a sixth of the world's population). Sixty percent of its population is aged between 15 and 59 years (Census of India, 2011). Consisting of 29 states and 7 union territories (centrally administered) spread over 3.29 million square kilometres, it is a country of cultural, linguistic, religious and ethnic diversity with a pluralistic worldview, synthesising mind-set and high context sensitivity. There are 22 official languages, 844 dialects, Hindi as the national language (spoken by 40 percent of the population) and English as the business language. India has a federal system of government with clear demarcation of powers between the central and the state governments.

India has high power distance, hence prior to Indian independence (1947) private owners dominated Indian industry, handling employee relations in an *ad hoc* manner (Meyers, 1959; Budhwar, 2003). HRM in India has evolved over the decades from a purely statutory labour welfare function to strategic HRM with 150 laws governing HRM practices (Venkataratnam, 1995).

Liberalisation of the Indian economy led to an inflow of foreign companies resulting in intense competition and expansion of organisational functions. Not only the MNCs but also the domestic firms moved towards HRM. A study of two firms by Amba-Rao (1994) posited that hierarchy and paternalism, though prevalent in Indian companies, have given way to adaptive and innovative styles and approaches for employee management. There is a strong emphasis on collectivism, power distance, and masculinity (Kanungo & Mendonca, 1994). The gender gap is high and work participation of women is 25.56 percent as against 51.7 percent for men (2011 Census of India). Though the Indian constitution grants gender equality and Indian women have been Prime Minister and President of the country, workplace issues relate to gender equity. Few women make it to the top due to socio-economic hurdles, prejudices and covert discrimination (Sharma Radha, 1982; Sharma, R. & Sharma N.P., 2015). Interpersonal relations are important and social, cultural, economic and political factors influence HRM policies and practices.

Economic Reforms and the Globalisation of India.

Since independence in 1947, India has planned its strategy for development through 5-year plans and has seen twelve '5-year plans' so far. All the 5-year plans aimed at steering India out of its socio-economically deprived state to a scientifically and technologically strong and self-reliant nation. This led to setting up state owned industry in all major fields including banks, to provide large-scale employment. Socialism, the dominant ideology of the government, later resulted in low productivity and caused problems of balance of payments. This necessitated economic reforms and in July 1991, the first wave of globalisation and liberalisation commenced comprising economic liberalisation, consumer focus, market orientation and competition. Realising the importance and strengthening the link between social development and economic growth, the Planning Commission of the government brought out a National Human Development Report, 2001. Consequently, banks were required to play a major role in accelerating country's socio-economic development. Therefore, banking reforms constituted a major part the economic reforms to bring about 'operational flexibility' and 'functional autonomy' to enhance 'efficiency, productivity, and profitability'. It also focused on changes in structure and HRM practices to strengthen the foundations of the banking system for greater stability, customer focus, performance, and profitability.

India categorises its economy and GDP as three sectors – agriculture, industry and services. The services sector includes banking, insurance, construction, retail, software, IT, communications, hospitality, infrastructure operations, education, and healthcare, among others where HRM assumes great significance. India has one of the world's fastest growing service sectors contributing 53 percent (2014) to the country's GDP (World Bank, 2014). The private IT companies were the largest private employers in the country.[2] The agricultural sector contributed 17 percent and industry sector 30 percent to the GDP in 2014 (World Bank, 2014), maintaining the trend for the past few years. The Indian government has launched 'Make in India' initiative in 2014 to boost manufacturing to focus on 25 sectors of the economy for job creation and skill enhancement. With more than 1,200 new ventures being set up, over USD 5 billion were invested in Indian start-ups in 2014.

Banking in India originated in the eighteenth century with the first government-owned bank established in 1806. After Indian independence its central bank (called the Reserve Bank of India) was nationalised in 1948, and with the enactment of the Banking Regulation Act in 1949 it was given powers 'to regulate, control, and inspect banks in India'. The government nationalised the 14 largest commercial banks in 1969 and later the next 6 largest banks in 1980. India has 93 scheduled commercial banks, of which 27 are public (government holding stake), 29 private, and 46 foreign banks. ICICI Bank is one of the private banks. As per the advance estimates by the World Bank, India's GDP is expected to grow by 7.5 percent in 2015–16 and 8 percent by 2018. Relationship management is extremely important in banking where women have an edge.

ICICI Bank: Aligning with Business Environment

Considering ICICI Bank was formed in 1994 as a subsidiary of the Industrial Credit and Investment Corporation of India Limited, it has made phenomenal progress in a short span under K. V. Kamath as its MD and CEO in its embryonic stage in 1996, and later under Ms Chanda Kochhar since 2009, succeeding Kamath. It was during Kamath's tenure that ICICI's strategy included the changing demands of the growing middle-class in India and introduced ATMs and cross-selling for convenience and business growth. He brought in direct selling agents to identify prospective customers to initiate dialogue and deliver personalised banking facilities, which changed the banking experience. Kamath's aggressive plans got ICICI Bank listed on the New York Stock Exchange (NYSE) in 1999, the first ever Indian financial institution to go down the American Depositary Receipts (ADR) route. In 2007 ICICI Bank created history by raising USD 5 billion in the largest-ever public offering with total bids worth over USD 25 billion from across the globe.

Meritocracy and performance were the most important criteria in recognising leaders and this strategy facilitated identifying the top 5 percent of the bank's talent who were treated differently. With a view to enhancing market share Kamath focused on identifying and nurturing leaders in the bank who could foresee business opportunities; he believed that women are more likely to articulate and take a stand on corporate matters than men. With the sustained strategy of leadership development ICICI Bank came to be known as a 'CEO factory', which produced leaders, including women, who headed businesses within and outside ICICI; Chanda Kochhar, the current MD & CEO is one of them.

Chanda Kochhar: The Woman Leader

Kochhar is the first woman to head an Indian private sector bank, commencing her career as a trainee at ICICI in 1984. Under her leadership, ICICI Bank leveraged the market, people and technology to provide innovative banking solutions to urban and rural customers, to script a new saga in the Indian banking industry. She spearheaded the bank's evolving retail business in 2000 to the top through her unrelenting efforts, focus on technology, innovation, and expansion of the distribution scale. She led ICICI Bank out of the 2008 financial crisis by re-defining the strategy from aggressive expansion to deliberate consolidation. ICICI transformed itself from a traditional development financial institution to a customer-centric private sector bank. Under Kochhar's leadership, ICICI Bank won the 'Best Retail Bank in India' award along with winner for the category of 'Best Internet Banking Initiative'. Kochhar ranked first in Fortune's list of 'Most Powerful Women' in Asia Pacific (2014) and has been appointed as the President of the International Monetary Conference (since 2015), member of the US–India CEO Forum (2015), member of the India–Japan Business Leaders' Forum (2015) and co-chair of the World Economic Forum's annual meeting (2011). She has also been awarded honorary Doctor of Law by Carleton University, Canada (2014) for her contribution to the financial sector and effective leadership during economic crisis (ICICI Bank, 2015).

Although ICICI Bank was mainly involved with retail banking, with Kochhar's vision it ventured into insurance, corporate banking, venture capital, to name but a few. It rolled out 101 electronic branches and launched many next-generation banking solutions including apps for customer convenience. For financial inclusion and providing banking services in rural areas ICICI bank introduced 'Branch on Wheels' (mobile branch with ATM).[3] On the sixtieth anniversary of the bank in 2015 Kochhar identified three areas for business focus i.e., leveraging technology for banking with the youth, partnership in infrastructure building and skill development for social responsibility.[4]

While Kamath, the earlier CEO, used to articulate the vision and mission for ICICI Bank from time to time, Kochhar is a woman leader of few words, with no long speeches on strategy and vision, but clear emphasis on details and plans. To quote: 'You don't want to micromanage every little thing and constrain the people in your team. But at the same time, you can't get so preoccupied with a vision or dream that you forget about your next big product launch or technology initiative', said Kochhar.[5]

Kamath saw an opportunity in the retail banking space and targeted the Indian middle class with a plan of customer-savvy banking strategies to create a niche for ICICI Bank; Kochhar furthered the vision by making ICICI Bank the first mover on digitising the banking platforms. ICICI Bank's strategy was based on the management principles of decentralisation, empowerment, risk taking, and learning from these, right recruitment and talent management across all levels.

When Kochhar took charge as CEO, the global financial crisis had hit ICICI Bank's profits but Kochhar quickly realised that ICICI Bank would require a paradigm shift in doing business. Though ICICI was the second largest bank by assets, some of its key financial metrics were not looking bright. Kochhar was in a deep dilemma whether to continue with the aggressive approach for business growth the bank had adopted over the years, which helped it attain market leadership, or whether it was time to re-think, in view of the economic volatilities in the environment and the growing size of the organisation.

However, Kochhar took a bold decision to shrink the business by consolidating it to strengthen the fundamentals of the bank. Kochhar, in consultation with her core team, worked out the new strategy of 4Cs focusing on cost, credit, CASA (current account and saving account) ratio, and capital. This was a significant shift from the then existing strategy of focus on growth through retail loans.[6]. She not only worked out the strategy for a turnaround but also wasted no time in convincing the board and getting its approval. She ensured that the decision making process was democratic and communicated both upwards and downwards to each and every employee.

With the backdrop of an uncertain economic environment, she reassured the customers through various communication channels and media and kept her word by the company's on-the-ground actions to keep the customers' faith. It was then that she decided that all the ATMs of the bank would have cash at all times, which was not an easy task given the size of India where the cities and rural areas are not so well connected. Her coolness in dealing with the situation helped ICICI Bank get out of the crisis in no time.[7]

Innovation in Banking Technology

ICICI Bank had been an early adopter of the latest technologies such as mobile banking, internet banking, tab banking, fully automated 24x7 touch banking, banking on Twitter, the digital wallet, among others, accessible to its customers not only in India but also in the UK and Canada. According to Kochhar: 'Our belief is – India's youths live around the fulcrum of digital, social and mobile. So all of us have to see how the business fits in with this.'[8] In view of the demographic trend of India, ICICI Bank wanted to use social media to capture the market share of the younger generation, which was more social media savvy. According to Kochhar, 'Youngsters spend a lot of time on social media platforms like Facebook and Twitter, and extensively use these for social interactions/transactions. ICICI Bank aims to help them complete the financial transactions also on social media.' ICICI Bank had 3.5 million fans on Facebook, which is the highest for any bank in India. The bank also launched its application on Twitter in 2015, which made it the first bank in Asia to provide the facility to transfer funds while on Twitter, as well as Facebook. The bank also launched India's first digital bank called 'Pockets' in 2015 (ICICI Bank, 2015).

Technology for Inclusive Growth in Rural India

Considering that the vast majority of India lives in rural areas, ICICI Bank started tapping into the micro-banking space in rural India, utilising partnerships with multinational and local agricultural institutions, leveraging technology. The bank assessed the situation in rural

India and installed low-cost ATMs, which had integrated power management systems and functioned despite the power failures experienced frequently by rural India. It also launched the Kisan (farmer) Loan Card to enable farmers to obtain loans through an electronic card with easy access to withdrawal of cash from the ATMs. In January 2015, Kochhar launched the 'digital village' project, aimed at providing cashless banking through digital platforms i.e., opening an account, and sale and purchase of a variety of products. The project also included digitising the school records such as the syllabus, teaching and learning tools.[9]

Technology for Employee Connect and Development

Under Kochhar's leadership, ICICI Bank has been leveraging technology not only for its external but also for internal customers (Sharma & Abraham, 2011a & b). Technology interventions were introduced to engage with employees in over 4,000 branches spread across the country (ICICI Bank, 2015). The CEO and the leadership team visited the branches 'virtually' through video conferencing apart from the regular onsite visits, making the leaders more connected with every employee. Also, the learning and training initiatives for the employees moved from brick-and-mortar classrooms to virtual classrooms, through the use of internal technology platforms making learning accessible and convenient according to learners' needs.

Accelerating Gender Diversity

ICICI Bank has been a front-runner in recognising female talent through gender equity initiatives. Women employees have felt comfortable with the bank's culture, free from gender bias. As Kamath put it 'Women leaders are also taken on board based on the intellect, ability, and entrepreneurial skills to lead teams.' In 2008 the bank had three women out of five executive board members and 13 women out of 40 in top managerial positions. The women executives at ICICI Bank have defied the odds and adopted an aggressive and risk-taking attitude to make it India's most diversified and customer-oriented bank. One wonders if it would have been possible without a conducive environment.

Kochhar has always maintained that ICICI has been a gender-neutral organisation adopting merit as the sole criterion for promotion and career advancement. The bank has demonstrated gender equity in practice by catering to the special requirements of women employees, to ensure that they grow and do not leave the organisation (Sharma, R.R. & Sharma, N.P., 2015). For example, when women employees were required to work till late evening for official work, special arrangements were made to ensure their safety in reaching home. ICICI Bank has also set up a Quick Response Team (QRT) to assist women employees who might experience distress while commuting. These QRT teams are equipped with GPS and medical equipments as well as medically trained staff to deal with medical emergencies, if any.

The bank has provision for protection of seniority for women employees who have taken maternity leave and for need based flexible timings. The female employees at ICICI Bank get not only their six-month maternity leave, but also childcare leave thereafter. In special cases the bank has the provision for fertility and adoption leave also for its employees. The women who avail themselves of maternity or other special leaves are appraised differently to ensure fair and unbiased performance appraisal (Sharma & Mukherjee, 2011). The bank has encouraged re-hiring of women who had left owing to motherhood and other compelling family demands and wanted to re-enter ICICI Bank. The women employees, who accepted a less challenging role at some point in their career due to their family responsibilities, were offered suitable opportunities later on request. 'It is crucial to support women in the middle years, so when it is time to choose a CEO the talent pool should have a fair number of women', said Kochhar.[10]

Bank's Culture: Shift from Aggressive to Caring Culture

With the global economic meltdown there was a change in business focus at ICICI Bank with emphasis on increasing the stickiness of deposits, improving credit quality and conserving capital. Therefore, Kochhar's efforts have been directed towards consolidation of verticals, strengthening and improving relationships with customers rather than only increasing the number of accounts through stretched targets. This required a change in attitude and work practices, therefore a change in the organisational culture was felt necessary. As customer service and retention would depend on how employees felt treated at the bank, it was considered necessary that employees were treated with care and compassion so that they manifested the same in their behaviour towards the customers. This principle led the bank to introduce its *Saath Apka* (your support) initiative for the employees which was similar to the *Khayaal Apka* (caring for you) programme for its customers, based on the same idea. This programme assured the employees that they were heard and cared for. For example, an illness in the family of an employee was given a patient hearing and strong transfer recommendations were made on an employee's request. This came out in one of Kochhar's interviews: 'I take all the stress on myself, so that others can work without the stress'.[5] In 2015 the bank conducted its third Employee Alignment Survey, post *Saath Apka*, which showed an improvement in the survey scores over the pre-initiative scores (ICICI Bank, 2015). Care and sensitivity have become important behavioural indicators for annual leadership potential assessment, stressing the importance of 'care for employees'.

ICICI Bank began to turn over a new leaf with respect to its culture in 2010 according to Ramkumar, the Executive Director, HR. The need for change from an 'aggressive' to a softer culture was felt due to the growing size of the organisation as well as the economic meltdown. 'It was a period of introspection for us', said Ramkumar, 'laying down aggressive targets, with a sharp performance and compensation differential, had the potential, in a large organisation like ours, for employees to take risks that are unacceptable to senior management.'[11] As the bank had consolidated, established itself on firm ground and had expanded into a much larger organisation, it was definitely a time to re-think, felt Ramkumar.

Before 2010, Sunday was a day for employees to finish the pending weekly work and take a day off during the week. As ICICI Bank emerged as the market leader from a challenger, working hours, workplace practices, Sundays and holiday were re-defined.[5] While change in the bank's culture could depend on a situation and the shift in the financial environment, much of it could also be attributed to the leadership (Sharma, 2007). Kochhar said, 'The aim is to nurture a culture of caring and supportive meritocracy of employees'.[11] She along with Ramkumar worked towards understanding the 'aggression' in the bank's culture and facilitating a change to a 'sensitive' yet meritocratic culture. It took Kochhar and her team a lot of effort to understand the employees' source of anxiety and apprehension with respect to 'a hire and fire' culture.

Changes in Performance Appraisal

The performance appraisal process also underwent a change at the bank. The top two ratings were increased to 40 percent of employees as against 25 percent prior to 2010. Variable pay for non-management and junior-management levels was reduced to 30 percent of the fixed pay, from 50 percent earlier. The speed of promotions was moderated, with a minimum of two to three years at a level, where a promotion every year was the norm earlier.[5] Those fast trackers felt a loss of trigger for keeping themselves motivated though the process of rating employees was more transparent with sharing of the rating with the employee before finalisation. If an employee was rated 1(1 being the highest, and 5 being the lowest) in a given year, and got rated 3 the next year, it would require the justification and authorisation of a senior manager (Deputy General Manager or General Manager), to explain the drop in performance. The system was made more objective with more quantifiable goals. For example, a regional sales manager would maintain a 'sales manager diary' to track daily goals of his sales team on a continuous basis. The mid-year feedback process gained importance over the last few years where every employee received detailed feedback from the reporting manager on each and every goal. This ensured timely course correction and kept the employee informed of individual performances throughout the year. While the changed system had reduced pressure and improved work–life balance, the employees used to the fast-track career felt upset and took time to adjust to the new system. They felt that identifying, grooming and fast tracking the talent was at the core of the bank's culture earlier; the changed system offered far fewer differential rewards or opportunities to the fast trackers and made some people feel de-motivated. On the other hand the management considered it as a strategy to manage talent and prevent talent loss in an era of talent shortage.

Talent Management at ICICI

ICICI Bank was ranked among the top five organisations in the world, in a global survey called 'Top Companies for Leaders' conducted by AON Hewitt in 2015. These rankings had taken into account the time and effort an organisation puts into building a leadership pipeline (ICICI Bank, 2015). The bank had not only built a leadership pipeline at the top level but also created a second line of leaders at critical positions in the middle level and in the important frontline roles. The bank provided functional knowledge and skills to its employees to develop them for higher responsibilities and roles. The bank leveraged its internal academies to train its employees, for example, Branch Banking Academy carried out the 'Branch Leadership Programme' to train and certify eligible employees to take on leadership roles at the branches. The high performing sales personnel were given a structured career progression plan under the programme 'STAR' (Sales Talent Acceleration and Recognition), launched in 2014, whereby the qualifying sales personnel are admitted into the Probationary Officers' programme of the bank. Also, in 2015 the Young Leaders Programme (YLP) was launched to offer a structured career progression at the junior management level of Assistant Managers. Given the ever-changing aspirations of the youth, the women employees wondered if it was gender equity, talent management or technological innovation that would contribute to their upward journey at ICICI.

Note: This is updated version of an earlier case 'Leveraging Human Capital for Business Growth: A case of ICICI Bank, India' authored by Sharma, Radha R. and Abraham, P.(2011). In James Hayton, Michal Biron, Liza Castro Christiansen and Bard Kuvaas (Eds.) Global HRM Casebook, Routledge, USA, pp 276–288.

Case Study Tasks

Questions for Class Discussion

1 Identify the leadership style of Chanda Kochhar, MD & CEO of ICICI Bank and compare it with that of her predecessor K.V. Kamath. How is it different?
2 Do you think Chanda Kochhar's caring and non-aggressive personality has dispelled the masculine view associated with leadership? Is this effective? Discuss.

Group Exercise

In your view is ICICI Bank focusing on gender equality or gender equity? Discuss the same in the context of your national culture; identify the gaps and suggest measures to mitigate them. Form groups of 10 and debate the issue.

Role-play Exercise

Chanda Kochhar entrusts the Executive Director, Human Resources (HR) to prepare a plan to facilitate ICICI's transition from a 'pace setting' culture to a 'soft' egalitarian culture and present it in the next meeting.

The Executive Director, HR instructs the following core HR team to prepare a plan for initiating, implementing and communicating the change:

- Manager–Performance Management
- Manager–Communications
- Manager–Organisational Development

   (a) Each role can be assigned to the participants in the class on voluntary basis.
   (b) They can select their team, develop and discuss the plans and present these to the role holder of Executive Director, HR who will discuss and finalise the plan to be presented to the MD & CEO.

Notes

1 http://reports.weforum.org/global-gender-gap-report-2015/the-global-gender-gap-index-2015/
2 www.livemint.com/Industry/bCLOgyaLGiIi6TuhmN0S7J/Indian-IT-services-exports-seen-growing-1214-in-year-ahead.html. Accessed on Sep. 29, 2015.
3 www.business-standard.com/content/general_pdf/010315_01.pdf. Accessed on November 5, 2015.
4 http://articles.economictimes.indiatimes.com/2015–01–04/news/57663583_1_chanda-kochhar-icici-bank-icici-group. Accessed on November 3, 2015.
5 http://www.mckinsey.com/insights/leading_in_the_21st_century/an_interview_with_chanda_kochhar. Accessed on October 4, 2015.
6 www.businesstoday.in/magazine/special/most-powerful-women-in-business-2011-chanda-kochhar/story/18327.html. Accessed on November 2, 2015.
7 http://fortune.com/2011/10/04/chanda-kochhar-how-a-star-ceo-keeps-her-bank-growing/. Accessed on November 2, 2015.
8 http://forbesindia.com/article/big-bet/chanda-kochhar-making-icici-banks-digital-strategy-click/41159/1#ixzz3sCGpj9Nv. Accessed on October 3, 2015.
9 www.businesstoday.in/sectors/banks/icici-launches-digital-village-project-adopts-gujarat-village/story/214196.html. Accessed on October 15, 2015.

10 http://economictimes.indiatimes.com/industry/how-icici-bank-has-emerged-as-a-ceo-factory-of-primarily-women-leaders/articleshow/31682254.cms. Accessed on October 5, 2015.

11 http://articles.economictimes.indiatimes.com/2013–12–03/news/44710492_1_icici-bank-chanda-kochhar-k-ramkumar. Accessed on November 5, 2015.

References

Amba-Rao, S. C. (1994). US HRM principles: cross-country comparisons and two case applications in India. *International Journal of Human Resource Management, 5*(3), 755–778.

Budhwar, P. S. (2003). Employment relations in India. *Employee Relations, 25*(2), 132–148.

Census of India. (2011). *Population Composition*. Retrieved from http://www.censusindia.gov.in/vital_statistics/SRS_Report/9Chap%202%20-%202011.pdf. Accessed on Nov 5, 2015.

Eagly, A. H. & Carli, L. L. (2003). The female leadership advantage: An evaluation of the evidence. *The Leadership Quarterly, 14*(6), 807–834.

Eagly, A. H. & Carli, L.L. (2007). *Through the labyrinth: The truth about how women become leaders*. Harvard Business Press.

Goleman, Daniel, Boyatzis Richard E., & Mckee, Annie (2002). *Primal leadership*. Boston, MA: Harvard Business School Press.

ICICI Bank. (2015). *2014–2015 Annual Report of ICICI Bank*. Retrieved from http://www.icicibank.com/managed-assets/docs/investor/annual-reports/2015/ICICI-Bank-Annual-report-FY2015.pdf. Accessed: November 1, 2015.

Kanungo, R. and Mendonca, M. (1994). Culture and Performance Improvement. *Productivity, 35*(4): 447–453.

Krotz, Joanna L. (2009). 'Do women make better managers?' Retrieved from http://www.microsoft.com/smallbusiness/resources/management/leadership-training/do-women-make-better-managers.aspx. Accessed on November 2, 2015.

Meyers, C.A. (1959). Labor Problems in the Industrialization of India. *International Executive, 1*(1), 7–8.

Sharma, Radha, R. (1982). Education of women in India: inequalities and bottlenecks. *Educ. Q.* 3, 20–27.

Sharma, Radha, R. (2007). Predicting Transformational Leadership and Locus of Control through Emotional Intelligence Competencies. In S. Subramony & S. Raj. (Eds), *Psychological Assessment in Personnel Selection*. New Delhi: Defense Institute of Personality Research.

Sharma, R. R., & Mukherji, S. (2011). Can Business and Humanism Go Together? The Case of the Tata Group with a Focus on Nano Plant. In *Humanistic Management in Practice* (pp. 247–265). Basingstoke, UK: Palgrave Macmillan.

Sharma, Radha R. & Abraham, P. (2011a) Leveraging Human Capital for Business Growth. In James Hayton, Michal Biron, Liza Castro Christiansen and Bård Kuvaas (Eds), *The Global Human Resources Casebook. Academy of Management* (pp. 276–288). New York: Routledge.

Sharma, Radha R. & Abraham, P. (2011b). ICICI Bank: The Emergent Bank of Emerging Economies. In Spitzeck, H., Pirson, M., & Dierksmeier, C. *Banking with Integrity – The winners of the financial crisis?* (pp. 115–128). New York: Palgrave Macmillan.

Sharma, R. R. (2013a). Primal Leadership: An Imperative for Effective Public Service Management. *Accountable Governance for Development-Setting an Agenda Beyond 2015*, 349.

Sharma Radha, R. (2013b). *Development and Standardization of Perceived Gender Equity Scale, Gender Diversity in India: An Unpublished Report*. Centre for Positive Scholarship, Management Development Institute, India.

Sharma Radha, R. and Sharma, N. P. (2015) Opening the gender diversity black box: causality of perceived gender equity and locus of control and mediation of work engagement in employee well-being. *Front. Psychol.* 6: 1371, 1–14. doi: 10.3389/fpsyg.2015.01371.

Singh, V. & Vinnicombe, S. (2004). Why so few women directors in top UK boardrooms? Evidence and theoretical explanations. *Corporate Governance: An International Review, 12*(4), 479–488.

Time. (2015). The 100 Most Influential People: Chanda Kochhar. April 16, 2015. http://time.com/3822610/chanda-kochhar-2015-time-100/. Accessed: Oct 26, 2015.

UNESCO. (2000). ABC of Women Worker's Rights and Gender Equality. Geneva: ILO.

Venkata Ratnam, V. CS. (1995). Economic liberalization and the transformation of industrial relations policies in India. In T. Kochan, R. Lansbury, & A. Verma (Eds.), *Employment relations in the growing Asian economies* (pp. 220–281). London, England: Routledge.

World Bank. (2014). Industry, value added (% of GDP). Retrieved from http://data.worldbank.org/indicator/NV.IND.TOTL.ZS. Accessed on November 12, 2015.

28

Singapore

Alexandra Hospital: Realizing the Value of Older Workers

Audrey Chia and Angeline Lim

As the population of Singapore ages, employers have had to address the question of how to recognize and realize the value of older employees. One such organization, Alexandra Hospital, has adopted innovative human resource (HR) policies for older employees, which are the focus of this case. However, Alexandra Hospital is itself in transition, as it prepares for a change of management. How can these innovative practices for older workers be passed on?

Background Information on Singapore

Singapore is a small island nation with a multi-ethnic, multi-religious population of 5.54 million of which 70.5 percent are residents (Singapore citizens and permanent residents) and 29.5 percent are non-residents (Singapore Department of Statistics, 2015a). As at 2010, the Singapore resident population comprises 74.1 percent Chinese, 13.4 percent Malays, 9.2 percent Indians, and 3.3 percent other ethnic groups (Singapore Department of Statistics, 2011). Of the resident population aged 15 years and older, 33.3 percent are Buddhists, 18.3 percent are Christians, 17.0 percent have no religion, 14.7 percent are Muslims, 10.9 percent are Taoists, 5.1 percent are Hindus, 0.4 percent are Sikhs and 0.4 percent practise other religions (Singapore Department of Statistics, 2011).

Over the last 50 years, Singapore has grown rapidly from a third world nation with poor infrastructure, limited capital, and a GDP per capita of US$500, to a first world nation with world-class infrastructure, huge national reserves, and a GDP per capita of about US$56,000 (Economic Development Board, 2015; Monetary Authority of Singapore, 2015). Unemployment rates as at December 2015 are low at 1.9 percent (Singapore Department of Statistics, 2016), and quality of life has been ranked the highest in Asia and twenty-sixth highest in the world (Mercer, 2015). Industries that have contributed most to Singapore's GDP are manufacturing (18.4 percent), wholesale and retail (17.5 percent), business services (15.8 percent), finance and insurance (12.5 percent), transportation and storage (6.9 percent), and construction (5.1 percent); (Singapore Department of Statistics, 2015b). In recent years, there was also greater emphasis on knowledge and innovation-intensive activities, with billions of dollars set aside to promote research and development, especially in the areas of environmental and water technology, biomedical sciences and interactive and digital media (Economic Development Board, 2015).

Singapore enjoys political stability, with a single dominant ruling party (the People's Action Party) since its independence. It also has a strong education system, with 69.5 percent of residents aged 25 years and over possessing secondary or higher qualifications, and a literacy rate of 96.7 percent of residents aged 15 years and over (Singapore Department of Statistics, 2015c). Education is a key focus for the government and is heavily subsidized, with financial assistance given to low-income families to ensure that every child has an equal opportunity to basic education. In the area of healthcare, Singapore was ranked sixth by World Health Organisation (World Health Organisation, 2000), and ranked first by Bloomberg for having the most efficient healthcare in the world (Bloomberg, 2014).

Despite its progress on many fronts, one of the key concerns that Singapore shares with many other countries is that of an aging population. Singapore's population is one of the fastest aging populations in the world. The median age of the resident labour force has increased from 40 years in 2006 to 43 years in 2015 (Ministry of Manpower, 2015a). Currently, 11.8 percent of the population is aged 65 and older; this has increased by 2.8 percent from just 5 years ago (Singapore Department of Statistics, 2015a). The life expectancy of Singaporeans has also increased to 80.5 years for males and 84.9 years for females (Singapore Department of Statistics, 2015d). The aging population implies that Singaporeans will need to extend their working lives to support themselves in their old age. In addition, Singapore's economy may have to depend on, among other things, Singaporeans working in their later years.

Attitude Toward Diversity

As a multi-ethnic, migrant society, Singapore's attitude toward diversity is that of equality and harmony. Great emphasis is also placed on fairness and meritocracy in the workplace. Article 12(2) of the Constitution of the Republic of Singapore forms the legislative backbone of this inclusive attitude. It outlaws

> discrimination against Singapore citizens based on religion, race, descent or place of birth in any law or in the appointment to any office or employment under a public authority or in the administration of any law relating to the acquisition, holding or disposition of property or the establishing or carrying on of any trade, business, profession, vocation or employment.

In 2006, the Tripartite Alliance for Fair Employment Practices (TAFEP) was established to "promote non-discriminatory employment practices and to shift mind-sets among employers, employees and the general public toward fair employment practices for all workers" (TAFEP, 2009). The founding of the alliance is timely as the changing characteristics of the workforce necessitate a more inclusive stance toward women, older workers, ex-offenders, disabled individuals, and other individuals whose membership in certain social groups renders them vulnerable to workplace discrimination other than that stipulated by Article 12(2). In 2014, TAFEP expanded its scope beyond fair employment practices and into work-life harmony and age management. This expansion resulted in a change of name to the Tripartite Alliance for Fair and Progressive Employment Practices, and the inclusion of a non-profit entity, the Employer Alliance, which advocates and champions work-life practice (TAFEP, 2014).

In 1999, the Retirement Age Act was introduced, officially extending the minimum retirement age from 60 to 62 years. To encourage the continued employment of older workers, however, employers are allowed, under the Act, to reduce the wages paid to employees aged 60 and older. Although the Act covers the notice period and criteria/justification for wage reduction and advises discretion on the part of employers, it also rather oddly allows wages to be cut more than once as long as each reduction is not more than 10 percent. It also allows employers to retire employees at the age of 60 or after if they cannot reach agreement on their post-60 wages. In 2011, the Act was revised and renamed the Retirement and Re-employment Act. Under this revised Act, companies are required to offer re-employment to workers above the age of 62, up to the age of 65.

To encourage workforce participation by older citizens and also to encourage employers to continue employing older workers, the Tripartite Committee on Employability of Older Workers was formed to improve their employability and competitiveness. This Committee comprised representatives from unions, employers, and the government. The Committee recommended a four-pronged strategy: expanding employment opportunities for older workers, enhancing their cost-competitiveness, improving their skills, and nurturing positive perceptions of older workers. Among the schemes that have been implemented is a retraining program for professionals and an incentive program for companies to redesign jobs for older workers. The Committee also highlighted positive examples of companies that had successfully integrated older workers into their workforce. In September 2014, the Committee recommended that the Government encourage employers to voluntarily raise the re-employment age from 65 to 67 years old. To guide employers to do so, the tripartite partners have also issued a Tripartite Advisory on re-employment of employees from age 65 to 67 (Ministry of Manpower, 2015b).

One of the positive outcomes of the Tripartite Committee's recommendations was the creation of the ADVANTAGE! Scheme. This scheme was piloted by the Singapore Workforce Development Agency (WDA), the National Trades Union Congress (NTUC), and the Singapore National Employers Federation (SNEF) in 2005 and introduced in 2006 to promote the employment of mature workers (age 40 and beyond) and the re-employment of older workers (age 62 and beyond) by giving businesses incentives to hire and retain mature and older workers.

Given Singapore's aging workforce, organizations face the challenge of strategically aligning their HRM practices to fit the demographics of the workforce. Ideally, they would leverage the experience and expertise of older workers.

Alexandra Hospital

Alexandra Hospital is a 400-bed, acute care hospital in the south of Singapore.

A fundamental component of Alexandra Hospital's philosophy is patient-centredness. Alexandra Hospital employees strive for a standard of care "good enough for our loved ones" and hold that the most important people in the hospital are the patients. Alexandra Hospital's implementation of organizational learning practices has earned it first place in Singapore's Patient Satisfaction Survey for public hospitals for six years in a row.

Strategic Fit Between Human Resources Practices and Medical Practice

In 1994, a Department of Geriatrics was established at Alexandra Hospital. The department was formed to cater to the elderly population in the Western region of Singapore. This was significant because of Alexandra Hospital's proximity to two housing estates (Queenstown and Bukit Merah) which had higher proportions of elderly residents. Besides providing medical services in Geriatrics, Alexandra Hospital also ran a Continence Clinic, Falls Clinic, Dementia Clinic and Care Program, Psychogeriatric Clinic, and a Palliative Care Service. It also housed a mock-up of a studio apartment that featured how homes could be equipped and designed for the elderly to live independently and safely. To educate the public, Alexandra Hospital conducted courses on health for older persons. These courses addressed topics such as nutrition, diseases, disability prevention, health risks, fitness, and cognitive capabilities.[1] Alexandra Hospital also engaged the community at large through various activities, among them a workshop in which bank employees spent time interacting with the elderly, tried to understand their needs, designed living spaces for the elderly, and presented their findings to the CEO and management of Alexandra Hospital.

Alexandra Hospital's strategic focus on geriatrics made it quite natural that the hospital's human resource policies would also give special attention to older employees. In the words of its then-CEO, Liak Teng Lit, "There was a time when an elderly person was supposed to be inactive, quiet and done with his years of work . . . Nowadays, most people in their fifties and sixties are physically healthy" (HRM Asia, March 7, 2009).

Re-employment and Retraining of Older Workers

The minimum retirement age in Singapore is currently 62 years, with employers being required to offer re-employment in the organization to eligible employees who turn 62, up to age 65. This legislation was passed in 2012, but Alexandra Hospital was far ahead of the deadline, and adopted a post-retirement employment policy for older workers in September 2007 (Singapore National Employers Federation [SNEF] Re-employment Portal, n.d.). Upon reaching retirement age, Alexandra Hospital employees could be re-employed, subject to their health and performance. They could be rehired in their former positions or in new ones but with no reduction in salary. For instance, a health attendant was rehired as an events coordinator, and an occupational therapist with a passion for gardening was rehired as a senior executive in charge of landscaping and environment (Tripartite Alliance for Fair Employment Practices, 2010). In 2009 at Alexandra Hospital, the proportion of employees older than 40 was 31 percent, with 15 percent of employees beyond the age of 50.

Alexandra Hospital recognized that retraining was an essential complement to re-employment. Besides retraining its employees for new positions after retirement, Alexandra Hospital also introduced a patient care associate (PCA) position in 2007, as a result of job redesign that combined support functions and patient care. Duties of PCAs included feeding, assisted bathing of patients, and housekeeping. Most of the PCAs were older than 40. Four-fifths had been jobless before working as PCAs, and most used to be homemakers or had been retrenched. The introduction of PCAs not only allowed for career development for these older workers but extended more personalized care to patients. In addition to PCAs, Alexandra Hospital also introduced a new position of environment service associate to tighten infection control, enhance cleanliness and maintain environmental standards comparable to those at five-star hotels (Fatimah, April 8, 2010).

Cultural Fit

There was a clear fit between Alexandra Hospital's focus on older workers and its work culture. A conscious effort was made by the HRM department to socialize Alexandra Hospital employees of all levels to see themselves as health ambassadors: "From the junior cook to the CEO, all those working in Alexandra Hospital attend training to become health ambassadors. They have to attend a compulsory health advocacy course to acquire skills and knowledge related to healthy living. This will help them to advocate healthy living to the patients and their families" (AHa! Alexandra Hospital in action, Jan.–Feb., 2009, p. 1).

Stretching over two days, the content of the health advocacy course included health advice, understanding nutrition and food labels, and nurturing good mental health. The belief was that employees would be more effective as health ambassadors if they kept themselves healthy. Alexandra Hospital's deputy director of HRM explained that employees who practise a healthy lifestyle would be more likely to encourage others to do likewise. "Human Resources hopes that staff on all levels can pass on healthy living messages to patients in everyday language, delivering a very personal and beneficial service to patients" (HRM Asia, January 12, 2010).

Older employees stepped up to their roles as health ambassadors not just as patients and the public but to their colleagues. Among them was a project specialist aged 59, who with some colleagues formed a brisk walking club. In her words, "We have a beautiful garden, so it's a very pleasant walk . . . colleagues . . . finish work at the same time, and we'll go walking together. It makes it more fun!" (AHa! Alexandra Hospital in action, Jan.–Feb. 2008, p. 2).

Health Initiatives at Alexandra Hospital

From 2000, Alexandra Hospital underwent a comprehensive restructuring to improve its services and environment. As part of this change, Alexandra Hospital also revamped its HRM policies and began to take a multi-pronged approach to promoting and maintaining the health of older workers and designing the workplace to make it friendly to older workers. These efforts were termed the Wellness for Older Workers (WOW) program.

Alexandra Hospital had a wellness initiative (Health for Life) for all employees to maintain a healthy workforce. Health for Life included health checks, exercise programs, weight management, an annual fitness challenge, and a healthy cafeteria with discounts for healthier choices. As part of Health for Life, a program called Health for Older Persons (HOP)@Work was specially designed. HOP@Work was funded by the Singapore Government's Advantage! Scheme.[2] With HOP@Work, older employees could learn how to better manage their health, to exercise and stay active, to eat healthily, and to be more aware of ergonomics at work. The program could also be customized to each employee's educational level and needs (SNEF Re-employment of Older Employees Portal, n.d.).

Besides HOP@Work, a Health Intervention Program (HIP) was developed to give older employees a deeper understanding of chronic diseases (e.g., hypertension, diabetes, and high cholesterol) and how they could be managed. Weight management was also part of HIP (SNEF Re-employment of Older Employees Portal, n.d.). Older employees were encouraged to exercise and stay active while having fun in programs that offered line dancing, gardening, stretching, and other exercises (Employer Alliance, Singapore, n.d.).

Another program bore the amusing name of MASH (musculo- and skeletal health) fitness program. Though HIP focused on health interventions, MASH complemented HIP on maintaining fitness and conditioning. MASH comprised assessments of musculoskeletal and joint fitness and training for fitness and good posture and strength (SNEF Re-employment of Older Employees Portal, n.d.).

The falls prevention program was introduced to identify older employees with a high risk for falls. These older employees were provided with training on balance trainers to improve their visual and musculoskeletal coordination. This program was credited with reducing the incidence of accidents and injuries to older workers at Alexandra Hospital.

Ergonomics at Work

Going beyond health interventions and fitness maintenance, Alexandra Hospital considered how the workplace could be designed to be more ergonomic and prevent work-related injuries. Effort went into educating older employees on ergonomics. There was an exhibit that showed what an ergonomic workstation looked like. Employees also learned about ergonomics in their specific work function via a multi-lingual video. Accompanying the exhibit was an "Ergonomic Peripherals Store" from which employees could borrow items to enhance the ergonomics of their own workspace.

The efforts to train and educate older workers in ergonomics were complemented by the redesign of work equipment. In the medical records office, the burden of having to push heavy trolleys laden with medical records was eased when the trolleys were motorized with the help of students from a local polytechnic. Hoists were installed to allow older employees to more easily lift or transfer patients to and from their beds.

Flex Time Scheme

Besides HRM policies specifically for the elderly, Alexandra Hospital also had a noteworthy flex time scheme. A survey of older workers in Singapore (part of a larger Global Survey on the Future of Retirement) revealed that 80 percent of the respondents wanted to continue working for as long as possible and that more than 70 percent wanted to work part-time or flexible hours (Basu, 2009). Alexandra Hospital's flex time scheme allowed older employees to work part-time, flexible hours and even share jobs:

> Patient-care associate Joseph Robert Roch, 57, also took a pay cut to work a four-day week at Alexandra Hospital, but said that with savings in the bank, money is not his main concern. The former shipping company executive now helps nurses feed or bathe patients and said he needs at least three days a week to enjoy leisure activities such as reading, walking his dog, watching movies or attending church.

This description indicated that older Alexandra Hospital employees could balance work with life and lead an active life while aging gracefully.

Results

For its holistic approach to managing older workers, Alexandra Hospital won the American Association for Retired Persons (AARP) International Innovative Employer Award in 2008 (AARP, September 2008). Alexandra Hospital also won HRM Singapore's 2010 Award for Best Mature Workforce Practices (HRM Awards, March 4, 2011).

The focus on healthy lifestyles, active aging, and ergonomics also reaped internal rewards. Among employees in general, there were fewer illness-related absences. The participants in the programs reported being happier and more satisfied with themselves. A nursing administrator was featured in Alexandra Hospital's newsletter in a *sarong kebaya*,[3] proudly reporting her weight loss, healthier dining patterns, and regular exercise with colleagues. Older employees became more health-conscious, aligning their health-conscious behaviours at work with similarly health-conscious actions outside of work, whether grocery shopping or choosing what to drink. They also reported feeling more energetic and alert (AHa! Alexandra Hospital in action, Jan–Feb 2009 p. 2).

Alexandra Health System

From 2008 to 2010, Alexandra Hospital began to prepare for a new phase of its development. Recognizing the good work that the team at Alexandra Hospital had done to transform the hospital, a public healthcare cluster under the name of Alexandra Health System was set up to take care of the needs of 700,000 residents in the northern part of Singapore (Lim, 2015, p. 244). Meanwhile, the running of Alexandra Hospital would be handed over to Jurong Health Services.

A transition period from December 2009 to August 2010 saw employees from both organizations working side by side. Through shadowing and observation, the Jurong Health staff learnt service standards, allowing for a smoother transition. Mixed clinical teams from both organizations also got together during the transition. From March 2010, Jurong Health began to assume responsibility for different aspects of the hospital's functioning and services.

Alexandra Health System now manages the new 590-bed hospital, Khoo Teck Puat Hospital (KTPH), which opened in 2010 in Yishun housing estate, in the north of Singapore. The core staff of Alexandra Hospital was transferred to KTPH. However, because KTPH was a larger hospital, many new staff had to be recruited. A job fair for positions at KTPH attracted more than 4,500 visitors and resulted in 2,500 applicants for 1,000 jobs. By March 2010, KTPH had a headcount of 2,300 (Neo, 2010, p. 1).

In December 2015, Alexandra Health System expanded to manage Yishun Community Hospital. In the next few years, Alexandra Health System will include Admiralty Medical Centre (opening in 2017), Sembawang Primary Care Centre, and Woodlands Integrated Health Campus (opening progressively from 2020) (Lim, 2015, p. 245).

Challenges

How would the employees who moved over from Alexandra Hospital be able to energize and enthuse the much larger KTPH workforce with the positive aspects of Alexandra Hospital, especially its programs for older workers? KTPH's staff would be made up of transferred staff from Alexandra Hospital and a complement of about 1,000 new employees (AHa! Alexandra Hospital in action, March–April 2008, p. 2). Would the policies and practices for older employees be transferable and sustainable on a large scale? What would have to be done to spread the message of health and active living and to build the identity of the new employees as health ambassadors? How would the employees who had moved from Alexandra Hospital be able to communicate their perceptions and views of mature and older workers to their newer colleagues?

Many Alexandra Hospital employees had moved on, but the Alexandra Hospital building, grounds, patients, and surrounding community were left behind. How would the philosophy of health for life, active aging, and the value placed on mature workers continue to flourish in those same surroundings and among the Jurong Health employees who had taken over the running of Alexandra Hospital? What could be done to pass on the message and practices that had worked so well?

Case Study Questions

1 To what extent have Alexandra Hospital's practices been encouraged or supported by Singapore's national agenda and public policies on mature workers? Compare this to your experiences in your own country or other countries in this book.

2 In your opinion, how successful is Alexandra Hospital's approach to older workers? Is there anything missing? What would you add or take away if you were the human resources director or CEO? How would you take Alexandra Hospital further in its quest to realize the value of mature workers?

3 What are the possible risks or challenges to Alexandra Hospital's culture of inclusion, especially with the move to bigger hospital premises and the inclusion of a large number of new employees?

Notes

1 The preceding information is obtained from the Alexandra Hospital website.
2 The Advantage! Scheme was introduced to encourage companies to hire or retain mature workers older than the age of 40 or re-employ workers beyond the official retirement age of 62.
3 Traditional Malay dress in a form-fitting cut.

References and Further Reading

AHa! Alexandra Hospital in action. (2008). Job Fair for Khoo Teck Puat Hospital attracts some 4,500 job seekers. (2008, March-April). *AHa! (Alexandra Hospital in action)*, Mar.–Apr., 19, 2.

AHa! Alexandra Hospital in action. (2008). Working boomers get serious about health: Getting on in years is no excuse for not exercising. *AHa! (Alexandra Hospital in action)*, Jan.–Feb., 18, 2.

AHa! Alexandra Hospital in action. (2009). Keeping Staff Healthy. *AHa! (Alexandra Hospital in action)*, 24, Jan–Feb., 1.

Alexandra Hospital. (n.d.). Retrieved from http://www.alexhosp.com.sg

American Association for Retired Persons. (2008, September). Alexandra Hospital, Winner, AARP International Innovative Employer Awards. Retrieved from http://www.aarp.org/work/employee-benefits/info-09–2008/alexandra_hospital_2008.html

Basu, R. (2009, February 28). Seniors want flexibility. *The Straits Times*, p. A24.

Bloomberg. (2014). Most Efficient Health Care 2014: Countries. Retrieved from http://www.bloomberg.com/visual-data/best-and-worst//most-efficient-health-care-2014-countries

Chia, A., & Lim, A. (2010). Singapore: Equality, harmony & fair employment. In A. Klarsfeld (Ed.), *International Handbook on Diversity Management at Work: Country Perspectives on Diversity and Equal Treatment* (pp. 198–217). London: Edward Elgar.

Economic Development Board. (2015). Our History: The Millennium. Retrieved from https://www.edb.gov.sg/content/edb/en/why-singapore/about-singapore/our-history/2000s.html

Employer Alliance, Singapore. (n.d.). *Success Stories: Alexandra Hospital*. Retrieved from http://www.employeralliance.sg/toolkit/toolkit/tk1_4_5a.html

Fatimah, M.K. (2010, April 8). *Managing mature workforce – Alexandra health story*. Presented at the Fair Employment Conference, Singapore. Retrieved from http://www.feconference.sg/workshop1.htm

HRM Asia. (2009, March 7). *Rocking on – Getting the most out of mature talent*. Retrieved from http://www.hrmasia.com/resources/mature-workers/rocking-on-getting-the-most-out-of-mature-talent/36345

HRM Asia. (2010, January 12). *Alexandra Hospital: Going places*. Retrieved from http://www.hrmasia.com/case-studies/alexandra-hospital-going-places/39454

HRM Awards, Singapore (2011, March 4). HRM Awards 2010 Singapore Winners. Retrieved from http://www.hrmawards.com/winners2010.cfm

Khoo Teck Puat Hospital. (n.d.). Retrieved from http://www.ktph.com.sg/main/pages

Lim, C. (2015). Alexandra Health System. In Lee, C.E., & Satku, K. (Eds.), *Singapore's health care system: What 50 years have achieved* (pp. 241–245). Singapore: World Scientific.

Mercer. (2015). Quality of Living Rankings, 2015. Retrieved from https://www.imercer.com/content/quality-of-living.aspx

Ministry of Manpower, Singapore. (2015a). Re-employment. Retrieved from http://www.mom.gov.sg/employment-practices/re-employment

Ministry of Manpower, Singapore. (2015b). Singapore Workforce, 2015. Retrieved from http://stats.mom.gov.sg/iMAS_PdfLibrary/mrsd-singapore-workforce-2015.pdf#page=7

Monetary Authority of Singapore. (2015). "An Economic History of Singapore: 1965–2065" Keynote Address by Mr Ravi Menon, Managing Director, Monetary Authority of Singapore, at the Singapore Economic Review Conference 2015 on 5 August 2015. Retrieved from http://www.mas.gov.sg/News-and-Publications/Speeches-and-Monetary-Policy-Statements/Speeches/2015/An-Economic-History-of-Singapore.aspx

Neo C, C. (2010, March 29). A hospital where your heart rate will not go up. *Today*, p.1.

Singapore Department of Statistics. (2011). Singapore Census of Population 2010: Statistical Release 1: Demographic Characteristics, Education, Language and Religion. Retrieved from http://www.singstat.gov.sg/docs/default-source/default-document-library/publications/publications_and_papers/cop2010/census_2010_release1/cop2010sr1.pdf

Singapore Department of Statistics. (2015a). Population Trends 2015. Retrieved from http://www.singstat.gov.sg/docs/default-source/default-document-library/publications/publications_and_papers/population_and_population_structure/population2015.pdf

Singapore Department of Statistics. (2015b). Share of GDP by Industry. Retrieved from http://www.singstat.gov.sg/statistics/visualising-data/charts/share-of-gdp-by-industry

Singapore Department of Statistics. (2015c). Latest Data: Education & Literacy. Retrieved from http://www.singstat.gov.sg/statistics/latest-data#19

Singapore Department of Statistics. (2015d). Complete Life Tables 2013–2014 for Singapore Resident Population. Retrieved from http://www.singstat.gov.sg/docs/default-source/default-document-library/publications/publications_and_papers/births_and_deaths/lifetable13–14.pdf

Singapore Department of Statistics. (2016). Summary Table: Unemployment. Retrieved from http://stats.mom.gov.sg/Pages/Unemployment-Summary-Table.aspx

Singapore National Employers' Federation, Re-employment of Older Employees Portal. (n.d.). Alexandra Hospital. Retrieved from http://www.re-employment.sg/web/contents/Contents.aspx?ContId=227xxx

Singapore Statutes Online. (n.d.). Constitution of the Republic of Singapore. Retrieved from http://statutes.agc.gov.sg/

Singapore Statutes Online. (n.d.). Retirement and Re-employment Act. Retrieved from http://statutes.agc.gov.sg/

Singapore Workforce Development Agency. (n.d.). Fact sheet – ADVANTAGE! Scheme. Retrieved from http://www.wda.gov.sg/content/dam/wda/pdf/PressRelease/15082008/Annex A.pdf

Tripartite Alliance for Fair Employment Practices, Singapore. (2009). Inaugural Conference on Fair Employment Practices celebrates milestone in Singapore's journey towards fair and inclusive workplaces. Retrieved from https://www.tafep.sg/inaugural-conference-fair-employment-practices-celebrates-milestone-singapore-s-journey-towards-fair

Tripartite Alliance for Fair Employment Practices, Singapore. (2010). *Leading Practices for Managing Mature Employees.* Retrieved from http://www.fairemployment.sg/resources.asp?subid=2

Tripartite Alliance for Fair and Progressive Employment Practices, Singapore (2014). Recipes for a Happy Workplace, Annual Review 2014. Retrieved from https://www.tafep.sg/sites/default/files/TAFEP%20Annual%20Review%20DPS%202014.pdf

World Health Organization. (2000). The World Health Report 2000. Health Systems: Improving Performance. Retrieved from http://www.who.int/whr/2000/en/whr00_en.pdf

29
Thailand
How Selection Practices Make a Difference:
A Case Study of a Global Thai Company

Chaturong Napathorn

Barbara, the director of ZZZ (Thailand)'s human resource management (HRM) department, was very proud that her company had been selected as one of the 500 most admired companies in 2015. She believed that the company's selection practices played an important role in this world-class ranking. The company has implemented these practices for over 40 years of operations in Thailand, and recently, it has begun to implement the practices in other countries.

Organizational Setting

ZZZ is considered one of the world's largest producers of animal feed, poultry, and shrimp. It has operated businesses in several countries across the globe, including Thailand, China, India, Morocco, Nigeria, Pakistan, Turkey, Russia, and Vietnam. ZZZ employs nearly 100,000 people worldwide. Approximately half of them are employed in Thailand. ZZZ's business model began with upstream production and then expanded to include downstream food and agro-processing businesses. In other words, ZZZ has remained almost completely vertically integrated across its supply chain. ZZZ began its business operations in the animal feed business. Its main policy is to purchase raw materials (e.g., soy bean meal) from several suppliers to produce animal feed. From the animal feed it produces, ZZZ feeds its own chicken, swine, ducks, and shrimp in its farming business. ZZZ has primarily operated its own farms both in Thailand and in foreign countries through subsidiaries. However, to respond to the growth of its businesses and to maintain positive relationships with the farmers and local communities surrounding its businesses, ZZZ has applied the 'contract farming' model, as it has also done in the animal feed business. ZZZ then processes its own meat from the 'contract farming' model to produce semi-cooked food products or ready-to-eat products. All of the products have typically been sold under the 'ZZZ' brand. Finally, in addition to exporting the processed meat and food products, ZZZ has also created its own retailers to help distribute products to end consumers. ZZZ entered the food business to satisfy its mission of 'Cuisine of the World', which means ZZZ's products must be distributed and sold in every part of the globe. ZZZ recently expanded its operations to cover a wider range of businesses, including telecommunications, real estate, and convenience stores.

ZZZ's main HRM strategy at its headquarters in Thailand is to rely on an internal labour market strategy to build a set of loyal Thai managers or to 'make' its own managerial and professional employees from scratch. ZZZ has emphasized that 'making' its own managerial and professional employees from scratch leads to a stronger and more powerful organization. Specifically, ZZZ recruits workers from younger generations and develops them over the long run. This strategy has strengthened the firm and represented a considerably better approach than 'acquiring' or 'buying' mid-career personnel from other companies. Of course, this process has been very slow; however, ZZZ has been able to obtain employees who truly understand its business operations and would like to remain with the company because ZZZ is 'ZZZ', not because ZZZ is 'a typical firm'. ZZZ has appeared fortunate enough to be able to recruit people who would like to remain with the firm and are willing to do anything for it, as reflected by the fact that most of ZZZ's top executives have worked for the company for approximately 30–35 years.

Background to the Case

Historical and Economic Background

Unlike many countries in Southeast Asia, Thailand was never colonized by European countries or the USA. However, Japan occupied the country for a brief period during World War II (Lawler and Atmiyanandana, 2003). Thailand reached a turning point in 1932, when it transitioned from an 800-year-old absolute monarchy to a constitutional monarchy (Gullaprawit, 2002). It then changed its name from Siam to Thailand. According to the current regime, the government or cabinet is divided into several levels: ministries and quasi-autonomous agencies, provinces, districts, municipalities, communes, and villages. The ministries responsible for the country's HRM practices are the Ministry of Education (which includes University Affairs), the Ministry of Labour, the Ministry of Social Development and Human Security, and the Ministry of Science and Technology.

In terms of its economic history, Thailand has fallen into the middle-income trap, which means the country has low rates of research and development (R&D) investment, innovation, and productivity growth. In this regard, the Thai economy has been unable to continue to grow sufficiently. Total productivity growth in Thailand between 1990 and 2008 was only 0.7 percent, which is much lower than that of China (4.7 percent), South Korea (1.6 percent), or Taiwan (1.3 percent) (Asian Productivity Organization, 2011). Additionally, relatively low rates of economic growth (3–5 percent per year) during the past decade have not helped to improve the well-being of the majority of Thais, who live in the outskirts of the capital city, Bangkok, and in rural areas.

One of the leading industries contributing to Thailand's economic growth is the food and agro-food processing industry. Thailand's food and agro-food processing industry is substantial and one of the most rapidly internationalizing industries in the country (Thirawat, Robins, & Baume, 2012). It began internationalizing in 1970. Since then, the industry has generated double-digit annual export growth rates, except for the year 2007, when the rate declined to below 10 percent (9.52 percent). However, in 2008, Thailand's overall food exports reached a 26 percent annual export growth rate (Thirawat, Robins, & Baume, 2012), which was very high. From 1980 to 2009, the food and agro-food processing industry accounted for an increasing share of total gross domestic product (GDP). In 1980, the industry contributed 42,412 million Thai baht to the economy, and this amount rose to approximately 250,979 million Thai baht in 2009 (National Economic and Social Development Board, 1980; 2009; Thirawat, Robins, & Baume, 2012).

Labour Market Dynamics

As in other developing countries, the labour market in Thailand can be classified as a 'segmented market' (Lawler and Atmiyanandana, 1995) with a surplus labour supply (Lawler and Atmiyanandana, 2003). The majority of the Thai labour force is engaged in agriculture and services. The agricultural sector has been the largest employer in Thailand for many years, employing more than 14.6 million workers. However, because the national industrialization strategy was implemented and Thailand's economy began to focus on manufacturing for export, a significant number of workers have moved from the agricultural sector to the manufacturing sector. Not surprisingly, the proportion of agriculture in the nation's GDP has continually decreased (Pholphirul, 2009). The government should pay attention to this shift. One interesting characteristic of the Thai labour market is the difference in agricultural workers' participation rates between the wet season (July to August) and the dry season (January to March) (Gullaprawit, 2002). During the wet season, the worker participation rate is high because every member of a farm household, including the children and elderly, participates in the harvest. During the dry period, however, some family members do not participate. Because only the main family workers harvest during the dry season, the national participation rate is lower at this time of year.

Another sector that should not be overlooked is the service sector. Thailand's service sector includes 6 million workers in wholesale and retail services, 2.6 million workers in hotel and restaurant services, and approximately 1 million workers in financial and real estate services. Thus, there are more than 10 million workers in the service sector. However, due to Thailand's policies regarding economic and financial liberalization as well as free trade agreements, Thai workers, especially in the service sector, need to develop their skills and abilities to survive and compete in the new international environment.

Population Size and Cultural Values

Currently, there are approximately 67.4 million people living in Thailand. The Thai population essentially consists of two main groups: the ethnic Thai people and individuals of Chinese descent. However, unlike other Southeast Asian countries, such as Malaysia and Singapore, where the Chinese communities do not intermingle with ethnically native residents, Chinese people in Thailand have a good relationship with ethnic Thais. Some Chinese people are married to Thai people, and their children are 'Sino-Thais' (Lawler and Suttawet, 2000). Not surprisingly, Thai family enterprises have been influenced by Chinese culture in terms of management and HRM practices (Lawler and Atmiyanandana, 2003). The Chinese management system seems to be influenced by Confucianism (Lawler and Siengthai, 1997). That is, managers demand loyalty from their subordinates, and the subordinates anticipate that the managers will take care of their needs.

Buddhism also plays an important role in shaping HRM practices in Thailand. Approximately 95 percent of the total population belongs to this religion (Lawler and Atmiyanandana, 2003). Theravada Buddhism encourages Thai people to believe in passive and contemplative ways of coping with life events or challenges (Siengthai and Vadhanasindhu,

1991). This religious practice is one of the reasons that Thai people are passive and unambitious in asserting their rights (Napathorn and Chanprateep, 2011a, 2011b). They attempt to avoid conflicts with others if possible. Thai people focus on values and attitudes such as 'Mai Pen Rai' (never mind), 'Jai Yen Yen' (take it easy), 'Kreng Jai' (be self-effacing, respectful, humble, and extremely considerate), and 'Boon Khun' (reciprocity). These values and attitudes tend to favour 'patron-client' relationships within the workplace (Siengthai, Tanlamai, and Rowley, 2008). Theravada Buddhism differs from the Mahayana Buddhism practised in East Asia, as the latter adheres to the belief that social activism is not wrong, as was demonstrated in the actions of monks during the Vietnam War (Lawler and Suttawet, 2000). Another important Thai value is 'Sa Nuk' (fun) (Lawler and Atmiyanandana, 2003). Thai people do not accept the value of high levels of stress at work. Instead, they believe that fun should be a part of their life and work. Thus, it is the responsibility of employees to incorporate 'fun' into their working life.

Ownership Structure and Selection Practices at ZZZ

The literature cites ownership structure as a factor that differentiates HRM practices in Thailand (Lawler and Atmiyanandana, 1995; Napathorn and Kuruvilla, forthcoming). Most family enterprises in Thailand have been influenced by Chinese culture, particularly by Confucianism, in terms of their management and HRM practices (Lawler and Atmiyanandana, 2003), although some of these firms, including ZZZ, have gone public and become publicly owned corporations. Buddhism also plays an important role in shaping HRM practices at ZZZ. However, because ZZZ went public in 1994, its management tends to be more professional. Many of ZZZ's managers and executives have educational degrees in management from the US, the UK, Australia, or from one of the many MBA programs offered by public and private universities in Thailand (Lawler, Siengthai, and Atmiyanandana, 1997). Thus, the managerial elite of this company has been to some extent 'Westernized'. Not surprisingly, ZZZ applies very interesting Thai-style selection practices while simultaneously employing some Western-style selection practices for its managerial and professional employees. Western-style selection practices are practices introduced in several Western HRM textbooks (e.g., Noe, Hollenbeck, Gerhart, and Wright, 2010) such as the use of internationally accepted application forms, reference checks, several written tests, interviews, and an assessment centre. Specifically, ZZZ pays attention to an applicant's date of birth, horoscope, and facial appearance when selecting its managerial and professional employees. For instance, the company's fortune teller typically sits in the interview room and observes the candidates. ZZZ hired its own fortune teller to help select or promote its managerial and professional employees. Here, horoscopes and face reading play a very important role, and they are believed to have helped to make the company a powerful organization. Specifically, there are two main Thai-style selection practices used at ZZZ related to the use of horoscopes and face reading.

Horoscopes

An advisor of ZZZ, an expert in the field of astrology and/or horoscopes, stated that the selection of applicants who are qualified and have good personalities is very important to every organization. At ZZZ, when selecting the best applicants, he has to pay attention to the Chinese zodiac year based on the 'applicant's date, month, and year of birth'. There are two principles used: the principle of reinforcement or compatibility (the so-called principle of 'Ha' in Thai) and the principle of disagreement or conflict (the so-called principle of 'Chong' in Thai). The applicant's date, month and year of birth must be compatible with those of his or her supervisor or boss. For instance, if the supervisor was born on June 3, 1953, which was the year of snake according to the Chinese zodiac, this supervisor must choose an applicant who was born in the Chinese zodiac's year of the monkey, rooster, or ox. This advisor then writes a report for the supervisor to provide information about this issue, so that the supervisor can use this information to select the most appropriate applicant.

According to this advisor, success is closely related to the date, month, and year of their birth. In this regard, if the date, month, and year of birth of two people are compatible, they will reinforce or support one another, and this will ultimately benefit the company. There is also another principle: the principle of triple reinforcement (the so-called 'Sa-Ha' in Thai). In this case, there are three Chinese zodiac years that are very compatible with one another. For instance, people who were born in the Chinese zodiac year of the rat are compatible with people were born in the year of the dragon and in the year of the monkey. People who were born in the Chinese year of the tiger are compatible with people who were born in the year of the horse and in the year of the dog. In this respect, if a supervisor intends to select a prospective employee, he or she will select one who was born in the Chinese zodiac year that is compatible with him or herself and with the other existing employee or supervisor in the department according to the principle of triple reinforcement. All three individuals should support one another in their job duties and responsibilities.

Regarding the principle of disagreement or conflict (the so-called principle of 'Chong' in Thai), if the supervisor was born in the Chinese zodiac year of the rat, he or she would not be compatible with any applicant who was born in the Chinese zodiac year of the horse. These two years are not compatible. They are likely to disagree with one another or have conflicts over their job duties. The other three examples in this case are that the year of the ox is not compatible with the year of the goat, the year of the rabbit is not compatible with the year of the rooster, and the year of the snake is not compatible with the year of the pig.

When the advisor has to select an applicant for any department, he has to know the date, month, and year of birth of the manager or supervisor of that department. Then, he will match the horoscope of the applicant with that of the manager or supervisor.

The situation is more sophisticated than the points mentioned above, however. If an employee in the department was born in the Chinese zodiac year that is not compatible with that of the supervisor, this does not mean that the supervisor has to shift this person to another department or dismiss this person from the company. The advisor offered the example that some people did not clearly understand the principle of disagreement or conflict and, sometimes, moved or dismissed employees who were born in the Chinese zodiac year that was not compatible with them. This was not the correct course of action. A person who was born in the Chinese zodiac year that is not compatible with that of the supervisor can still work in the department or for the company if there is someone working between this person and the supervisor in the organization's hierarchy. For example, an immediate supervisor who was born in the year that is compatible with this person can supervise this person before this person reports to the boss.

The year of birth, month of birth, date of birth and time of birth have different meanings. The year of birth reflects healthiness and stamina. The month of birth is indicative of one's career and success in one's career, while the date of birth affects the relationship between each person and his or her family members. Finally, the time of birth affects love and success in love.

Face Reading

ZZZ's top executives have invested their effort, time, and financial resources in hiring several advisors who are experienced in face reading or physiognomy. One of the advisors stated that the selection of employees at ZZZ based on the applicants' facial appearance is classified into two groups: the selection of managerial employees and the selection of professional employees (i.e., white collar workers). The use of face reading plays a very important role in selection practices at ZZZ, as indicated below.

> The nose of applicants indicates the applicants' insights, ideology, health conditions, and responsibility for family members and / or spouses. A male with a fleshy nose demonstrates that he loves his family very much. The eyes of applicants indicate the intellectual ability and mind of applicants. If an applicant has triangle-shaped eyes, this person may be dishonest and should not be selected.

The main responsibilities of this face-reading advisor are that he must read the facial appearance of at least three applicants per day to determine whether these applicants are eligible for managerial positions at ZZZ. In addition to acting as the advisor to the CEO of ZZZ, he serves as a face-reading advisor for several other companies in Thailand. In terms of selection criteria, this advisor suggested that there is no best practice in selecting good managerial and professional employees. (Actually, for ordinary staff, both horoscopes and face reading can also be used to select this group of employees. Due to resource constraints, however, the company primarily applies these two selection practices to managerial and professional employees.) This advisor has to pay attention to the overall appearance of an applicant. He cannot judge an applicant by examining one aspect of the applicant's face. For instance, the height of the forehead demonstrates the creativity of an applicant. The straightness of an applicant's nose indicates his or her decision-making style, and the eyebrows reflect the applicant's intellectual ability and prudence.

When selecting a professional marketer or a marketing manager, this advisor must pay attention to the facial shape of applicants. The advisor noted that a professional marketer or a marketing manager should have an oval-shaped face. He or she should have clear eyes and stretched ears. The nose should be straight, and the height of the forehead should be appropriate. When selecting an accountant, he or she should have a fleshy face with a large chin. The cheeks should also be fleshy. The hair should be soft and delicate. The eyebrows should be well-groomed. The hair and eyebrows of an applicant are reflective of his or her prudence and delicacy. They also indicate whether the applicant is good-hearted. Before the company ultimately makes a hiring decision, each applicant must pass at least 80 percent of the preliminary face-reading review for each position. For instance, the cheeks of applicants must be fleshy because this indicates that they are responsible. The nose should also be fleshy. Applicants with a small and sharply pointed nose are not acceptable. A pointed chin indicates that the person is not responsible.

A male applicant with thin shoulders may be impatient or less patient than an applicant with broad shoulders. An applicant having beautifully shaped ears demonstrates that he or she is a very responsible person because the outer ears indicate intellectual ability and the inner ears reflect a person's performance potential. As an example, the advisor suggested that a person who has a face that is shaped like that of a monkey and a body similar to one of the billionaires in Thailand who passed away several years ago would be highly capable of caring for his family members and subordinates. This face-reading advisor, however, concluded that ZZZ does not pay attention only to the facial appearance of applicants. The company also focuses on other elements of the application such as transcripts. However, face reading plays a very important role in selecting managerial and professional employees at ZZZ. If face reading were not necessary, the advisor reported that he would be unemployed. Some people have noted that such assessment is unreasonable. However, the practice has been taught for thousands of years, and nobody has been able to prove that it is unreasonable.

Thai-style and Western-style Selection Practices at ZZZ

As mentioned above, ZZZ has employed both Thai-style and Western-style practices in selecting its managerial and professional employees. In stage 1, the company uses Western-style selection practices, as set forth in Western HRM textbooks (e.g., Noe, Hollenbeck, Gerhart, and Wright, 2010), such as the use of internationally accepted application forms, reference checks, several written tests, interviews, and an assessment centre to create the pool of qualified applicants – particularly in terms of their knowledge, skills, abilities, aptitude, and attitudes. Thai-style selection practices – such as the use of horoscopes and face reading – are applied in stage 2 of the selection process to ensure that applicants have personalities and attitudes that are suited to the positions they have applied for and to the organization's culture and, ultimately, to determine who is actually hired. These practices are used to ensure that applicants have a better 'person – organization fit' and to achieve congruence between the norms and values of two parties: organizations and employees.

Thai-style selection practices, therefore, complement Western-style selection practices in determining the managerial and professional employees that best fit with the company's culture. Although, from a scientific point of view, Western-style selection practices are valid selection methods, whereas Thai-style selection practices, specifically horoscopes and face reading, are not (Schmidt and Hunter, 1998), both styles are designed to create long-term employment and stability, as evidenced by the long years of service exhibited in the majority of ZZZ's employees. Additionally, Thai-style selection practices appear to be a necessary and integral component that results in high retention among its managerial and professional employees, and contribute – to the company's success as one of the 500 most-admired companies in 2015.

What Does the Future Hold?

ZZZ has internationalized its businesses to include several countries across the globe in recent years. The company intends to become a global entity driven by local managerial and professional employees in each country instead of a global entity dominated by expats from headquarters.

Barbara (the director of ZZZ's HRM department) felt that she had reached a turning point again. She was not certain that Thai-style selection practices, such as horoscopes and face reading, could be implemented in foreign subsidiaries. These practices are based primarily on the Confucianism and Buddhism found in Asian countries such as China. However, the company intends to expand its business operations to European countries and the US. 'How could these practices be applied in these countries?' Barbara wondered, as she believes that these Thai-style practices are considered a significant component of ZZZ's HRM practices, and result in high retention among managerial and professional employees and the long-term stability of the company. Should the company apply only some Western-style or standardized selection practices in European countries and the US? How could one guarantee long-term employment and stability for the company in these countries if ZZZ were to only apply those Western-style selection practices? If ZZZ intends to apply both Thai-style and Western-style selection practices in Western countries, what should it do? What would be the best way to do it?

Note: For confidentiality reasons, and due to the sensitive nature of the subject matter, a pseudonym is used and certain details concerning the organization's titles, details, and activities have been altered.

Case Study Tasks

Questions for Group/Class Discussion

1 In your opinion, do you think that Thai-style selection practices play a role in the long-term employment and stability of ZZZ in Thailand? If so, why? If not, why not?
2 Should the company apply only Western-style or standardized selection practices when selecting local employees to work in its subsidiaries in European countries and the US? Why or why not?
3 What would be the best way to select managerial and professional employees at ZZZ's other foreign subsidiaries, given that the company intends to become a global entity driven by local managerial and professional employees in each country, instead of a global entity dominated by expats from headquarters? Why?

Role-play Exercise

Barbara, the HRM director of ZZZ in Thailand, decides to arrange a meeting with key people at ZZZ in Thailand to consider the best way to select managerial and professional employees at ZZZ's other foreign subsidiaries. Those key people are as follows:

1 ZZZ's CEO.
2 Country managers of ZZZ's main subsidiaries, such as those in China, India, Russia, and Vietnam.
3 ZZZ's advisors and experts in horoscopes and face readings.
4 Head of ZZZ's recruitment and selection section in Thailand.

Your tasks are as follows:

(a) Allocate roles to individuals.
(b) Each individual should take 10–15 minutes to prepare the issues and/or arguments that are considered relevant to his/her role.
(c) Hold a meeting in which the HRM director of ZZZ in Thailand states her case together with her ideas and/or concrete plans. Then, other meeting participants should offer their reactions, ideas, plans, or concerns.
(d) Each participant in the meeting should keep in mind that win-win solutions should be proposed in future action plans.
(e) Present the executive summary to the Board of Directors regarding the final solutions and action plans.

Acknowledgements

The author would like to thank Thammasat Business School at Thammasat University in Bangkok, Thailand for partially funding this research.

References

Asian Productivity Organization. (2011). *APO Productivity Databook 2011.* www.apo-tokyo.org/files/ind-45-apo_pdb-2011.pdf), October 30, 2015.

Gullaprawit, C. (2002). Thailand. In M. Zanko (Ed.), *The Handbook of Human Resource Management Policies and Practices in Asia-Pacific Economies.* Volume 1. USA: Edward Elgar.

Lawler, J.J. and Atmiyanandana, V. (1995). Human Resource Management in Thailand. In L.F. Moore and P.D. Jennings (Eds), *Human Resource Management on the Pacific Rim: Institutions, Practices, and Attitudes.* Berlin: de Gruyter.

Lawler, J.J. and Atmiyanandana, V. (2003). HRM in Thailand: A Post-1997 Update. *Asia Pacific Business Review,* 9(4): 165–185.

Lawler, J.J. and Siengthai, S. (1997). Human Resource Management and Strategy in the Thai Banking Industry. *Research and Practice in Human Resource Management,* 5(1): 73–88.

Lawler, J.J., Siengthai, S., and Atmiyanandana, V. (1997). HRM in Thailand: Eroding Traditions. *Asia Pacific Business Review,* 3(4): 170–196.

Lawler, J.J. and Suttawet, C. (2000). Labor Unions, Globalization and Deregulation in Thailand. *Asia Pacific Business Review,* 6(3–4): 214–238.

Napathorn, C. and Chanprateep, S. (2011a). Recent Labor Relations and Collective Bargaining Issues in Thailand. *Interdisciplinary Journal of Research in Business,* 1(6): 66–81.

Napathorn, C. and Chanprateep, S. (2011b). Reasons Why Thai Employees Want to Join Labor Unions: Evidence in Private Companies and State Enterprises. *International Journal of Business and Management,* 6(12): 58–64.

Napathorn, C. and Kuruvilla, S.C. (forthcoming). Indonesia, Malaysia, and Thailand. In F.L. Cooke and S. Kim (Eds), *Routledge Handbook of Asian HRM.*

National Economic and Social Development Board. (1980). *National Income of Thailand.* http://www.nesdb.go.th/Default.aspx?tabid=94, November 5, 2014.

National Economic and Social Development Board. (2009). *National Income of Thailand 2009.* Bangkok: National Economic and Social Development Board.

Noe, R.A., Hollenbeck, J.R., Gerhart, B., and Wright, P.M. (2010). *Human resource management: Gaining a competitive Advantage* (7th edn). New York: McGraw-Hill/Irwin.

Pholphirul, P. (2009). Thai workers under wave of globalization. *NIDA Development Journal,* 49(3): 39–74.

Schmidt, F.L., & Hunter, J.E. (1998). The validity and utility of selection methods in personnel psychology: Practical and theoretical implications of 85 years of research findings. *Psychological bulletin,* 124(2): 262–274.

Siengthai, S. and Vadhanasindhu, P. (1991). Management in a Buddhist Society – Thailand. In Joseph M. Putti (Ed.), *Management: Asian Context.* Singapore: McGraw-Hill.

Siengthai, S., Tanlamai, U., and Rowley, C. (2008). The Changing Face of Human Resource Management in Thailand. In C. Rowley and S. Abdul-Rahman (Eds), *The Changing Face of Management in Southeast Asia.* London: Routledge.

Thirawat, N., Robins, F., & Baume, G. (2012). Internationalization Factors of Thai Multinationals and Thailand's Bilateral trade policy. *Journal of Asia-Pacific Business,* 13(2): 143–176.

Part VI
The Americas

Part VI

30

Canada

Building a Culture of Inclusion at the Royal Bank of Canada:
Strategies for Aboriginal Peoples and Newcomers to Canada

Maria Rotundo

This case is about the ongoing commitment of the Royal Bank of Canada (RBC) ongoing commitment to managing diversity and building a culture of inclusion. RBC is an example of a company that strives for more than increasing the numbers of minority group members – to creating an environment of inclusion, in which every member has the opportunity to reach his or her full potential. This case shares some of RBC's strategies for achieving inclusion. It would be difficult to cover adequately in this short case RBC's efforts with respect to all designated groups. Thus, this case focuses on Aboriginal peoples and newcomers to Canada.

Organizational Setting

The history of the Royal Bank of Canada (RBC) dates back to 1864 when it was founded as a private commercial bank – The Merchants Bank in Halifax, Canada, adopting the name The Royal Bank of Canada in 1901; it now operates under the brand name RBC. RBC had its beginnings on the east coast, and it wasn't long before the bank expanded west through the rest of Canada, south to the Caribbean and the Americas, abroad to Britain, and to countries in Europe and Asia.

RBC is Canada's largest bank (as measured by assets and market capitalization) and the eighteenth largest bank globally, based on market capitalization. As of 2015, it has approximately 81,000 employees, serves more than 16 million clients, and operates in approximately 40 countries around the world. It provides personal and commercial banking, wealth management services, insurance, investor services and capital markets products and services on a global basis. RBC helps communities prosper, supporting a broad range of community initiatives through donations, sponsorships and employee volunteer activities. In 2015, it contributed more than $111 million to causes worldwide.

Historical Background of the Case

Canada's population is estimated to be 35,851,800.[1] It covers approximately 9.98 million square kilometers in the northern part of North America and consists of ten provinces and three territories. Canada became a self-governing colony on July 1, 1867 and is a federal constitutional monarchy with a democratic parliamentary system of government and a Prime Minister as the Head of Government. The indigenous Aboriginal peoples inhabited the land for thousands of years. The British and Europeans explored and settled the land around the 1500s and provided the main source of population growth up until the 1960s when they were joined by newcomers from several other nations. Inspired by dreams of a better life and attracted to a land of opportunity rich in natural resources, immigrants were and continue to be a major force in Canada's development. Centuries of the cohabitation of indigenous Aboriginal peoples and settlers from around the world shaped the country's history, culture, and values resulting in a unique blend of tradition and customs.

Canada evolved into one of the most progressive, diverse, and inclusive countries in the world. Women were granted the right to vote before many other developed countries. Canada was the fourth country to legalize the marriage of same-sex couples. Employment and pay equity legislation aims to achieve equality in the workplace for all Canadians. Government programs offer Canadians universal health care, pension plans, parental leave, and child benefit plans, among other programs designed to improve social welfare. In 2011, Canada placed second among 34 industrialized nations on overall quality of life, having received the highest scores on housing, education, health, and life satisfaction.[2] In a survey of prosperity and well-being, Canada ranked sixth among 142 countries and ranked first on personal freedom, which considers tolerance and civil liberties.[3] Canadians rate the *Charter of Rights and Freedoms* as important to their national identity and believe that their fellow citizens share the values of human rights, respect for the law, and gender equality.[4]

Canadians tend to be engaged citizens. They participate in sports or cultural organizations, professional associations, school, community, or religious groups.[5] For the most part, they exercise their right to vote with the 2015 federal election seeing the highest voter turnout in almost twenty years, at 68.49 percent.[6] Of the 338 seats that were being elected, 26 percent were filled by women,[7] 14.2 percent by visible minorities,[8] 11 percent by peoples who were born outside of Canada,[9] 3 percent by Aboriginal peoples,[10] and 1.8 percent by lesbian, gay, bisexual, and transgendered peoples.[11] The diversity among the elected officials affords these groups the opportunity to exercise their voice.

Diversity in Canada

While Canada's population stands just over 35 million, various projections support continued growth in the years ahead with estimates pointing to a population of anywhere between 40 million and almost 64 million by 2063.[12] The aging population, increased life expectancy, and a sustained decline in the Canadian fertility rate make population growth solely from natural increases improbable. Thus, the majority of the population growth is projected to be from immigration as has been the case over the last twenty-five years. Canada ranks highest among other G-7 countries in the rate of immigration.[13] Recent reports indicate that it has accounted for about 60 percent of the population growth,[14] and that Canada receives some

250,000 immigrants each year.[15] Recently, the three countries from which a majority of the permanent residents came were China, India, and Philippines.[16]

Aboriginal peoples in Canada total 1,400,685 or 4.3 percent of the population as of 2011, representing an increase of about 20 percent from the previous five years compared to an increase of 5.2 percent in the non-Aboriginal population.[17] The Aboriginal population is on the younger side with a median age of 28 years, 18.2 percent youth, and 28 percent younger than fifteen years of age compared to a median age of 41 years, 12.9 percent youth, and 16.5 percent younger than fifteen years of age in the non-Aboriginal population.[18] Thus, Aboriginal peoples are at a prime age to play an important role in Canada's labour market and to advance their social, cultural, and economic wellbeing.

Challenges in Managing Diversity

Canada's labour market has been improving since the recent economic recession. It has realized an increase of 6.3 percent employed Canadians and an increase in real wages as well as high labour force participation including for women, an excellent employment-to-population ratio, and a lower long-term unemployment rate.[19] However, the labour market outcomes are not as favorable for all groups of individuals. The unemployment rate is higher for immigrants, and they can also experience lower earnings even when they hold a university degree.[20] More immigrants report working in temporary positions or being over qualified for their positions especially if they arrived in the previous five or so years.[21] Some of these outcomes are believed to be related to language barriers, illiteracy, skills mismatch, or delayed recognition of credentials.[22] Although Canada has been successful at attracting international students, who make-up about 7 percent of post-secondary enrolment, other OECD countries report rates of 15 percent or higher.[23] This differential could present an opportunity for Canada to pursue student enrolment which helps alleviate the growing skills gap and labour shortage.

Aboriginal peoples experience challenges as well. Their labour market availability in the federally regulated private sector stands at about 3.5 percent and their representation at 2.1 percent.[24] Their unemployment rate continues to be high,[25] and they report lower rates of high school completion and postsecondary qualifications.[26] However, levels of education are higher for younger Aboriginal people,[27] which may improve labour market availability and present better labour market opportunities for future generations.

The Canadian government is taking steps to improve the labour force participation of under-represented groups. It has invested funds to improve on reserve primary and secondary education and to help Aboriginal peoples develop work skills.[28] The government has also provided financial support for programs that help newcomers integrate into the economy including training programs.[29] Nevertheless, there is room for employers to join the efforts in leveraging diversity as these less favorable labour market outcomes represent unfulfilled potential and lost opportunities.

Achieving an Environment of Inclusion at RBC

RBC has long considered the interests of minority group members and worked toward achieving its goal for inclusion. Female employees of RBC achieved many firsts beginning around 1968 when the first female manager was appointed. This appointment was followed by the first female to sit on RBC's Board of Directors (1976), the first female executive (1979), the first female Vice-Chairman (1999), the first female Chief Financial Officer (2004), and the first female Chair of the Board (2014). These appointments helped RBC demonstrate its commitment toward not only hiring members of designated groups but also developing this talent.

Achieving these milestones across all designated groups takes time. It also necessitates an understanding of the barriers that members of each group face and concrete plans to address or eliminate these barriers. RBC's efforts in this regard became more formalized starting in the 1970s with the appointment of an Equal Employment Opportunity coordinator (1977), the implementation of an Employment Equity survey (1987), and the establishment of the Diversity Business Council (1996). These initiatives brought greater awareness of the needs of its workforce and paved the way for RBC to devise a diversity and inclusion strategy that included realistic goals and timelines.

The support of leaders is paramount to the success of any critical initiative. It is also an indication of the importance and commitment that institutions and organizations place on these initiatives. In 1991 the Prime Minster of Canada, Brian Mulroney, established the Royal Commission on Aboriginal Peoples. The Commission sought to better understand the challenges of the Aboriginal peoples including the economic gap that existed between the Aboriginal population and the rest of the Canadian population. In 1996 the Commission released a 4,000- page report recommending change. One year later and in response to the Commission's report, RBC's CEO and Chairman John Cleghorn co-sponsored a conference called 'The Cost of Doing Nothing' to raise awareness in Corporate Canada of the social and economic costs of ignoring Aboriginal economic development issues. They urged the business community to lend its support to the Commission's goals and led by example by implementing several initiatives themselves.

In 2001, Gordon Nixon, who was the next president and CEO, established the RBC Diversity Leadership Council, which comprised senior RBC executives representing all businesses and functions. The Council's primary purpose was to develop and monitor diversity enterprise strategies and to align the diversity strategies across all business units. In line with the previous leadership, the Council took its mission one step further and advocated for the importance of diversity to governments and other business leaders across Canada. In the fall of 2005 RBC released a report entitled *The Diversity Advantage: A Case for Canada's 21st Century Economy* and presented it at a conference.[30] The report made the strong case for the social and economic benefits of diversity and why diversity was critical to Canada's future prosperity.

Shortly after this the Council released the *RBC Diversity Blueprint 2009–2011*, which set out RBC's corporate diversity priorities, which was followed by the subsequent release of the *RBC Diversity Blueprint 2012–2015* outlining RBC's enhanced diversity objectives, priorities, and action plans. Dave McKay assumed the role of President and CEO in 2014 and continues to advocate for diversity and inclusion.

Corporate values are another signal of what leaders deem to be important. Among RBC's five core values is *Diversity & Inclusion*. RBC's vision with respect to diversity and inclusion is "To have a diverse workforce in an inclusive workplace that unleashes the talents of all employees to create value, deliver a superior client experience and develop innovative solutions for the markets and the communities we serve."[31] This communication conveys the breadth over which their efforts at leveraging diversity span. These efforts focus not only on the workplace but also on clients and more broadly on communities as well. RBC believes that "Simply having differences is interesting; doing something with them is powerful".[32]

This value and vision is reflected in RBC's *Integrated Model for Diversity and Inclusion* (see Figure 30.1).[33]

RBC believes that any meaningful progress in achieving diversity and inclusion should be visible and reflected in three main areas the bank has the capability to influence. These areas include Talent, Clients, and Communities. More specifically, in the Talent pillar RBC's reach is global with a focus on leadership positions and the commitment to improve the representation of women and visible minorities. They continue to strive to unleash the full potential of their talent by providing workplace experiences and opportunities to develop critical skills. Their approach is to maximize success in these assignments by creating a developmental and supportive environment. In the Clients pillar, RBC's commitment is to grow new markets and help underserved groups by customizing products and services

Figure 30.1 RBC's Integrated Model for Diversity and Inclusion

to meet the needs of potential clients in diverse markets. They aim to improve their service to existing clients by making products and services more accessible and improving the ease of access to funds. RBC also seeks to improve the diversity of its suppliers in North America. In the Communities pillar, RBC's focus is on social and economic development with a commitment to be leaders in this development through collaborative efforts in research, strategic partnerships, donations and sponsorships. RBC recognizes that there are synergies across these pillars and it is possible for some initiatives to have a positive impact across all three.

RBC has a long history of leveraging diversity for its many stakeholders, making it difficult to describe all of it here. RBC will continue to support education and training, mentoring and employee development for diverse groups, as well as enable economic independence and community development with a particular focus on Aboriginal peoples and newcomers to Canada.

Education and Training

RBC long recognized the important role that education plays in opening doors and in helping youth achieve success in life. Throughout the 1990s it introduced several programs that supported education for Aboriginal youth. One such program now called the *RBC Aboriginal Student Awards Program* provides funding for Aboriginal students who attend a Canadian university or college. As of 2015 RBC awarded 148 scholarships. Another program called the *Aboriginal Stay-in School Program* employs high school students across Canada for one month each summer at the branch level. The *Aboriginal Summer Internship Program* is a three-year program designed to prepare individuals who are pursuing postsecondary education for roles as Client Advisors or Banking Advisors. Since program inception, RBC has hired more than 200 Aboriginal summer interns. More recently, the RBC Law Group established the *Aboriginal Articling Program*, which is designed to provide law students with experiences to develop their business and legal skills. RBC donated funds to Canada's first Aboriginal College and the only one operated by First Nations people and continues to provide financial support for other educational programs (e.g., Pathways to Education-2010; Martin Aboriginal Education Initiative–2011).

RBC supports various initiatives that help newcomers acquire relevant Canadian work experience. RBC is the founding sponsor of a community-based internship program for new immigrants. This program, *Career Bridge*, is designed to connect newcomers with small and medium-sized businesses to work in roles that match their skills and previous global work experience. RBC and other sponsors cover the cost of the first four months, enabling the clients to grow their businesses through the employment of qualified talent. Since the program's inception in 1996 RBC has hired 600 interns from three different internship programs. RBC has a longstanding relationship with *ACCES Employment*, a newcomer-focused employment agency. As of 2015, RBC hosted over 90 speed mentoring and job-related networking events, which resulted in the hiring of 200 newcomers from *ACCES Employment*.

RBC is a founding member of the Toronto Region Immigrant Employment Council (TRIEC), a multi stakeholder agency that brings together public, private and community leaders with the goal of improving access to employment for newcomers in the Toronto region. The TRIEC Advisory Council has been chaired by RBC's CEO and CHRO since 2010. RBC employees are active participants in the TRIEC Mentorship Partnership, a four-month program that not only helps develop and make connections for new immigrants but also provides employees with the opportunity to enhance cultural awareness and give back to the community.

Other ways in which RBC advocates for newcomers is by sharing its strategies for successfully recruiting and integrating immigrants into its own work environment. One avenue through which they achieve this is a partnership with 'hireimmigrants.ca,' a website designed for small and medium-sized Canadian businesses. The website includes tools and resources for hiring and mentoring newcomers, recognizing foreign credentials, and breaking down cultural barriers.

RBC has supported other initiatives that sought to help newcomers prepare to join the Canadian labour market even while they were still in their home country. In 2007, the Government of Canada funded the *Canadian Immigration Integration Project* of which RBC was an employment partner through to 2010. The aim of the project was to assist skilled immigrants to integrate more quickly into the labour market before they arrive in Canada.

Mentoring and Employee Development

RBC believes that nurturing strong relationships is critical to achieving an inclusive workforce, to retaining talent, and to improving employee wellbeing. These relationships can exist between junior and more experienced employees as well as among peers. Members of under-represented groups typically experience fewer opportunities to develop important workplace relationships. Thus, RBC has implemented two mentoring initiatives – one that pairs junior and senior employees and another one focused on peer mentoring. *Diversity Dialogues*, which was created in 2006, is designed to stimulate discussion about diversity related topics by matching diversity group members with senior leaders. The relationship can be described as a mutual exchange whereby senior leaders gain increased awareness about different cultures and knowledge about the unique experiences of diverse group members. Leaders in turn have the opportunity to coach the employee on his or her career. Almost 3,000 employees have participated in this program.

Employee resource groups are self-governing grassroots peer networking organizations whose members support one another personally and professionally. It is an opportunity to raise awareness about culture, share experiences, coach, and mentor each other. Groups that are formally recognized by RBC receive an annual budget and communications support. As of 2015 RBC supported 21 different employee resource groups involving over 17,000 RBC employees. The *Royal Eagles* was established in 1990 for Aboriginal employees and was RBC's first employee resource group. Recently, RBC has shifted attention to not only attracting Aboriginal peoples but retaining them. With this goal in mind, in 2014 RBC partnered with Royal Eagles to launch the *Aboriginal Group Mentoring Program*, which focused on the onboarding experience of Aboriginal employees as they join RBC or assume a new role. Another employee resource group, *MOSAIC*, was established in 2008 as a network to support visible minorities and newcomers to Canada. In 2014 *MOSAIC* hosted a *Diversity Dialogue* titled *Leadership in Action*. Through this event *MOSAIC* reached out to RBC's partners in the community to share successful strategies for creating inclusiveness in Canada. The event was videotaped and attended by over 120 RBC leaders, MOSAIC members, and community partners.

Furthermore, RBC believes in the value that role models play in achieving an inclusive environment and therefore sponsors several awards that recognize diversity champions.

For example, RBC is the title and founding sponsor of the *RBC Top 25 Canadian Immigrant Awards*, which honors immigrants who have made important contributions to Canada whether these are in the community, or as athletes, professionals, or humanitarians, among other possible contributions.

Economic Independence

RBC understands that achieving inclusion entails reaching beyond the workplace and into the daily lives of all individuals to help them achieve economic independence. RBC has a history of working with businesses, the government, and Aboriginal peoples to identify and resolve economic issues in Aboriginal communities. In 2007, the Assembly of First Nations reached out to Canadian businesses through a corporate challenge, to which RBC responded. It signed a two-year Memorandum of Understanding, which outlined RBC's commitment to local and regional economic development.

Achieving economic independence arguably begins with obtaining access to banking services and capital. Throughout the 1990s, RBC worked with Aboriginal communities across Canada to understand their banking needs, which led to the opening of on-reserve branches across Canada that were staffed primarily by Aboriginal peoples. RBC was among the first to provide on-reserve mortgage and housing programs and financing for capital projects. It also worked to educate the Aboriginal peoples on personal financial matters through workshops in Aboriginal communities.

RBC has implemented several initiatives that help immigrants get established financially beginning in their home country. In 2006, RBC introduced a website in three languages called *Newcomer to Canada* followed by a *Welcome to Canada Banking Package*, and now the *RBC Newcomer Advantage*. In late 2014/2015, RBC introduced policy changes that allow newcomers to access credit without any previous credit history for their first credit card, car, and home.

Supporting them with their banking helps newcomers get settled and established quickly and easily. In addition, RBC implemented a telephone service that serves clients in over 200 languages by phone and was the first financial institution in Canada to offer this multi-language telephone service through its branch network enabling clients to interact in their preferred language. RBC continues to update these packages and services to satisfy the emerging needs of newcomers.

Community Development

RBC understands that success for many Canadians involves more than economic prosperity. It is about preserving social and cultural values and investing in community and social development. RBC continues to finance infrastructure projects and supports initiatives that help preserve the environment and cultural heritage. In 2007, it released *RBC's Environmental Blueprint*, which detailed its global environmental policy, priorities, and objectives followed by a report of its achievements in 2013. In 2014 it released an updated version that detailed its new commitments leading up to 2018. RBC continually tracks its own performance in-house and works with suppliers in an effort to reduce its indirect energy use, material consumption and greenhouse gas emissions. RBC committed 50 million dollars over 10 years to the *Blue Water Project*, which aims to reduce RBC's own "water footprint". The project funds grants focused on water conservation and preservation and has supported 1,157 projects in 15 countries.

RBC sponsored the 2014 North American Indigenous Games, a sporting event held in Saskatchewan that saw over 4,000 athletes compete. The event celebrated Aboriginal culture as much as it showcased sports. RBC continues to celebrate National Aboriginal Day at which time it profiles RBC employees and leaders across Canada and shares stories highlighting RBC's commitment to the Aboriginal Community.

Diversity and Inclusion Outcomes

RBC's longstanding commitment to achieving an inclusive workplace is reflected further in the importance RBC places on accountability for results. RBC tracks several statistics and qualitative indicators of progress toward achieving its annual objectives, which are measured against each of the three pillars: Talent, Clients, and Communities. It shares these outcomes annually in the *Diversity and Inclusion* report. One critical sign of progress is the employment, retention, and advancement of its workforce. As of 2014, RBC employed over 644 individuals of Aboriginal descent, which represented 1.5 percent of RBC's total employee population in Canada, compared to 1.1 percent in 2000. In 2014, 32 percent of RBC employees were from racialized groups and 31 percent were in management. These numbers were only 14 and 14 percent, respectively in 2000.

In an effort to measure progress toward employee engagement, RBC conducts an annual employee opinion survey (EOS) in which employees can voice their opinion about how well RBC is delivering on what matters most to them. The overall results are analyzed for each of the designated groups, are reviewed by the Diversity Leadership Council and business leads, and action plans are developed to help close any identified gaps. In 2006, a Diversity and Inclusion Index was introduced as part of the survey to measure inclusiveness in the workplace, with year over year scores exceeding North American high performing norms and benchmarks.

RBC continues to be recognized by several groups for its innovative approaches to building a culture of inclusion. RBC earned the 2010 *Catalyst Diversity Award* for its commitment and progress towards advancing women and minorities. For several years, RBC has been recognized as one of *Canada's Best Diversity Employers* by Mediacorp Canada Inc. for its best-in-class diversity and inclusiveness programs. For seven consecutive years, RBC has been recognized as one of the *Best Workplaces in Canada* for it workplace culture (*Great Place to Work©* Institute). RBC and several of its leaders have received other awards and recognitions most of which have made note of some of the initiatives that have been described here as well as other initiatives that are aimed at building an inclusive workplace.

RBC believes that achieving an inclusive workplace is a journey, and one that is to be taken together. It hopes to learn from its experiences and to share its story so that others will join RBC on this journey.

Case Study Tasks

1 Think about your personal experiences with diversity and inclusion in the workplace.

   (a) Based on this experience describe the one thing that you feel is critical to achieving inclusion.

   (b) In what ways does your previous experience with diversity and inclusion differ from RBC's approach?

2 RBC is interested in your input on its efforts at building a culture of inclusion. They have hired you as an outside consultant to evaluate their initiatives against best practices that can be found in the research on achieving diversity and inclusion. What recommendations would you make?

3 What are your reactions to the research literature on diversity and inclusion? Explain.

Acknowledgment

The author would like to thank RBC for their assistance in reviewing and editing drafts of this case. The author received permission from RBC to publish this case study.

Notes

1 This estimate is as of July 1, 2015. (Statistics Canada, 2015).
2 Organization for Economic Co-operation and Development Better Life Initiative Survey as featured in Abma and O'Neil (2011).
3 Legatum Institute's 2015 Legatum Prosperity Index as featured in Kohut (2015).
4 Statistics Canada, General Social Survey 2013 as reported in Sinha (2015).
5 Statistics Canada, General Social Survey 2013 as reported in Turcotte (2015).
6 Reported October 20, 2015 as per Paperny (2015).
7 Maclean's *The Shape of the House* as reported by Shendruk & Taylor-Vaisey.
8 *Ibid.*
9 Library of Parliament, retrieved from http://www.lop.parl.gc.ca/parlinfo/Compilations/Parliament/BornOutsideCanada.aspx?Country=&Show=MP&Curr ent=True
10 *Ibid.*
11 National Democratic Party of Canada, retrieved from http://ndp-lgbt-npd.ca/blog/canada-election-2015-ndp-out-lgbt-members-of-parliament/
12 Medium-growth projection scenario as reported in Statistics Canada (2014).
13 Figure: Inflow of Permanent Immigration as a Share of Total Population, OECD Countries, 2011 as reported on p. 40, Department of Finance (2014).
14 For the years spanning 2014/2015 as reported in Statistics Canada (2015).
15 p. 192. OECD (2015).
16 *Ibid.*
17 National Household Survey, 2011 as reported on p. 4. Statistics Canada (2013a).
18 *Ibid.*
19 p. 7, 13, 14, 16, 41. Department of Finance, Canada (2014).
20 p. 19. Department of Finance, Canada (2014).
21 For the year 2008. Statistics Canada (2009).
22 p. 19. Department of Finance, Canada (2014).
23 p. 25. Department of Finance, Canada (2014).
24 As of June 1, 2014. Employment and Social Development Canada (2014).
25 p. 19. Department of Finance, Canada (2014).
26 2012 Aboriginal Peoples Survey as reported in Bougie, Kelly-Scott, and Arriagada (2013). National Household Survey, 2011 as reported on p. 4. Statistics Canada (2013a).
27 National Household Survey, 2011. Statistics Canada (2013b).
28 p. 51. Department of Finance, Canada (2014).
29 *Ibid.*
30 RBC Financial Group (2005).
31 RBC (2014).
32 RBC (2015).
33 N. Tombari & M. Najafi (personal communication, May 3, 2016)

References

Abma, D., & O'Neil, P. (2011, May 24). Canada gets high score on quality of life index: study. *National Post*. Postmedia News. Retrieved October 14, 2015, from http://news.nationalpost.com/news/canada/canada-scores-near-the-top-of-quality-of-life-index-study

Bougie, E., Kelly-Scott, K., & Arriagada, P. (2013). The Education and Employment Experiences of First Nations People Living Off Reserve, Inuit, and Métis: Selected Findings from the 2012 Aboriginal Peoples Survey. *Statistics Canada Catalogue no. 89–653-X — No. 001*. Ottawa, Ontario, Canada: Statistics Canada: Social and Aboriginal Statistics Division. Retrieved October 29, 2015, from http://www.statcan.gc.ca/pub/89-653-x/89-653-x2013001-eng.pdf

Department of Finance Canada. (2014). Jobs Report: The State of the Canadian Labour Market. *Catalogue no. F1–23/3–2014E*. Ottawa, Ontario, Canada. Retrieved October 29, 2015, from http://www.budget.gc.ca/2014/docs/jobs-emplo is/pdf/jo bs-emplois-eng.pdf

Employment and Social Development Canada. (2014). Labour Program 2014. *Employment Equity Act Annual Report, Catalogue no. Em5–2/2014E-PDF*. Ottawa, Ontario, Canada. Retrieved October 20, 2015, from http://www.labour.gc.ca/eng/standards_equity/eq/pubs_eq/annual_reports/2014/docs/eear2014.pdf

Kohut, T. (2015, November 2). Canada ranked first for 'personal freedom' by annual prosperity index. *Global News*. Canada: Global News. Retrieved November 2, 2015, from http://globalnews.ca/news/2314236/canada-ranked-first-fo r-personal-freedom-by-annual-prosperity-index/

Library of Parliament. *Members of the House of Commons: Born outside Canada*. Retrieved February 9, 2016, from http://www.lop.parl.gc.ca/parlinfo/Compilations/Parliament/BornOutsideCanada.aspx?Country=&Show=MP&Current=True

Library of Parliament. *Members of the House of Commons: Inuit, Métis or First Nation origin*. Retrieved February 9, 2016 from http://www.lop.parl.gc.ca/parlinfo/Compilations/Parliament/Aboriginal.aspx?Role=MP&Current=True&NativeOrigin=

National Democratic Party of Canada. (2015, October 24). *Canada election 2015 results: NDP openly out LGBT MPs (Canada's 42nd Parliament)*. Retrieved February 9, 2016, from http://ndp-lgbt-npd.ca/blog/canada-election-2015-ndp-out-lgbt-members-of-parliament/

Organisation for Economic Co-operation and Development (OECD). (2015). *International Migration Outlook 2015*, 11–13, 59–103, 192–193. Paris, France: OECD Publishing. doi:10.1787/migr_outlook-2015–11-en

Paperny, A.M. (2015, October 20). Federal election 2015: Voter turnout highest in decades. *Global News*. Canada: Global News. Retrieved October 29, 2015, from http://globalnews.ca/news/2287464/federal-election-2015-voter-turnout-hig hest-since-1997/

RBC. (2014). *2014 Diversity and Inclusion Report*. Retrieved August 25, 2015, from http://www.rbc.com/diversity/docs/2014_RBC_Diversity_and_Inclusion_Report_ENG.pdf

RBC. (2015). *An RBC value*. Retrieved December 22, 2015, from http://www.rbc.com/diversity/an-rbc-value.html

RBC Financial Group. (2005, October 20). *The Diversity Advantage: A Case for Canada's 21st Century Economy*. Paper presented at the 10th International Metropolis Conference: Our Diverse Cities: Migration, Diversity, and Change, Toronto, ON.

Shendruk, A., & Taylor-Vaisey, N. The shape of the house: An interactive exploration of the 42nd parliament. *Maclean's Magazine*. Retrieved February 9, 2016, from http://www.macleans.ca/shape-of-the-house/

Sinha, M. (2015, October 1). Canadian Identity, 2013. *Statistics Canada Catalogue no. 89–652-X2015005*. Ottawa, Ontario, Canada. Retrieved October 15, 2015, from http://www.statcan.gc.ca/pub/89-652-x/89-652-x2015005-eng.pdf

Statistics Canada. (2009, November 23). Study: Quality of employment in the Canadian immigrant labour market. *The Daily*. Ottawa, Ontario, Canada. Retrieved October 30, 2015, from http://www.statcan.gc.ca/daily-quotidien/091123/dq091123b-eng.htm

Statistics Canada. (2013a). Aboriginal Peoples in Canada: First Nations People, Métis, and Inuit. *Statistics Canada Catalogue no. 99–011-X2011001*. Ottawa, Ontario, Canada. Retrieved November 1, 2015, from http://www12.statcan.gc.ca/nhs-enm/2011/as-sa/99–011-x/99-011-x2011001-eng.cfm

Statistics Canada. (2013b, June 26). 2011 National Household Survey: Education in Canada: Attainment, field of and location of study. *The Daily, Statistics Canada Catalogue no. 11–001-X*. Ottawa, Ontario, Canada. Retrieved October 15, 2015, from http://www.statcan.gc.ca/daily-quotidien/130626/dq130626a-eng.pdf

Statistics Canada. (2014, September 17). Population projections: Canada, the provinces and territories, 2013 to 2063. *The Daily, Statistics Canada Catalogue no. 11–001-X*. Ottawa, Ontario, Canada. Retrieved October 15, 2015, from http://www.statcan.gc.ca/daily-quotidien/140917/dq140917a-eng.pdf

Statistics Canada. (2015, September 29). Canada's population estimates: Age and sex, July 1, 2015. *The Daily, Statistics Canada Catalogue no. 11–001-X*. Ottawa, Ontario, Canada. Retrieved October 15, 2015, from http://www.statcan.gc.ca/daily-quotidien/150929/dq150929b-eng.pdf

Turcotte, M. (2015, September 14). Civic engagement and political participation in Canada. *Statistics Canada Catalogue no. 89–652-X2015006*. Ottawa, Ontario, Canada. Retrieved October 15, 2015, from http://www.statcan.gc.ca/pub/89-652-x/89-652-x2015006-eng.pdf

Additional Reading

Andrevski, G., Richard, O. C., Shaw, J. D., & Ferrier, W. J. (2014). Racial diversity and firm performance: The mediating role of competitive intensity. *Journal of Management, 40(3)*, 820–844.

Eagly, A. H. & Chin, J. L. (2010). Diversity and leadership in a changing world. *American Psychologist, 65(3)*, 216–224.

Kulik, C. T., & Roberson, L. (2008). Diversity initiative effectiveness: What organizations can (and cannot) expect from diversity recruitment, diversity training, and formal mentoring programs. In A. P. Brief (Ed.) *Diversity at Work* (pp. 265–317). New York, NY: Cambridge University Press.

Miller, D. I., Eagly, A. H., & Linn, M. C. (2015). Women's representation in science predicts national gender-science stereotypes: Evidence from 66 nations. *Journal of Educational Psychology, 107(3)*, 631–644.

Nielsen, B. B., & Nielsen, S. (2013). Top management team nationality diversity and firm performance: A multilevel study. *Strategic Management Journal, 34*, 373–382.

31
Chile
Development of Self-Managed Teams at S.C. Johnson & Son in Chile

Andrés Raineri

This case has been prepared based on public records and interviews with people involved in the events. Its purpose is to serve as material for class discussion and not to illustrate good practices or inadequate management of organizations.

The author thanks Jaime de la Horra whose work gave rise to this case and who allowed the interviews and subsequent surveys conducted with the participants in the change program. Thanks are also extended to research assistants Rafael Pizarro and Cecilia Gutierrez.

Introduction

While boarding the plane to Buenos Aires, Jaime de la Horra reflected on the self-managed teams' initiative that was being implemented at SC Johnson's Viña del Mar wax production plant in Chile. Jaime was concerned about the impact that the company's new strategy, which had been articulated at its headquarters in Wisconsin, was having on the production lines. In recent months this plant had experienced a job redesign process, complemented with an employee development program that prepared workers to take part in self-managed teams (SMTs). Jaime was considered an ardent advocate of SMTs. He held the Operations Manager position at the plant, and led the SMT implementation process. However, sometimes he doubted whether the process would be successful, given the difficulties encountered.

Company History

SC Johnson was founded in Racine, Wisconsin, USA in 1886 by Samuel Curtis Johnson, dedicated to the manufacture of wooden floors. In a few years, consumer demand led the company to produce floor wax, its flagship product. In 1914 a process of international expansion was started. A subsidiary was opened in Britain, followed by Australia and Canada. Today SC Johnson operates in over 70 countries.

The beginnings of SC Johnson in Chile dates back to 1960 when a local businessman Alvaro Montt, who owned a local wax factory, contacted the SC Johnson headquarters and reached an agreement to produce licensed waxes. After the death of Alvaro Montt in 1967 the family sold the facilities to SC Johnson. From that year on the company took control of the factory, where production was increased to meet local market demands, with well-known brands such as Raid, Glade, Bravo and Ziploc, and it started to export products to Peru, Uruguay and Argentina.

In the 1990s the company made efforts to adapt its structure to the needs of a global market: Internationally the company reorganized its operations into clusters of countries. This large-scale worldwide agenda required the development of change programs that transformed not only the organization's structure and work processes, but also local organizational cultures shared by workers in different countries.

Country Background

Chile is composed of a long narrow strip of land in Latin America', on the west side of the southern cone, Eastern Island (Oceania), and part of the Antarctic region. Its estimated population surpasses 18 million people, mostly a mixture of pre-Hispanic native people who blended with Spanish and other countries' immigrants from the sixteenth century onwards. Nearly 6 percent of its people still consider themselves members of several aboriginal ethnic groups. Additionally, in recent years Chile has received migrant workers from other Latin-American countries searching for a better economic future.

Chile, a democratic, presidential republic, has been ranked by The Economist Intelligence Unit (2014) first in Latin America, and 13th across the world, in terms of its business climate. Schwab (2015) points out the country's strengths, such as a strong institutional setup (ranked 28th worldwide), low levels of corruption (25th), an efficient government (21st), and solid macroeconomic stability (22nd). Areas in need of improvement are highlighted by the World Bank (2015), including its educational system and energy supply. In 2010 Chile became the first South American country to join the Organization for Economic Cooperation and Development (OECD), setting for itself high standards in the development of policies to improve the economic and social well-being of its people. Exports of goods and services account for one-third of Chile's GDP, commodities represent three-quarters of national exports, and copper provides 19 percent of government revenues. Other important exports in Chile are sulphate, wood-pulp, fish sub-products, fruit and wood (World Bank, 2015).

Quality of life indicators in Chile have shown significant progress over the last decades. The unemployment rate has remained close to 6 percent in the last few years (World Bank, 2015). Chile has the highest income per capita in Latin America, but has a Gini Index coefficient close to the regional mean, reflecting high economic inequality. When compared to developed countries, Chile ranks below the average in civic engagement, health status, jobs and earnings, social connections, work–life balance, housing, personal security, education and skills, and environmental quality (OECD, 2015). Despite the above, according to the PISA report (2012), Chile has one of the best primary and secondary education systems in Latin America. According to the OECD (2014), 18 percent of the Chilean adult population holds a complete tertiary education, less than the 32 percent average of the OECD countries, but above the 12 percent average in Latin America (World Bank, 2015).

HRM in Chile: Historical Perspective and Current State

During the last century labour laws and HRM practices in Chile have been pushed by sustained social movements and political initiatives. Current labour laws in the private sector

(Law 19759) include a 45-hour per week work schedule, severance pay in the case of dismissal, the right to form unions, and collective bargaining (Codigo del Trabajo, 2015). The legal system protects employees' rights in the judicial courts with effectiveness. Discrimination in HRM is explicitly prohibited by law. However, employment levels and compensation gaps disfavouring female and young workers are among the highest in the OECD (OECD, 2015).

The Global Competitiveness Report (Schwab, 2015), highlights Chile's labour market rigidities, ranking the country in the 120th position across the world. Labour law requires employers to pay workers sizable tenure-dependent severance compensation at the moment of dismissal. Additionally, temporary workers cannot be contracted for longer than three months, after which period a permanent contract becomes legally binding. Maternity immunity protects women from the beginning of pregnancy until one year after the first twelve post-natal weeks, preventing employers from terminating their work contract. The law also requires mandatory pre and post-natal rest periods, of six and twelve weeks respectively. Finally, social security deductions from employee compensation are mandatory in Chile, which represent roughly 21 percent of the first US$2,500 of monthly gross income for every employee, and cover health insurance, unemployment insurance, and pension funding.

In the last 40 years, human resources departments of most larger companies have become highly professionalized, in part because of the impact of competition, understanding of the contribution of employees to organizational results, and the development of university level education programs which have trained many generations of human resources managers (Perez-Arrau Eodes & Wilson, 2012). This situation has led to an improvement in the reputation of human resources departments in larger Chilean companies. Nevertheless, in smaller companies, a struggle to develop their informal HRM practices still persists.

In Chile, work culture varies from company to company. In some firms HRM practices and values reflect a culture of professionalization and efficiency, while in other firms values of authoritarianism, high power distance and paternalism are common. These latter traditional work values, which probably originated in the nineteenth- and early twentieth-century agrarian and mining industries, can be a hindrance to the development of work designs that require collaboration and proactive behaviour, as is the case with SMTs (Raineri, 2003). The Viña del Mar production plant was an example of a company which shared, for most of its history, the traditional work values of authoritarianism and paternalism, values which needed to change, in order to implement SMTs.

The Viña del Mar Plant

After purchasing the plant, SC Johnson moved its administrative offices to Santiago. Soon, marketing, finance, accounting and human resources departments, and a general manager position, were created. At the Viña del Mar plant were kept only the production facilities and a human resources representative. While from the start SC Johnson brought its own management style, which promoted confidence in people, employees' development opportunities, and open communications, the inherited hierarchical organizational structure remained in place until the late 1990s. The plant had several hierarchical levels, with low employee participation. Decisions were centralized, with occasional consultations with lower levels. This structure blended well with the pre-existing work culture. Each production line was headed by a 'Line Supervisor', a position not formally recognized, but historically respected. Such a position was usually held by a machine operator, with many years of experience, with a strong paternalistic leadership ascendancy over his peers. This position reported to company managers for productivity outcomes, loss of materials, performance,

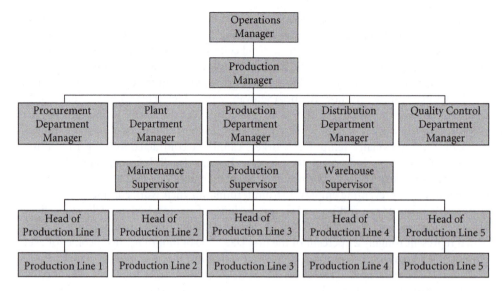

Figure 31.1 SC Johnson's Viña del Mar plant Operations Department structure held prior to the SMTs implementation

and other issues. Line Supervisors had very basic academic preparation. Most of them had only a few years of secondary education, limited interpersonal skills, with no immediate potential to develop professionally beyond a line operator post. Production workers held routine ridden positions in the production line, where they followed instructions from managers, with few opportunities to participate in work design and decisions. The Operations Department structure had six hierarchical levels (see Figure 31.1).

For 20 years the company operated with this structure, with very low employee rotation, and consistent growth. Most of the time the work climate was positive, and management succeeded in overcoming crises and productivity problems. Company benefits were distributed to all members of the organization through a profit sharing program.

The Change Program

The globalization process, experienced by most of the world's economies during the 1990s, forced companies to redesign their strategies. Following other mass products companies, SC Johnson integrated some of its activities throughout Latin America, centralizing its production and management in a few countries. The decision to locate facilities depended on a variety of issues such as access to raw materials, workers' competencies, social and macroeconomic stability, and market size. In 1998 SC Johnson grouped its activities in South America within clusters of countries. Production facilities were consolidated in a lead location, from where products were distributed to other countries. The activities in Chile were attached to the Southern Cone Cluster. In this cluster manufacturing was settled in two plants in Argentina and the Viña del Mar plant in Chile. This last plant had approximately 100 employees. Management was centralized in Argentina, due to market size and the local success of the firm's products. Business results and management reports were sent to

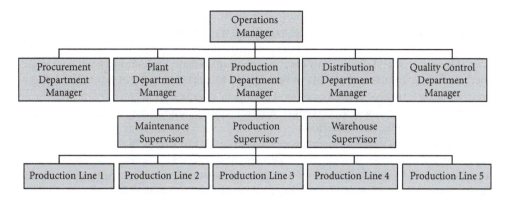

Figure 31.2 New structure implemented at Viña del Mar plant Operations Department

the USA from Argentina. Back office administrative functions were created in Argentina, and front office administrative functions were kept in countries where business was developed. Many functions that were previously performed in Chile began to be executed in Argentina, such as Production Engineering, Accounting, Finance and Human Resources. In order to adjust to new workloads, terminations were made in Chile, and new recruitments were made in Argentina.

The Director of Operations for the region met several times with the Chilean General Manager. They concluded that a major change in the organizational structure and production processes at the Viña del Mar plant was necessary. The excessive number of hierarchical levels was not compatible with the company's new production objectives. One of the first decisions made was to remove the Operations Manager and the Production Manager. The former position was offered to Jaime de la Horra, and the latter position was eliminated, as was the informal position of 'Line Supervisor'. The latter was a significant change for production workers, accustomed to receive work instructions from their supervisors on a daily basis. A voluntary outplacement program was offered to line supervisors. Most of them were close to retirement age and willing to accept the generous financial offer, which included technical training that would enhance their job market value. The new structure had only four hierarchical levels (see Figure 31.2). In each production line the firm decided to develop SMTs, replicating changes made at plants in other countries.

Initiating the Self-Managed Teams

A few years earlier, the company had conducted similar changes in its plants in the USA, England and Argentina, where experience in the formation of SMTs was gained. The new work system required the delegation of responsibilities previously held by supervisors to the production line workers. At the Viña del Mar plant, the plan was to form teams at each line, ranging from 5 to 15 members each. Team leadership roles were defined in the areas of Production, Quality Assurance, Maintenance, Financial Resources, Security, Hygiene and Environment and Human Resources. These roles did not imply endorsement of responsibilities. All team members were expected to handle these tasks through collaboration. Team duties in Human Resources included participating in the selection process of new hires, recommending the termination of team members who repeatedly performed below expectations, solving conflicts within the team and scheduling work shifts. A set of values (i.e. collaboration, participative decision making, and self-management) was also promoted.

The company developed communication procedures for the SMTs, including formal meetings, reports, and production data information folders. Evaluation systems were created, including annual assessments of team goals' attainment, and a bi-annual 360-degree individual performance evaluation. Team members' compensations received no significant changes, remaining almost 90 percent of workers' compensation fixed, and small incentives dependent on production indicators.

In Chile the SMTs' development process began with a meeting in 1998, where Argentina's Operations and Human Resources units presented their SMTs' implementation experience to other South American countries' managers. Jaime attended this meeting, where he was invited to lead the SMTs implementation in Chile. Initial stages of the SMTs program at Viña del Mar were supported by the HRM and Operations 'back office' from Argentina, taking advantage of their previous experience.

The new work system offered SC Johnson more flexible structure and processes, development of a participative culture, delegating operations and management responsibilities to lower hierarchical levels, and the enhancement of relationships across production units. Additionally, the project allowed for employees' development opportunities, creating a more motivating and challenging work experience, and facilitated traineeship in new technologies. Employees had an opportunity to develop a wider range of skills, more autonomy, and a more comprehensive understanding of the business. Changes also allowed more attractive jobs to be offered to new applicants.

SMTs' Implementation Strategy

To deploy the SMTs the company used a change implementation structure consisting of three work groups (see Figure 31.3).

The Steering Committee: Formed by senior executives responsible for implementing global strategies; included the Human Resources and Operations Directors for the Americas and directors in analogous positions at the Southern Cone Cluster level. Some of them had participated in the implementation of SMTs in the USA and Argentina.

The Implementation Committee: Included 'back office' executives from Argentina and 'front office' executives from Chile. The group held the responsibility to lead the SMTs program in Chile. This committee included the Human Resources Managers in Argentina and Chile as well as Jaime, the Operations Manager in Chile, and Edita Olivares, the Production Department Manager in Chile.

Support Group: Formed by four plant workers, selected based on their leadership skills, technical capabilities and influence among peers. They served as 'hands-on' change facilitators.

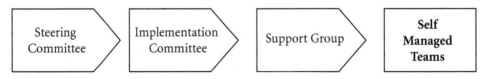

Figure 31.3 Parallel structures developed at the Viña del Mar plant in order to implement the SMTs in its production lines

Members had their job descriptions redesigned in order to accommodate their SMTs support duties. One member came from Quality Control, two were production line operators and the fourth a crane operator. Their new positions became part of a new unit called 'Operations', reporting directly to Jaime. This group was responsible for transmitting information from the lines to management and vice versa, and for explaining to other employees, on the job, how the new system worked. One of its members described their new role: 'to listen carefully to the problems faced by production line workers during the SMTs implementation, explain and facilitate the emergence of cooperation, make them accountable for their actions, and ultimately help in the formation of SMTs.'

Through several months the Support Group received training in topics such as 'Communications Tools', 'Teamwork Values' and 'Managing Change'. Additionally, they took trips to visit the plants in Argentina, to learn from their experiences. One member described his experience: '. . . we had to stand up to higher levels of expertise and responsibility in order to lead the change process at the operational level'. Another member said that they became '. . . closer to each other and to the line workers'. Another member stated that 'we felt appreciated by the executive staff . . . our motivation and commitment to the company increased'.

In order to analyse the challenges facing the implementation of SMTs at the plant, the Implementation Committee conducted a SWOT analysis (Strengths, Weaknesses, Opportunities & Threats). The analysis showed that the organization was partially prepared to initiate the SMTs (see Figure 31.4).

Major strengths

- Supervisors and workers highly committed to the organization.
- High level of participation and motivation in the use of new equipment recently acquired.
- Medium to low resistance to change.

Major opportunities

- Potential to improve productivity.
- SMTs offer an opportunity to develop employees leading to higher levels of satisfaction and commitment.
- Opportunity to become more competitive for future scenarios.
- Facilitate direct communications and agility in operations.
- Develop organizational flexibility.

Major weaknesses

- Line operators academic standards are low.
- Employees are used to report to the position of "head of production line", even though it is a not a formal position in the organizational structure.
- Elder staff have less academic training compared to younger employees (i.e. computer).
- Operations processes need the presence of temporary staff during periods of increased production (December to March).

Main threats

- Supervisors or natural leaders might feel threatened and resist the SMT program.
- Increased perception among employees that the SMT program might be used to execute dismissals.
- Staff employees fear more stress arising from new challenges.

Figure 31.4 Key findings of the SWOT analysis conducted by the Implementation Committee

To assess workers' perceptions towards the change program the Implementation Committee conducted a survey labelled 'First Social Analysis' at the plant. In the words of a Support Group member: 'This first survey was a failure. People did not understand what SMTs were about. Additionally, the survey had over 60 questions which generated a lot of confusion among workers.' The survey's failure suggested to the Implementation Committee how far the program was from success. Workers showed difficulties in understanding basic concepts such as the nature and benefits of SMTs, and the need for an increase in their participation. These concepts were foreign to their habitual way of doing things at work, as well as an unfamiliar way of looking at themselves and their roles in the plant. In reaction to these survey results, the Implementation Committee decided first to explain to the employees what the objectives, purpose and benefits of the SMTs program. After selling the program across the production plant, the Implementation Committee decided to apply a 'Second Social Analysis' survey, consisting of 20 questions aimed at understanding the perceptions employees had about their current work situation, as well as their desired future work conditions. This second analysis indicated the need to improve communications at the company. Workers felt that their opinions were not being considered. Employees' needs for career development were also detected, and their wish to have more involvement in decisions concerning their own work, including the desire of operators to choose their work team mates themselves.

While collecting responses to the second survey an Implementation Committee member was surprised when a worker arrived at her office with tears in his eyes. The worker had heard rumours that they would use new computer equipment. The worker knew that his inability to read would be discovered and feared losing his job. Soon the Implementation Committee concluded that the plant had many workers with literacy problems, who were also hiding their weaknesses, partly because of embarrassment and partly out of fear. A plant manager commented: 'Some employees may ask for directions many times, even though written instructions may be attached to their machines. Some workers seem to have constant problems with their eyesight. . . . The truth is they simply can't read.'

The Pilot Program

The Implementation Committee decided, in a first stage, to launch the SMTs at one production line as a pilot program. The line chosen was 'Doypack', the flexible packaging line. If success was achieved, other production lines would follow. The first activity with workers at the Doypack line is described by an Implementation Committee member:

> "We met with all members of the line. We explained to them the reasons for change, emphasizing recent opinions of dissatisfaction from customers, the advantages of SMTs, such as providing more flexibility and better quality control in production. We also explained that SMTs were being introduced first at their line, how this would be a gradual transition process, and how we should all learn and participate in the process. I remember a lot of scepticism and doubts from employees about what we were proposing. It was hard to gain their commitment, but we also made it clear that this was a one-way street, mandated from headquarters."

The Doypack line had state of the art technology and a motivated workforce. But workers at the line had uneven education levels. Some had not completed high school and others had received extensive technical training. An individual evaluation was conducted to assess the competencies of each employee at the Doypack line. As a consequence, the Company sent some employees to complete their high school education, and paid for their tuition. Others were sent to training workshops in topics such as Computers, Boilers, Electro-mechanics and Inventory Management. All Doypack employees also received training specifically geared towards developing SMTs skills. Courses were dictated by members of the Support Group and by an outside consulting company, about topics such as interpersonal communications, team meetings and self-management. Education would gradually help them develop the skills necessary to work in SMTs. According to Edita Olivares, member of the Implementation Committee: 'The objectives of the training program were fulfilled step by step . . . We trained 90 percent of the workers. Emphasis was placed in introducing computers into the work processes. Everybody wanted to learn how to use them.'

Pilot Program Progress

Three months after launching the pilot program, Edita and Jaime engaged in informal conversations with Doypack employees. The intention was to diagnose the progress of the program. Results confirmed that the training received by employees had positive effects that went beyond the workplace. However, problems were also detected, as employees comments in those interviews show:

> 'Education has improved my quality of life. I feel closer to my family. Now I can help my children do their homework when they get back from school . . . it keeps me close to them.'
> 'I have a better understanding of how other areas of the company work. Computers allow me to see what happens with other operators, discover when they have problems, and help them. Last month supermarkets had run out of red wax. Computers allowed operators preparing white wax to recognize the situation. They changed the production routine and manufactured red wax.'
> 'Changes have generated stress on workers. Sometimes we spend hours discussing how to do something. We find it hard to agree on work procedures. This is exhausting. We lose lots of time arriving at agreements.'
> 'Now I can perform all tasks at the line . . . We also make decisions that benefit our work. For example, we changed the packaging line process so that the boxes stay closer to the product, reducing the processing time. The relocation of the machines also created a more comfortable work environment.'

Jaime and Edita decided to communicate their findings to the Support Group, and requested them to meet with Doypack workers, in order to tackle several issues: (1) Communicate and celebrate progress, (2) Seek mechanisms to decrease stress for workers, (3) Identify and dismantle within-group conflicts, and (4) Strengthen the sense of self-efficacy by providing additional training or coaching as needed.

The Support Group met with the Doypack line workers. They started the meeting by thanking them for the effort delivered. They pledged to help workers find better ways to organize work, reduce stress, and create a greater balance in their workloads. Individualized coaching programs were offered to those in need. They decided to take an afternoon off, and celebrate progress with team members at a barbecue.

Throughout the following summer Edita and Jaime continued engaging in informal talks with Doypack line employees. Improvements were detected. As several workers recounted: "There are many decisions we have agreed upon and need not discuss again. We did a mapping of our work processes, and improved them." "We can change the production line in a few hours, if we need to. We call for a meeting, decide what to do, and distribute the work." "We are closer to each other. We even share our personal family lives. That did not happen before."

However, some employees still indicated dissatisfaction:

"I'm afraid to be wrong. Accepting more responsibilities increases errors. . . . There was this person who ignored technical problems at the line and tried to avoid the situation. His team mates confronted him, the Support Group pressed him to help. On similar events he still ignored the group. Soon he was changed to another production line. In the future he could be dismissed."

The interviews also indicated that employees were aware that the company had not adapted the pay systems to the new responsibilities. Complains stated that '. . . we have not been rewarded for the new achievements . . . It seems the company does not plan any changes in compensation. They believe that more work and responsibilities are compensated by the training we received.'

Jaime knew he needed to decide whether to expand the SMTs program to the other production lines. While flying to Buenos Aires, he missed the high altitude views over the Andes mountains, without appreciating the beauty that nature offered him. He was absorbed in deciding how to give a second wind to the SMTs program on his return to Viña del Mar.

Discussion Questions

1 Are the changes proposed for the Viña del Mar plant appropriate? What benefits does SC Johnson seek with the incorporation of SMTs?
2 Did the local culture hinder or help in the implementation of SMTs? Why?
3 Has the implementation of SMTs affected the human resource practices of the company? Which ones? In what way?
4 Consider the problems emerging during the SMTs implementation. How can these problems be solved?

References

Código del Trabajo (2015). Dirección del trabajo, Chile. Downloaded November 17, 2015. https://www.imf.org/external/pubs/ft/scr/2015/cr15227.pdf
OECD (2014). Education at a Glance 2014: OECD Indicators, OECD Publishing.
OECD (2015). In It Together: Why Less Inequality Benefits All. OECD Publishing.
Perez-Arrau, G., Eades, E., & Wilson, J. (2012). Managing human resources in the Latin-American context: the case of Chile. *The International Journal of Human Resource Management*, 23(15), 3133–3150.

Raineri, A. (2003). El impacto de la cultura nacional en la administración de equipos de trabajo en Chile. *Estudios de Administración*, 10(2), 28–57.

Schwab, K. (Ed.). (2015). *The global competitiveness report 2014–2015*. Geneva: World Economic Forum.

The Economist Intelligence Unit (2014). Business Environment Rankings: Which country is best to do business in? The Economist Intelligence Unit Report. http://pages.eiu.com/rs/eiu2/images/BER_2014.pdf Downloaded November 17, 2015.

The World Bank. (2015). Chile Overview. http://www.worldbank.org/en/country/chile/overview#1 Downloaded November 17, 2015.

32

Mexico

Mexican Experiences from a Danish Firm: "Changing" Mexican Culture

Jacobo Ramirez and Laura Zapata-Cantú

Organisational Setting

Global Care[1] is a Danish company that is a world leader in the healthcare industry. The company has the broadest healthcare product portfolio in the industry, including the most advanced products within the area of hormone systems. According to Global Care reports from September 2015, the firm had more than 40,300 full-time employees in 75 countries and marketed its products in 180 countries. The company's internationalisation strategy is intended to expand its market to Latin America and other emerging economies. In 2004, Global Care established a commercialisation and distribution site in Mexico for its pharmaceutical products, which employed 180 full-time employees in September 2015.

Global Care has developed a people management framework that integrates its principles, policies, and practices into its human resource management (HRM) system. The company's implementation of its HRM system within all of its subsidiaries around the world is key to providing employees with a framework in which to work consistently in line with the firm's core values. The present case exposes the challenges and opportunities with respect to the implementation of Global Care's HRM system in the Mexican institutional context.

Background of the Case[2]

Mexico is located in North America, where it borders the United States in the north and Guatemala and Belize in the south. In 2016, Mexico was the eleventh most populated country in the world (120 million inhabitants). For almost 30 years, Mexico has pursued a path towards greater economic development, with consistent, solid and stable macroeconomic systems to reduce investment risk. However, aspects such as organised crime and violence, and particularly narcoterrorism, characterise the Mexican context. Indeed, the "war against drugs", which was transformed into an inter-cartel competition and has led to a string of crime and violent executions and the destruction of infrastructure, has directly and indirectly shaped firm operations in Mexico, particularly with respect to HRM.

HRM in Mexico: Historical Perspective and Current State

The national business culture (i.e., "premises and belief about work") and management style (i.e., a "particular approach to management"; Schein, 1989) in Mexico are deeply rooted in Mexican society and remain so despite the implementation of "modern" HRM systems, as well as the increasing rate of crime and violence since 2006. Typically, researchers addressing HRM systems – a group of separate but interconnected HRM practices, principles, policies and programs (e.g., Lawler, Chen, Wu, Bae, & Bai, 2011) that shape the pattern of interactions between and among managers and employees – in the Mexican context have highlighted (1) values such as family, dignity and loyalty and (2) cultural dimensions such as high power distance, collectivism (House, Hanges, Javidan, Dorfman, & Gupta, 2004) and hierarchical (top-down) decision making in portraying such systems in Mexico and thus in designing HRM systems.

The traditional management style in Mexico involves the application of strong family values in the workplace, including a strong hierarchy and high power distance (House *et al.*, 2004). CEOs and firm owners are commonly considered paternal figures and frequently use an autocratic management style (Elvira & Davila, 2005). In this context, it is common to encounter a "boss worship" business culture (*una cultura del culto al jefe*) in which authority (*autoridad*) plays a special role in management (De Forest, 1994). The national business culture in Mexico is generally intended to reward submission, direction, and loyal personal service to the person in authority. Workers are thus expected to be loyal to their supervisors and to avoid questioning their decisions. In this context, it is not acceptable to contradict a supervisor's opinion in public, especially across hierarchical levels (e.g., Stephens and Greer, 1995). Further, Mexican workers tend to expect instruction, decision making is generally based on status roles, and workers have little individual control over their tasks or work processes. They also frequently respond warmly to formal and dignified treatment – in other words, workers seem to appreciate such treatment when authority is not abused. In general terms, the ideal working conditions in Mexico are based on the family model. In this model, everyone works together according to their designated roles. Supervisors tend to be understanding (*compresivo*). Moreover, they aim to keep their distance and address workers formally, patiently demonstrate tasks, and remain sufficiently flexible to lend a hand occasionally. These work-related characteristics are commonly observed and expected in Mexico and are regarded as a "paternalistic" employer obligation. Correspondingly, workers are expected to show unquestioning respect to their employer (rather than engage in a simple economic exchange in which they receive a salary). Some Mexican employees develop such a strong allegiance to their company, which they commonly view as an extended family. These work-related characteristics underlie the assumptions and unspoken expectations that seem to be found in Mexican workplaces today.

Mexico is frequently described as a low-trust society (e.g., Kühlmann, 2005) in which reluctance to share information is common. Typically, senior managers are unwilling to share power. Further, power, authority, knowledge, and information travel from the top to the bottom in the organisational hierarchy. Such a hierarchy is visible even in Mexican labour law, which separates workers into two groups: At the supervisor level and above, employees are called *empleados de confianza*, which means "trusted employees" or "confidential employees". The other group (*empleados sindicalizados*) comprises "blue-collar workers" – unionised employees. This classification indicates an implicit separation between Mexican employees that also has additional implications. For example, in some organisations, there are separate cafeterias for confidential and blue-collar employees.

The Mexican interpretation of "being on time" may be argued to differ from the European or North American interpretations. Such a time dimension is also evidenced in verbal communications, since it can be difficult to understand the "real" meaning of what some Mexicans say, as Mexicans often use the diminutive form in speech. For example, *esperame* means "wait for me", whereas *esperame una rato* means "wait a moment for me". However, a Mexican would more often say *esperame un ratito*. In this phrase, "*ratito*" is the diminutive form of "*rato*", meaning "a very short moment". The ability to read between the lines thus seems to be an important asset in understanding Mexican business culture. Nevertheless, the so-called tomorrow (*mañana*) syndrome appears to be in decline, as some academic studies show, for example, that Mexican workers are good at meeting deadlines and that they score well on performance-related assessments (e.g., Elvira & Davila, 2005).

The recurring Mexican financial crisis of recent decades and the current "war on drugs" have rendered non-monetary compensation systems a more important motivating factor for Mexican employees. HRM systems designed to build employees' commitment to decrease turnover, for example, by integrating flexible work schedules are not new in Mexico. Emerging HRM systems in Mexico indicate that managers understand employees' absenteeism or lateness due to the Mexican context of violence and crime. The design of humanistic policies and practices, such as counselling or work-from-home arrangements, as well as pragmatic investment in security hardware and calculative policies and practices based on strict candidate and employee control, including employee screening (to avoid hiring a candidate related to drug cartels), presents an inherent duality in Mexico: HRM systems must have (1) strong and strict employee protection and screening and (2) a humanistic orientation, such as flexibility. Thus, the balance between stability and flexibility is one of the strategic dilemmas of designing HRM systems in Mexico.

The paternalist nature of employers appears to have induced employees to perceive firms as obliged to provide them with the following services as part of their non-monetary compensation: free company bus services (given that some employees are afraid to take public transportation), healthcare services for family members, a canteen (normally a hot meal is provided to employees), and counselling programs to employees and their families, among others. A common practice in Mexico is for individual workers to receive premiums for attendance, punctuality and overtime. Moreover, Mexican labour law requires companies to pay employees a Christmas bonus (known as the *aguinaldo*) equal to 15 days' salary. Normally, firms pay this bonus on the same day as their Christmas party (the *posada*, which is a company party that involves dancing, dinner, gifts, and so forth). The message inherent in treating employees well by providing such services is likely to build loyalty among Mexican workers who respond well to monetary and non-monetary rewards that emphasise emotional appeals, family support, and social support.

A lack of education, particularly among blue-collar workers, may translate into low self-confidence and low expectations. Overall, 22.3 percent of the population above 15 years of age has finished secondary education[3] (INEGI, 2015). In Mexico, it is common to find workers who may not have developed the analytical and communication skills required for schemes such as self-management. Therefore, several managers argue that even with extensive employee training and careful selection, HRM systems still need to be modified and made consistent with certain aspects of the Mexican context. In other words, before "modern" HRM systems are implemented, managers should consider "unspoken" employer and employee expectations rooted in the Mexican national business culture, which includes employees with only a basic education and a work environment characterised by loyalty, submission and respect.

Mexicans are inclined towards face-saving, which means that they are reluctant to admit failure or error; thus, they tend to avoid openly saying that they do not know something. The influence of the *machismo* ethic (e.g., Pelled & Xin, 2000), which discourages the admission of mistakes, is a challenge in Mexico. Mexicans typically may not admit to mistakes, and they will try not to communicate bad news because they feel uncertain about how their boss will react. Likewise, the authoritarian style of many Mexican managers does not encourage communication or feedback from the lower levels of the hierarchy to the upper levels. Economic fear in the workplace is a reality in many Mexican companies, and employees justifiably worry about making errors. Although Mexican legislation softens the blow of terminations, mandates such as severance compensation may not provide an adequate economic buffer against the loss of a job that pays above the minimum wage level. In Mexico, there is no unemployment insurance; therefore, Mexicans make every effort to keep their jobs.

The HRM Context in Global Care Mexico

HRM System

Global Care has developed a people management framework for helping Global Care managers and employees to act in accordance with the firm's core values. According to a manager in Denmark, "The people management framework is a system that combines modern value-based management with traditional control, (e.g., a respectful, healthy and engaging working environment, optimised way of working, ambitious goals and pursuit of excellence)".

Global Care has implemented its people management framework in Mexico through an HRM system, which is presented as the configuration of high-performance HR practices[4] in Table 32.1.

The HRM manager in Mexico has commented that "The Charter for companies in the Global Care Group and the people management framework established a new way of thinking and working across the company." The HRM Department has four employees in the

Table 32.1 Configuration of high-performance HRM practices

HRM Subsystem	Dimension	
	Resource and Control-Based HRM Practices	Sample HRMPractices
People flow	Staffing Training Mobility (internal & external) Job security	Selective training More extensive general skills training and development Broad career paths Guaranteed job security
Appraisal and rewards	Appraisal Rewards	Long-term, results-oriented appraisal Extensive, open-ended rewards
Employment relations	Job design Participation	Broad job description; flexible job assignments Encouragement of participation and teamwork

following functional areas: Recruitment, Selection and Career Development, Operational Personnel Management, and Communication and General Service. The corporate building is located in an exclusive area of Mexico City in Lomas de Chapultepec, and the workplace is spacious, creating an open and pleasant atmosphere. Further, the coffee bar has fresh fruit, water and tea, but there are no soft-drink vendor machines in the building because Global Care aims to promote a healthy lifestyle among its employees and thus avoids offering sugar-based drinks in the workplace.

HRM Subsystem: People Flow

Regarding the People Flow subsystem, Global Care Mexico has made changes in its recruitment and selection processes to adapt them to the Mexican national business environment. For example, in Denmark, the recruitment channels are mainly firms' websites, university fairs and specialised recruitment agencies. In Mexico, Global Care's brand was not well known in 2004 and thus, the firm faced the challenge of attracting potential employees willing to work at an "unknown" firm. The HRM manager expressed the idea as follows: "This is a reality. We are new in the Mexican market. We are very small in comparison to our competition: e.g., Eli Lilly. It was difficult for applicants to understand Global Care's philosophy, [and the same was true] for many of the employees." The HRM manager also indicated that employees' personal networks (word of mouth) form a basic source in the recruitment process for Global Care Mexico. According to prior research, "word of mouth" tends to be a powerful recruitment channel in the Mexican business culture, which is characterised by strong relationships between friends and family members which assist them in handling work- and non-work-related issues (Elvira & Davila, 2005).

Global Care Mexico has established a bonus system to reward employees who recommend a candidate. This policy seems to aim to motivate employees not only because they wish to receive the monetary bonus but also because the firm trusts its employees' recommendations in the recruitment process. An employee in Mexico commented, "Global Care is a very open organisation. This openness helps us to learn from each other and the environment."

However, to avoid any discriminatory practices within the hiring process, managers in Global Care Mexico recruit and select their employees based on their job profile, and Global Care aligns the selection process with the competences required for the position. The recruitment and selection manager explained,

> We have access to the main HRM operational processes of the firm; however, we needed to adapt it to the Mexican legislation. However, Global Care's philosophy is completely different from [that of] other companies that I have worked for (USA and Mexico). Now, I have to make sure that there is no discrimination in any of our HRM subsystems.

According to the HRM manager, demographic aspects, such as age, gender, and marital status (e.g., being a single mother), might negatively influence hiring decisions in Mexico. Global Care views these demographic considerations as discriminatory hiring practices, as they seem to attract employees with a "submissive" profile in order to maintain a pattern of following orders without question, which tends to be appreciated in Mexico.

As the recruitment and selection manager in Mexico stated, "Our starting point is the job description. We develop an assessment based on the competences [required]." A special feature of the selection process is a psychological test completed via the Internet. The recruitment and selection supervisor sends the web link to the candidate, and he/she can complete the test any time and anywhere. This is quite a unique approach in the Mexican context, where psychological testing is traditionally conducted under the strict supervision of a firm's recruitment and selection department because of the low-trust society in Mexico (e.g., Kühlmann, 2005). Indeed, giving a candidate total freedom to complete a psychological test online tends to be unexpected in Mexico. However, Global Care Mexico's approach is based on the fundamental values of trust and honesty, and the firm claims to have an equal opportunity policy and absolute respect for individuals as human beings. As the HRM manager explained, "Sadly, in Mexico, we do not trust employees. However, we depart from this basic principle in the selection process." Another manager in Mexico commented on this subject: "There is a complete lack of trust in some firms in Mexico, and of course when you arrive at an organisation like Global Care Mexico, you say 'Can this really be true?' You have to pinch yourself to make sure you're not dreaming."

In terms of training and development, the challenge that Global Care Mexico faces concerns how to make employees change their way of thinking. The procedure that the firm follows starts with an induction process and continues with manager training/coaching and assessment based on competencies and feedback. Employees are responsible for their own development, and the firm provides training programs aligned with the balanced scorecard approach. According to the HRM manager, "The biggest challenge in Mexico is to 'erase' the type of behaviours that contradict the Danish culture and the Global Care people management framework. We need to de-skill our 'old' Mexican skills [and teach them] the 'new' method of management." In this sense, Global Care has three types of employees. The first type are employees who have work experience at other firms that share Global Care's values to some extent. For this type of employee, Global Care's management framework is not completely "new." The second type of employees have work experience only in Mexican firms and thus are more likely to need to unlearn old work habits based on "typical Mexican" management styles. The firm needs to coach these individuals so that they will understand and perform their work according to Global Care principles. The third group of employees comprises individuals with no work experience. For these employees, it is relatively easy to learn Global Care's management framework. As the HRM manager commented, "Across Global Care, we are working hard to implement a learning culture to help people build new competencies quickly." Global Care's challenge in Mexico seems to be to ensure that employees believe in the firm's values and to encourage them to practise these values. Such efforts will likely focus on the second group of employees. As a manager in Mexico explained, "We cannot tolerate a double standard or a false standard. We cannot use certain values at work and others at home. The goal would be that after we start [using them in our lives], it affects our daily life at home, with friends, etc."

HRM Subsystem: Appraisal and Rewards

The process of appraising performance at Global Care is based on a balanced scorecard. According to the HRM manager, employees know the firm's strategy and the required achievements at different organisational levels. Together with their supervisor, they set the goals that will be measured at the end of the assessment period, in a process of open communication in which the goals are established fairly for the employee and the firm. In this way, everyone is evaluated based on the same procedure.

Regarding rewards, the HRM manager noted, "Our compensation system is competitive in the local market. In addition, all employees have the right to a productivity bonus, from an office boy to the director of the Mexican subsidiary."

Global Care is working to ensure that employees can maintain a natural balance between work and leisure time. To help employees achieve such a balance, Global Care has implemented policies worldwide such as telecommuting, flexible scheduling, and extended maternity/paternity leave. The company aims to establish a balance that ensures that employees have a full life that includes enjoyment and fulfilment at both work and home. In Mexican business culture, such policies are not commonly implemented; however, because of the current security risk in Mexico, such practices are more common in Mexico today.

HRM Subsystem: Employment Relations

The employment relations subsystem encourages employee participation, and the HRM department seems to be searching for ways to encourage open communication. On this subject, one manager in Denmark noted, "On our team, there is no way to avoid participation in decision-making processes. This is a typical characteristic of Danish culture". Another employee in Denmark noted,

> Here everything takes time. Perhaps [allowing] too much democracy is not right for all processes. We have several rounds of discussions, trying to reach a consensus and consider all opinions in making decisions. This slows down all processes and makes the decision-making process difficult.

In Denmark, this tendency seems to have been developed by a long tradition of democratic decision making within the political system.

The HRM manager in Mexico commented, "It has been difficult to implement Global Care's management framework in Mexico. In Mexico, we are not used to having too much openness. We do not know what to do with it. We do not know what to do with too much liberty." In Mexico, unlike in Denmark, decisions are made by one person: the boss is the boss, and "masculine society" (House *et al.*, 2004) makes decisions. One of the most significant challenges that Global Care Mexico has faced is the openness and freedom given to Mexican employees, as these characteristics seem to be in direct opposition to the modes of functioning, direction/delegation, organisational structures, decision making and types of control used in HRM in Mexico. Table 32.2, the Configuration of High-Performance HRM Practices in Global Care Mexico, shows these characteristics of the firm in Mexico.

Problems and Issues in the Case Scenario

Culture is a dynamic concept, and it is difficult to make a single statement about Mexican business culture, as it is constantly undergoing changes. Denmark tends to have a more stable business environment, and it has been described as a stable society in terms of its political and economic developments (e.g., Schramm-Nielsen, 2000). The *Global Care* HRM system (see Table 32.2) seems to be derived from the Scandinavian model,

Table 32.2 Configuration of high-performance HRM practices in Global Care Mexico

HRM Subsystem	Dimension	
	Resource and Control-based HRM Practices	Global Care Mexico Operation of HRM Practices
People flow	Staffing Training Mobility (internal & external) Job security	• Online psychological test • Panel interview based on competences • Employees are responsible for career development • Zero discrimination • Opportunities for worldwide mobility within the firm
Appraisal and rewards	Appraisal Rewards	• Based on a balanced scorecard • Productivity bonus given to all employees without regard to hierarchy
Employment relation	Job design Participation	• Job design based on competence • Encourage participation in decision-making processes • Based on the Global Care Management Framework

in which institutions (e.g., Scott, 2014) play a key role. In particular, the Scandinavian model is characterised by (1) stable labour relations, (2) reforms of work culture, and (3) strong governments that, in alliance with trade unions, are strongly committed to supporting an extensive welfare and social security system with full employment as an absolute objective (Grenness, 2003, p. 19).

Although Denmark is as an individualistic society (House *et al.*, 2004), with regard to decision making, Danes are group oriented. In Denmark, when particular subjects are discussed, all possible perspectives are typically considered, and an agreement is reached. Danes tend to view themselves as tolerant and egalitarian people (House *et al.*, 2004). Further, they pay little attention to rank and status and tend to have equal respect for everyone. Danish workplaces typically do not feature the highly hierarchical structures found in Mexico; rather, they tend to be characterised as flat organisations. The distance between the boss and employees is thus short, and in principle, everyone—regardless of their education, position or social status—is regarded as equal. Employees are also commonly not exposed to tight control. Finally, in Denmark, asking colleagues for advice is not considered a sign of weakness. The ability to cooperate is highly regarded, and people help each other across status and professional categories. Criticism is thus considered to focus on with one's work rather than to constitute a personal attack, and it is acceptable to make mistakes.

Summary of the Case's Main Features

There are two main pillars of the HRM system (see Table 32.2) in Global Care Mexico. First, the national business culture and management style seem to be important to HRM systems, but they do not entirely determine the assimilation of an HRM system originally designed in Denmark and implemented in Mexico. Second, trust, openness, participation, non-discrimination, and honesty, among other values, are used to support HRM-performance subsystems and to create a strong corporate culture that employees will endorse.

Mexico is unique in its economic development and features both a different social dynamic and different patterns of relationships within organisations. Specifically, Mexico is characterised by higher levels of power distance and a lower level of egalitarianism (House *et al.*, 2004): decisions tend to be made based on the hierarchy. Nevertheless, there is evidence of the strong influence of Global Care's people management framework in establishing a management style that is in some ways contradictory to the Mexican context. In particular, highly selective recruitment, information sharing, investment in training and participation in decision making are HRM practices that Global Care has implemented in Mexico, and these practices have been implemented while considering factors inherent to the Mexican context. For example, employee personal networks are important sources for recruitment. Online psychological testing, job design based on competence, and rewards based on a balanced scorecard are common practices that must be supported by information technology. The implementation of these practices has been a challenge for Global Care Mexico, because it cannot rely on the way institutions work in Mexico in seeking to implement HRM practices as they have been implemented in Denmark.

The main insight gained from this study is that Global Care Mexico must acknowledge the contextual factors at play when implementing a model of high-performance HRM practices and devote particular attention to the factors that affect investments in professional development. Nevertheless, Global Care does not necessarily need to change its core values to implement HRM subsystems in Mexico. Rather, Mexican employees need to adapt to Global Care's people management framework. However, Global Care's HRM system is not a completely new method of management in Mexico, as other organisations operate under the same types of universal values and management strategies. Thus, this case invites us to rethink the configuration of HRM practices designed elsewhere and implemented in Latin American countries.

Case Study Tasks

Questions for Group/Class Discussion

1 Given the Mexican and Danish business cultures, what are the most important HRM challenges that Global Care Mexico faces? What does the company need to do to succeed?
2 What are the key strengths of Global Care in implementing its management framework in Mexico? How did the firm leverage these advantages given the history and current state of HRM in Mexico?
3 What is the "right" HRM strategy for Global Care Mexico – hybrid or centralised? Why? Evaluate the different options (with the pros and cons).

Group Activity

Lead the participants in breaking into small groups to perform the following tasks:

• The Global Mobility Department at Global Care in Denmark requests that your group conducts Internet-based research in order to determine (1) what the relative cost of living in Mexico City is as of this year and (2) what expatriate support services are available in Mexico.
• Each group should develop a list of available services and provide details for at least one organisation that could provide services. These services should then be listed

in order of priority for expatriates according to the business environment found in Mexico.
- Each group should be ready to justify its reasons for prioritising the services that Global Care Mexico will provide.

Notes

1 Because of confidentiality reasons and the sensitive nature of the subject matter, a pseudonym is used, and certain details concerning the organisation's titles and activities have been altered.
2 This case is based on fieldwork conducted between 2009 and 2010, and it builds on the findings published in Ramirez, J., Madero, S. and Muñiz, C. (2015). The impact of narcoterrorism on HRM systems, *The International Journal of Human Resource Management*, DOI: 10.1080/09585192.2015.1091371.
3 Secondary education is the third level of basic education (after elementary and primary education); it provides the knowledge needed to begin graduate studies. It is also the minimum level of education that a blue-collar employee must have to be hired for a job.
4 The high-commitment model was developed by Bamberger and Meshoulam (2000, pp. 66–67).

References

Bamberger, P., & Meshoulam, I. (2000). *Human resource strategy: Formulation, implementation, and impact.* London: Sage Publications.
De Forest, M. E. (1994). Thinking of a plant in Mexico? *Academy of Management Perspectives, 8*(1), 33–40. doi:10.5465/AME.1994.9411302385.
Elvira, M. M., & Davila, A. (2005). Special research issue on human resource management in Latin America. *International Journal of Human Resource Management, 16*(12), 2164–2172. doi:10.1080/09585190500358539.
Grenness, T. (2003). Scandinavian managers on Scandinavian management. *International Journal of Value-Based Management, 16*(1), 9–21. doi:10.1023/A:1021977514976.
House, R. J., Hanges, P. J., Javidan, M., Dorfman, P. W., & Gupta, V. (2004). *Culture, leadership, and organizations: The GLOBE study of 62 societies.* London: Sage Publications.
INEGI (2015). Instituto Nacional de Estadística y Geografía (National Institute of Statistics and Geography). Census 2010. Retrieved November 15, 2015 from http://www3.inegi.org.mx/sistemas/temas/default.aspx?s=est&c=19004
Kühlmann, T. M. (2005). Formation of trust in German–Mexican business relations. In K. Bijlsma-Frankema & R. K. Woolthuis (Eds.), *Trust under pressure: Empirical investigations of trust and trust building in uncertain circumstances* (pp. 37–54). Cheltenham, UK: Edward Elgar.
Lawler, J. J., Chen, S., Wu, P., Bae, J., & Bai, B. (2011). High-performance work systems in foreign subsidiaries of American multinationals: An institutional model. *Journal of International Business Studies, 42*(2), 202–220. doi:10.1057/jibs.2010.42.
Pelled, L. H., & Xin, K. R. (2000). Relational demography and relationship quality in two cultures. *Organization Studies, 21*(6), 1077–1094. doi:10.1177/0170840600216003.
Ramirez, J., Madero, S., & Muñiz, C. (2015). The impact of narcoterrorism on HRM systems. *The International Journal of Human Resource Management, 27*(19), 2202–2232, doi:10.1080/09585192.2015.1091371.
Schein, L. (1989). *A manager's guide to corporate culture.* Research Report No. 926. Washington, D.C: The Conference Board.
Schramm-Nielsen, J. (2000). How to interpret uncertainty avoidance scores: A comparative study of Danish and French firms. *Cross Cultural Management: An International Journal, 7*(4), 3–11. doi:10.1108/13527600010797129.
Scott, W. R. (2014). *Institutions and organizations, ideas, interests and identities.* Thousand Oaks, CA: Sage.
Stephens, G. K., & Greer, C. R. (1995). Doing business in Mexico: Understanding cultural differences. *Organizational Dynamics, 24*(1), 39–55. doi:10.1016/0090–2616(95)90034-9.

Index